외투기업의 No.1 노무법인
KangNam Labor Law Firm

Practical Manual
for Labor Law (10/20)

Manual on Bullying and Sexual Harassment in the Workplace

직장 내 괴롭힘과 성희롱 예방 매뉴얼

by El-lim Kim
Professor Emeritus of KNOU, Ph.D. in Law
한국방송통신대학교 명예교수 **김 엘 림** (법학박사)
Bongsoo Jung
Labor Attorney of KLLF, Ph.D. in Law
강남노무법인 대표 공인노무사 **정 봉 수** (법학박사)

강남노무법인

Preface

I visited a large bookstore while sightseeing in Kyoto, Japan in June 2019. While there, I was surprised about two things: one was the number of labor management books in the labor law section, while the other was that those labor books were divided into practical guides and volumes on research & theory. In Korea, not only are there few books on labor management, but most are simply academic and do not lend themselves well as practical guides.

For some time, I have wanted to write practical manuals that can be immediately helpful in business. I have selected as themes 20 most important aspects of labor management that can be used immediately in practice, and related examples, case studies, practical application guidelines, and related forms were included in detail to form a series of guidebooks for HR managers and ordinary workers.

This Manual on Preventing Workplace & Sexual Harassment deals with labor issues that have become front and center at workplaces in recent years. As the provisions on preventing workplace harassment were introduced to the Labor Standards Act in 2019, numerous conflicts between superiors and subordinates, which had been simmering at the workplace, are rising to the surface. While working on several cases involving workplace bullying and conducting some sessions on preventing it, I felt that now is the time for a manual to help businesses (and employees) facing these issues. It is for this purpose that this book has been published. Of special note is that Professor Kim El-lim of Korean National Open University (KNOU), who was the first president of the Society for Gender Law and an expert on sexual harassment in the workplace, joins me in this volume. I had the privilege of having her as a teacher and she was gracious enough to contribute a chapter on preventing sexual harassment in the workplace, which I have the honor of publishing herein. As such, this manual contains practical examples and ways to prevent workplace sexual harassment as well as workplace bullying.

This manual is structured in the following way. Chapter 1 explains the basic concepts of workplace harassment and sexual harassment. Chapter 2 contains specific cases of workplace harassment that have been handled in practice. Chapter 3 covers the legal system around and preventive measures against workplace sexual harassment, as well as case analysis data. Finally, Chapter 4 presents a variety of workplace and sexual harassment cases that have been dealt with by the Ministry of Employment and Labor and the courts, providing readers with a diverse range of practical examples.

I would like to express my deep gratitude to Ms. Kim Hye-min and Ms. Park Cheney, who provided English editing and proofreading services, and Mr. Jung Young-cheol for his editing and publication of this book. In particular, I would like to thank my long-time friend, Dave Crofton, who has been responsible for English editing. I believe that this manual, which reflects the efforts of many people, is not solely the work of the author, but a collaborative achievement.

June 1, 2023

Bongsoo Jung / Labor Attorney, PhD in Law

머 리 말

2019년 6월, 일본 교토 관광을 하면서 대형서점을 들렀다. 그곳에서 노동법 섹션에 꽂혀있는 노무관리 책들이 참으로 다양하다는 사실과 실무와 연구서적을 구분하여 저술활동이 이루어지고 있다는 사실을 깨닫고 느낀 바가 많았다. 한국의 경우 노무관리 책들이 많지 않을 뿐만 아니라, 그나마 나와 있는 책들도 학술서적이 대부분이다.

그동안 내가 집필해왔던 기고문이나 서적 등이 실생활과는 동떨어져 있다는 생각을 하던 것이 사실인지라 이번에는 기업에서 바로 도움이 될 수 있는 실무 매뉴얼을 작성하고자 하였다. 실무에서 곧바로 활용할 수 있는 중요한 노무관리 부분만을 20개 테마로 선정하여 관련근거, 사례연구, 실무적용 지침과 관련 양식까지도 자세히 수록하여 실무자들의 업무처리 지침서로 만들고자 하였다.

이번에 출간된 「직장 내 괴롭힘과 성희롱 예방 매뉴얼」은 최근에 사업장에서 가장 많은 이슈가 되는 노동문제를 다루고 있다. 직장 내 괴롭힘 방지법이 2019년 「근로기준법」으로 도입됨에 따라 그동안 직장 내에서 수면 아래에 잠재해 있었던 직원 상하간의 수많은 갈등이 수면위로 올라오고 있다. 저자는 직장 내 괴롭힘에 대한 여러 사건을 처리하기도 하고, 직장 내 괴롭힘 예방교육도 실시하면서, 이러한 직장 내 괴롭힘에 대한 예방매뉴얼이 절실히 필요하다고 느꼈다. 그러한 취지에 이 책을 출간하게 되었다. 특히, 국립방송통신대학교(방송대) 김엘림 교수님은 본 저자의 스승이자 한국젠더법학회의 초대회장으로 직장 내 성희롱 문제에 대한 전문가이시다. 김 교수님께 특별히 부탁드려 직장 내 성희롱 예방에 관한 원고를 받아서 공저자로서 같이 출판하게 되는 영광을 가지게 되었다. 따라서 이 매뉴얼은 직장 내 괴롭힘 뿐만 아니라 직장 내 성희롱에 대한 실무사례와 예방에 대한 내용도 담고 있다.

이 매뉴얼의 구성은 다음과 같다. 제1장은 직장 내 괴롭힘과 성희롱에 관한 기본적 이해로서 직장 내 인권 존중에 관한 권리의무와 필요성, 직장 내 괴롭힘과 성희롱의 개념과 문제, 법적 대응 등에 관해 설명하고 있다. 제2장은 실무에서 처리했던 직장 내 괴롭힘 사례에 대해 구체적인 내용을 담고 있고, 제3장은 현행법이 사업주에게 요구한 직장 내 성희롱의 예방 조치와 발생 시 조치, 그리고 실제로 사업장에서 사업주, 상급자, 근로자에 의해 발생된 사건들과 이에 대한 법원과 국가인권위원회 등의 분쟁처리기관 들의 사건처리사례들을 담고 있다. 그리고 제4장은 고용노동부와 법원에서 다루었던 다양한 괴롭힘과 성희롱 사례를 담아서 독자들에게 다양한 경험을 하도록 하였다.

본서 출간에 있어 영문 편집과 교정을 해주신 김혜민 사무장님과 박채늬 노무사님께 무한한 감사를 드린다. 그리고 이 책이 빛을 볼 수 있도록 편집과 출판을 해 주신 정영철 사장님께 감사드린다. 특히 나의 오랜 친구이자 영문교정을 맡고 있는 Dave Crofton에게도 감사드린다. 여러 사람의 노력이 배어있는 본 매뉴얼은 결코 저자 혼자만의 작품이 아닌 공동작업의 성과물이라고 생각한다.

2023년 6월 1일 선릉 사무실에서
공동저자 공인노무사/법학박사 정 봉 수

Chapter I — Understanding Workplace Harassment and Sexual Harassment

Section 1: Employer's Obligation to Protect (El-lim Kim, Bongsoo Jung) ········ 05
  Ⅰ. Rights and Obligations of Labor and Management Respecting the Human Rights ······ 05
  Ⅱ. Employer's Obligation to Protect and Impact of Violations ················· 12

Section 2. Basic Understanding of Workplace Harassment (Bongsoo Jung) ············· 16
  Ⅰ. Concept & Criteria of Determining Workplace Harassment ················· 17
  Ⅱ. The Workplace Harassment Prevention Law and the Employer's Duty ············ 22

Section 3. Basic Understanding of Sexual Harassment (El-lim Kim) ················· 27
  Ⅰ. Definition of "Sexual Harassment" and "Workplace Sexual Harassment" ············ 27
  Ⅱ. Definition of "Sexual Harassment" and "Workplace Sexual Harassment" under Korean Law ················· 30
  Ⅲ. Characteristics of Sexual Harassment and its Relationship to Workplace Harassment, Sexual Assault, and Gender Discrimination ················· 37
  Ⅳ. Problems and Harms Caused by Sexual Harassment ················· 43

Chapter II — Workplace Harassment: Prevention and Response (Bongsoo Jung)

  Ⅰ. Workplace Harassment Resolved through Recognition of an Accident as Related to Work ················· 54
  Ⅱ. A Case of Workplace Harassment and the Criteria for Recognizing Consequent Mental Illness as an Occupational Accident Related to Work ············ 59
  Ⅲ. When Workplace Harassment Occurs, What Measures Should an Employer Take? ················· 66
  Ⅳ. A Case Study on Workplace Harassment against a New Employee ·············· 72
  Ⅴ. Cases of Workplace Bullying & Sexual Harassment and Disciplinary Committee Decisions ················· 78
  Ⅵ. Workplace Bullying and Sexual Harassment: A Case Analysis
    - Supreme Court Ruling on November 25, 2021, 2020da270503 - ··········· 85

차 례

제1장 직장 내 괴롭힘과 성희롱에 관한 기본적 이해

제1절 직장 내 인권 존중의 권리의무와 필요성(김엘림, 정봉수) …… 05
Ⅰ. 근로관계에서의 인권 존중의 중요성과 필요성 ………………… 05
Ⅱ. 근로계약상 사용자의 보호의무와 위반의 효력 ………………… 12

제2절 직장 내 괴롭힘의 기본적 이해(정봉수) ……………………… 16
Ⅰ. 괴롭힘의 개념과 판단기준 ……………………………………… 17
Ⅱ. 직장 내 괴롭힘 방지법과 사용자의 의무 ……………………… 22

제3절 직장 내 성희롱의 기본적 이해(김엘림) ……………………… 27
Ⅰ. '성희롱'과 '직장 내 성희롱'이란 용어의 뜻 …………………… 27
Ⅱ. 현행법의 '성희롱'과 '직장 내 성희롱'의 개념 정의 …………… 30
Ⅲ. 성희롱의 특성과 직장 내 괴롭힘·성폭력·성차별과의 관계 …… 37
Ⅳ. 성희롱의 문제와 피해 …………………………………………… 43

제2장 직장 내 괴롭힘 사건 사례와 예방조치(정봉수)

Ⅰ. 직장 내 괴롭힘 원인제거를 통한 해결 사례 …………………… 54
Ⅱ. 직장 내 괴롭힘 사례와 산재인정 요건 ………………………… 59
Ⅲ. 직장 내 괴롭힘 사건 사례를 통해서 본 사업주의 적절한 조치 …… 66
Ⅳ. 직장 내 괴롭힘 처리 사례 (신입직원) …………………………… 72
Ⅴ. 직장 내 괴롭힘, 성희롱 사건과 기각 결정 사례 ……………… 78
Ⅵ. 직장 내 괴롭힘과 성희롱에 관한 판례 해석
　　(대법원 2021.11.25. 선고, 2020다270503 판결) ……………… 85

Chapter III — Workplace Sexual Harassment: Prevention and Response (El-lim Kim)

Section I. Measures to Prevent Workplace Sexual Harassment 93
    I. Prohibiting Workplace Sexual Harassment 93
    II. Preventing Workplace Sexual Harassment 94

Section 2. Responding to Reported Incidents of Workplace Sexual Harassment 99
    I. Responding Inside the Workplace 99
    II. Handling of Incidents by the Labor Relations Commission 107
    III. Handling of Incidents by the Minister of Employment and Labor 115
    IV. Handling of Incidents by the National Human Rights Commission of Korea 117
    V. Handling of Incidents by Investigative Agencies and the Courts 125

Section 3. Issues and Related Cases in Handling Workplace Sexual Harassment Incidents 128
    I. The Criteria for Judgment by Courts and National Human Rights Commissions 128
    II. Precedents and Decisions related to Workplace Sexual Harassment 137
    III. Court Rulings and Decisions related to Sexual Harassment by Superiors 143
    IV. Court Rulings and Decisions related to Sexual Harassment of Employees 155

Chapter IV — Case Studies for Workplace and Sexual Harassment (Bongsoo Jung)

Section 1. Cases Studies for Workplace Harassment (MOEL) 161
Section 2. Labor Cases related to Workplace Harassment 169
Section 3. Sexual Harassment Case and Procedures for Handling this Case (for Sales Workers) 180
Section 4. Sexual Harassment Case in the Workplace & Lessons Learned (for Production Workers) 185
Section 5. Labor Cases related to Sexual Harassment 192

제3장 직장 내 성희롱의 예방과 발생시 조치 및 사건처리 사례(김엘림)

제1절 직장 내 성희롱 금지와 예방조치 ······ 93
Ⅰ. 직장 내 성희롱의 금지 ······ 93
Ⅱ. 직장 내 성희롱의 예방조치 ······ 94

제2절 직장 내 성희롱 발생 시 조치와 사건처리 ······ 99
Ⅰ. 사업장 내 발생시 조치와 사건처리 ······ 99
Ⅱ. 노동위원회의 사건 처리 ······ 107
Ⅲ. 고용노동부장관의 사건 처리 ······ 115
Ⅳ. 국가인권위원회의 사건 처리 ······ 117
Ⅴ. 수사기관과 법원의 사건 처리 ······ 125

제3절 직장 내 성희롱 사건 처리 사례 ······ 128
Ⅰ. 법원과 국가인권위원회의 판단기준 등 ······ 128
Ⅱ. 사업주의 성희롱 사건과 관련 판례·결정례 ······ 137
Ⅲ. 상급자의 성희롱 사건과 관련 판례·결정례 ······ 143
Ⅳ. 근로자의 성희롱 사건과 관련 판례·결정례 ······ 155

제4장 직장 내 괴롭힘과 성희롱 사건 사례와 판단 (정봉수)

제1절 고용노동부의 직장 내 괴롭힘 판단 사례 ······ 161
제2절 직장 내 괴롭힘 관련 주요 사례 ······ 169
제3절 직장 내 성희롱 사건사례 (영업직 직원) ······ 180
제4절 직장 내 성희롱 사건사례 (사무직 직원) ······ 185
제5절 직장 내 성희롱 관련 주요 사례 ······ 192

Chapter 1. Understanding Workplace Harassment and Sexual Harassment

Section 1. Employer's Obligation to Protect
 (El-lim Kim, Bongsoo Jung)
  Ⅰ. Rights and Obligations of Labor and Management respecting the Human Rights
  Ⅱ. Employer's Obligation to Protect and Impact of Violations

Section 2. Basic Understanding of Workplace Harassment
 (Bongsoo Jung)
  Ⅰ. Concept & Criteria of Determining Workplace Harassment
  Ⅱ. The Workplace Harassment Prevention Law and the Employer's Duty

Section 3. Basic Understanding of Sexual Harassment (El-lim Kim)
  Ⅰ. Definition of "Sexual Harassment" and "Workplace Sexual Harassment"
  Ⅱ. Definition of "Sexual Harassment" and "Workplace Sexual harassment" under Korean Law
  Ⅲ. Characteristics of Sexual Harassment and Its Relationship to Workplace Harassment, Sexual Assault, and Gender Discrimination
  Ⅳ. Problems and Harms Caused by Sexual Harassment

제1장 직장 내 괴롭힘과 성희롱에 관한 기본적 이해

제1절 직장 내 인권 존중의 권리의무와 필요성
(김엘림, 정봉수)
 Ⅰ. 사용자와 근로자의 인권 존중에 관한 권리의무
 Ⅱ. 근로계약상 사용자의 보호의무와 위반의 효력
제2절 직장 내 괴롭힘의 기본적 이해(정봉수)
 Ⅰ. 괴롭힘의 개념과 판단기준
 Ⅱ. 직장 내 괴롭힘 방지법과 사용자의 의무
제3절 직장 내 성희롱의 기본적 이해(김엘림)
 Ⅰ. '성희롱'과 '직장 내 성희롱'이란 용어의 뜻
 Ⅱ. 현행법의 '성희롱'과 '직장 내 성희롱'의 개념 정의
 Ⅲ. 성희롱의 특성과 직장 내 괴롭힘・성폭력・성차별과의 관계
 Ⅳ. 성희롱의 문제와 피해

Section 1: Employer's Obligation to Protect

I. Rights and Obligations of Labor and Management respecting the Human Rights

1. The Relationship between labor law, employment relationships, and respect for human rights[1]

Labor law is a legal framework that regulates the relationship between workers and employers in capitalist societies. It encompasses norms governing employment, working conditions, and labor-management relations, with the aim of guaranteeing a dignified life for workers, who are economically and socially vulnerable, and promoting industrial peace and balanced development of the national economy.

The rights and obligations between workers and employers, known collectively as the labor-management relationship, are established through the labor contract, which the Labor Standards Act defines as "a contract concluded for the purpose of a worker providing labor to an employer, and the employer paying wages in return" (Article 2, paragraph 1, clause 4). Therefore, the labor relationship is fundamentally based on the worker's obligation to provide labor and the right to claim wages, as well as the employer's right to receive labor and the obligation to pay wages.

In a capitalist society, workers provide labor in exchange for wages to support themselves and their families and to sustain their economic and social lives. In reality, job opportunities are limited, making it quite challenging for individuals seeking employment to secure positions in their desired locations. Moreover, once employed, workers are not able to autonomously provide their labor, but rather must comply with the employer's directives based on the rights of business operation and personnel management. A worker who violates the employer's directives may face contract termination or disciplinary actions such as dismissal. Consequently, in a capitalist society, workers find themselves in a position of dependency and subordination to employers, lacking equal standing. As a result, ensuring the legitimacy, legality, appropriateness of the employer's directives, as well as safeguarding the rights of workers such as freedom and equality, becomes a fundamental and essential issue in regulating the labor relationship.

---

[1] El-lim Kim, Bongsoo Jung, Yonggeun Choi, 「Labor Protection Law」 (revised edition in 2020), January 2020, Korea National Open University Press, pp. 5-7, pp. 307-308.

제1절 직장 내 인권 존중의 권리의무와 필요성 (김엘림, 정봉수)

I. 근로관계에서의 인권 존중의 중요성과 필요성

1. 근로관계와 인권 존중의 관계[1]

노동법이란 자본주의 사회에서 근로자와 사용자 및 국가의 관계를 규율하며 취업과 근로조건 및 노사관계에 관하여 규정한 규범들의 총체로서 경제적·사회적 약자인 근로자의 인간다운 생활을 보장하여 산업평화와 균형 있는 국민경제의 발전을 이루고자 하는 법이다.

근로자와 사용자 사이의 권리의무 관계 즉 근로관계는 근로계약의 체결로 성립된다. 「근로기준법」은 근로계약을 "근로자가 사용자에게 근로를 제공하고 사용자는 그 대가로 임금을 지급하는 것을 목적으로 체결된 계약"(제2조제1항제4호)으로 정의하고 있다. 그러므로 근로관계는 근로자의 근로 제공 의무와 임금청구권, 사용자의 노동력 수령권과 임금 지급의무를 기본으로 한다.

그런데 자본주의 사회에서 근로자는 자신과 가족의 생계와 경제적·사회적 생활을 위해 노동력을 제공하고 그 대가로 임금을 받아야 하는데 일자리는 적고 취업하고자 하는 사람들이 많은 현실에서 자기가 원하는 곳에 취업하기가 상당히 어렵다. 그리고 취업을 하면 근로자는 노동력을 자율적으로 제공할 수 있는 것이 아니라 사용자의 사업 운영을 위한 경영권과 인사권에 기초한 지휘·명령에 따라 제공해야 한다. 사용자의 지휘·명령을 어긴 근로자는 근로계약을 해지당하거나 해고 등의 징계를 받게 된다. 그리하여 자본주의 사회에서 근로자는 사용자와 실질적으로 대등한 지위에 있지 않고 사용종속 관계에 있게 된다. 그러므로 사용자의 지휘·명령의 정당성과 적법성·적절성, 근로자의 자유와 평등 및 인간다운 생활을 할 권리 등의 인권 보장은 근로관계를 규율하는 기본적이고 핵심적인 문제가 된다.

---

[1] 김엘림·정봉수·최용근, 「근로보호법」(2020년 개정판), 2020., 한국방송통신대학교 출판문화원, 5~7면, 307~308면.

Section 1: Employer's Obligation to Protect (El-lim Kim, Bongsoo Jung)

2. The meaning of human rights and international guarantees[2]

(1) The meaning of human rights

Every person possesses inherent dignity, worth, freedom, and rights, known as human rights. Human rights are characterized by their natural quality applicable to all individuals regardless of their status, location, or circumstances and inviolability, requiring respect and prohibiting infringement under any situation or by anyone.

(2) International trends in ensuring human rights

The United Nations (UN), an international organization joined by nearly all countries worldwide, enunciates the attributes of these human rights, establishes international norms to guarantee and promote their realization, and urges member states to implement these norms. The International Labour Organization (ILO), a specialized agency of the UN, develops international standards concerning actions to be taken by governments and employers to ensure the protection of workers' human rights and to enable them to live dignified lives in work and social security. The ILO also urges member countries to implement these standards. Among the international norms (treaties, declarations, recommendations, codes of conduct, etc.) adopted by the UN and the ILO, there are norms that guarantee the human rights of workers, focusing on eliminating discrimination and violence. Norms aimed at eliminating discrimination include the UN's Universal Declaration of Human Rights, the International Covenant on Economic, Social and Cultural Rights, the International Covenant on Civil and Political Rights, the Convention on the Elimination of All Forms of Discrimination Against Women, and the International Convention on the Elimination of All Forms of Racial Discrimination. The ILO's international standards include the Equal Remuneration Convention (No. 100), the Discrimination (Employment and Occupation) Convention (No. 111), and the Maternity Protection Convention (No. 183), which address equal pay for work of equal value, discrimination in employment, and equal opportunities and treatment for male and female workers with family responsibilities, respectively. Norms aimed at eliminating violence include the UN's Declaration on the Elimination of Violence Against Women, which was unanimously adopted by the UN General Assembly on December 12, 1993, and the ILO's Convention concerning the Elimination of Violence and Harassment in the World of Work (Convention No. 190), adopted at the ILO Centenary International Labour Conference on June 21, 2019.

---

[2] Kim, El-rim. "Gender Equality and the Law" (2022 Revised Edition), KNOUPRESS (Korea National Open University Press), 2022, pp. 33-48; Kim, El-rim, "Sexual Harassment: Law and Dispute Resolution Cases," Episteme, 2023, pp. 110-112.

2. 인권의 의의와 국제적 보장 [2]

(1) 인권의 의의와 속성

모든 사람은 인간으로서의 존엄과 가치 및 자유와 권리 즉 인권(Human Rights)을 가진다. 인권은 인간이면 누구나 태어날 때부터 가지는 자연성, 어떠한 지위와 장소 및 상황에서든 누구나 가지는 보편성, 누구에 의해서든 어떠한 상황이든 존중받아야 하고 침해되어서는 아니 되는 불가침성을 가진다.

(2) 인권의 보장에 관한 국제적 동향

세계 거의 모든 국가가 가입한 국제기구인 UN(국제연합)은 이러한 인권의 속성을 천명하고 인권을 보장하고 구현하기 위한 국제규범을 채택하여 가입국에 이를 이행할 것을 촉구하고 있다. UN의 전문기구인 국제노동기구(ILO)는 고용과 사회보장 부문에서 근로자들이 인권을 보장받고 인간다운 생활을 할 수 있게 하기 위해 국가와 사용자가 해야 할 조치에 관한 국제규범을 채택하고 가입국에 그 이행을 촉구하고 있다.

UN과 ILO가 채택한 국제규범(협약, 선언, 권고, 행동강령 등)에는 차별을 철폐하기 위한 국제규범과 폭력을 철폐하기 위한 국제규범이 있다. 차별을 철폐하기 위한 국제규범에는 UN의 「세계인권선언」, 국제인권규약(「경제적·사회적·문화적 권리에 관한 국제규약」, 「시민적·정치적 권리에 관한 국제규약」), 「여성에 대한 모든 형태의 차별철폐협약」(약칭: 여성차별철폐협약), 「인종차별철폐협약」 등이 있다. ILO의 국제규범 중에는 「남녀 동일가치노동의 동일보수에 관한 협약」(제100호 협약), 「고용차별에 관한 협약」(제111호 협약), 「가족부양 책임을 가진 남녀근로자의 고용기회와 대우에서의 평등에 관한 협약」(제123호 협약) 등이 있다. 폭력을 철폐하기 위한 규범에는 UN이 1993년 12월 20일, 총회에서 만장일치로 채택한 「여성에 대한 폭력철폐선언」(약칭: 여성폭력철폐선언)과 ILO가 2019년 6월 21일, ILO 설립 100주년 기념 총회에서 채택한 「일의 세계에서의 폭력과 괴롭힘 철폐에 관한 협약」(제190호 협약) 등이 있다. UN의 「장애인의 권리에 관한 협약」 등과 같이 차별과 폭력, 학대의 철폐를 모두 포함하고 있는 국제협약도 있다.

---

[2] 김엘림, 「남녀평등과 법」(2022년 전면개정판), 한국방송통신대학교 출판문화원, 2022, 33~48면: 김엘림, 「성희롱: 법과 분쟁처리사례」, 에피스테매, 2023, 110~112면.

However, until the mid-1980s, the focus of the UN and ILO was primarily on eliminating discrimination. It was in 1985 when they first explicitly addressed sexual harassment and sexual and other forms of violence as human rights issues and called for their eradication. The substantial development of norms specifically targeting violence began in the 1990s. The UN's Declaration on the Elimination of Violence Against Women stated that "violence against women, including sexual harassment, sexual violence, domestic violence, and prostitution, is a form of discrimination against women as it deepens their subordinate status and violates their human rights as defined in the Convention on the Elimination of All Forms of Discrimination Against Women." When member countries submit national reports on their implementation of the Convention on the Elimination of All Forms of Discrimination Against Women to the UN, they are required to include measures to eliminate violence against women. This declaration, especially regarding sexual harassment, garnered global attention. Sexual harassment is defined as unwelcome behavior or demands of a sexual nature from someone using their position or in relation to work, which causes mental or physical harm, infringes upon human rights, and leads to work-related harm or damage to the victim. Here, sexual harassment primarily targets women.

The ILO recognizes that workplace sexual harassment not only violates the rights of workers but also undermines their motivation, performance, productivity, and creates a hostile and uncomfortable work environment, and that it also adversely affects both the workplace and its employees. Therefore, the ILO strongly urges governments and employers to develop measures to address these issues. Since the 2000s, the ILO has issued warnings about the pervasive nature of human rights violations, including workplace violence and harassment, and has begun developing strategies to tackle them. The culmination of these efforts is reflected in the International Convention on the Elimination of Violence and Harassment in the World of Work (Convention No. 190) and the Violence and Harassment Recommendation (No. 206).

UN and ILO have adopted various international norms to guarantee human rights by eliminating discrimination, harassment, and abuse. As a result, countries have developed and implemented legislation and policies to ensure human rights in the workplace.

3. Necessity of Ensuring Human Rights for Personal and Socio-economic Development

The international human rights norms of the UN and ILO explicitly state that

그런데 UN과 ILO는 1980년대 중반까지는 차별철폐 문제에 주력하였다. 성희롱·성폭력 등의 폭력문제를 인권문제로 국제규범에 처음 명시하고 국가와 사용자에게 철폐를 촉구한 때는 1985년이며 본격적으로 폭력철폐 규범을 마련하기 시작한 때는 1990년대이다. UN의 「여성폭력철폐선언」은 "성희롱, 성폭력, 가정폭력, 성매매 등의 여성에 대한 폭력은 남녀가 불평등한 관계에서 발생하여 여성의 종속적 지위를 심화시키고 여성의 인권을 침해하므로 「여성차별철폐협약」이 규정한 '여성에 대한 차별'에 해당된다."라고 하였다. 그리고 가입국이 「여성차별철폐협약」의 국가이행보고서를 UN에 제출할 때에 여성폭력을 철폐하는 조치를 포함할 것을 요구하였다. 이 선언 채택을 계기로 특히 'sexual harassment'(성희롱)은 세계적 주목을 받았다.

성희롱이란 업무와 관련하거나 지위를 이용하여 상대방이 원하지 않는 성적 언동이나 요구를 하여 상대방과 사업장 등에 심신의 손상과 인권침해, 업무상의 피해를 초래하는 행위를 말한다. 그런데 성희롱은 권위주의적 사회와 조직문화에서 주로 우월적 지위에 있는 사람이 비교적 취약한 지위에 있는 사람을 대상으로 자행하는 권력성과 폭력성, 그리고 가부장적 사회와 조직문화에서 주로 남성이 여성을 대상으로 자행하는 차별성을 가지는 특성이 있다.

ILO는 고용관계에서 이루어지는 '직장 내 성희롱'이 근로자의 인격권을 침해할 뿐 아니라 근로권도 침해하고 근로의 의욕과 실적이나 생산성을 저하하고 근로환경을 적대적이고 불편하게 만들어 피해자뿐 아니라 사업장과 그 종사자에게도 악영향을 준다는 해악성을 경고하고 국가와 사용자에게 대책을 마련할 것을 촉구하였다. 그런데 ILO는 2000년대 이후에는 직장 내 성희롱을 포함한 직장 내 폭력과 괴롭힘 등의 인권침해 문제의 대책을 마련하기 시작하였다. 이러한 성과로 이루어진 국제규범이 「일의 세계에서의 폭력과 괴롭힘 철폐에 관한 협약」(제190호 협약)과 권고(제206호) 이다.

이와 같이 UN과 ILO는 차별과 성희롱, 괴롭힘 등의 철폐를 통하여 인권을 보장하기 위한 다양한 국제규범을 채택하였다. 그 영향으로 국가들은 사업장에서의 인권을 보장하는 법령과 정책을 마련하여 시행하고 있다.

3. 인권 보장의 개인적·사회경제 발전에의 필요성

UN과 ILO의 국제인권 규범들은 인권 보장이 개인의 인간다운 생활과 존엄,

guaranteeing human rights is a fundamental requirement for individuals to lead a dignified, peaceful, and fulfilling life. Moreover, they emphasize the need to create a culture and system free from discrimination, harassment, and human rights violations, which promotes the maximum development of individual abilities, encourages social participation, and maximizes human resource utilization in workplaces and society. This understanding is based on the recognition that these factors are essential for the development of workplaces, societies, and nations.

For example, the "Convention on the Elimination of All Forms of Discrimination against Women" has been ratified by 190 countries, becoming a universal international norm. The Convention explicitly states in its preamble that discrimination against women violates the principles of equality and human dignity, obstructs women's participation in political, social, economic, and cultural aspects of life on equal terms with men, hampers the well-being and development of society and families, and hinders the full development of women's potential in the service of the nation and humanity. It further emphasizes the conviction that for the complete development of nations and the well-being and peace of humanity, it is essential for women to participate as equals in all fields with men.

Similarly, ILO Convention No. 190, in its preamble, points out that violence, harassment, and sexual harassment in the world of work are grave human rights violations and threats to the development of workplaces and society. It calls for the recognition of the need to protect the rights of workers in relation to this issue.

"It recognizes the right of all individuals to be free from violence and harassment, including gender-based violence and harassment, in the world of work. It acknowledges that violence and harassment in the world of work constitute human rights violations, threats to equal opportunities, and are incompatible with decent work. It recognizes the importance of fostering a culture of respect and dignity based on mutual respect for human beings to prevent violence and harassment. Member states have a significant obligation to promote an overall environment of zero tolerance towards violence and harassment in order to prevent such acts and practices. All actors in the world of work must refrain from, prevent, and address violence and harassment.

It acknowledges that violence and harassment in the world of work impact

안녕과 행복추구를 가능하게 하는 기본적인 요건이 된다는 것을 명시하고 있다. 뿐만 아니라 차별과 괴롭힘, 성희롱 등의 인권침해가 없는 문화와 제도를 조성하여 개인의 최대한의 능력계발과 발휘 및 사회참여를 촉진시키고 이를 통해 사업장과 사회의 인력활용 극대화를 이루게 하여 사업장, 사회와 국가를 발전시키는 데 필수적인 요건이 된다는 인식에 기초하고 있다.

예를 들면, 현재 190개 국가가 비준하여 보편적 국제 규범이 되고 있는 「여성차별철폐협약」은 전문에서 "여성에 대한 차별은 권리평등 및 인간의 존엄성의 존중 원칙에 위배되며, 여성이 남성과 동등한 조건하에 국가의 정치적·사회적·경제적 및 문화적 생활에 참여하는 데 장애가 되며, 사회와 가정의 번영의 증진을 어렵게 하며, 국가와 인류에 대한 봉사에 있어 여성의 잠재력의 완전한 개발을 더욱 어렵게 함을 상기하고, …국가의 완전한 발전과 인류의 복지 및 평화를 위해서는 여성이 모든 분야에 남성과 평등한 조건으로 최대한 참여하는 것이 필요함을 확신하고,…"라는 문구를 명시하였다.

또한 ILO 제190호 협약은 전문에서 다음과 같이 일의 세계(사업장)에서의 폭력과 괴롭힘, 성희롱이 중대한 인권침해이며 사업장과 사회 발전의 위협임을 지적하고 이에 대한 근로자의 인권보호의 필요성에 관하여 천명하였다.

"모든 사람이 일의 세계에서 젠더에 기반한 폭력과 괴롭힘을 포괄하는 폭력과 괴롭힘으로부터 자유로울 권리를 인정하며, 일의 세계에서의 폭력과 괴롭힘은 인권침해이고 기회균등에 대한 위협이며, 양질의 일자리에 용납할 수도 양립할 수도 없음을 인식하고, 폭력과 괴롭힘을 방지하기 위한 인간에 대한 상호 존중과 존엄에 기반한 일 문화의 중요성을 인식하고,

회원국들은 폭력과 괴롭힘 행위와 관행의 예방을 도모하기 위해 폭력과 괴롭힘에 대한 전반적인 무관용의 환경을 촉진할 중요한 의무를 지니며, 일의 세계의 모든 행위자들은 폭력과 괴롭힘을 삼가고, 예방하고, 고심해야 함을 상기하고,

일의 세계에서의 폭력과 괴롭힘이 개인의 정신적·신체적·성적 건강, 존엄, 가족 및 사회적 환경에 영향을 미침을 인정하고, 폭력과 괴롭힘은 또한 공공과 민간 서비스의 질에 영향을 주고, 개인들, 특히 여성들이 노동시장에 진입하고, 머무르고, 나아가지 못하게 막을 수 있음을 인지하고,

폭력과 괴롭힘은 지속가능한 기업의 촉진과 양립할 수 없고, 작업편성, 작업장 관계, 노동자 참여, 기업 평판, 생산성에 부정적인 영향을 줌에 주목하고,

individuals' mental, physical, and sexual well-being, dignity, family, and social environment. It also recognizes that violence and harassment have an impact on the quality of public and private services and can hinder individuals, especially women, from entering, staying, and advancing in the labor market. It highlights that violence and harassment are incompatible with the promotion of sustainable enterprises and have negative effects on job organization, workplace relations, worker participation, corporate reputation, and productivity.

It acknowledges that gender-based violence and harassment disproportionately affect women and girls. It recognizes that an inclusive, integrated, and gender-sensitive perspective that addresses underlying causes and risk factors such as gender stereotypes, intersecting and overlapping forms of discrimination, and unequal gender-based power relations is crucial in ending violence and harassment in the world of work."

In this context, "gender" refers to the perception of distinctions and differences based on sex, including male and female.

The UN and the ILO, through attempts to eliminate discrimination, violence, harassment, and abuse, have influenced the majority of countries worldwide to establish and enforce legislation and policies that guarantee human rights in the workplace.

4. Protection of workers' human rights in South Korean law and court rulings

In South Korea, various laws and policies have been established and implemented to ensure the protection of workers' human rights.

(1) Guarantee of Workers' Human Rights in the "Constitution".

The nation's supreme law and fundamental law, the "Constitution," contains various provisions to guarantee the human rights of workers, among which the following are the most important:

1) "All citizens shall possess human dignity and value as individuals and have the right to pursue happiness. The state shall confirm and guarantee the inviolable fundamental rights of individuals." (Article 10)
2) "All citizens are equal before the law and shall not be discriminated against in political, economic, social, or cultural life on the grounds of sex, religion, or

젠더에 기반한 폭력과 괴롭힘은 여성과 소녀들에게 편중되게 영향을 끼침을 인정하고, 젠더 고정관념, 중복과 교차 형태의 차별, 불평등한 젠더 기반 권력관계 등 근본적인 원인과 위험 요소들에 맞서는 포용적·통합적·성인지적인 관점이 일의 세계에서의 폭력과 괴롭힘을 끝내는 데 핵심적임을 인지한다."

그리고 제190호 협약은 '일의 세계에서의 폭력과 괴롭힘'(violence and harassment in the world of work)을 "그 발생이 일회성이든 반복적이든, 신체적·정신적·성적·경제적 피해를 목표로 하거나, 초래하거나, 초래할 개연성이 있어 용납할 수 없는 일련의 행위나 관행, 혹은 위협을 뜻하며 젠더에 기반한 폭력과 괴롭힘을 포함한다."(제1조제1항(a))라고 정의하였다. 그리고 '젠더에 기반한 폭력과 괴롭힘'(gender-based violence and harassment)을 "성별과 젠더(gender)를 이유로 인간에게 향하는, 혹은 특정 성 혹은 젠더에 편중되게 영향을 주는 폭력과 괴롭힘을 의미하며, sexual harassment를 포함한다."(제1조제1항(b))라고 정의하였다. 그리하여 직장 내 성희롱은 '젠더에 기반한 폭력과 괴롭힘'의 일종이며 '젠더에 기반한 폭력과 괴롭힘'은 일과 관련된 다양한 유형의 폭력과 괴롭힘의 일종으로 정리하였다. 여기서 '젠더(gender)'란 남성, 여성 등의 성의 구분과 차이에 관한 인식을 말한다.

4. 우리나라 법과 판례의 근로자의 인권 보장

우리나라에서도 근로자의 인권을 보장하기 위한 다양한 법과 정책이 마련되어 시행되고 있다.

(1) 「헌법」의 근로자 인권 보장

국가의 최고법과 기본법인 「헌법」은 근로자의 인권 보장을 위하여 다양한 조항을 두고 있는데 그중 가장 중요한 조항은 다음과 같다.

1) 모든 국민은 인간으로서의 존엄과 가치를 가지며, 행복을 추구할 권리를 가진다. 국가는 개인이 가지는 불가침의 기본적 인권을 확인하고 이를 보장할 의무를 가진다.(제10조)
2) 모든 국민은 법 앞에 평등하다. 누구든지 성별·종교 또는 사회적 신분에 의하여 정치적·경제적·사회적·문화적 생활의 모든 영역에 있어서

social status." (Article 11, Paragraph 1)
3) Regarding the right to work, Article 32 stipulates the following:
   ① "All citizens have the right to work. The state shall make efforts through social and economic measures to promote the employment of workers and guarantee appropriate wages and shall implement a minimum wage system as provided by law." (Paragraph 1)
   ② "The standards for working conditions shall be prescribed by law to ensure the dignity of human beings." (Paragraph 3)
   ③ "Women shall receive special protection in labor and shall not be subject to unfair discrimination in employment, wages, and working conditions." (Paragraph 4)
   ④ "Child labor shall receive special protection." (Paragraph 5)
   ⑤ National merit workers, disabled veterans, and families of deceased soldiers and police officers shall be given priority in employment opportunities as provided by law. (Paragraph 6)
4) Article 33 regulates the rights of collective action, known as the three labor rights (the right to organize, the right to collective bargaining, and the right to collective action):
   ① Workers have the right to voluntary organization, collective bargaining, and collective action for the improvement of working conditions.
   ② Public officials who are workers shall have the right to organization, collective bargaining, and collective action within the limits prescribed by law.
   ③ The right to collective action of workers engaged in major defense industries designated by law may be restricted or not recognized as provided by law.

(2) Guarantee of workers' human rights in the "Labor Standards Act".

According to Article 32, Clause 3 of the Constitution, the representative law that establishes standards for working conditions to guarantee human dignity is the "Labor Standards Act." Since its enactment on May 10, 1953, this law has included provisions on non-discrimination, equal treatment, prohibition of forced labor, prohibition of assault, protection of civil rights exercise during working hours, and other regulations related to guaranteeing human rights in terms of working conditions and treatment of workers by employers. These provisions serve as fundamental norms that guide the direction of employment relationships and the working conditions and treatment of workers. Additionally, in accordance with Article 32, Clauses 4 and 5 of the Constitution, this law includes special protection provisions for the labor of women and minors.

Furthermore, in response to cases where workers' rights are violated and extreme choices are made due to workplace harassment, the "Labor Standards Act" introduced the "Chapter 6-2: Workplace Harassment" on January 15, 2019, to

차별을 받지 아니한다.(제11조제1항)
3) 제32조에서는 근로권에 관하여 다음과 같이 규정하고 있다.
① 모든 국민은 근로의 권리를 가진다. 국가는 사회적·경제적 방법으로 근로자의 고용의 증진과 적정임금의 보장에 노력하여야 하며, 법률이 정하는 바에 의하여 최저임금제를 시행하여야 한다.(제1항)
② 근로조건의 기준은 인간의 존엄성을 보장하도록 법률로 정한다.(제3항)
③ 여자의 근로는 특별한 보호를 받으며, 고용·임금 및 근로조건에 있어서 부당한 차별을 받지 아니한다.(제4항)
④ 연소자의 근로는 특별한 보호를 받는다.(제5항)
⑤ 국가유공자·상이군경 및 전몰군경의 유가족은 법률이 정하는 바에 의하여 우선적으로 근로의 기회를 부여받는다.(제6항)
4) 제33조에서는 집단적 활동의 권리인 노동(근로) 3권(단결권, 단체교섭권, 단체행동권)에 관하여 다음과 같이 규정하고 있다.
① 근로자는 근로조건의 향상을 위하여 자주적인 단결권·단체교섭권 및 단체행동권을 가진다.
② 공무원인 근로자는 법률이 정하는 자에 한하여 단결권·단체교섭권 및 단체행동권을 가진다.
③ 법률이 정하는 주요방위산업체에 종사하는 근로자의 단체행동권은 법률이 정하는 바에 의하여 이를 제한하거나 인정하지 아니할 수 있다.

(2) 「근로기준법」의 근로자 인권 보장

「헌법」 제32조제3항에 따라 근로조건의 기준을 인간의 존엄성을 보장하도록 정한 대표적 법률이 「근로기준법」이다. 이 법은 1953년 5월 10일에 제정될 때부터 사용자의 근로자에 대한 근로조건과 대우에서의 차별금지와 균등처우, 강제근로의 금지, 폭행의 금지, 근로시간 중에의 공민권 행사 보장 등 인권 보장에 관한 규정들을 두고 있다. 이 규정들은 근로관계, 근로자의 근로조건과 대우의 방향을 제시한 기본규범이 된다. 그리고 이 법은 「헌법」 제32조의 제4항과 제5항에 따라 여성과 소년의 근로에 대하여 특별히 보호하는 규정들을 두고 있다.

한편, 직장 내 괴롭힘으로 근로자들이 사업장에서 인권을 침해당하고 극단적

prevent such harassment within the workplace. The "Industrial Safety and Health Act" and the "Industrial Accident Compensation Insurance Act" also introduced provisions on the prohibition of workplace harassment, protection of affected workers, and measures to be taken in case of its occurrence. The "Labor Standards Act" further strengthened the protection of workers' human rights from workplace harassment through its amendment on April 13, 2021.[3]

(3) Guaranteeing Workers' Human Rights under the "Equal Employment Act"

The "Equal Employment Act" is a special law enacted to ensure the prohibition of gender discrimination and promote gender equality in a concrete manner, as stipulated in the "Constitution" and the "Labor Standards Act." This law, enacted on December 4, 1987, prohibits gender discrimination throughout all stages of employment, including recruitment, hiring, wages, benefits, education, placement, promotion, retirement, and dismissal. Specifically, it regulates equal pay for equal work to address wage discrimination based on equal value of work.

The first introduction of the concept and regulations regarding education and measures for defining and preventing workplace sexual harassment in South Korea came after a landmark Supreme Court ruling (98Na12180, announced on February 10, 1998) that addressed a lawsuit involving sexual harassment. It was on February 8, 1999, that these regulations were first incorporated into the "Equal Employment Act," making it the first time sexual harassment was recognized as a significant issue in the country. When the "Equal Employment Act" was comprehensively revised on August 4, 2001, the concept of workplace sexual harassment was further refined. It was categorized under the second section of Chapter 2, titled "Equal Opportunities and Treatment of Men and Women in Employment," specifically addressing the "Prohibition and Prevention of Sexual Harassment in the Workplace." The revised law included provisions prohibiting workplace sexual harassment, mandating prevention education, specifying actions to be taken in the event of an occurrence, and establishing sanctions for employers who engage in such behavior. Subsequently, the "Equal Employment Act" further strengthened the provisions related to workplace sexual harassment to protect victims and whistleblowers, especially in response to the sexual harassment lawsuit involving R Automobile Company. Through amendments, including those made on May 18, 2021, by the Labor Relations Commission and the Ministry of Employment and Labor, the law introduced dispute resolution provisions and enhanced protection of workers' human rights.

(4) Legal principles and Precedents on the protection of workers' rights

Workers' rights encompass the right to fair treatment and employment, the right

---

[3] However, unlike the provisions of the "Equal Employment Act" regarding sexual harassment in the workplace, the "Labor Standards Act" does not include provisions on the prevention of workplace bullying. This is seen as a legislative loophole.

선택을 하는 경우들이 발생하자 그 대책으로 「근로기준법」은 2019년 1월 15일, 직장 내 괴롭힘을 방지하기 위하여 "제6장의 2 직장 내 괴롭힘"을 신설하여 사용자와 근로자의 직장 내 괴롭힘을 금지하고(제76조의2), 발생 시 조치에 관한 규정(제76조의3)을 도입하였다. 그리고 2021년 4월 13일의 개정으로 발생 시 조치에서 직장 내 괴롭힘에 대한 조사 규정을 구체화하고(제2항), 조사 관련자들의 비밀누설 금지의무를 명시하였다.(제7항) 제12장 벌칙에서는 사용자의 친족이 행한 직장 내 괴롭힘에 대한 제재도 마련하였다(제116조제1항).[3]

(3) 「남녀고용평등법」의 근로자 인권 보장

「헌법」과 「근로기준법」의 성차별금지와 남녀평등 대우를 구체적으로 보장하기 위하여 제정된 특별법이 「남녀고용평등법」이다. 1987년 12월 4일에 제정된 이 법은 모집·채용, 임금, 복리후생, 교육·배치·승진, 정년·퇴직·해고 등 고용의 모든 과정에서의 성차별을 금지하고 있다. 특별히 임금차별에 관해서는 동일가치노동 동일임금으로 규제하고 있다.

이 법이 직장 내 성희롱의 개념을 정의하고 예방을 위한 교육과 조치에 관한 규정을 처음 도입한 때는 우리나라 최초로 성희롱을 문제 삼은 소송에 관한 대법원 판결(1998.2.10.선고 98나12180판결)이 선고된 이후인 1999년 2월 8일이다. 「남녀고용평등법」이 2001년 8월 4일에 전부개정될 때, 직장 내 성희롱의 개념을 변경하고, [제2장 고용에 있어서 남녀의 평등한 기회보장 및 대우 등]의 제2절의 제목을 "직장 내 성희롱의 금지와 예방"으로 하여, 직장 내 성희롱의 금지, 예방교육, 발생 시 조치, 행위자인 사업주에 대한 제재 규정들을 두었다. 그 후 「남녀고용평등법」은 R자동차 회사의 성희롱 소송사건을 계기로 피해자와 신고자의 보호를 강화하기 위하여 2017년 11월 28일, 직장 내 성희롱 관련 규정들을 더욱 구체화하였고, 2021년 5월 18일의 개정으로 노동위원회와 고용노동부장관의 분쟁처리 규정들을 마련하여 근로자 인권 보장을 더욱 강화하였다.

(4) 근로자의 인권 보장의 법리와 판례

근로자의 근로권에는 정당한 대우를 받으며 일할 권리, 사업장에서 차별 및 괴롭힘과 성희롱을 당하지 않고 인권을 존중받으며 일할 권리, 안전하고 쾌적한

---
[3] 다만, 「근로기준법」은 「남녀고용평등법」의 직장 내 성희롱에 관한 규정들과 달리 직장 내 괴롭힘의 예방에 관한 규정들을 두지 않고 있는데 이것은 입법의 불비라고 보여진다.

to work without experiencing harassment or sexual harassment in the workplace while having their human rights respected, and the right to work in a safe and conducive environment that promotes good health.

The legal regulations regarding workplace harassment and sexual harassment serve as institutional mechanisms to ensure the dignity and human rights of individuals in the labor field by promoting a work environment that is friendly to human rights. Employers, who operate businesses utilizing the state and workers, have the obligation to guarantee the labor rights of their employees.

The Supreme Court, in its ruling on April 23, 1996 (Case No. 95Da6823), stated that "a worker is a human being with dignity and value, and the provision of labor by a worker in the employment relationship cannot be separated from their entire personality, considering that a worker's entire personality is being invested in the employer's workplace." It further emphasized that "unless there are special circumstances otherwise, an employer, through the conclusion of an employment contract, has a duty, based on the principle of good faith, to consider enabling the worker to realize their personality within the exercise of their authority to direct and give orders in the scope that harmonizes with the worker's rights."

Additionally, the Supreme Court, in its ruling on February 10, 1998 (Case No. 95Da39533), stated that "the employment relationship or labor relationship is a continuous creditor-debtor relationship based on personal trust. Therefore, regarding the obligation of the employee to provide labor faithfully in the employment contract, the employer, in addition to the obligation to provide remuneration, has a duty to respect and protect the employee's personality, to seek necessary measures to ensure that the employee does not suffer harm while fulfilling their obligations, and to provide a pleasant working environment, including facilities related to the employee's life, health, and well-being, thus fulfilling the duty to protect and support the employee."

II. Employer's Obligation to Protect and Impact of Violations

The employment contract is a legal agreement entered into for a worker to offer work and for an employer to pay wages for that work. Here, the main

근로환경에서 건강하게 일할 권리가 있다.

직장 내 괴롭힘과 성희롱에 관한 법규정들은 인권친화적 근로환경 조성을 통해 노동현장에서 인간의 존엄성과 인권을 보장하는 제도적 장치이다. 국가뿐 아니라 근로자를 사용하여 사업을 운영하는 사용자는 근로자의 근로권을 보장할 의무가 있다.

근로자의 인권 보장에 관하여 대법원(1996. 4. 23. 선고 95다6823 판결)은 "근로자는 인간으로서의 존엄과 가치를 지닌 인격체이고, 근로자는 자신의 전 인격을 사용자의 사업장에 투입하고 있는 점에서 근로관계에 있어서 근로자의 근로제공은 자신의 인격과 분리될 수 없다." "사용자는 특별한 사정이 없는 한 근로계약의 체결을 통하여 자신의 업무지휘권과 업무명령권의 행사와 조화를 이루는 범위 내에서 근로자가 자신의 인격을 실현시킬 수 있도록 배려하여야 할 신의칙상의 의무를 부담한다."라고 판시하였다.

또한 대법원(1998.2.10. 선고 95다39533 판결)은 "고용관계 또는 근로관계는 이른바 계속적 채권관계로서 인적 신뢰관계를 기초로 하는 것이므로, 고용계약에 있어 피용자가 신의칙상 성실하게 노무를 제공할 의무를 부담함에 대하여, 사용자로서는 피용자에 대한 보수지급의무 외에도 피용자의 인격을 존중하고 보호하며 피용자가 그 의무를 이행하는 데 있어서 손해를 받지 아니하도록 필요한 조치를 강구하고 피용자의 생명, 건강, 풍기 등에 관한 보호시설을 하는 등 쾌적한 근로환경을 제공함으로써 피용자를 보호하고 부조할 의무를 부담한다."라고 판시하였다.

한편, 사업장에서 타인의 인권을 존중할 의무는 인권의 자연성·보편성·불가침성의 속성상 사용자 뿐 아니라 근로자도 당연히 가진다. 이러한 점을 고려하여 「근로기준법」은 "사용자 또는 근로자"는 '직장 내 괴롭힘'을 하여서는 아니된다고 규정하고 있고, 「남녀고용평등법」은 "사업주, 상급자, 근로자"는 '직장 내 성희롱'을 하여서는 아니된다고 규정하고 있다.

II. 근로계약상 사용자의 보호의무와 위반의 효력

근로계약은 근로자가 사용자에게 근로를 제공하고 사용자는 이에 대하여 임금을 지급하는 것을 목적으로 체결된 계약이다. 여기서 근로자와 사용자의 주된

Section 1: Employer's Obligation to Protect (El-lim Kim, Bongsoo Jung)

obligations of workers is to provide work, and employers to pay wages in return. Workers must faithfully provide the work specified in the employment contract at a fixed time and place. If the worker fails to do so for reasons attributable to the worker, the employer may claim compensation for damages or terminate the employment contract (Article 390 of the Civil Act). Even if the employer fails to receive the worker's work, the entire wage must be paid for work already performed (Article 538 of the Civil Act). The Civil Act governs relations between equal parties and places clear responsibilities in the event of a breach of obligations. However, the Labor Standards Act imposes separate restrictions against violation of the main obligations between parties to ensure workers' right to life and so that employers pay wages promptly.

Employers are obligated to protect workers in accordance with the principle of good faith inherent in the employment contract. Typical examples are the duty to consider safety, the using employer's duty to dispatched workers, and the duty to prevent workplace and sexual harassment.[4]

1. Obligation to consider safety

Employers are obligated to take the necessary measures to prevent harm to life, body, and health while workers are providing labor in good faith in accordance with the employment contract. If the employer fails in these obligations, resulting in a worker being injured in some way, the employer shall be liable for neglect resulting in injury.[5] Also, a using employer is responsible for the dispatch employees it uses as if the using employer was the original employer in the event of an accident.

(1) **Case:** A worker fell from a ladder while working and was injured. While the worker was working on the ladder, the employer had a safety obligation to take measures so that other workers would secure the ladder to the ground so that the worker would not slip off the ladder. The employer neglected to do so. Therefore, the employer must compensate the worker for injury. Since the worker neglected to take action him or herself to prevent an accident, the

---

[4] Ha, Kaprae, 「The Labor Standards Act」 33rd Ed., Joongang Economy, 2020, pp. 149-165.
[5] Supreme Court ruling on Feb. 23, 1999: 97 da 12082.

의무는 근로제공과 임금 지급이다. 근로자는 근로계약서에 기재된 업무를 정해진 시간과 장소에서 성실하게 제공해야 하는데 근로자의 귀책사유로 근로제공 의무를 이행하지 못하게 되면, 사용자는 근로자에게 손해배상을 청구하거나 근로계약을 해지할 수 있다(「민법」 제390조). 또한 사용자가 근로자의 근로를 수령하지 못한 경우에도 임금 전액을 지급해야 한다(「민법」 제538조). 「민법」은 대등한 당사자간의 관계이므로 의무 위반에 명확한 책임을 가하고 있다. 그러나 「근로기준법」은 당사자의 주된 의무위반에 대해 근로자의 생존권 보장과 사용자의 신속한 급여지급을 위해 별도의 제한 규정을 두고 있다.

사용자는 근로계약에 내재된 신의성실원칙에 따른 근로자를 보호해야 하는 의무를 진다. 대표적인 것이 안전을 배려할 의무, 파견근로자에 대한 사용사업주의 의무, 직장 내 괴롭힘과 성희롱예방 의무 등이다.[4]

1. 안전을 배려할 의무

사용자는 근로계약에 수반되는 신의성실 원칙에 따라 근로자가 노무를 제공하는 과정에서 생명, 신체, 건강을 해치는 일이 없도록 필요한 조치를 마련하여야 할 보호의무를 부담한다. 이러한 의무를 위반하여 근로자가 손해를 입은 경우 채무불이행으로 인한 손해배상책임을 진다.[5] 또한, 근로자파견관계에 있어 근로계약이 없는 파견근로자가 사용사업주 업무를 수행하다가 업무상 사고를 당한 경우 사용사업주는 그 재해를 당한 파견근로자에 대해 사용자 책임을 진다.

(1) **사례** : 이 사건 근로자가 사다리에 올라가 작업하다가 떨어져 부상을 입었다. 당시 근로자가 사다리 위에 올라가서 작업을 하고 있었을 때 사용자는 근로자에게 사다리에서 미끄러지지 않도록 지상에서 고정하여 줄 다른 근로자와 공동작업을 할 수 있도록 조치할 안전을 배려할 의무가 있었다. 사용자는 근로자가 안전하게 작업할 수 있도록 필요한 조치를 취하여야 할 의무가 있음에도 불구하고 이를 게을리한 과실이 있다. 따라서 사용자는 근로자가 입은 손해를 배상할 책임이 있다. 근로자도 스스로 사고를 방지하려는 노력을 소홀히 한 과실이 있으므로 회사의

---

[4] 하갑례, 「근로기준법」 제33판, 중앙경제, 2020, 149-165면.
[5] 대법원 1999.2.23. 선고 97다12082 판결.

company's responsibility is limited to 70%.[6]

(2) **Case:** An accident occurred in which a worker was hit in the left eye by some bent rebar (resulting in blindness in that eye) during rebar removal work. The employer was obligated to conduct safety training and provide and require the wearing of safety equipment, but neglected to do so. Therefore, the company's liability is limited to 80% in calculating the amount of compensation that the company should pay.[7]

(3) **Case:** An industrial accident occurred that involved a worker who had signed an employment contract with a dispatching company but was working at the using employer's workplace. On November 15, 2005 at 3:35 am, while removing debris from a plastic injection machine, the worker's right arm and hand were crushed and lacerated. The worker demanded additional civil injury compensation from the using employer in 2010 after having received the treatment and disability compensation in lump sum form through the dispatch company's industrial accident insurance. The using employer claimed that there was no relationship between it and the dispatched worker, and the extinctive prescription for illegal activities had expired since 3 years had passed since the incident. In response, the Supreme Court stated in its ruling, "Although the using employer did not have any direct employment contract with the plaintiff, the using employer was able to control and manage the plaintiff's labor through a worker dispatch contract. This is regarded as an employer-worker relationship. Therefore, it is fair to say that the using employer is obligated to consider safety as if it were a using employer." The employer's duty to protect was recognized as grounds for injury compensation (Article 390 of the Civil Act), with the extinctive prescription determined to be 5 years instead of 3 years.[8]

2. Obligation to prevent workplace and sexual harassment

Employers must ensure a work life free from workplace and sexual

---

[6] Chuncheon District Court ruling on Aug. 10, 2016: 2014 gadan 11050.
[7] Daegu District Court ruling on Apr. 19, 2019: 2018 gadan 115280.
[8] Supreme Court ruling on Nov. 28, 2013: 2011 da 60247.

과실 책임은 70%로 제한한다.[6]

(2) **사례** : 근로자가 철근제거작업 중 휘어진 철근에 눈을 가격당하여 왼쪽 눈이 실명된 사고가 발생하였다. 이 산재사건에 대해 사용자는 안전교육을 실시하고 안전장비를 지급하고 착용하도록 해야 하는 의무가 있었다. 그러나 사용자는 필요한 안전교육을 하지 않았고, 안전장비를 갖추지 않았고, 장비를 착용하게 하여 사고를 미연에 방지해야 함에도 이를 게을리하였다. (중략) 이에 회사가 배상해야 할 손해액 산정에 있어 회사의 책임을 80%로 제한한다.[7]

(3) **사례** : 근로자가 파견회사와 근로계약을 체결한 후 사용사업주에게 파견되어 업무를 시작한지 6일째 되는 날, 산재사고가 발생하였다. 근로자는 2005년 11월 15일 03시 35분경 플라스틱 사출기에 이물질을 제거하던 중 오른쪽 손과 팔 부분이 압착되어 절단되는 사고가 발생하였다. 재해자는 파견회사의 산재보험으로 치료 및 장해보상 일시금을 모두 받은 후, 2010년경 사용사업주에게 민사상 손해배상을 청구한 사건이다. 이에 대해 사용사업주는 파견근로자와 근로계약 관계가 없고, 불법행위에 따른 소멸시효도 3년이므로 시효가 지났다고 주장하였다. 이에 대해 대법원은 "사용사업주와 원고 사이에 직접적인 고용계약은 존재하지 않지만 근로자파견계약에 의해 원고의 노무를 지배·관리할 수 있었고, 이러한 양자의 관계는 고용계약 및 근로자파견계약을 매개로 한 실질적인 사용자와 근로자 관계라고 본다. 따라서 사용사업주는 원고에 대해 사용자로서 안전배려의무가 있다고 할 것이다."라고 판단하였다. 사용자의 보호의무는 채무불이행에 따른 손해배상(민법 제390조) 규정으로 인정하고 그 소멸시효도 3년이 아닌 5년으로 판단하였다.[8]

2. 직장 내 괴롭힘과 성희롱예방 의무

사용자는 직장 내 괴롭힘과 성희롱이 없는 직장 생활을 보장해야 한다.

---

[6] 춘천지방법원 2016.8.10. 선고 2014가단11050 판결.
[7] 대구지방법원 2019.4.19. 선고 2018가단115280 판결.
[8] 대법원 2013.11.28. 선고 2011다60247 판결.

harassment. In the event sexual harassment occurs in the workplace, the employer shall take action to prevent recurrence, as well as suitable disciplinary action towards the instigator of the sexual harassment. The employer shall endeavor to make relief efforts and prevent secondary damage to the victim. If the employer fails in this obligation, the employer shall be liable for damages due to illegal acts as well as criminal punishment for violating the Equal Treatment Act.

- Related case: A worker (the plaintiff) complained about sexual harassment in the workplace and asked for prompt and appropriate remedy. However, not only did the defendant (company) ignore the complaint, but they also took disciplinary and other unfavorable actions, such as a suspension from work, against the plaintiff. The company also took discriminatory and unfair disciplinary actions against fellow workers who helped the plaintiff, thereby preventing the plaintiff from receiving any help from friendly colleagues in the workplace and isolating her from other colleagues. As a result of the company's actions, the plaintiff received "secondary damage" in which he was exposed to negative reactions, negative public opinion, disadvantageous treatment, and mental anguish for complaining about sexual harassment in the workplace and "causing a problem." The mental stress suffered by the plaintiff is believed to be considerable. In accordance with Article 756 of the Civil Act, the company shall compensate the plaintiff for mental injury incurred by its violation of Article 14 (2)[9] of the Equal Employment Act and as an employer in violation of its duty to protect.[10]

Workers are obligated to provide labor and employers are obligated to pay wages. These are the main obligations of parties to employment contracts. In addition, there are also secondary obligations according to the good-faith principle: workers are to protect confidentiality, be faithful, and comply with company rules. If any of these are violated, workers may be subject to dismissal or other forms of discipline. For their part, employers are obligated to provide safety for their workers and prevent workplace and sexual harassment. If these obligations are not carried out, employers shall be liable for damage and/or punishment for violating related labor laws.

---

[9] Article 14 (Measures to Be Taken in case of Sexual Harassment at Work) (2) Upon receiving a report as prescribed in paragraph (1) or discovering an occurrence of sexual harassment in the workplace, the employer shall immediately conduct an investigation to confirm the facts. In such cases, the employer must ensure that the worker who has reportedly suffered from sexual harassment on the job or who has claimed that sexual harassment occurred (hereinafter referred to as the "employee victim etc.") does not feel sexually humiliated during the investigation process.

[10] Seoul High Court ruling on Apr. 20, 2018: 2017 na 2076631.

직장 내 성희롱이 발생한 경우, 필요한 조치를 통해 성희롱 가해자에 적합한 징계 등을 통해 징계와 함께 재발방지를 위해 노력해야 하고, 피해자에게도 구제노력과 제2의 피해가 가지 않도록 노력해야 한다. 이를 위반한 경우에는 사용자는 「남녀고용평등법」을 위반한 형사처벌 뿐만 아니라 불법행위에 따른 손해배상 책임을 진다.

■ 사례 : 피고(회사)는 근로자인 원고가 이 사건 직장 내 성희롱으로 인한 피해를 호소하며 신속하고 적절한 구제조치를 취해 줄 것을 요청하는데도 이를 무시하고 오히려 성희롱 피해를 입은 원고에게 근거 없는 혐의를 씌워 부당한 징계처분을 하거나 대기발령 등의 불리한 조치를 하였다. 더구나 피고는 원고를 도와준 동료 근로자에게 까지 차별적이고 부당한 징계처분을 함으로써 원고로 하여금 직장 내에서 우호적인 동료들의 도움을 받을 수 없도록 하였고, 다른 동료들로부터 고립되는 처지에 놓이게 하였다. 피고의 이러한 행위로 인해 원고는 이 사건 직장 내 성희롱 피해 사실을 알리고 문제를 삼는 과정에서 오히려 부정적 반응이나 여론, 불이익한 처우 또는 그로 인한 정신적 피해에 노출되는 이른바 '2차 피해'를 입었고, 그로 인해 원고가 입은 정신적 고통은 상당할 것으로 판단된다. 따라서 피고는 원고에 대하여 「남녀고용평등법」 제14조제2항[9]을 위반하였고, 또한 사용자로서 보호의무를 위반하였기에 원고가 입은 정신적 손해를 배상할 책임이 있다.[10]

근로계약에 따른 주된 당사자의 의무로 근로자는 근로제공과 사용자는 임금지급 의무를 진다. 이러한 주된 의무 외에도 당사자는 근로계약에 신의칙 의무에 따른 부수적 의무를 진다. 이 부수적 의무로 근로자는 비밀유지의무, 충실의무, 사규준수 의무 등이 있다. 이를 위반하는 경우 근로자는 해고 등의 징계를 받을 수 있다. 이에 반해 사용자도 근로계약의 당사자인 근로자에 대해 안전한 사업장을 제공해야 하는 안전배려의무, 직장 내 괴롭힘과 성희롱 방지 의무 등을 진다. 이를 위반한 경우에 사용자는 채무불이행 또는 관련 노동법령 위반에 따른 불법행위 책임을 진다.

---

[9] 제14조(직장 내 성희롱 발생 시 조치) ② 사업주는 제1항에 따른 신고를 받거나 직장 내 성희롱 발생 사실을 알게 된 경우에는 지체 없이 그 사실 확인을 위한 조사를 하여야 한다. 이 경우 사업주는 직장 내 성희롱과 관련하여 피해를 입은 근로자 또는 피해를 입었다고 주장하는 근로자가 조사 과정에서 성적 수치심 등을 느끼지 아니하도록 하여야 한다.
[10] 서울고등법원 2018.4.20. 선고 2017나2076631 판결.

Section 2 Basic Understanding of Workplace Harassment

(Bongsoo Jung)

The Workplace Anti-Bullying Act was enacted in January 2019 and came into effect in July of the same year. Three incidents contributed to enactment of this law. The first case is known as the "nut rage" incident involving an executive of Korean Air in 2014. Vice President Cho 00, a daughter of Korean Air's owners, exploded in rage that her macadamia nuts were served in a bag, not on a plate, verbally abusing the flight attendant and the chief flight attendant and forcing both to kneel and apologize to her. Ms. Cho then ordered the plane—heading for a runway at New York's John F. Kennedy Airport to fly to Seoul—to return to the boarding gate where she ordered the chief flight attendant to get out. Then, the plane departed.[11] In 2019, Korean Air was ordered by the court to pay 70 million won to former chief flight attendant Park 00, for the personnel disadvantages received as a result of the incident.[12] The second case involves a nurse who killed herself, leaving a suicide note that said, "Workplace harassment makes it difficult to work." In March 2019, the Labor Welfare Corporation's Disease Judgment Committee recognized the incident as an industrial accident caused by workplace harassment. In the third case, at the end of 2018, a video surfaced of Yang 00, chairman of WeDisk, a start-up IT company, calling in an ex-employee and brutally assaulting him in the office. Yang is currently in prison for this and other illegal business activities.[13]

Until recently, investigation and treatment of workplace harassment has been entirely up to companies.[14] There were only two related rules when the Workplace Anti-Bullying Act was enacted. First, rules of employment had to include procedures for dealing with workplace harassment and for remedy. Second, employers were to be punished if they disadvantage those who report harassment in the workplace. The procedures for handling reports of bullying were entirely up to the employer, which did little to actually resolve the problem. Accordingly, in April 2021, the following five employer obligations were added

---

[11] Moon, Kangboon, "Is this workplace harassment?" 2020. Gadian, p. 34.
[12] Seoul High Court ruling on Nov. 5, 2019.
[13] Moon, Kangboon, "Is this workplace harassment?" 2020. Gadian, pp. 35-36.
[14] Shin, Kwonchul, "Legal Concepts and Criteria for Determining the Occurrence of Bullying in the Workplace," Labor Law (69), Korean Labor Law Association, Mar. 2019, p. 228.

제2절 직장 내 괴롭힘의 기본적 이해

(정봉수)

직장 내 괴롭힘 방지법이 2019년 1월에 도입되어 동년 7월부터 시행되었다. 직장 내 괴롭힘 방지법 제정에 결정적인 계기가 되었던 3가지의 관련된 사건이 사회적 이슈가 되었다. 첫 번째 사건은 2014년, D항공의 '땅콩 회항' 사건이다. D항공 소유주 일가인 조○○ 부사장이 마카다미아(Macadamia) 땅콩을 봉지 채 서비스한 것을 문제 삼아 승무원에게 폭언을 하고 사무장을 불러 무릎을 꿇리고 빌도록 했는데, 그래도 화가 안 풀려 뉴욕공항에서 서울로 향하던 항공기를 돌려 사무장을 내려놓은 뒤 출발한 사건이다.[11] 2019년 이 사건으로 인사상 불이익을 받은 박○○ 전 사무장에게 D항공이 7000만 원 배상을 해야 한다는 판결이 나왔다.[12] 두 번째 사건은 2018년 2월 서울아산병원의 신입 간호사가 "태움(병원 내 집단 괴롭힘) 때문에 일하기 힘들다"는 유서를 남기고 자살한 사건이다. 이 사건에 대해 2019년 3월 근로복지공단의 질병판정위원회는 직장 내 괴롭힘으로 인해 발생한 산업재해로 인정하였다. 세 번째 사건은 2018년 말 신생 IT 기업 WD의 양○○ 회장이 퇴사한 직원을 불러 사무실에서 무차별 폭행을 하는 동영상이 공개된 사건이다. 그는 현재 이 사건과 더불어 불법 기업활동으로 법정 구속되어 형을 살고 있다.[13]

직장 내 괴롭힘에 대한 조사와 처리는 전적으로 회사에 맡겨져 있다.[14] 이 직장 내 괴롭힘 법령 도입 시에는 관련 규칙이 두 가지만 있었다. 첫째 직장 내 괴롭힘에 대한 내용과 구제절차를 취업규칙의 필수기재 사항으로 하였고, 둘째 직장 내 괴롭힘을 신고한 자에게 불이익을 주는 경우 해당 사업주를 처벌하도록 하는 내용이었다. 이러한 취업규칙에 근거하여 괴롭힘 사건을 처리하는 방식은 사업주에게 전적으로 맡겨 놓았기 때문에 실질적 문제해결이 되지 못했다. 이에 2021년 4월 「근로기준법」 개정을 통해, 사용자의 실질적인 직장 내 괴롭힘에 대한 국가적 관여를 강제하면서 다음의 5가지 사항을 추가

---

11) 문강분, "이것도 직장 내 괴롭힘 인가요?" 2020. 가디언, 34면.
12) 서울고등법원 2019.11.5.선고 2019나2004517 판결.
13) 문강분, 위 출판물, 35-36면.
14) 신권철, "직장 내 괴롭힘의 법적 개념과 요건", 노동법학(69), 한국노동법학회, 2019.3. 228면.

in amendments to the relevant laws. Employers are now obligated to: ① Prohibit bullying in the workplace, ② Conduct objective investigations of reported bullying incidents in the workplace, ③ Take appropriate actions to protect alleged victims, ④ Establish and carry out disciplinary action in response to bullying in the workplace, and ⑤ Comply with confidentiality requirements related to harassment investigations in the workplace, with fines levied for negligence.

When determining whether bullying has occurred in the workplace, the criteria are somewhat complex given the blur between the employer's discretionary personnel rights and the employee's personal rights. I will take a look at the related details and criteria for judgement herein.

Ⅰ. Concept & Criteria of Determining Workplace Harassment

The Labor Standards Act (Article 76-2) prohibits harassment in the workplace, which is defined as "an act of inflicting physical or mental pain on other workers or worsening the working environment through an abuse of the superior position of the employer or relationships in the workplace." There are four components to workplace harassment: ① Defined target: employer or employee, ② Abuse of position: Using position or work relationship against the target, ③ Repeated actions towards the target, or assigning of tasks, unnecessary for performance of contracted work: Actions beyond the appropriate scope of work, ④ Infringements of human rights and/or degradation of the working environment: Any action that causes physical or mental pain or worsens the working environment. All four factors above must be met for an incident to qualify as workplace harassment.

1. Explanation of the factors in harassment[15]

(1) Defined target: Employer or employee

The Labor Standards Act (Article 2 (2)), defines an employer as someone in charge of managing the business, or a person who acts on behalf of the employer with respect to matters related to workers. Someone in charge of managing the business does not have to be the business owner but is in charge

---

[15] Ministry of Employment and Labor, "Manual for Judgment and Prevention of Harassment in the Workplace," 2019, pp. 24-27.

하였다. ① 사업주의 직장 내 괴롭힘 금지의무, ② 직장 내 괴롭힘 사건에 대해 객관적 조사 실시의무, ③ 피해근로자에 대한 적절한 보호조치의무, ④ 직장 내 괴롭힘 행위자에 대한 필요한 징계조치, ⑤ 직장 내 괴롭힘 조사와 관련된 내용에 대해 비밀준수 의무 등 신설조항과 과태료 조항의 도입이다.

직장 내 괴롭힘을 판단하면서 사용자의 재량적 인사권과 근로자의 인격권 사이에서 직장 내 괴롭힘 판단기준에 대해 다소 애매모호한 점이 많아 이와 관련된 내용과 판단기준에 대해 구체적으로 살펴보고자 한다.

I. 직장 내 괴롭힘의 개념과 판단기준

「근로기준법」제76조의2는 직장 내 괴롭힘을 금지하고 있다. 직장 내 괴롭힘을 "사용자 또는 근로자는 직장에서의 지위 또는 관계 등의 우위를 이용하여 업무상 적정범위를 넘어 다른 근로자에게 신체적·정신적 고통을 주거나 근무환경을 악화시키는 행위"로 규정하고 있다. 직장 내 괴롭힘의 구성요소는 다음의 4가지이다. ① 주체 : 사용자 또는 근로자, ② 지위의 활용 : 직장에서의 지위나 관계 등에서의 우위, ③ 업무일탈 : 업무의 적정범위 이상의 행위, ④ 인적, 환경적 침해행위 : 근로자에게 신체적, 정신적 고통을 주거나 근무 환경을 악화시키는 행위. 위의 4가지 요소를 모두 충족해야만 직장 내 괴롭힘에 해당한다.

1. 괴롭힘의 판단요소[15]

(1) 주체 : 사용자 또는 근로자

직장 내 괴롭힘에서 금지의 주체는 사용자와 근로자이다. 「근로기준법」(제2조제2항)에서 사용자라고 하면 사업주 또는 사업 경영 담당자, 그 밖에 근로자에 관한 사항에 대하여 사업주를 위하여 행위 하는 자를 말한다. 사업 경영담당자는 사업주가 아니면서 사업경영 일반을 책임지는 자로서, 사업주로부터 사업 경영의 전부 또는 일부에 대해 포괄적인 위임을 받고 대외적으로 사업을 대표하거나 대리하는 자를 말한다. 근로자에 관한 사항에 대해

---

[15] 고용노동부, "직장 내 괴롭힘 판단 및 예방 대응 매뉴얼", 2019. 24-27면.

of general business management, and refers to someone who represents a business externally after comprehensive delegation from the business owner for all or part of the business management. Anyone who acts on matters related to workers for the business owner is delegated authority from the business owner or the person in charge of business management, and is involved in making personnel decisions, such as hiring and dismissal of those within their own realm of responsibility, directing and supervising the workers on the job, and working conditions. It also refers to someone who can decide and execute matters related to working conditions. Relatives of the employer are included in the scope of "employer" with revision of the Labor Standards Act in 2021 (Article 116). "Employer" includes those with an advantage over other workers, such as via position or work relationship.

In the worker dispatch relationship, according to the Act on the Protection, etc., of Dispatched Workers, a bullying agent in the workplace can also include an employer who directly supervises and directs the work of a dispatched worker.

(2) Abuse of position: Using position or work relationship, etc., against the target

Harassment in the workplace mainly occurs in places where there is a strong organizational culture or authoritarian hierarchy. It occurs mainly in the form of actions by people with superior social or economic status using their power and superior status against those less socially privileged.[16]

A superior relationship refers to one in which it is likely to be difficult for those in lower positions to resist any bullying behavior. An abuse of position refers to an offender using their superiority against someone in a command-and-control relationship, or even if it is not a direct command-order relationship, it is to use the higher position or rank system. Workplace harassment does not occur unless it involves the abuse of superiority in position or relationship.

(3) Repeated actions towards the target, or assigning of tasks, unnecessary for performance of contracted work: Actions beyond the appropriate scope of work

Actions that are inappropriate and recognized as exceeding the scope of work can be classified into the following seven categories.

① Violence and intimidation: Actions that involve direct physical force or the threat

---

[16] Lee, Soo-Yeon, "The Concept of Workplace Harassment and Judgment Criteria", Ewha Gender Law 10(2), Ewha Womans University Gender Law Research Institute, Aug. 2018, p. 119.

사업주를 위하여 행위하는 자는 사업주 또는 사업경영 담당자로부터 권한을 위임받아 자신의 책임 아래 근로자 채용, 해고 등 인사처분을 할 수 있고, 직무상 근로자의 업무를 지휘, 감독하며 근로조건에 관한 사항을 결정하고 집행할 수 있는 자를 말한다. 2021년 「근로기준법」 개정으로 직장 내 괴롭힘을 행한 사용자에 대한 벌칙(1천만 원 이하의 과태료)을 부과하는 조항(제116조)이 신설되었다. 이 벌칙은 사용자의 배우자, 4촌의 혈족과 인척이 해당 사업 또는 사업장의 근로자이면서 직장 내 괴롭힘을 행한 경우에도 부과된다(시행령 59조의3). 여기서 금지의 주체인 근로자라고 하면 다른 근로자에 대해 직장에서의 지위나 관계 등의 우위를 가진 자를 말한다.

근로자파견관계에서는 파견법에 따라 파견 중인 근로자의 경우 직접 업무를 감독하고 지시하는 사용사업주도 직장 내 괴롭힘 행위자로 인정된다.

(2) 지위의 활용 : 직장에서의 지위나 관계 등에서의 우위

직장 내 괴롭힘은 조직문화나 권위주의적 위계질서가 강한 곳에서 주로 발생한다. 이는 사회적 경제적으로 우월한 지위에 있는 사람들이 사회적 약자를 대상으로 권력형, 우월적 지위를 이용한 행위의 형태로 주로 발생한다.[16]

우위성이라고 하면 피해자가 괴롭힘 행위에 대해 저항 또는 거절이 어려울 가능성이 높은 관계를 의미한다. 지위의 우위는 괴롭힘 행위자가 지휘명령 관계에서 상위에 있거나 직접적인 지휘명령 관계가 아니어도 직위, 직급체계상 상위에 있음을 이용하는 것이다. 관계의 우위는 행위자가 피해자와의 관계에서 우위에 있는지는 특정 요소에 대해 사업장 내에서 통상적으로 이루어지는 평가를 바탕으로 판단한다. 따라서 직장에서의 지위나 관계 등의 우위를 이용한 것이 아니라면 직장 내 괴롭힘에 해당되지 않는다.

(3) 업무일탈 : 업무의 적정범위 이상의 행위

업무의 적정범위를 넘는 것으로 인정되는 행위는 다음의 7가지로 분류할 수 있다.
① 폭행 및 협박 행위 : 신체에 직접 폭력을 가하거나 물건에 폭력을 가하는 등 직, 간접의 물리적 힘을 행사하는 폭행이나 협박행위는 업무상 적정범위를

---
[16] 이수연, "직장 괴롭힘의 개념과 판단기준에 관한 판례법리", 이화젠더법학 10(2), 이화여자대학교 젠더법학연구소, 2018.8. 119면.

of physical force, such as directly or indirectly inflicting violence on an object.

② Verbal behavior, such as violent, abusive language or gossip: If it is determined that gossip is spread to a third party, such as in an open place, to damage the victim's reputation, it is beyond the appropriate scope for work. In particular, continuous and repetitive verbal abuse or abusive language can seriously harm the victim's personal rights and cause mental pain, so engaging in it constitutes an act beyond the appropriate scope for work.

③ Orders to perform tasks related to assistance with non-work affairs: These are orders that exceed the appropriate scope of work and beyond what is considered normally acceptable in human relations. Examples include continuous and repetitive instructions to run personal errands related to daily life.

④ Bullying and exclusion: Intentional disregard and exclusion in the process of performing work are acts that are beyond the appropriate scope of work and beyond the social norm. Examples include intentionally not providing important information related to work or excluding someone entitled to participation in the decision-making process without justifiable reason, forcing someone to move or leave the department without good reason, discriminating against someone in training, promotion, rewards, or routine benefits without good reason, etc.

⑤ Repetitive instructions for work unrelated to the employment contract: If instructions are given to an employee repeatedly to do work that is unrelated to that specified at the time the labor contract was signed, and if a justifiable reason is not recognized, it amounts to an act beyond the appropriate scope for work. Examples including menial tasks only when an employee was hired for specific other tasks, or giving the employee little work without justifiable reason.

⑥ Assigning an excessive amount of work: If the action is judged to be inappropriate, such as not allowing even the minimum amount of time physically necessary for the task, without unavoidable reasons, it is beyond the appropriate scope of work.

⑦ Interfering with smooth business performance: Actions that interfere with smooth business performance, such as not providing essential equipment (computers, telephones, etc.) necessary for business, or blocking access to the Internet or company intranet, are beyond social norms and inappropriate for business.

(4) Infringements of human rights and/or degradation of the working environment
This refers to actions of an employer or a worker that inflict physical or

넘은 행위이다.
② 폭언, 욕설, 험담 등 언어적 행위 : 공개된 장소에서 이루어지는 등 제3자에게 전파되어 피해자의 명예를 훼손할 정도인 것으로 판단되면 업무상 적정범위를 넘은 행위이다. 특히, 지속 반복적인 폭언이나 욕설은 피해자의 인격권을 심각하게 해치고 정신적인 고통을 유발할 수 있으므로 업무상 적정범위를 넘는 행위이다.
③ 사적 용무 지시 : 개인적인 심부름을 반복적으로 시키는 등 인간관계에서 용인될 수 있는 부탁의 수준을 넘어 행해지는 것은 업무상 적정범위를 넘은 행위이다. 예)사적인 심부름 등 개인적인 일상생활과 관련된 일을 하도록 지속적, 반복적으로 지시하는 것
④ 집단 따돌림과 배제시킴 : 업무수행 과정에서의 의도적 무시와 배제는 사회통념을 벗어난 업무상 적정 범위를 넘어선 행위이다. 예) 정당한 사유 없이 업무와 관련된 중요한 정보제공이나 의사결정 과정에서 배제시키는 것. 정당한 이유 없이 부서이동 또는 퇴사를 강요하는 것. 정당한 이유 없이 훈련, 승진, 보상, 일상적인 대우 등에서 차별하는 것 등.
⑤ 업무와 무관한 일을 반복 지시 : 근로계약 체결 시 명시했던 업무와 무관한 일을 근로자의 의사에 반하여 지시하는 행위가 반복되고 그 지시에 정당한 사유가 인정되지 않는다면 업무상 적정범위를 넘어선 행위이다. 예)근로계약서 등에 명시되어 있지 않은 허드렛일만 시키거나 일을 거의 주지 않는 것.
⑥ 과도한 업무 부여 : 업무상 불가피한 사정이 없음에도 불구하고 해당업무 수행에 대해 물리적으로 필요한 최소한의 시간마저도 허락하지 않는 등 그 행위가 타당하지 않은 것으로 판단되면 업무상 적정범위를 넘어선 행위이다.
⑦ 원활한 업무수행을 방해하는 행위 : 업무에 필요한 주요 비품(컴퓨터, 전화 등)을 제공하지 않거나, 인터넷 사내 인트라넷 접속을 차단하는 등 원활한 업무수행을 방해하는 행위는 사회 통념을 벗어난 행위로서 업무상 적정 범위를 넘어선 행위이다.

(4) 인적, 환경적 침해행위
사용자나 근로자가 다른 근로자에게 직장 내 괴롭힘을 통해 근로자에게

mental pain on another worker through harassment in the workplace or worsening the working environment. It can be said that the working environment has been degraded if an employer intentionally moves certain workers to work in front of the washroom, embarrassing them or creating an environment in which workers cannot perform their duties properly. Intention of the offender is not a prerequisite to determining that actions directly cause physical or mental pain or worsen the working environment.

2. Criteria for Determining Workplace Harassment

(1) Conflict between the employer's right to order work and the employee's personal rights

In determining whether or not bullying has occurred in the workplace, there are cases in which the employer's right to order work and the employee's personal rights are in conflict. In labor disputes, an employer's exercise of personnel rights in a way that violates the employee's personal rights is often viewed as illegal under the Civil Act.

The employer's right to command work is one of the personnel rights, which is an authority unique to the employer and necessary to maintain and establish corporate order. The courts have ruled that employers have considerable discretion in determining the extent of personnel management necessary for business, since they are responsible for personnel.[17] In contrast, the Constitutional Court argues that the right to work includes not only the "right to a place to work" but also "the right to a reasonable environment in which to work," with the latter a basic right to protect against infringement on human dignity. It has ruled that this right includes the right to demand a healthy working environment, fair compensation for work, and guarantee of reasonable working conditions.[18]

Here, in determining the appropriate scope of work, it is necessary to determine whether the employer's right to order the work or the worker's personal rights should take precedence. In this case, it is necessary to determine whether or not it is illegal to determine certain work as falling within the appropriate scope for a job through an "evaluation of conflicting fundamental rights."[19] Of the requirements for determining whether an action constitutes workplace harassment, whether or not it departs from the appropriate scope of

---

[17] Supreme Court ruling on July 22, 2003: 2002do7225, and many similar rulings.
[18] Constitutional Court decision on Nov. 28, 2002: 2001hunba50; Constitution Court decision on Aug. 30, 2007: 2004hunma670.
[19] Naver Korean dictionary: An evaluation to compare and judge the legal interests of conflicting fundamental rights.

신체적, 정신적 고통을 주거나 근무환경을 악화시키는 행위이다. 사업주가 의도적으로 특정 근로자를 화장실 앞으로 업무자리를 옮겨 창피를 주거나 근로자가 제대로 된 업무를 수행할 수 없는 환경을 조성하는 경우 근무환경을 악화시켰다고 볼 수 있다. 행위자의 의도가 없었더라도 그 행위로 인해 신체적, 정신적 고통을 느꼈거나 근무환경이 예전보다 나빠졌다면 인정될 수 있다.

2. 직장 내 괴롭힘의 판단기준

(1) 사용자의 업무지시권과 근로자의 인격권과 충돌

직장 내 괴롭힘 여부를 판단함에 있어서 사용자의 업무지시권과 근로자의 인격권이 충돌되는 경우가 있다. 노동분쟁에서 사용자의 인사권 행사가 근로자의 인격권을 침해한 경우에는 민법상의 불법행위로 구성되는 경우가 많다.

사용자의 업무지시권은 인사권으로 기업질서의 유지와 확립을 위해 사용자가 가지는 고유한 권한이다. 사용자의 인사명령에 대해 법원은 인사권자인 사용자의 권한에 속하므로 업무상 필요한 범위에서는 상당한 재량을 가진다고 한다.[17] 이에 반해, 헌법재판소는 근로의 권리가 "일할 자리에 관한 권리" 뿐만 아니라 "일할 환경에 관한 권리"도 함께 내포하고 있고, 후자는 인간의 존엄성에 대한 침해를 방어하기 위한 자유권적 기본권의 성격도 갖고 있어 건강한 작업환경, 일에 대한 정당한 보수, 합리적인 근로조건의 보장 등을 요구할 수 있는 권리 등을 포함한다고 밝히고 있다.[18]

여기서 업무의 적정범위에 대한 판단에 있어 사용자의 업무 지시권을 우위에 두어야 하는지 아니면 근로자의 인격권 보호를 우위에 두어야 하는지를 판단해야 한다. 이 경우 업무상 적정범위는 '이익형량[19]'을 통해서 위법성 여부가 판단되어야 한다.[20] 직장 내 괴롭힘의 성립요건 중 '업무상 적정범위 일탈' 여부는 사용자와 근로자의 기본권이 상호 조화적으로 해결될 수 있도록 목적에 부합하는 이익형량이 요구된다. 즉, 두 기본권이 충돌할 경우 어느 기본권을 우위에 두어야 하는지의 여부는 사회공동체의 건전한 상식과 관행에 비추어

---

[17] 대법원 2003.7.22. 선고 2002도7225 판결 등. 다수
[18] 헌법재판소 2002. 11. 28. 선고 2001헌바50 결정; 헌법재판소 2007. 8. 30. 선고 2004헌마670 결정.
[19] 법률사전: 서로 충돌하는 기본권의 법익을 비교하고 판단하여 결정하는 일.
[20] 이상곤, "직장 내 괴롭힘 법제의 개선방안 연구", 아주대학교 대학원 박사학위 논문, 2020. 8. 163-164면.

work needs to be determined so that conflicts over the basic rights of the employer and employee can be harmoniously resolved.[20] This is determined in the light of sound common sense and practices of the social community, and whether there is rationality or substantiality in common social concepts, etc., which shall be judged individually and in relationship to each other.[21] However, since the problem of workplace harassment arises on the premise of an imbalance of power and infringes on the personal rights of workers, an evaluation of conflicting fundamental rights is required from the perspective of the victim, and should focus more on the protection of personal rights.[22]

(2) Criteria for determining whether workplace harassment has occurred

The factors and criteria suggested by the court can be used to determine whether workplace harassment has occurred. This shall be decided by considering and evaluating the following collectively: "
① the relationship between the offender and victim,
② the motive and intention of the act,
③ the timing, place, and situation,
④ the details of the victim's explicit or presumed reaction,
⑤ the content and extent of the act, and
⑥ the repetition or continuity of the act."[23]

Simply put, it is possible for an employer to infringe on human and personal rights or worsen the employment environment with position (power relations), related work (work relations), or other actions unwanted by the receiving party that are outside the scope of the relevant work (harassment, abusive language, etc.).[24]

The employer is the exerciser of authority, while the employee has voluntarily consented to perform subordinate duties. Therefore, it is not easy to distinguish if harassment has occurred or if the employee is simply unhappy with work duties.[25] Nevertheless, if the above criteria are individually reviewed and judged comprehensively, it is believed that clarity will emerge in each individual case as

---

[20] Lee, Sang-Gon, "A Study on Improvement of the Law on Bullying in the Workplace," PhD Thesis, Graduate School of Ajou University, Aug 2020, pp. 163-164.
[21] Supreme Court ruling on Feb. 10, 1998: 95da39533: Whether the employer is liable for compensation for harassment in the workplace.
[22] Lee, Sang-Gon, "A Study on Improvement of the Law on Bullying in the Workplace," PhD Thesis, Graduate School of Ajou University, Aug. 2020, p. 165.
[23] Supreme Court ruling on Feb. 10, 1998: 95da39533.
[24] Kim, Elim, "Gender Equality and Law," Korea National Open University Press and Culture Center, 2013, p. 242.
[25] Shin, Kwonchul, "Legal Concepts and Criteria for Determining the Occurrence of Bullying in the Workplace," p. 243.

볼 때 용인될 수 있는 정도의 것인지, 사회통념상 합리성이 없거나 상당성 결여 여부 등을 종합하여 개별적, 상대적으로 판단해야 할 것이다.[21] 다만, 직장 내 괴롭힘의 문제는 힘의 불균형을 전제로 하여 발생되고 근로자의 인격권을 침해한다는 점에서, 인격권 보호에 주안점을 두고 피해근로자의 관점에서 다소 상향된 이익형량이 요구된다.[22]

(2) 직장 내 괴롭힘의 판단기준

법원이 제시한 직장 내 성희롱의 위법성 판단요소와 기준을 살펴보면 직장 내 괴롭힘 여부를 판단하는 기준으로 삼을 수 있을 것이다. 괴롭힘 행위인지의 여부는
① 위법행위와 관련한 행위자와 피해자의 관계
② 행위의 동기와 의도
③ 시기와 장소 및 상황
④ 피해자의 명시적 또는 추정적 반응의 내용
⑤ 행위의 내용과 정도
⑥ 행위의 반복성이나 지속성 등을 종합하여 노동인격의 침해여부를 가려야 할 것이다.[23]

이를 단순히 정리하면, 사용자가 지위를 이용하여(권력관계), 업무와 관련하여(업무관련성), 상대방이 원하지 않는 행동(괴롭힘, 언동 등)을 함으로써, 인권 및 인격권을 침해하거나 고용환경을 악화시키는지 여부를 판단하는 것이다.[24]

직장 내 괴롭힘의 판단에 있어 행위자인 사용자는 권한 행사자로서 외관을 갖추고 있고, 피해자인 근로자는 근로의무의 수행원으로서 자발적 동의에 의해 이루어진다. 따라서 이를 구분하기는 쉽지 않다.[25] 그럼에도 불구하고 위의 기준을 가지고 개별적으로 검토하여 종합적으로 판단한다면 직장 내 괴롭힘 여부 판단에 있어 개별 사안별로 분명한 기준이 나올 것이라고 본다.

2019년 7월 시행된 직장 내 괴롭힘 방지법은 직장 내에서 기존의 가부장적 권위주의적 조직 문화를 개선하고 근로자들의 인격권 보장에 큰 역할을 하였다. 그럼에도 불구하고 회사의 자율에 맡겨져 노사간 스스로 문제해결을 시도

---
21) 대법원 1998.2.10. 선고 95다39533 판결: 직장 내에서 성희롱 관련 사용자의 배상책임 여부.
22) 이상곤, "직장 내 괴롭힘 법제의 개선방안 연구", 위의 논문, 165면.
23) 대법원 1998.2.10. 선고 95다39533 판결
24) 김엘림, "남녀평등과 법", 한국방송통신대학교 출판문화원, 2013, 242면.
25) 신권철, "직장 내 괴롭힘의 법적 개념과 요건", 위의 논문, 243-244면.

to whether or not workplace harassment has occurred.

The Workplace Anti-Bullying Act, introduced in July 2019, is a major influence on reducing the existing patriarchal authoritarian culture in the workplace and guaranteeing the personal rights of workers. Nevertheless, if resolving workplace harassment is left up to companies, there will be no effective results any time an employer deals with bullying half-heartedly. Amendment to the Workplace Anti-Bullying Act in April 2021 includes provisions to punish employers for engaging in or failing to take the appropriate action for workplace harassment, and obligate employers to conduct an objective investigation if they become aware of workplace harassment. This amendment is particularly helpful to workers. In the future, when harassment occurs in the workplace, the Ministry of Employment and Labor will thoroughly review the incident and actively intervene and punish any employers who fail to take appropriate action, which will work to drastically reduce recurrence. Actions to prevent workplace harassment and provide practical remedies when it does happen can be expected to occur at the same time.

II. The Workplace Harassment Prevention Law and the Employer's Duty

Recently workplace harassment within large corporations has become a social problem. Every day it seems that the executives of these companies are reported by the media on issues such as abusive language, assault, and inhumane treatment of their employees, but these acts which are revealed to the public are but the tip of the iceberg. According to a survey by the Korea Labor Institute,[26] 66.3% of respondents said that they had experienced direct harassment at their workplace in the past five years. Also, according to the Human Rights Commission's survey,[27] 73.3% of respondents experienced workplace harassment over the past year. The average number of harassment was 10.0 cases, the experience of personal harassment was 39.0%, and the experience of collective harassment was 5.6%. These workplace harassments have resulted in negative reactions such as consideration of resignation (66.9%), less confidence in the company and its senior officials (64.9%), a decline in work performance and concentration (64.9%), and a reluctance to relate with peers (33.3%).

The damage due to workplace harassment continues to grow and so the

---

[26] Keunjoo Kim/Kyunghee Lee, 「A Survey of Workplace Harassment and The Countermeasures」, Korean Labor Institute, December 2017.

[27] Sungsoo Hong et al, 「A Survey of Workplace Harassment」, The National Human Rights Commission of Korea, November 2017.

하면서, 사용자가 실질적으로 직장 내 괴롭힘 사건에 있어 큰 열의가 없을 경우에는 실효적 효과를 가져올 수가 없었다. 그래서 이번 2021년 4월에 새롭게 도입된 직장 내 괴롭힘 방지법에서는 사용자가 직장 내 괴롭힘 행위자인 경우 처벌을 할 수 있는 조항이 신설되었고, 사용자가 직장 내 괴롭힘을 인지한 경우 객관적 조사를 하여야 할 의무조항이 도입되어 실질적으로 근로자에게 도움이 된다는 것에 그 의미가 있다. 앞으로 직장 내 괴롭힘 사건 발생시 고용노동부에서는 적극적 개입을 통해 사용자가 사건을 철저히 조사하여 관련자를 처벌하게 할 것이고, 이로 인해 차후 사건 재발을 방지할 수 있는 획기적인 변화를 가져올 것이다. 이를 통해 직장 내 괴롭힘 사건에 대한 실질적 구제조치와 예방조치가 동시에 이루어질 수 있을 것이라 기대한다.

II. 직장 내 괴롭힘 방지법과 사용자의 의무

최근 대기업의 직장 내 괴롭힘이 언론에 보도되는 사회 문제가 되고 있다. 이들 회사의 임원들이 직원에 대한 폭언, 폭행, 비인간적인 대우 등의 문제가 사실로 드러난 괴롭힘의 행위이지만 여전히 이것은 빙산의 일각이라 할 수 있다. 한국노동연구원의 조사에 따르면, 과거 5년간 직장 내 괴롭힘에 대해 '직접적 피해 경험'이 있다고 응답한 응답자가 전체 응답자 중 66.3%로 나타났다.[26] 또한 국가인권위원회의 조사에 따르면, 1년간의 직장 내 괴롭힘 피해를 경험하였다고 응답한 응답자는 전체 응답자의 73.3%였고, 피해 경험 행위의 개수는 평균 10.0개로 나타났으며, 괴롭힘 경험 중 개인적 괴롭힘 경험이 39.0%, 집단적 괴롭힘 경험이 5.6%로 나타났다. 이러한 직장 내 괴롭힘으로 인해 이직을 고민(66.9%)하거나, 상급자나 회사에 대한 신뢰가 하락(64.9%)하고, 그 밖에 업무 능력이나 집중도 하락(64.9%) 동료들과의 관계가 멀어짐(33.3%) 등의 부정적 영향이 발생하고 있다.[27]

직장 내 괴롭힘의 피해가 커지고 있고, 이에 대한 개선을 위한 사회적 요구로 인하여 직장 내 괴롭힘 금지 관련 「근로기준법」, 「산업재해보상보험법」, 「산업안전보건법」이 개정되었다. 아래에서는 직장 내 괴롭힘법의 주요내용과

---

[26] 김근주, 이경희, 「직장 내 괴롭힘 실태와 제도적 규율 방안」, 한국노동연구원, 2017.12.
[27] 홍성수외 7명, 「직장 내 괴롭힘 실태조사」, 국가인권위원회, 2017.11.

II. The Workplace Harassment Prevention Law and the Employer's Duty

Workplace Harassment Prevention Law was enacted because of public demand for improvement. The details are described below.

1. Content of the Workplace Harassment Prevention Law

(1) The employer's obligation to prohibit workplace harassment

Article 76-2 (Prohibition of Workplace Harassment) in the Labor Standard Act: the employer or an employee shall not cause physical or mental suffering or deteriorate the working environment, exceeding the appropriate level of bearable limits, by taking advantage of his or her position or relationship in the workplace.

(2) Obligations of the employer in case of an occurrence of workplace harassment (Article 76-3 of the LSA)

① Anyone who has learned the occurrence of workplace harassment may report such fact to the employer.

② Where an employer receives a report under paragraph (1) or becomes aware of the occurrence of workplace harassment, the employer shall, without delay, conduct an objective investigation of the persons involved to ascertain the fact.

③ Where necessary to protect employees who suffer or claim to suffer workplace harassment (hereinafter referred to as "victimized employees, etc.") while investigation under paragraph (2) is conducted, the employer shall take appropriate measures for the victimized employees, etc., such as transferring their place of work or ordering them a paid leave of absence. In such cases, the employer shall not take measures contrary to the will of the victimized employees, etc.

④ Where the occurrence of workplace harassment is verified as a result of investigation under paragraph (2), the employer shall take appropriate measures for the victimized employees, etc., such as transferring their place of work, giving them a lateral transfer or ordering them a paid leave of absence, if the victimized employees, etc. make a request.

⑤ Where the occurrence of workplace harassment is verified as a result of investigation under paragraph (2), the employer shall, without delay, take necessary measures, such as taking disciplinary measures against the perpetrator of workplace harassment or transferring his or her place of work. In such cases, before taking disciplinary measures, etc., the employer shall hear opinions of the victimized employees, etc. on such measures.

실무적 적용에 대해 구체적으로 살펴보고자 한다.

1. 직장 내 괴롭힘 방지법 내용

(1) 사용자의 직장 내 괴롭힘 금지의무 명시

「근로기준법」제76조의2(직장 내 괴롭힘의 금지): 사용자 또는 근로자는 직장에서의 지위 또는 관계 등의 우위를 이용하여 업무상 적정범위를 넘어 다른 근로자에게 신체적·정신적 고통을 주거나 근무환경을 악화시키는 행위를 하여서는 아니 된다.

(2) 직장 내 괴롭힘 발생 시 사용자의 조치 의무(근기법 제76조의3)

① 누구든지 직장 내 괴롭힘 발생 사실을 알게 된 경우 그 사실을 사용자에게 신고할 수 있다.

② 사용자는 제1항에 따른 신고를 접수하거나 직장 내 괴롭힘 발생 사실을 인지한 경우에는 지체 없이 당사자 등을 대상으로 그 사실 확인을 위하여 객관적으로 조사를 실시하여야 한다.

③ 사용자는 제2항에 따른 조사 기간 동안 직장 내 괴롭힘과 관련하여 피해를 입은 근로자 또는 피해를 입었다고 주장하는 근로자(이하 "피해근로자등"이라 한다)를 보호하기 위하여 필요한 경우 해당 피해근로자등에 대하여 근무장소의 변경, 유급휴가 명령 등 적절한 조치를 하여야 한다. 이 경우 사용자는 피해근로자등의 의사에 반하는 조치를 하여서는 아니 된다.

④ 사용자는 제2항에 따른 조사 결과 직장 내 괴롭힘 발생 사실이 확인된 때에는 피해근로자가 요청하면 근무장소의 변경, 배치전환, 유급휴가 명령 등 적절한 조치를 하여야 한다.

⑤ 사용자는 제2항에 따른 조사 결과 직장 내 괴롭힘 발생 사실이 확인된 때에는 지체 없이 행위자에 대하여 징계, 근무장소의 변경 등 필요한 조치를 하여야 한다. 이 경우 사용자는 징계 등의 조치를 하기 전에 그 조치에 대하여 피해근로자의 의견을 들어야 한다.

⑥ 사용자는 직장 내 괴롭힘 발생 사실을 신고한 근로자 및 피해근로자등

Ⅱ. The Workplace Harassment Prevention Law and the Employer's Duty

⑥ No employer shall dismiss employees who report the occurrence of workplace harassment, victimized employees, etc., or treat them unfavorably.

⑦ No person who investigates the occurrence of workplace harassment pursuant to paragraph (2), who receives a report on the details of investigation, or who participates in the investigation process of workplace harassment shall divulge confidential information learned in the course of investigation to any other persons against the will of the victimized employees, etc.: Provided, That the same shall not apply where the investigator reports matters relating to the investigation to the employer or provides necessary information at the request of a relevant institution.

(3) Amendment to the Industrial Accident Compensation Insurance Act

Article 37 (1) of the IACI Act, which lists reasons for acceptance as occupational diseases, has added "illness caused by work-related mental stress, such as workplace harassment and abuse of the worker pursuant to Article 76-2 of the Labor Standards Act".

(4) Amendments to the Industrial Safety and Health Act

Article 4 of the ISH Act (Government obligations) added a new item: "10. Establishment, guidance and support of measures to prevent workplace harassment pursuant to Article 76-2 of the Labor Standards Act".

2. Explanation of Workplace Harassment

(1) Definition of workplace harassment

It is meaningful that the definition of workplace harassment clearly defines the obligations of the related employer and the standard of related harassment incidents. Until this concept was established, the labor law had no legal obligation or liability for workplace harassment. It is very meaningful that the Labor Standards Act has stipulated a definition of workplace harassment in order to strengthen the obligations of employers and to protect the workers with measures to receive remedy for workplace harassment. Therefore, under the existing legal system, the measures that a victim who had been harassed in the workplace could take to the employer included

① a claim for damages based on the liability of the victim for illegal acts (Article 750 of the Civil Act),

에게 해고나 그 밖의 불리한 처우를 하여서는 아니 된다.
⑦ 제2항에 따라 직장 내 괴롭힘 발생 사실을 조사한 사람, 조사 내용을 보고받은 사람 및 그 밖에 조사 과정에 참여한 사람은 해당 조사 과정에서 알게 된 비밀을 피해근로자등의 의사에 반하여 다른 사람에게 누설하여서는 아니 된다. 다만, 조사와 관련된 내용을 사용자에게 보고하거나 관계 기관의 요청에 따라 필요한 정보를 제공하는 경우는 제외한다.

(3) 「산업재해보상보험법」 개정

업무상 질병으로 인정하는 사유를 열거한 「산업재해보상보험법」 제37조 1항에 "「근로기준법」 제76조의2에 따른 직장 내 괴롭힘, 고객의 폭언 등 업무상 정신적 스트레스가 원인이 되어 발생한 질병"을 추가되었다.

(4) 「산업안전보건법」 개정

「산업안전보건법」 제4조(정부의 책무)에서 "「근로기준법」 제76조의2에 따른 직장 내괴롭힘 예방을 위한 조치기준 마련, 지도 및 지원"(제10호)을 신설하였다.

2. 직장 내 괴롭힘 방지법 설명

(1) 직장 내 괴롭힘 정의 규정

직장 내 괴롭힘의 정의를 규정함으로써 관련된 사업주의 의무와 업무상 재해의 기준을 명확하였다는 점에서 의미가 있다. 이 개념이 정립되기 전에는 노동법상 직장 내 괴롭힘에 대한 법적인 의무나 책임관계를 갖지 못했다. 일반적으로 근로자들이 직장 내 괴롭힘을 이유로 권리구제를 받는 경우가 거의 없었다는 점에서, 이번 「근로기준법」에 직장 내 괴롭힘의 정의를 명문화함으로써 사업주의 의무를 강화하고 근로자의 보호방안을 마련하였다는데 큰 의미가 있다. 따라서 현재의 법제하에서 직장 내 괴롭힘을 당한 피해근로자가 사용자를 대상으로 취할 수 있는 조치로는
① 가해근로자의 불법행위에 대한 사용자 책임을 이유로 한 손해배상 청구소송(「민법」 제750조),

II. The Workplace Harassment Prevention Law and the Employer's Duty

② a suit for damages (violation of the obligation of safety considerations by labor contract) (Article 390 of the Civil Act), and

③ a complaint under Article 30 (Human Rights Violation) of the National Human Rights Commission Act.

④ By informing the labor inspector and the Minister of Employment and Labor of the damages incurred, an employee can seek redress directly through filing a legal complaint for violation of Article 116.

(2) Establishment of the employer's duty for action in case of workplace harassment

In case of workplace harassment, the victim or a third party can notify the employer. An employer who has been informed of the occurrence of workplace harassment must conduct an investigation to confirm the fact. In the course of this investigation, measures should be taken to protect the victim and, if the investigation confirms the workplace harassment, disciplinary action should be taken without delay.

(3) The addition of 'workplace harassment' in the required items of the Rules of Employment

An employer who routinely employs 10 or more workers must fill out the 12 required items in the Rules of Employment and report them to the Minister of Employment and Labor (Article 93 of the LSA). Here is the required item added in relation to workplace harassment: "11. Matters concerning prevention and measures in case of occurrence of workplace harassment." In other words, it is stipulated in the Rules of Employment that the company has implemented measures related to workplace harassment.[28]

(4) Penalties applicable for unfavorable treatment by an employer

It is regulated as the employer's duty, in the self-governing rules, that the employer should explore preventive measures against workplace harassment and take appropriate measures. However, if disadvantageous treatment of victims is taken, the employer should and can be severely punished, similar to the Equal Employment Act. In other words, Article 110 of the Labor Standards Act stipulates "imprisonment for up to three years or a fine of not more than KRW

---

[28] Labor Ministry Guideline: "Operational Guides for the Rules of Employment", LSA Dept-1119, April 24, 2009.

② 채무불이행(근로계약상 안전배려의무 위반)을 이유로 한 손해배상 소송(「민법」 제390조),
③ 「국가인권위원회법」 제30조(인권침해)에 기한 진정제기
④ 근로감독관, 고용노동부장관에 피해를 통보, 진정할 수 있고 제116조 위반으로 검사에게 직접 고소할 수 있는 방법이 생겼다.

(2) 직장 내 괴롭힘 발생 시 사용자의 조치 의무 신설

직장 내 괴롭힘 발생시에 피해근로자나 제3자가 사용자에 신고할 수 있다. 신고를 받았거나 직장 내 괴롭힘 발생을 인지한 사용자는 그 사실관계 확인을 위한 조사를 실시하여야 한다. 이 조사과정에서 피해근로자를 보호를 위한 조치를 하여야 하고, 조사결과 직장 내 괴롭힘이 사실로 확인되는 경우에는 지체 없이 징계조치를 하여야 한다.

(3) 취업규칙의 필요적 기재사항 중 직장 내 괴롭힘 추가

취업규칙은 상시 10명이상의 근로자를 사용하는 사용자는 필요적 기재사항 12가지를 기재한 취업규칙을 작성하고 고용노동부장관에게 신고하도록 하고 있다(「근로기준법」 제93조). 여기에 필요적 기재사항으로 "11. 직장 내 괴롭힘의 예방 및 발생 시 조치 등에 관한 사항"이 추가되었다. 즉, 직장 내 괴롭힘과 관련한 자체적인 회사의 조치 사항을 취업규칙에 명문화하여 이를 준수하도록 하고 있는 것이다.[28]

(4) 직장 내 괴롭힘을 신고한 근로자와 피해자에 대한 해고 등 불이익 처우 시 벌칙

직장 내 괴롭힘에 대한 예방과 발생시 조사하여 합당한 조치를 하여야 하는 사업주의 의무는 법적인 의무가 자치규정으로 사업주 스스로 지켜야 하도록 규정화 되어 있다. 그러나 이러한 과정에서 피해근로자에 대한 불이익 처우에 대해서는 사용자가 강력한 처벌을 받을 수 있도록 「남녀고용평등법」과 동일하게 사용자의 법적 의무를 부과하고 있다. 즉, 「근로기준법」 제110조에 "이 법 제76조의3인 6항 위반 시, 3년 이하의 징역 또는 3천만 원 이하의 벌금"을 규정하고 있다.

---

[28] "취업규칙 해석 및 운영지침", 근로기준과-1119, 2009.4.24.

II. The Workplace Harassment Prevention Law and the Employer's Duty

30 million in violation of Article 76-3 (Paragraph 6) of this Act".

(5) Amendment to the Industrial Accident Compensation Insurance Act

The current Article 37 (1) of the IACI Act did not recognize occupational accidents caused by workplace harassment, but the revised law does recognize an occupational accident due to "illness caused by work-related mental stress such as workplace harassment", and so this article will provide a legal basis to occupational accidents. Diseases caused by workplace harassment were difficult to have recognized as a work-related injury by the Korea Workers' Welfare Corporation, and were accepted exceptionally only after complicated legal disputes. However, with the revised law, the Welfare Corporation has opened the way for victims to be recognized more quickly in the first work-related accident assessment stage.

(6) Amendments to the Industrial Safety and Health Act

Workplace harassment has an adverse effect on the mental and physical health of the workers, undermining their opportunity to work in a healthy environment. Therefore, the amendment to Article 4 of the ISH Act, to prevent illness caused by workplace harassment, imposes upon the government an obligation to act. In this regard, the Ministry of Employment and Labor has prepared 'A Practical Manual for the Prevention of Workplace Harassment and Countermeasures Against It', which will be distributed to all companies. Unfortunately, this obligation to prevent workplace harassment is defined as an obligation of the state rather than a direct obligation of the employer, so that the employer is not responsible for violations of the ISH Act.

3. The Effect of the Workplace Harassment Prevention Law

It is not easy for ordinary workers to take legal action for harassment against a workplace because such matters take a considerable amount of time and money. However, the amendment to the Labor Standards Act clarifies the concept of workplace harassment, and in particular the obligation of prohibition of workplace harassment by an employer, along with the obligation to implement relief procedures that will enable victims to receive protection and relief from workplace harassment more quickly.

(5) 「산업재해보상보험법」 개정

현행 산업재해보상보험법」 제37조 1항에는 직장 내 괴롭힘에 의한 업무상 재해를 인정하지 않았으나, 개정법은 "직장 내 괴롭힘, 고객의 폭언 등 업무상 정신적 스트레스가 원인이 돼 발생한 질병"도 업무상 재해로 인정받을 수 있는 법적 근거를 마련했다. 기존의 직장 내 괴롭힘으로 발생한 질병은 근로복지공단에서 업무상 재해로 인정받기 어려웠고, 공단의 불승인 결정에 불복하여 법원에서 힘겹게 다투고 나서야 권리를 구제받을 수 있었다. 그러나, 이번 개정법으로 인해 앞으로는 근로복지공단의 최초 업무상 재해 심사 단계에서 더욱 신속하게 피해를 구제 받을 수 있는 길이 열리게 되었다.

(6) 「산업안전보건법」 개정

직장 내 괴롭힘은 근로자의 정신적, 신체적 건강에 악영향을 끼쳐 해당 근로자의 건강한 근로의 기회를 훼손하게 되므로 직장 내 괴롭힘으로 발생하는 질병을 예방하는 차원에서 산업안전보건법 개정안 제4조는 직장 내 괴롭힘 예방에 관한 정부의 조치의무를 부과하고 있다. 이와 관련하여 고용노동부는 직장 내 괴롭힘에 대한 '직장 내 괴롭힘 판단 및 예방·대응 실무 매뉴얼'을 제작하여 기업에서 배포할 예정이다. 아쉬운 것은 이러한 직장 내 괴롭힘 예방의 의무를 사업주의 직접 의무가 아닌 국가의 의무로 규정함으로써 사업주가 산업안전보건법 위반으로부터는 책임을 면하고 있다는 점이다.

3. 직장 내 괴롭힘 방지법의 효과

기존에도 직장 내 괴롭힘이 발생한 경우에는 경우에 따라 그에 대한 민사상 손해배상이나 형사상 고소가 가능하였으나 그러한 법적 조치를 취한다는 것은 상당한 시간과 비용이 들기 때문에 일반 근로자가 현실적으로 직장 내 괴롭힘으로부터 구제받는 것은 쉽지 않았다. 그러나 이번 「근로기준법」 개정안은 직장 내 괴롭힘의 개념을 분명히 하였고, 특히 사업주의 직장 내 괴롭힘 금지와 구제 절차 이행 의무를 규정함으로써 피해근로자가 직장 내 괴롭힘으로부터의 보호와 구제를 더욱 신속하게 받을 수 있게 되었다.

Section 3. Basic Understanding of Sexual Harassment

(El-lim Kim)

Ⅰ. Definition of "Sexual Harassment" and "Workplace Sexual Harassment" [29]

1. Origin and internationalization of the term 'sexual harassment'

The term "sexual harassment" is a translation of "성희롱" (性戱弄) and was first used in the United States in the mid-1970s. From the mid-1980s, it has been widely used internationally as well. In the United States, "sexual harassment" refers to the incidents where female (or male) employees in the workplace are subjected to mental and physical harm and human rights violations by male (female) superiors or colleagues who use their superior status to attempt to get away with making unwelcome sexual remarks, actions, or demands. Feminists[30] first coined the term "sexual harassment" as a specific description distinguished from "gender discrimination/violence." Subsequently, U.S. courts and the Equal Employment Opportunity Commission (EEOC) reflected this view in recognizing "sexual harassment" as a violation of Title VII of the Civil Rights Act, which prohibits employment discrimination. Therefore, it became a legal term in the United States.

As a result, international interest in 'sexual harassment' increased. In 1985, the United Nations (UN) adopted the "Nairobi Forward-looking Strategies for the Advancement of Women" at the Third World Conference on Women, where for the first time in the history of international human rights documents, the International Labour Organization (ILO) pointed out that 'sexual harassment' violates women's labor rights and equality, hinders their ability to perform and their motivation to work, and hampers women's development. They called for national measures to address this issue. Consequently, the European Community (EC) adopted the

---

[29] Elim Kim, 「Sexual Harassment: Law and Cases of Dispute Handling」, Episteme, 2023.
[30] Feminists are people who pursue feminism, a belief system that seeks to identify and address the causes of unfair treatment of women. Today's feminists aim to change the existing male-centered social structure and culture, to guarantee women's rights and gender equality.

제3절 직장 내 성희롱의 기본적 이해

(김엘림)

I. '성희롱'과 '직장 내 성희롱'이란 용어의 뜻[29]

1. '성희롱' 용어의 어원(sexual harassment)과 국제화

'성희롱'(性戱弄)이란 용어는 1970년대 중반부터 미국에서 먼저 사용되다가 1980년대 중반부터 국제적으로 통용되고 있는 'sexual harassment'(섹슈얼 하라스먼트)란 용어의 번역어이다.

미국에서 'sexual harassment'란 용어는 사업장에서 여성근로자들이 수적으로나 지위상 우월한 남성 사용자나 근로자들의 불쾌한 성적인 말과 행동, 요구에 의해 정신적·육체적 피해와 인권침해를 당하고 근로조건과 근로 의욕 및 근로환경, 실적에 악영향을 받는 현상을 여성주의자(페미니스트)들[30]이 성차별이나 성폭력과 다른 새로운 여성 문제로 특화하여 처음 고안, 사용하였다. 그 후 미국의 법원과 연방 고용기회평등위원회(EEOC)는 여성주의자들의 의견을 반영하여 'sexual harassment'를 고용차별을 금지하는 「민권법」 제7편(Civil Rights Act Ⅶ)을 위반하는 행위로 인정하였다. 그리하여 이 용어는 미국에서 1980년 초부터 법률용어가 되었다.

그 영향으로 국제적으로 'sexual harassment'에 관한 관심이 높아졌다. 1985년에 UN은 제3차 세계여성대회에서 채택한 「2000년을 향한 여성의 진보를 위한 나이로비 미래지향 전략」에서, ILO는 총회에서 채택한 「여성근로자의 기회 및 대우의 평등을 촉진하기 위한 결의」에서 국제인권문서 사상 처음으로 'sexual harassment'가 여성의 근로권과 평등권을 침해하고 능력 발휘와 근무 의욕 나아가 여성발전을 저해하는 문제를 가짐을 지적하고 국가적 대책이 필요함을 촉구하였다. 이에 따라 유럽공동체(EC)가 1990년에 「직장에서의

---

[29] 김엘림, 「성희롱: 법과 분쟁처리사례」, 에피스테매, 2023. 5~26면.
[30] 여성주의자(페미니스트)들이란 여성들이 억압받는 원인과 현상을 규명하고 문제해결을 위해 기존의 남성중심적 사회구조와 문화를 변화시켜 여성의 인권과 성평등을 보장하려는 사상체계이자 이 사상을 구현하려는 운동인 페미니즘(feminism)을 추구하는 사람이나 조직체를 말한다.

Section 3. Basic Understanding of Sexual Harassment

"Resolution on the Dignity and Protection of Women and Men in the Workplace" in 1990, followed by the "Resolution on Measures to Combat Sexual Harassment" in 1991. Since the 1990s, many countries have started implementing various forms of measures to address sexual harassment.

International human rights documents and the laws and court precedents and decisions in various countries also include the term "sexual harassment." The definition refers to behavior 1) that causes harm (mental/physical, human rights violations, or workplace harm) to another person, 2) through unwanted sexual advances (speech, actions, or demands) related to work, 3) using one's position to put pressure on another person to accept or give in (even though the action is resisted by the other person and causes them to feel uncomfortable).

2. Usage and legal terminology of the term 'sexual harassment' in Korea

In Korea, the term "sexual harassment" is referred to as "성희롱" (seong-hui-rong). This became a subject of legal and social discourse after the first sexual harassment lawsuit was filed in October 1993. A woman who worked as a laboratory assistant on a contract basis at S National University, was dismissed before the end of her contract period. She claimed that her dismissal was in retaliation for her rejection of unwarranted and inappropriate sexual advances made by her supervising professor. She argued that it was "sexual harassment" and that it resulted in a violation of her right to personal dignity and also amounted to employment discrimination. She sued the professor, the president of S University, and the Republic of Korea for damages. This lawsuit marked the beginning of the widespread use of the term "sexual harassment" in the 1990s.

However, the Korean language dictionary defines 희롱 (hui-rong) as "teasing with speech or behavior without any substance." However, there has been criticism that the term "성희롱" does not fully express the essence or seriousness of the problem of sexual harassment and may be misunderstood as only sexual advances that are trivial in nature. Suggestions have been made to replace the term with "sexual humiliation" or the English term itself, "sexual harassment." The Second Trial Court ruling on the first sexual harassment lawsuit (Seoul High Court verdict on

여성과 남성의 존엄 보호에 관한 결의」, 1991년에 「성희롱에 대처하기 위한 행동 결의」를 채택한 것을 비롯하여 1990년대부터 많은 국가에서 성희롱에 관한 다양한 형태의 대책이 마련되기 시작하였다.

그런데 'sexual harassment'의 개념을 정의한 국제인권문서들과 여러 국가의 법규나 지침을 살펴보면, 각각 표현에 차이가 있지만, 대체로 1. 업무와 관련하거나 지위를 이용하여, 2. 상대방이 원하지 않는 성적인 언동을 하여, 3. 피해를 발생시키는 행위의 세 가지 요건으로 개념을 구성하고 있다고 보여진다. 여기서 '상대방이 원하지 않는 성적 언동'이란 상대방이 거부하는, 상대방의 의사에 반한, 상대방에게 성적 굴욕감이나 혐오감, 수치심이나 불쾌감을 주는 성적인 말이나 행동, 요구를 의미한다. 또한 '피해'란 상대방의 정신적·육체적 손상, 인격권·성적 자기결정권·평등권 등 인권의 침해뿐 아니라 업무의욕과 실적의 저하, 업무환경의 악화 등의 업무상의 피해도 포함한다. 업무상의 피해는 피해자 개인만이 아니라 사업장과 그 사업장의 종사자에게도 악영향을 미친다.

2. 우리나라에서의 '성희롱' 용어의 사용과 법률용어화

우리나라에서 'sexual harassment'가 '성희롱'으로 지칭되고 이 용어가 법적 논의와 사회적 주목의 대상이 된 것은 1993년 10월에 최초의 성희롱 소송이 제기된 것을 계기로 한다. 당시 국립대였던 S대에서 실험실 조교로 근무하다가 계약기간 만료 전에 해임된 여성은 자신의 해임이 담당 교수의 업무상 불필요하고 부적절한 성적 언동을 거부한 것에 대한 보복적 조치이며 이는 'sexual harassment' 곧 '성희롱'이라고 주장하였다. 그리고 성희롱으로 인해 인격권 침해와 고용상 성차별을 당하였다며 교수, S대 총장, 대한민국에 대하여 손해배상을 청구하였다. 이 소송을 계기로 '성희롱'이란 용어가 1990년대부터 널리 사용되기 시작하였다.

그런데 최초의 성희롱 소송에 대한 제2심 법원(서울고등법원 1995.7.25 선고 94나15358 판결)은 '성적 괴롭힘'이란 용어를 사용하면서 이를 "고용과 관련하여 불쾌한 성적 접근에 응하기를 요구하는 행위를 포함한 성적인 성격을 가진 일체의 성적 언동으로서 그 성적인 성격이 노골적이고 성적인 의도가

Section 3. Basic Understanding of Sexual Harassment

July 25, 1995, 94Na15358) used the term "sexual harassment," which it defined as "any sexual conduct, including unwanted demands for sexual favors, that has an explicit sexual nature and clear sexual intent, and must be serious and thorough, including being repeated persistently against the victim's will." The court also issued a judgment against the plaintiff's claim, saying that the defendant professor's sexual behavior was minor and benign, and did not constitute "sexual harassment" due to lack of evidence. This decision was criticized by feminist activists.

Against this backdrop, the Framework Act on Women's Development was enacted on December 30, 1995, to promote women's social participation. The Act stipulates that "the state, local governments, and employers must take necessary actions to create an equal work environment, including the prevention of sexual harassment" (Article 17, paragraph 3).

As a result, the term "sexual harassment" became a legal term. However, the first law to legally define "sexual harassment" in Korea was the Act on Gender Discrimination Prohibition and Relief, which was enacted on February 8, 1999. This was after the first Supreme Court ruling on the first sexual harassment lawsuit (Supreme Court ruling on Feb. 10. 1998, 95Da39533).

3. Use and legal terminology of the term "sexual harassment in the workplace"

In the United States, the term "sexual harassment" initially referred to sexual advances towards female (or male) employees in the workplace. But now it includes sexual advances in various settings, such as in schools and public institutions. As a result, the term "sexual harassment at work" or "sexual harassment in the workplace" is specifically used to describe sexual harassment in the workplace.

In South Korea, the first sexual harassment lawsuit involved sexual advances towards a professor's assistant. The plaintiff, her legal team, and women's rights activists who supported her called it "sexual harassment in the workplace." The first and only law in South Korea to define the concept of "sexual harassment in the workplace" was the Equal Employment Act(enacted February 28, 1998.)

분명히 간취될 수 있어야 하며, 피해자의 의사에 반하여 집요하게 반복적으로 이루어지는 등으로 중대하고 철저한 행위가 되어야 성립한다."라고 판시하였다. 그리고 피고 교수의 성적 언동에 관한 원고의 주장 상당수는 증거가 없을 뿐 아니라 '성적 괴롭힘'에 해당되지 않는 경미하고 호의적인 것에 불과하다며 원고 패소판결을 내렸다. 이 판결에 대하여 여성주의자들은 'sexual harassment' 용어의 취지를 이해하지 못하고 성희롱의 인정요건과 범위를 지나치게 엄격하고 좁게 해석하였다며 강하게 비판하고 성희롱에 대한 법적 대책을 요구하였다.

이러한 배경으로 1995년 12월 30일에 여성의 사회참여를 촉진하기 위한 여성정책의 기본법으로 제정된 「여성발전기본법」에 "국가·지방자치단체 또는 사업주는 성희롱의 예방 등 평등한 근무환경 조성을 위하여 필요한 조치를 하여야 한다."라고 규정한 조항(제17조제3항)이 마련되었다. 그리하여 '성희롱'이란 용어는 법률용어가 되었다. 그런데 성희롱의 법적 개념을 처음 정의한 법은 최초의 성희롱 소송에 대한 대법원 판결(1998.2.10 선고 95다39533 판결)이 선고된 후인 1999년 2월 8일에 제정된 「남녀차별금지및구제에관한법률」이다.

3. '직장 내 성희롱'이란 용어의 사용과 법률용어화

미국에서 'sexual harassment'란 용어는 처음에 일반 사업장에서 여성근로자들에 대한 성적 언동을 문제 삼았다가 그후 학교, 공공기관, 군대 등 다양한 곳에서의 성적 언동으로 문제의 대상을 확장하였다. 이러한 배경으로 사업장에서의 성희롱을 특화하여 'sexual harassment at work', 'sexual harassment in workplace'란 용어가 사용되었다.

우리나라에서는 최초의 성희롱 소송의 사안이 대학교수의 조교에 대한 성적 언동이었는데 이를 원고와 원고의 변호인단, 원고를 지원하던 여성주의자들이 '직장 내 성희롱'으로 명명하였다. 1999년 2월 8일에 개정된 「남녀고용평등법」은 이러한 상황을 고려하여 우리나라 법 중 최초로 '직장 내 성희롱'의 개념을 정의하였다.

Section 3. Basic Understanding of Sexual Harassment

II. Definition of "Sexual Harassment" and "Workplace Sexual harassment" under Korean Law[31]

The current Korean laws that define "sexual harassment" are the Framework Act on Gender Equality and the National Human Rights Commission of Korea Act. The Equal Employment Act defines sexual harassment and regulates actions in the context of sexual harassment in the workplace.[32] These three laws have different purposes and uses, with each expressing the criteria for determining whether sexual harassment has occurred somewhat differently.

1. Definition and use of the term in the Framework Act on Gender Equality

(1) Definition of sexual harassment and criteria for establishing whether it has occurred

Article 2-2 of the Framework Act on Gender Equality defines sexual harassment as "actions taken by employees, employers, or workers of public agencies (hereinafter referred to as "government agencies") designated by Presidential decree or local autonomous entities in work, employment, or other relationships that cause the other party to feel sexual humiliation or hatred due to sexual advances or demands related to their position or work, or that offer benefits with the condition of causing disadvantage if the other party does not comply with sexual advances or demands." "Institutions or organizations designated by Presidential decree as 'public agencies'" include "schools of all levels established under the Elementary and Secondary Education Act, the Higher Education Act, and other laws, and public interest-related organizations announced by the head of the Personnel Innovation Agency in the government gazette pursuant to Article 3-2. (2) 2 of the Regulation on Ethics of Public Officials Enforcement (institutions and organizations that have been excluded from public interest-related organizations pursuant to Clause 3 of the same Article are excluded)" (Article 2 of the Enforcement Regulation).

Therefore, for any conduct to be considered sexual harassment under the Framework Act on Gender Equality, the following criteria must be met in relation to the actors (perpetrator and victim), circumstances, means, harm, and behavior, as seen in Table 1.

---

[31] Kim, El-lim. "Sexual Harassment: Law and Case Studies." Episteme, 2023, pp. 172, 185-189, 260.

[32] The "Act on the Prohibition of Sex Discrimination and Remedies thereof" was abolished on March 30, 2005, and the "Basic Law for Women's Development" was converted to the "Gender Equality Basic Law" on May 28, 2014. The "Act on the Equal Employment of Men and Women" was transformed into the "Act on the Promotion of Gender Equality in Employment and Support for Work-Family Reconciliation" on June 22, 2005.

Ⅱ. 현행법의 '성희롱'과 '직장 내 성희롱'의 개념 정의[31]

현행법 중 '성희롱'의 개념을 규정한 법은 「양성평등기본법」과 「국가인권위원회법」이다. 「남녀고용평등법」은 고용과 관련한 성희롱을 '직장 내 성희롱'으로 규정하고 그 개념을 정의하고 있다.[32] 이 세 가지 법은 각기 목적과 쓰임새가 다르다. 그리하여 각 법마다 성희롱의 요건에 관하여 다소 다르게 표현하고 있다.

1. 「양성평등기본법」의 개념 정의와 용도

(1) '성희롱'의 개념 정의와 성립요건

「양성평등기본법」은 '성희롱'을 " 업무, 고용, 그 밖의 관계에서 국가기관·지방자치단체 또는 대통령령으로 정하는 공공단체(이하 "국가기관등"이라 한다)의 종사자, 사용자 또는 근로자가 다음 각 목의 어느 하나에 해당하는 행위를 하는 경우를 말한다. 가. 지위를 이용하거나 업무 등과 관련하여 성적 언동 또는 성적 요구 등으로 상대방에게 성적 굴욕감이나 혐오감을 느끼게 하는 행위 나. 상대방이 성적 언동 또는 성적 요구에 따르지 아니한다는 이유로 불이익을 주거나 그에 따르는 것을 조건으로 이익 공여의 의사표시를 하는 행위"(제2조제2호)라고 정의하고 있다. 여기서 '대통령령으로 정하는 공공단체'란 "① 「초·중등교육법」, 「고등교육법」 및 그 밖의 다른 법률에 따라 설치된 각급 학교 ② 「공직자윤리법 시행령」 제3조의2제2항에 따라 인사혁신처장이 관보에 고시한 공직유관단체(같은 조 제3항에 따라 공직유관단체에서 제외된 것으로 보는 기관 및 단체는 제외한다)"이다(시행령 제2조).

그러므로 어떠한 언동이 「양성평등기본법」에서 말하는 '성희롱'이 되려면 다음 <표 1>에서 정리한 당사자(행위자와 상대방), 경위, 수단, 피해와 행태의 요건을 갖추어야 한다.

---

[31] 김엘림, 「성희롱: 법과 분쟁처리사례」, 에피스테매, 2023., 172면, 185~189면, 260면.
[32] 「남녀차별금지 및 구제에 관한 법률」은 2005년 3월 30일에 폐지되었고, 「여성발전기본법」은 2014년 5월 28일에 「양성평등기본법」으로 전환되었다. 「남녀고용평등법」은 2005년 6월 22일에 「남녀고용평등과 일·가정 양립지원에 관한 법률」로 법률명이 변경되었다.

Section 3. Basic Understanding of Sexual Harassment

<Table 1> Criteria for Establishing 'Sexual Harassment' under the Framework Act on Gender Equality

Perpetrator	Employee, employer, or worker of a public entity (hereinafter referred to as "state institutions") designated as such by Presidential decree or local governments in the course of their work, employment, or other relationships.
Victim	Unspecified
Occurrence	In the course of work, employment, or other relationships
Means	Sexual behavior, demands, or requests, etc.
Behavior	<ul><li>Actions that cause the victim to feel sexual humiliation or aversion through sexual behavior, demands, or requests, etc. used in connection with work or employment that involve the perpetrator exploiting his or her position[33]</li><li>Actions that result in unfavorable treatment of the victim for refusing sexual behavior, demands, or requests</li><li>Actions that promise benefit in exchange for sexual behavior, demands, or requests from the victim</li></ul>

(2) Use of the term "sexual harassment"

To fulfill the principle of gender equality in the Constitution of the Republic of Korea (Article 1), The Framework Act on Gender Equality aims to achieve gender equality in all areas (politics, economics, society, and culture) by stipulating the basic matters related to the duties of the state and local governments.

The concept of "sexual harassment" in this law is mainly used as a target for the sexual harassment prevention measures that should be implemented by heads of public institutions (state agencies, local governments, schools of all levels, and public officials in charge of family and women's affairs).

2. Definition and use of the term "sexual harassment" under the National Human Rights Commission Act

(1) Definition and elements of 'sexual harassment'

---

[33] This law places "using one's position or in relation to work, etc." before the act of sexual harassment, which is one form of sexual harassment that causes the other party to feel sexual humiliation or disgust through sexual advances or demands, in contrast to the National Human Rights Commission Act and the Equal Employment Opportunity Act. However, this requirement is a fundamental element for establishing sexual harassment, so it is believed that the amendment of the legal text is necessary.

Ⅰ. 성희롱의 개념

<표 1>   「양성평등기본법」의 '성희롱' 성립요건

행위자	국가기관·지방자치단체·각급 학교·공직유관단체의 종사자, 사용자 또는 근로자
상대방	불특정
경위	업무, 고용, 그 밖의 관계에서
수단	성적 언동 또는 성적 요구 등
행태	■ 지위를 이용하거나 업무 등과 관련하여[33] 성적 언동 또는 성적 요구 등으로 상대방에게 성적 굴욕감이나 혐오감을 느끼게 하는 행위 ■ 상대방이 성적 언동 또는 성적 요구에 따르지 아니한다는 이유로 불이익을 주는 행위 ■ 상대방에게 성적 언동 또는 성적 요구에 따르는 것을 조건으로 이익 공여의 의사표시를 하는 행위

(2) '성희롱' 개념의 용도

「양성평등기본법」은 "「대한민국헌법」의 양성평등 이념을 실현하기 위한 국가와 지방자치단체의 책무 등에 관한 기본적인 사항을 규정함으로써 정치·경제·사회·문화의 모든 영역에서 양성평등을 실현하는 것"을 목적으로 한다.(제1조)

이 법의 '성희롱' 개념은 주로 공공기관(국가기관·지방자치단체·각급학교·공직유관단체)의 장과 여성가족부장관이 실시해야 할 방지조치의 대상으로 사용된다.

2. 「국가인권위원회법」의 성희롱 개념 정의와 용도

(1) '성희롱'의 개념 정의와 성립요건

---

[33] 이 법은 "지위를 이용하거나 업무 등과 관련하여"를 「국가인권위원회법」과 「남녀고용평등법」의 경우와 달리 성희롱의 형태 중 하나의 형태인 "성적 언동 또는 성적 요구 등으로 상대방에게 성적 굴욕감이나 혐오감을 느끼게 하는 행위" (제2조제2호 가목)앞에 두었지만 이 요건은 성희롱의 기본적 성립요건이므로 법조문의 수정이 필요하다고 본다.

Section 3. Basic Understanding of Sexual Harassment

Under the National Human Rights Commission of Korea Act, sexual harassment refers to "actions by employees, employers, or workers of public institutions (referring to national or local government agencies, schools of all levels established under the Elementary and Secondary Education Act, the Higher Education Act, and public officials' ethics organizations established under Article 3-2 (1) of the Act on Public Official's Standards of Conduct) that use their position or their job to cause sexual humiliation/revulsion through sexual advances or to give employment-related disadvantages for refusing such demands or actions" (Article 2, section 3, subsection 1).

Therefore, for any behavior to be deemed sexual harassment according to the National Human Rights Commission of Korea Act, the requisites listed in Table 2 must be met, regarding the parties involved (the perpetrator and victim), the context, the means, the harm, and the behavior.

<Table 2> Requisites of Sexual Harassment according to the
National Human Rights Commission of Korea Act

Perpetrator	Employee, employer, or worker of a "public institution" (national institution, local autonomous entity, school at any level established according to the Elementary and Secondary Education Act and the Higher Education Act, or Public Service-related Organization established according to Article 3-2 (1) of the Public Officials Ethics Act).
Victim	Unspecified
Occurrence	During work, employment or other work-related activity, using one's position
Means	Sexual behaviors, etc.
Behaviors	■ Behaviors that cause the victim to feel sexual humiliation or hatred ■ Behaviors that cause disadvantage to the victim's employment relations for refusing sexual advances or demands[34]

(2) Use of the concept of "sexual harassment"

The purpose of the National Human Rights Commission of Korea Actis to protect and enhance the fundamental, inalienable human rights of all individuals through establishment of the National Human Rights Commission. It is also meant to realize the dignity and value of human beings and contribute to establishing the

---

[34] Although the Act defines sexual harassment as "behaviors that cause employment-related disadvantage to the victim for refusing sexual advances or demands," it is not limited to employment-related experiences but also applies to sexual harassment that causes educational disadvantage. Therefore, it is reasonable to revise "employment-related disadvantage" to simply "disadvantage."

「국가인권위원회법」에서 '성희롱'이란 "업무, 고용, 그 밖의 관계에서 공공기관(국가기관, 지방자치단체, 「초·중등교육법」 제2조, 「고등교육법」 제2조와 그 밖의 다른 법률에 따라 설치된 각급 학교, 그 밖의 「공직자윤리법」 제3조의2제1항에 따른 공직유관단체를 말한다)의 종사자, 사용자 또는 근로자가 그 직위를 이용하여 또는 업무 등과 관련하여 성적 언동 등으로 성적 굴욕감 또는 혐오감을 느끼게 하거나 성적 언동 또는 그 밖의 요구 등에 따르지 아니한다는 이유로 고용상의 불이익을 주는 것"(제2조제3호라목)을 말한다.

그러므로 어떠한 언동이 「국가인권위원회법」에서 말하는 '성희롱'이 되려면 다음 <표 2>에서 정리한 당사자(행위자와 상대방), 경위, 수단, 피해와 행태의 요건을 갖추어야 한다.

<표 2> 「국가인권위원회법」의 '성희롱' 성립요건

행위자	국가기관·지방자치단체·각급 학교·공직유관단체의 종사자, 사용자 또는 근로자
상대방	불특정
경위	업무, 고용, 그 밖의 관계에서 그 직위를 이용하여 또는 업무 등과 관련하여
수단	성적 언동 등
행태	■ 상대방에게 성적 굴욕감이나 혐오감을 느끼게 하는 행위 ■ 상대방이 성적 언동 또는 성적 요구에 따르지 아니한다는 이유로 고용상의 불이익[34]을 주는 행위

(2) '성희롱' 개념의 용도

「국가인권위원회법」은 "국가인권위원회를 설립하여 모든 개인이 가지는 불가침의 기본적 인권을 보호하고 그 수준을 향상시킴으로써 인간으로서의 존엄과 가치를 실현하고 민주적 기본질서의 확립에 이바지함"을 목적으로 한다.(제1조)

---

34) 이 법은 성희롱의 행태 중의 하나로 "상대방이 성적 언동 또는 성적 요구에 따르지 아니한다는 이유로 고용상의 불이익을 주는 행위"를 규정하고 있지만, 이 법은 고용 영역에 한정하여 적용되지 않고 교육 영역 등 다양한 영역에서의 성희롱에도 적용되므로 "고용상의 불이익"은 "불이익" 으로 개정하는 것이 타당하다. 다양한 영역에 적용되는 「양성평등기본법」은 불이익으로 표기하고 있다.

Section 3. Basic Understanding of Sexual Harassment

basic order of democracy (Article 1).

Accordingly, the National Human Rights Commission of Korea Act specifies corrections for violations of rights and discriminatory acts that infringe on the right to equality (Article 19, paragraphs 2 and 3). Sexual harassment is a type of discriminatory act that infringes on the right to equality. Therefore, "sexual harassment" in this law is used to define the scope of conduct for which the victim can apply for remedy and the National Human Rights Commission to conduct investigations and provide such remedy.

3. Definition and application of "sexual harassment in the workplace" in the Equal Employment Act"

(1) Definition of "sexual harassment in the workplace"

The Equal Employment Act defines sexual harassment in the workplace as any act of an employer, superior, or employee using their position in the workplace or work-related relationship to cause another employee to feel sexual humiliation or disgust due to sexual advances or demands, or to inflict disadvantageous employment conditions and consequences on them for refusing such advances or demands (Article 2-2).

(2) Requirements for establishing that sexual harassment in the workplace has occurred

To be recognized as "sexual harassment" as defined by the National Human Rights Commission Act, the requisites in Table 3 must be met, regarding the perpetrator and the victim, the context, the means, the harm, and the behavior.

<Table 3> Requisites for Establishing that Sexual Harassment in the Workplace Has Occurred" (according to the Equal Employment Act)

Perpetrator	Employer, superior, or employee
Victim	Employee
Occurrence	Using one's position in the workplace or work relationship
Means	Sexual language or gestures
Behaviors	▪ Behaviors that cause the victim to feel sexual humiliation or hatred ▪ Behaviors that result in the victim suffering disadvantageous employment conditions or treatment due to refusing to comply with sexual advances or demands

이 법에 따라 국가인권위원회는 '인권침해행위'와 '평등권 침해의 차별행위'에 대한 권리구제업무를 한다(제19조제2호·제3호). 이 법에서 성희롱은 '평등권 침해의 차별행위'의 일종이다. 그러므로 이 법의 '성희롱' 개념은 피해자가 피해를 진정하고 국가인권위원회가 조사하며 권리구제를 할 수 있는 행위의 범위이다.

3. 「남녀고용평등법」의 '직장 내 성희롱'의 개념 정의와 용도

(1) 직장 내 성희롱'의 개념 정의

「남녀고용평등법」은 '직장 내 성희롱'을 "사업주·상급자 또는 근로자가 직장 내의 지위를 이용하거나 업무와 관련하여 다른 근로자에게 성적 언동 등으로 성적 굴욕감 또는 혐오감을 느끼게 하거나 성적 언동 또는 그 밖의 요구 등에 따르지 아니하였다는 이유로 근로조건 및 고용에서 불이익을 주는 것"(제2조제2호)으로 정의하고 있다.

(2) '직장 내 성희롱'의 성립요건

그러므로 어떠한 언동이 「남녀고용평등법」에 말하는 '직장 내 성희롱'이 되려면 다음 <표 3>에서 정리한 당사자(행위자와 상대방), 경위, 수단, 피해와 행태의 요건을 갖추어야 한다.

<표 3> 「남녀고용평등법」의 '직장 내 성희롱' 성립요건

행위자	사업주, 상급자 또는 근로자
상대방	근로자
경위	직장 내의 지위를 이용하여 또는 업무와 관련하여
수단	성적 언동 등
행태	■ 상대방에게 성적 굴욕감 또는 혐오감을 느끼게 하는 행위 ■ 상대방이 성적 언동 또는 그 밖의 성적 요구에 따르지 아니하였다는 이유로 근로조건 및 고용에서 불이익을 주는 행위

Section 3. Basic Understanding of Sexual Harassment

1) Parties involved

According to the Labor Standards Act, "employer" refers to "a business owner, a person responsible for management of a business, or a person who works on behalf of a business owner with respect to matters relating to workers" (Article 2 (1) 2). However, the Equal Employment Act defines a perpetrator of sexual harassment in the workplace as "an employer, superior, or employee" instead of using only the term "employer." Here, "superior" refers to an individual in a higher position than the victim, whether or not they assist the employer with management authority and responsibilities.

Meanwhile, again according to the Labor Standards Act, the term "employee" refers to "any person who provides labor to a business or workplace for the purpose of receiving wages, regardless of the type of occupation" (Article 2 (1) 1). However, the Equal Employment Act defines the receiver (victim) of sexual harassment in the workplace as "an employee," which refers to "any person employed by an employer or any person who intends to be employed" (Article 2-4).

Therefore, sexual harassment in the workplace also occurs when an employer, superior, or employee uses his or her status during the recruitment and hiring process by engaging in sexual behaviors that cause a job seeker to feel humiliated or disgusted. The Prevention and Response Manual for Sexual Harassment in the Workplace, published by the Ministry of Employment and Labor in 2020, states that job seekers and employees who receive wages and provide labor in a workplace, regardless of their job title or employment status, are all considered employees. Examples of "job seekers and employees" include regular employees, job seekers, non-regular employees (fixed-term employees, short-term employees, dispatched workers, etc.), and workers from subcontractors and partner companies.[35]

However, this law limits the scope of "sexual harassment in the workplace" to sexual acts by an employer, superior, or employee against another employee. Therefore, sexual behaviors executed by employees against employers are not considered "sexual harassment in the workplace." Furthermore, although this law includes Article 14-2 (Prevention of Sexual Harassment by Customers, etc.), "sexual behaviors by customers and other business-related persons" is considered as separate from sexual harassment in the workplace.

2) Circumstances

---

[35] Ministry of Employment and Labor, "Prevention and Response Manual for Sexual Harassment in the Workplace", 2020, pp. 8-9.

1) 당사자

「근로기준법」에서 '사용자'란 "사업주 또는 사업 경영 담당자, 그 밖에 근로자에 관한 사항에 대하여 사업주를 위하여 행위하는 자"(제2조제1항제2호)를 말한다.

그런데 「남녀고용평등법」은 직장 내 성희롱의 행위자를 '사용자'로 하지 않고 '사업주와 상급자, 근로자'로 하고 있다. 여기서 '상급자'란 사용자뿐 아니라 사용자의 경영상의 권한과 책무를 지지 아니하더라도 피해자보다 상위의 직급에 있는 사람을 말한다.

한편, 「근로기준법」에서 '근로자'란 "직업의 종류와 관계없이 임금을 목적으로 사업이나 사업장에 근로를 제공하는 사람"(제2조제1항제1호)을 말한다. 「남녀고용평등법」은 직장 내 성희롱의 상대방(피해자)을 "다른 근로자"로 규정하고 있는데 이 법에서 '근로자'란 "사업주에게 고용된 사람과 취업할 의사를 가진 사람"(제2조제4호)을 말한다. 그러므로 모집·채용과정에서 사업주·상급자 또는 근로자가 지위를 이용하거나 업무와 관련하여 구직자에게 성적 굴욕감 또는 혐오감을 느끼게 하는 성적 언동을 하는 경우도 직장 내 성희롱에 해당된다. 고용노동부가 2020년에 발간한 「직장 내 성희롱 예방·대응 매뉴얼」은 "구직자와 임금을 받고 사업장에서 근로를 제공하는 근로자는 명칭과 고용형태 여하에 관계없이 모두 근로자에 포함된다."라고 기술하고 이에 해당하는 근로자에 정규직 근로자, 구직자 및 비정규직 근로자(기간제 근로자, 단시간 근로자, 파견근로자 등)과 하청업체와 협력업체의 근로자를 예시하였다.[35]

그런데 이 법은 '직장 내 성희롱'의 범위를 사업주, 상급자, 근로자가 다른 근로자에게 하는 성적 언동으로 제한한다. 그러므로 근로자가 사용자에게 성적 언동을 하는 경우에는 직장 내 성희롱에 해당되지 않는다. 또한 이 법은 제14조의2(고객 등에 의한 성희롱 방지)를 두고 있지만, 고객, 거래처 관계자 등 업무와 밀접한 관련이 있는 사람이 근로자에게 하는 성적 언동과 직장 내 성희롱을 구별하여 다르게 취급하고 있다.

2) 경위

---

[35] 고용노동부, 「직장 내 성희롱 예방·대응 매뉴얼」, 2020, 8~9면.

Section 3. Basic Understanding of Sexual Harassment

This law defines the circumstances of sexual harassment in the workplace as "using one's position in the workplace or engaging in work-related actions." Therefore, work-relatedness is an essential factor in deeming whether sexual harassment has occurred in the workplace. Unwanted sexual behaviors that occur in places related to work, such as on business trips or at social gatherings, dinners, or a residence belonging to one of the parties, are all recognized as sexual harassment in the workplace.

3) Means

This law defines sexual harassment in the workplace as involving "sexual language and behaviors," which in turn refer to physical relations between a man and woman or physical, linguistic and visual behaviors in relation to the male or female physical appearance.

As summarized in Table 4, the Enforcement Decree to this law classifies "sexual language and behaviors" as "physical acts," "verbal acts," "visual acts," or "other language or behavior recognized as causing sexual humiliation or disgust according to social norms."

<Table 4> Examples of "Sexual Language and Behaviors" according to the Enforcement Decree to the Equal Employment Act

Physical Behaviors	■ Physical contact such as kissing, hugging from in front or behind ■ Touching private parts of the body, like the breast, backside, etc. ■ Behaviors such as forcing a massage or caressing
Verbal Behaviors	■ Saying a filthy joke or speaking lustful and indecent words, including in telephone conversations ■ Likening appearance to sexual things ■ Asking about sexual relationships or facts, or intentionally distributing information of a sexual nature ■ Forcing or requesting sexual relations ■ Forcing a woman to sit close and fill glasses at a dinner meeting, etc.
Visual Behaviors	■ Putting up or displaying lustful photos, pictures, drawings, etc., including distribution by email or fax

I. 성희롱의 개념

이 법은 직장 내 성희롱의 경위를 "직장 내의 지위를 이용하거나 업무와 관련하여"라고 규정하고 있다. 그러므로 업무관련성은 직장 내 성희롱의 요건이 된다. 사업장 내 뿐 아니라 출장지, 야유회, 회식 장소, 당사자의 거주지도 업무와 관련되는 행위가 이루어지거나 업무가 수행되는 경우에는 직장 내 성희롱의 발생 장소로 인정된다.

3) 수단

이 법은 직장 내 성희롱의 수단을 "성적 언동 등으로"라고 규정하고 있다. '성적 언동'이란 성적 성질을 가지는, 성적 의미가 내포된 말과 행동을 말하는데 성적 요구도 포함된다.

이 법의 시행규칙 [별표1]은 <표 4>에서 정리한 바와 같이 직장 내 성희롱에 해당하는 성적 언동을 '육체적 행위', '언어적 행위' '시각적 행위' '그 밖에 사회통념상 성적 굴욕감 또는 혐오감을 느끼게 하는 것으로 인정되는 언어나 행동'로 구분하여 예시하고 있다.

<표 4> 「남녀고용평등법 시행규칙」의 '성적 언동' 예시

육체적 행위	■ 입맞춤, 포옹 또는 뒤에서 껴안는 등의 신체적 접촉행위 ■ 가슴·엉덩이 등 특정 신체부위를 만지는 행위 ■ 안마나 애무를 강요하는 행위
언어적 행위	■ 음란한 농담을 하거나 음탕하고 상스러운 이야기를 하는 행위 (전화통화를 포함한다) ■ 외모에 대한 성적인 비유나 평가를 하는 행위 ■ 성적인 사실 관계를 묻거나 성적인 내용의 정보를 의도적으로 퍼뜨리는 행위 ■ 성적인 관계를 강요하거나 회유하는 행위 ■ 회식자리 등에서 무리하게 옆에 앉혀 술을 따르도록 강요하는 행위
시각적 행위	■ 음란한 사진·그림·낙서·출판물 등을 게시하거나 보여 주는 행위 (컴퓨터통신이나 팩시밀리 등을 이용하는 경우를 포함한다)

Section 3. Basic Understanding of Sexual Harassment

	■ Intentionally exposing or touching one's own physical parts in a sexual manner
Other language or behavior which makes other workers feel sexually humiliated or offended as a socially accepted notion.	

4) Behaviors

This law defines sexual harassment behaviors in the workplace as "actions that cause the other person to feel sexual humiliation or aversion" and "taking disadvantageous actions regarding the employee's working conditions or employment because they did not comply with sexual advances or other sexual demands."

Attached Form 11 of the Enforcement Decree to this law provides behavioral examples of sexual harassment in the workplace, such as "unfair treatment in employment such as failure to hire, demotion, promotion denial, job transfer, suspension, leave of absence, or termination."

(3) Criteria for determining whether sexual harassment in the workplace has occurred

In the "Note" to Attached Form 1 of the Enforcement Decree to this law, there is a standard for evaluating whether or not sexual harassment has occurred in the workplace, stating that "when determining whether sexual harassment has occurred in the workplace, the subjective circumstances of the victim should be taken into account."

It also considers "how a reasonable person would evaluate and respond to behavior that would be problematic from the victim's perspective according to social norms, and ultimately assessing whether such behavior creates a threatening or hostile work environment that impairs work efficiency."[36]

(4) Use of the concept of "sexual harassment in the workplace"

The "Equal Employment Act" aims to guarantee equal opportunities and

---

[36] However, when this law was amended on February 8, 1999, the concept of "sexual harassment in the workplace" was defined as "using one's position as an employer, superior, or employee to sexually harass another employee through sexual language or behavior related to work, or by causing employment-related harm or humiliation through such language or behavior." The criteria presented in the Enforcement Decree to this Act took account of this definition. However, this definition was revised on August 4, 2001, and the phrase "creating disadvantage in their employment" was removed. Therefore, it would be inconsistent with the revised legal definition of sexual harassment in the workplace to keep the standard of the current Enforcement Decree to this Act which says, "ultimately assessing whether such behavior creates a threatening or hostile work environment that impairs work efficiency."

	■ 성과 관련된 자신의 특정 신체부위를 고의적으로 노출하거나 만지는 행위
	그 밖에 사회통념상 성적 굴욕감 또는 혐오감을 느끼게 하는 것으로 인정되는 언어나 행동

4) 행태

이 법은 직장 내 성희롱의 행태를 "상대방에게 성적 굴욕감 또는 혐오감을 느끼게 하는 행위"와 "상대방이 성적 언동 또는 그 밖의 성적 요구에 따르지 아니하였다는 이유로 근로조건 및 고용에서 불이익을 주는 행위"로 규정하고 있다.

이 법의 시행규칙은 [별표 1]에서 직장 내 성희롱의 행태 중 "고용에서 불이익을 주는 것"에 대하여 "채용탈락, 감봉, 승진탈락, 전직(轉職), 정직(停職), 휴직, 해고 등과 같이 채용 또는 근로조건을 일방적으로 불리하게 하는 것"으로 예시하고 있다.

(3) '직장 내 성희롱'의 판단기준

이 법의 시행규칙은 [별표 1]의 '비고'에서 "직장 내 성희롱 여부를 판단하는 때에는 피해자의 주관적 사정을 고려하되, 사회통념상 합리적인 사람이 피해자의 입장이라면 문제가 되는 행동에 대하여 어떻게 판단하고 대응하였을 것인가를 함께 고려하여야 하며, 결과적으로 위협적·적대적인 고용환경을 형성하여 업무능률을 떨어뜨리게 되는지를 검토하여야 한다."라고 판단기준을 제시하고 있다.[36]

(4) '직장 내 성희롱' 개념의 용도

「남녀고용평등법」은 "「대한민국헌법」의 평등이념에 따라 고용에서

---

[36] 그런데 이 법은 1999년 2월 8일에 개정될 때, '직장 내 성희롱'의 개념을 "사업주, 상급자 또는 근로자가 직장 내의 지위를 이용하거나 업무와 관련하여 다른 근로자에게 성적인 언어나 행동 등으로 또는 이를 조건으로 고용상의 불이익을 주거나 또는 성적 굴욕감을 유발하게 하여 고용환경을 악화시키는 것"으로 처음 정의하였다. 이 법의 시행규칙에서 제시한 판단기준은 이러한 '직장 내 성희롱'의 개념을 고려한 것이다. 그런데 '직장 내 성희롱'의 법적 개념은 2001년 8월 4일에 개정되어 '고용환경을 악화시키는 것"이란 문구가 삭제되었다. 그러므로 현행 시행규칙이 "결과적으로 위협적·적대적인 고용환경을 형성하여 업무능률을 떨어뜨리게 되는지를 검토하여야 한다."라는 판단기준을 유지하는 것은 '직장 내 성희롱'의 개정된 법적 개념과 맞지 않는다.

Section 3. Basic Understanding of Sexual Harassment

treatment for men and women in employment, promote maternity protection and women's employment, and support the reconciliation of work and family life in order to improve the quality of life for all citizens in accordance with the equality principles of the "Constitution of the Republic of Korea" (Article 1). This law includes provisions on the prohibition and prevention of workplace sexual harassment in Chapter 2, Section 2 (Prohibition and Prevention of Workplace Sexual Harassment) of the "Guarantee of Equal Opportunities and Treatment between Men and Women in Employment." Therefore, the concept of "workplace sexual harassment" in this law refers to actions that employers, superiors, and employees must not engage in and the measures that employers must take to ensure equal opportunities and treatment between men and women.

(5) Scope of application of regulations regarding 'workplace sexual harassment'

The law also stipulates the actions that employers must take to ensure equal opportunities and treatment for men and women and applies to all businesses or workplaces (hereinafter referred to as "businesses") that employ workers (Article 4). However, the entire law does not apply to businesses consisting solely of close relatives living together or domestic workers (Article 2 of the Enforcement Decree).

III. Characteristics of Sexual Harassment and Its Relationship to Workplace Harassment, Sexual Assault, and Gender Discrimination

Sexual harassment encompasses elements of work-relatedness, power dynamics, violence, and discrimination. In this regard, sexual harassment shares similarities and differences with workplace bullying, sexual violence, and gender discrimination.[37]

1. Work-relevance of sexual harassment and its relationship with workplace harassment

Sexual harassment is connected to sexual behavior related to work or the use of position. Such behavior is mainly directed towards individuals in a vulnerable position by those with authority and higher positions. For example, if sexual harassment occurs in a regular workplace, the employer or a superior is often the perpetrator. In a university, it might be a professor. Therefore, sexual harassment is both relevant to power and work.

2. Relationship between sexual harassment and workplace harassment

---

[37] Kim El-lim, "Sexual Harassment: Law and Dispute Resolution Cases," Episteme, 2023, pp. 27-43.

남녀의 평등한 기회와 대우를 보장하고 모성 보호와 여성 고용을 촉진하여 남녀고용평등을 실현함과 아울러 근로자의 일과 가정의 양립을 지원함으로써 모든 국민의 삶의 질 향상에 이바지하는 것을 목적으로 한다."(제1조).

이 법은 직장 내 성희롱의 금지와 예방 등에 관한 규정들을 [제2장 고용에서 남녀의 평등한 기회보장 및 대우등]의 제2절(직장 내 성희롱의 금지 및 예방)에 편성하고 있다. 그러므로 이 법의 '직장 내 성희롱' 개념은 남녀의 평등한 기회 및 대우를 보장하기 위하여 사업주, 상급자, 근로자가 해서는 아니되는 행위와 사업주가 해야 할 조치를 규정한 것이다.

(5) '직장 내 성희롱' 관련 규정의 적용범위

이 법은 근로자를 사용하는 모든 사업 또는 사업장(이하 "사업"이라 한다)에 적용한다(제4조). 다만, 동거하는 친족만으로 이루어지는 사업과 가사사용인에 대하여는 법의 전부를 적용하지 아니한다(시행령 제2조).

Ⅲ. 성희롱의 특성과 직장 내 괴롭힘·성폭력·성차별과의 관계

성희롱은 업무관련성과 권력성, 폭력성, 차별성을 가진다. 이 점에서 성희롱은 직장 내 괴롭힘, 성폭력, 성차별과 공통점과 차이점을 가진다.[37]

1. 성희롱의 업무관련성과 '직장 내 괴롭힘'과의 관계

성희롱은 업무와 관련하거나 지위를 이용하여 행한 성적 언동을 기본요건으로 한다. 그런데 이러한 언동은 주로 권한이 많고 지위가 높은 사람이 취약한 지위를 가지는 사람을 대상으로 하여 많이 행해진다. 예를 들면, 일반 사업장에서는 사업주와 사용자 또는 상급자가, 대학에서는 교수가 행위자가 되는 경우가 많다. 그리하여 성희롱은 업무관련성과 권력성을 가진다.

2. 성희롱과 '직장 내 괴롭힘'과의 관계

---

[37] 김엘림, 「성희롱: 법과 분쟁처리사례」, 에피스테매, 2023., 27~43면.

Section 3. Basic Understanding of Sexual Harassment

(1) Definition of workplace harassment and "gap-jil" ("power harassment")

As mentioned in Chapter 1, when the Labor Standards Actwas revised on January 15, 2019, regulations were added to prevent workplace harassment and to handle victims' grievances. According to this law, "workplace bullying" refers to "behavior by an employer or employee who uses their superior position or relationship in the workplace to cause physical or mental pain to other employees beyond the reasonable scope of work or to worsen the working environment" (Article 76-2 (1)).

Meanwhile, government departments jointly announced "Guidelines for Eradicating Workplace Harassment in the Public Sector" on February 18, 2019. These guidelines define "power harassment" as "unfair demands or treatment imposed on another person by someone who holds a superior position in social or economic relationships, or who exercises practical influence derived from that position."

However, on December 30, 2021, the Enforcement Rule of Disciplinary Actions for Public Officials replaced the term "power harassment" in the disciplinary standards (Appendix 1) with the term "unfair conduct, such as causing physical or mental pain to other civil servants by using one's superior position or relationship beyond the reasonable scope of work." This behavior is now included as a type of violation of the duty to respect the dignity of others. It is defined as "the act of a civil servant, using their superior position or relationship, that causes physical or mental pain beyond the reasonable scope of work, against: (a) another civil servant; (b) employees of the institution to which the civil servant belongs, the institution to which that civil servant belongs, and the affiliated institutions as defined in Article 4, paragraph 1 of the Act on the Operation of Public Institutions and Organizations; and (c) job-related persons according to the "Code of Conduct for Civil Servants" (If the job-related persons are a corporation or group, it means their employee)."

(2) Similarities and differences between sexual harassment and workplace harassment

Sexual harassment, workplace harassment, gap-jil(power harassment), and unfair acts such as using one's superior position to inflict physical and mental pain on other civil servants all involve harassment and human rights violations. They also

(1) '직장 내 괴롭힘', '갑질'의 의의

「근로기준법」은 2019년 1월 15일에 개정될 때, '직장 내 괴롭힘'을 방지하고 피해자의 고충을 처리하는 규정들을 신설하였다. 이 법에서 '직장 내 괴롭힘'이란 "사용자 또는 근로자가 직장에서의 지위 또는 관계 등의 우위를 이용하여 업무상 적정범위를 넘어 다른 근로자에게 신체적·정신적 고통을 주거나 근무환경을 악화시키는 행위"(제76조의2제1항)를 말한다.

한편, 정부 관계부처는 합동으로 2019년 2월 18일, 「공공분야 갑질 근절을 위한 가이드라인」을 발표하였다. 이 가이드라인은 '갑질'을 "사회·경제적 관계에서 우월적 지위에 있는 사람이 권한을 남용하거나, 우월적 지위에서 비롯되는 사실상의 영향력을 행사하여 상대방에게 행하는 부당한 요구나 처우"라고 정의하였다.

그런데 「공무원 징계령 시행규칙」은 2021년 12월 30일, 징계기준(별표1)에 '갑질'이란 용어 대신에 '우월적 지위 등을 이용하여 다른 공무원 등에게 신체적·정신적 고통을 주는 등의 부당행위'라는 용어를 사용하고 이를 품위 유지의무 위반의 행위 유형에 포함하였다. 그리고 그 의미에 관하여 "공무원이 자신의 우월적 지위나 관계 등의 우위를 이용하여 업무상 적정범위를 넘어 다음 각 목의 사람에게 신체적·정신적 고통을 주거나 근무환경을 악화시키는 행위를 말한다. 가. 다른 공무원 나. 공무원 자신이 소속된 기관, 그 기관의 소속기관 및 산하기관(「공직자윤리법」 제3조의2 제1항에 따른 공직유관단체와 「공공기관의 운영에 관한 법률」 제4조제1항에 따른 공공기관을 말한다)의 직원 다.「공무원 행동강령」에 따른 직무관련자(직무관련자가 법인 또는 단체인 경우에는 소속 직원을 말한다)"라고 규정하였다.

(2) 성희롱과 '직장 내 괴롭힘'의 공통점과 차이점

성희롱은 주로 우월적 지위를 가진 사람들이 비교적 취약한 지위에 있는 사람들을 대상으로 인권침해와 업무상의 피해를 주는 점에서 '직장 내 괴롭힘', '갑질', '우월적 지위 등을 이용하여 다른 공무원 등에게 신체적·정신적 고통을 주는 등의 부당행위'와 공통점을 가진다.

제1장에서 서술한 바와 같이, ILO(국제노동기구)가 2019년 6월 21일에 개최한 제108차 총회(ILO 설립 100주년 기념 총회)에서 채택한 「일의 세계에서의 폭력과 괴롭힘 철폐에 관한 협약」(제190호)에서 '성희롱'(sexual harassment)은

cause work-related harm to relatively vulnerable individuals targeted by those in superior positions.

Convention 190 concerning the Elimination of Violence and Harassment in the World of Work, adopted at the 108th session of the International Labour Organization (ILO) on June 21, 2019 (commemorating the 100th anniversary of the ILO's establishment), clarifies the relationship between workplace harassment and sexual harassment. This convention defines violence and harassment in the world of work as "a series of actions or practices, or threats thereof, whether occurring once or repeatedly, that aim at or result in physical, mental, sexual, or economic harm that is unacceptable, including gender-based violence and harassment" (Article 1(1)(a)). It further defines gender-based violence and harassment as "violence and harassment that is directed against a person because of their gender, or that disproportionately affects persons of a particular gender which includes sexual harassment" (Article 1(1)(b)). In other words, this convention defines sexual harassment as a type of workplace harassment centered on sexual behavior.

However, those in superior positions are not the only ones who might sexually harass someone else. A colleague or student can also be guilty of this. It also differs from workplace harassment because sexual behavior is the constituent requisite.

3. The Violence of sexual harassment and its relationship with sexual assault

(1) The violence of sexual harassment

Sexual harassment is considered violent because it involves making unwanted or non-consensual sexual advances towards someone, causing them physical and psychological harm, infringing upon their human rights, and causing them harm in the workplace.

(2) Relationship between sexual harassment, sexual assault, and other sexual crimes

1) Definition of sexual assault and crimes and its bias towards women

"Sexual assault" (violence) is a term commonly used internationally to refer to unwanted sexual behavior that involves violent acts that violate a victim's physical

"성별과 젠더(gender)를 이유로 인간에게 향하는, 혹은 특정 성 혹은 젠더에 편중되게 영향을 주는 폭력과 괴롭힘"을 의미하는 '젠더에 기반한 폭력과 괴롭힘'(gender-based violence and harassment)의 일종이다. '젠더에 기반한 폭력과 괴롭힘'은 "그 발생이 일회성이든 반복적이든, 신체적·정신적·성적·경제적 피해를 목표로 하거나, 초래하거나, 초래할 개연성이 있어 용납할 수 없는 일련의 행위나 관행, 혹은 위협"을 의미하는 '일의 세계에서의 폭력과 괴롭힘'(violence and harassment in the world of work)의 일종이다.

그런데 한편, 성희롱은 우월적 지위를 이용한 사람들에 의해서만 발생하는 것은 아니며 동료 근로자나 학생에 의해서도 발생할 수 있는 점, 성적 언동을 성립요건으로 하는 점, 특정 성에게 편중되어 발생하는 점에서 '직장 내 괴롭힘'과 차이가 있다.

3. 성희롱의 폭력성과 '성폭력'과의 관계

(1) 성희롱의 폭력성

성희롱은 상대방이 원하지 않는(거부하는, 상대방의 의사에 반한, 상대방에게 성적 굴욕감이나 혐오감 또는 수치심이나 불쾌감을 주는) 성적 언동을 자행하여 상대방 등에게 심신의 피해, 인권침해, 업무상의 피해를 주는 점에서 폭력성을 가진다.

(2) 성희롱과 '성폭력' 및 '성폭력범죄'와의 관계

1) 성폭력 및 성폭력범죄의 의의와 여성편향성

'성폭력'이란 국제적으로 널리 사용되고 있는 'sexual violence', 'sexual assault'를 지칭하는 용어다. 상대방이 원하지 아니한 성적 언동을 수반하는 모든 폭력행위로서 피해자에게 심신의 피해와 인격권과 성적 자기결정권을 침해하는 행위를 말한다. '성폭력범죄'란 성폭력 중에서 죄질이 나쁘고 피해가 심해 국가가 형벌로 처벌하는 행위를 말한다.

그런데 우리나라 법은 성폭력과 성폭력범죄를 같은 행위로 보고 있다. 즉 「성폭력방지 및 피해자 보호 등에 관한 법률」(약칭: 성폭력방지법)은 '성폭력'을 "「성폭력범죄의 처벌 등에 관한 특례법」(약칭: 성폭력처벌법) 제2조제1항에

Section 3. Basic Understanding of Sexual Harassment

and psychological well-being, as well as their right to sexual self-determination. "Sexual crimes" refer to acts of sexual assault that are punished by the state because they are severely damaging.

However, in South Korea, sexual assault and sexual crimes are considered the same behavior. The Sexual Assault Prevention Act defines sexual assault as "an act that corresponds to the crime specified in Article 2 (1) of the Act on Special Cases Concerning the Punishment Etc. of Sexual Crimes." However, Article 2 (1) of the same Act only lists the types of sexual crimes without giving a solid definition of sexual assault. It also designates various sexual crimes specified in the Criminal Act and new sexual crimes added in Chapter 2 (Article 3-15) of this law as sexual assault crimes. These sexual crimes include offenses related to rape, molestation, adultery, obscenity, invasion of privacy in multi-use places for sexual purposes, and illegal filming.

The majority of victims of sexual assault and sexual crimes are women, a phenomenon that is common throughout the world. Therefore, the UN General Assembly adopted a "Declaration on Violence against Women" unanimously on December 12, 1993, which defines "violence against women" as "any act of gender-based violence occurring in public or in private life that results in, or is likely to result in, physical, sexual, or psychological harm or suffering to women, including threats of such acts, coercion or arbitrary deprivation of liberty." It points out sexual harassment, sexual assault, domestic violence, and forced prostitution as representative examples of violence against women. South Korea's Framework Act on the Prevention of Violence against Women aims to "clarify the responsibilities of the state and local governments to prevent violence against women, protect and support victims, and promote comprehensive and systematic policies to prevent violence against women to contribute to the enhancement of human dignity and human rights of individuals" (Article 1).

(2) Comparing sexual harassment and sexual assault

Sexual harassment and sexual assaults or sexual crimes share the common characteristic of involving the use of sexually oriented behavior that goes against

규정된 죄에 해당하는 행위"라고 규정하고 있다. 「성폭력처벌법」 제2조제1항은 성폭력의 개념을 정의하지 않고, 성폭력범죄에 해당되는 범죄를 열거하고 있다. 「성폭력처벌법」은 「형법」에 규정된 다양한 성범죄와 이 법 제2장(제3조~제15조)에서 새로이 추가한 성범죄를 모두 성폭력범죄로 규정하고 있다. 이러한 성폭력범죄의 행태는 다양한데 강간 관련죄, 추행 관련죄, 간음 관련죄, 음란 관련죄, 다중이용장소의 성적 목적 침입 관련죄, 불법 촬영·반포 관련죄의 6개의 유형으로 구분할 수 있다.

그런데 성폭력, 성폭력범죄의 주된 피해자는 여성이다. 이러한 현상은 거의 세계 공통적인 현상이다. 그리하여 UN 총회는 1993년 12월 20일, 만장일치로 「여성폭력철폐선언」(Declaration on Violence against Women)을 채택하였다. 이 선언은 '여성에 대한 폭력'을 "공사 모든 영역에서 여성에게 신체적, 성적 혹은 심리적 손상이나 괴로움을 주거나 줄 수 있는, 젠더에 기반한 (gender-based) 폭력행위와 그러한 행위를 하겠다는 협박, 강제, 임의적인 자유 박탈"로 정의하고 그 대표적 유형으로 성희롱, 성폭력, 가정폭력, 강제적 성매매 등을 예시하였다. 우리나라 「여성폭력방지기본법」은 "여성폭력방지와 피해자 보호·지원에 관한 국가 및 지방자치단체의 책임을 명백히 하고, 여성폭력방지정책의 종합적·체계적 추진을 위한 기본적인 사항을 규정함으로써 개인의 존엄과 인권 증진에 이바지함"(제1조)을 목적으로 2018년 12월 24일에 제정되었다. 이 법은 "여성폭력방지정책의 추진을 통하여 모든 사람이 공공 및 사적 영역에서 여성폭력으로부터 안전할 수 있도록 하고 이를 지속적으로 발전시킴으로써 폭력 없는 사회를 이루는 것"을 기본이념으로 한다(제2조). 2019년 8월 25일에 시행된 이 법에서 '여성폭력'이란 "성별에 기반한 여성에 대한 폭력으로 신체적·정신적 안녕과 안전할 수 있는 권리 등을 침해하는 행위로서 관계 법률에서 정하는 바에 따른 가정폭력, 성폭력, 성매매, 성희롱, 지속적 괴롭힘 행위와 그 밖에 친밀한 관계에 의한 폭력, 정보통신망을 이용한 폭력 등"(제3조제1호)을 말한다.

(2) 성희롱과 '성폭력'의 공통점과 차이점

성희롱과 성폭력·성폭력범죄는 상대방의 의사에 반하는 성적 언동을 수단으로 하는 폭력성을 가지는 점, 피해자에게 신체적·정신적 피해를 주고 인격권과

Section 3. Basic Understanding of Sexual Harassment

the will of the other party. Also, it has a violent nature that causes physical and mental harm to the victim, violating their personality and sexual self-determination. They are also both considered a form of "violence against women" under the UN Declaration on the Elimination of Violence against Women and South Korea's Framework Act on the Prevention of Violence against Women, since women are the most common victims.

However, sexual harassment differs from sexual assault as it requires a work-related or hierarchical relationship as a basic criteria for determining whether it has occurred. In contrast, sexual assault, including sexual crimes specified in Article 303 of the Criminal Act (Sexual Intercourse by Abuse of Occupational Authority) and Article 10 of the Punishment Act for Sexual Assault (Sexual Molestation Committed by Force or Coercion), requires the existence of a power relationship, but not necessarily a work-related one. Additionally, not all sexual assault or sexual crimes require work-related or hierarchical relationships as basic criteria. Furthermore, while all sexual assault or sexual crimes are subject to criminal punishment under current law, not all cases of sexual harassment are subject to criminal punishment. However, if the behavior/conduct of sexual harassment meets the standard for sexual assault or sexual crime, the perpetrator shall be subject to criminal punishment.

4. The discriminatory nature of sexual harassment and its relationship with gender discrimination

(1) The discriminatory nature of sexual harassment

Sexual harassment is discriminatory in nature, as it primarily targets women and results in unjustified disadvantages (such as mental distress, violation of human rights, and harm to work performance).

(2) Relationship between sexual harassment and gender discrimination

1) Definition of gender discrimination and gender bias

"Gender discrimination" refers to treating a specific gender unfairly without rational justification based on perception of that gender. The National Human Rights Commission of Korea Act defines "discrimination that violates equal

성적 자기결정권을 침해하는 행위인 점, UN의 「여성폭력철폐선언」과 우리나라 「여성폭력방지기본법」이 정의한 '여성폭력'의 일종으로서 주로 여성이 피해자가 되는 점에서 공통점을 가진다.

그런데 성희롱은 업무와 관련하거나 지위를 이용하여 이루어지는 업무관련성을 기본요건으로 하는 점에서 이를 기본요건으로 하지 않는 성폭력과 구별된다. 성폭력범죄 중 「형법」의 제303조(업무상 위력 등에 의한 간음)와 「성폭력처벌법」 제10조(업무상 위력 등에 의한 추행 등)가 규정한 성폭력범죄는 업무관련성을 구성요건으로 하지만 모든 성폭력, 성폭력범죄가 업무관련성을 기본요건으로 하지 않는다. 또한 현행법상 모든 성폭력범죄는 형사처벌의 대상이 되지만, 모든 성희롱이 형사처벌의 대상이 되는 것은 아니라는 점에서도 차이가 있다. 그러나 성희롱의 행위 행태가 성폭력범죄에 해당되는 경우에는 행위자는 형사처벌을 받게 된다.

4. 성희롱의 차별성과 '성차별'과의 관계

(1) 성희롱의 차별성

성희롱은 주로 여성을 대상으로 하여 행해지고 여성에게 성적 언동과 관련하여 합리적 이유 없이 불이익(심신의 피해, 인권침해, 업무상의 피해)을 초래하는 점에서 차별성을 가진다.

(2) 성희롱과 성차별과의 관계

1) 성차별의 의의와 여성편향성

'성차별'이란 성별에 관한 인식에 기초하여 특정 성에게 합리적 이유 없이 불리하게 대우하는(불이익을 주는) 행위를 말한다.

「국가인권위원회법」은 '평등권 침해의 차별행위'의 개념을 규정하고(제2조제3호) 차별의 사유를 성별을 포함한 19가지[38]로 예시하고 있다. 차별의 영역과 경위에 대해서는 3가지(① 고용(모집, 채용, 교육, 배치, 승진, 임금 및 임금 외의 금품 지급, 자금의 융자, 정년, 퇴직, 해고 등을 포함한다)과 관련하여,

---

[38] 성별, 종교, 장애, 나이, 사회적 신분, 출신 지역(출생지, 등록기준지, 성년이 되기 전의 주된 거주지 등을 말한다), 출신 국가, 출신 민족, 용모 등 신체 조건, 기혼·미혼·별거·이혼·사별·재혼·사실혼 등 혼인 여부, 임신 또는 출산, 가족 형태 또는 가족 상황, 인종, 피부색, 사상 또는 정치적 의견, 형의 효력이 실효된 전과(前科), 성적(性的) 지향, 학력, 병력(病歷) 등

Section 3. Basic Understanding of Sexual Harassment

rights" (Article 2, paragraph 3) and provides 19 examples of categories of discrimination[38], including gender. The scope and process of discrimination are limited to three areas: ① employment (including recruitment, hiring, education, placement, promotion, payment of wages and other benefits, loans, resignation, retirement, dismissal, etc.), ② supply or use of goods, services, transportation, commercial facilities, land, and residential facilities, ③ education and training in education facilities or vocational training institutions. Discriminatory behavior is "favoring, excluding, or treating a particular person (including groups of specific persons) differently or unfairly." The concept of "gender discrimination in employment" in this provision refers to "treating a specific person or group differently or unfairly in employment and conditions of work without rational justification based on gender." However, "the establishment, amendment, and implementation of laws or policies that temporarily favor a specific person or group in order to eliminate existing discrimination (such as "Affirmative Action") shall not be considered as "discrimination that violates equal rights" (Proviso to Article 2-3).

Meanwhile, the Equal Employment Act defines discrimination as "cases where employers unreasonably differentiate in employment or working conditions based on gender, marriage, status within the family, pregnancy, childbirth, or other reasons [including cases where, even if employers apply the same employment or working conditions equally, the conditions are significantly lower for one gender compared to the other and this results in unfair outcomes for a specific gender, and the employer cannot prove that it is legitimate]."

However, the following cases are excluded: a) cases where a specific gender is inevitably required based on the nature of the job, b) cases where measures are taken for protection of maternity, such as pregnancy, childbirth, and breastfeeding by female workers, c) cases where active employment improvement measures are taken in accordance with this Act or other laws (Article 2 (1)). "Active employment improvement measures" in this Act refer to "measures to eliminate

---

[38] Gender, religion, disabilities, age, social status, region of origin (place of birth, registered residence, primary place of residence before reaching adulthood, etc.), country of origin, ethnic background, physical attributes such as appearance, marital status (married, unmarried, separated, divorced, widowed, remarried, in a de facto relationship, etc.), pregnancy or childbirth, family structure or family situation, race, skin color, beliefs or political opinions, previous criminal record with legal effect, sexual orientation, education level, medical history, etc.

② 재화·용역·교통수단·상업시설·토지·주거시설의 공급이나 이용과 관련하여, ③ 교육시설이나 직업훈련기관에서의 교육·훈련이나 그 이용과 관련하여)로 제한하고 있다. 그리고 차별의 행태를 "특정한 사람(특정한 사람들의 집단을 포함한다)을 우대·배제·구별하거나 불리하게 대우하는 행위"로 규정하고 있다. 다만, "현존하는 차별을 없애기 위하여 특정한 사람이나 집단을 잠정적으로 우대하는 행위와 이를 내용으로 하는 법령의 제정·개정 및 정책의 수립·집행"은 예외로 규정하고 있다(제2조제3호 단서). 이러한 「국가인권위원회법」의 차별의 개념에 관한 규정에서 '고용상의 성차별'의 개념을 구성하면 "합리적인 이유 없이 성별을 이유로 고용과 근로조건, 직업훈련기관의 이용과 관련하여 특정한 사람 또는 그 집단을 우대·배제·구별하거나 불리하게 대우하는 행위(다만, 현존하는 차별을 없애기 위하여 특정한 사람이나 집단을 잠정적으로 우대하는 적극적 조치는 예외로 한다)"이다.

한편, 「남녀고용평등법」은 '차별'을 "사업주가 근로자에게 성별, 혼인, 가족 안에서의 지위, 임신 또는 출산 등의 사유로 합리적인 이유 없이 채용 또는 근로의 조건을 다르게 하거나 그 밖의 불리한 조치를 하는 경우 [사업주가 채용조건이나 근로조건은 동일하게 적용하더라도 그 조건을 충족할 수 있는 남성 또는 여성이 다른 한 성(性)에 비하여 현저히 적고 그에 따라 특정 성에게 불리한 결과를 초래하며 그 조건이 정당한 것임을 증명할 수 없는 경우를 포함한다]"로 개념 정의하고 있다(제2조제1호). 그런데 이 법은 "① 직무의 성격에 비추어 특정 성이 불가피하게 요구되는 경우, ② 여성 근로자의 임신·출산·수유 등 모성보호를 위한 조치를 하는 경우, ③ 그 밖에 이 법 또는 다른 법률에 따라 적극적 고용개선조치를 하는 경우"는 차별로 보지 아니한다(제2조제1호 단서). 이 법에서 '적극적 고용개선조치'란 "현존하는 남녀 간의 고용차별을 없애거나 고용평등을 촉진하기 위하여 잠정적으로 특정 성을 우대하는 조치"(제2조제3호)를 말한다.

그런데 성차별은 남성 중심의 가부장적 사회구조와 조직문화에서 주로 여성에 대하여 행해진다. 이것은 거의 세계 공통적인 현상이다. UN은 인구의 거의 반수를 차지하는 여성에 대한 차별이 여성의 인권을 침해하고 여성의 능력 개발과 사회참여, 인력활용을 저해하여 여성의 발전 뿐 아니라 사회 및 국가, 인류의 발전을 저해한다는 인식에서 성차별 철폐를 적극적으로 추진하고 있다.

or alleviate existing employment discrimination between men and women, or to promote equal employment opportunities for men and women, such as affirmative action measures."

(3) Comparing sexual harassment and gender discrimination

Sexual harassment is similar to gender discrimination in that it primarily occurs in patriarchal societies where men target women, resulting in unfair and unfavorable work situations for women. In fact, laws and judicial precedents in countries like the United States and Canada consider sexual harassment as a form of gender discrimination. In South Korea, the National Human Rights Commission of Korea Actdefines sexual harassment as a type of "discriminatory act that violates the right to equality" (Article 2-3 (d)). The Equal Employment Actincludes provisions related to sexual harassment in the workplace in its Chapter 2, "Guarantee of Equal Opportunities and Treatment for Men and Women in Employment."

On the other hand, gender discrimination refers to acts that unjustly prefer, exclude, differentiate, or treat individuals unfavorably in terms of opportunities or treatment without reasonable justification, thereby violating their right to equality. Sexual harassment is distinguished from gender discrimination, because it involves acts that infringe upon the right to dignity, sexual self-determination, and equality through the use of one's position or engaging in unwanted sexual behavior related to work.

IV. Problems and Harms Caused by Sexual Harassment[39]

1. Problems related to sexual harassment

Sexual harassment is a complex issue that arises from structural problems such as the abuse of dominant power and authority within hierarchical structures, patriarchal social structures, and organizational cultures. It poses negative effects on labor, including infringements on workers' rights, decreased motivation and performance, deteriorating work environments, and increased labor-management conflicts. It also intersects with industrial accidents, human rights concerns, and educational issues. Furthermore, disputes related to sexual harassment exhibit trends and challenges in terms of escalation, prolonged duration, collective impact,

---

[39] Kim El-lim, "Sexual Harassment: Law and Dispute Resolution Cases," Episteme, 2023, pp. 47-106.

1979년 12월 18일에는 「여성차별철폐협약」(Convention on the Elimination of All Forms of Discrimination against Women)을 채택하였다. 이 협약에서 '여성에 대한 차별'이란 "정치적, 경제적, 사회적, 문화적, 시민적 또는 기타 분야에 있어서 결혼여부에 관계없이 남녀 동등의 기초위에서 인권과 기본적 자유를 인식, 향유 또는 행사하는 것을 저해하거나 무효화하는 효과 또는 목적을 가지는 성에 근거한 모든 구별, 배제 또는 제한"(제1조)을 말한다.

(3) 성희롱과 '성차별'의 공통점과 차이점

성희롱은 가부장적 사회에서 주로 남성이 여성을 대상으로 하여 이루어지는 점, 여성에게 불합리하고 부당한 업무 상황을 초래하여 불이익을 주는 점에서 성차별과 공통점을 가진다. 그리하여 미국, 캐나다 등의 법과 판례·결정례는 성희롱을 성차별의 일종으로 보고 있다. 우리나라에서도 「국가인권위원회법」은 성희롱을 "평등권 침해의 차별행위"의 일종으로 규정하고 있다(제2조제3호라목). 「남녀고용평등법」은 직장 내 성희롱의 금지와 예방, 발생시 조치에 관한 규정들을 [제2장 고용에서 남녀의 평등한 기회보장 및 대우 등]의 제2절에 편성하고 있다.

그런데 성차별은 합리적 이유 없이 기회나 대우에서 우대·배제·구별하거나 불리하게 대우하여 평등권을 침해하는 행위이지만, 성희롱은 지위를 이용하거나 업무와 관련하여 상대방이 원하지 않는 성적 언동을 하여 인격권, 성적 자기결정권, 평등권을 침해하는 행위라는 점에서 성차별과 차이가 있다.

Ⅳ. 직장 내 성희롱의 문제와 피해[39]

1. 직장 내 성희롱의 문제

직장 내 성희롱은 권위주의적이고 가부장적 사회구조와 조직문화에서 발생된다. 그리고 노동문제와 산업재해 문제, 인권문제, 학교사업장의 교육문제 등의 부정적 효과를 발생시킨다. 성희롱과 관련한 분쟁은 증가와 장기화, 집단화, 강경화, 사회문제화, 법적 분쟁화되는 경향을 보이며 그로 인하여

---
[39] 김엘림, 「성희롱: 법과 분쟁처리사례」, 에피스테매, 2023., 47~106면.

Section 3. Basic Understanding of Sexual Harassment

hardening of positions, societal problematization, and legal disputes.

(1) Structural factors in the occurrence of sexual harassment

1) Abuse of authority and misuse of power in hierarchical structures

When analyzing data from surveys and legal cases related to sexual harassment, it can be observed that sexual harassment often occurs in environments with strong hierarchical structures, such as workplaces, schools, public institutions, the military, healthcare, the arts, and sports, where individuals in positions of authority misuse or abuse their power against those in vulnerable positions. For example, in workplaces, sexual harassment is frequently reported against irregular workers who are particularly vulnerable.

The problem with hierarchical and authoritarian structures is that it is difficult to prevent the abuse of power by those in superior positions, and victims often find themselves in situations where they cannot resist due to fear of reprisal, despite suffering unjust harm. The use of the term "sexual humiliation" in Korean laws, precedents, and decisions related to sexual harassment indicates the consideration for such situations.

From this perspective, sexual harassment can be considered a form of "power-based sexual assault" or "sexual crimes using a superior position" where socially and economically privileged individuals exploit and harass socially disadvantaged individuals, akin to "harassment by those in power."

2) Patriarchal social structures and organizational culture

Sexual harassment occurs predominantly against women in patriarchal social structures and organizational cultures where men hold superior positions. In incidents recognized by the National Human Rights Commission, 95.4% of perpetrators were men and only 4.5% were women.[40] Of the 131 court cases that acknowledged sexual harassment by professors, the gender of all perpetrators were men. Only six court rulings—related to three incidents—showed that the victims were male students, and in the remaining 125 cases (95.4%), all victims were women.[41] Also, court rulings related to sexual harassment and violence against university students showed that all perpetrators were men, except for

---

[40] National Human Rights Commission, "Compilation of Cases for Corrective Recommendations on Sexual Harassment" (Appendix: Statistics on Sexual Harassment Incidents), Vol. 9, July 2020, p. 382.

[41] Kim, Elim, "Legal Disputes on Professor's Sexual Harassment," Journal of Law, Vol. 20, No. 3, Ewha Law Research Institute, March 2016, p. 292.

개인과 사업장, 사회에 악영향을 주는 문제를 가진다.

(1) 성희롱 발생의 구조적 문제

1) 위계적 구조에서의 우월적 지위의 권한 오·남용

성희롱에 관한 실태조사자료들과 판례·결정례를 분석한 자료들을 살펴보면, 성희롱 사건은 직장이나 학교, 공공기관, 군대, 의료계, 예술계, 스포츠계 등에서와 같이 권위주의적 위계질서가 강한 곳에서 우월적 지위를 가진 사람들이 취약한 지위를 가진 사람들을 대상으로 권한을 오용하거나 남용하여 발생하는 경우가 많다. 예를 들면, 사업장에서는 사용자가 근로자에게 특히 취약한 상황에 있는 비정규직 근로자에게 성희롱을 하는 경우가 많다.

위계적·권위주의적 구조는 우월적 지위를 가진 사람들의 권한 오·남용을 제지하기 어렵고 피해자들은 부당한 피해를 당하면서도 불이익이 두려워 저항하지 못하는 상황을 초래한다. 우리나라 성희롱에 관한 법과 판례·결정례에서 "성적 굴욕감"이란 표현을 하는 것은 이러한 성희롱 발생 상황을 감안한 것으로 보여진다.

이러한 점에서 성희롱은 사회적·경제적으로 우월한 사람들이 사회적 약자를 대상으로 횡포를 부리는 소위 '갑질'의 일종으로서 '권력형 성폭력', '우월적 지위를 이용한 성범죄' 해당된다고 볼 수 있다.

2) 가부장적 사회구조와 조직문화

성희롱은 남성이 여성보다 우월적 지위가 많은 가부장적 사회구조와 조직문화에서 주로 여성을 대상으로 하여 많이 발생한다. 국가인권위원회가 성희롱 발생을 인정하고 시정권고를 한 사건에서 남성이 행위자(피진정인)인 경우는 95.4%, 여성이 행위자인 경우는 4.5%였다.[40] 법원이 교수가 성희롱을 하였음을 인정한 판례 131개에서 당사자의 성별을 조사해보면, 행위자인 교수는 모두 남성이었다. 피해자는 3종의 사건에 관한 6개의 판례에서만 남학생이었고 그 외 125개 판례(95.4%)는 모두 여성이었다.[41] 대학생의 성희롱·성폭력에 관한 판례·결정례에서 행위자는 모두 남성이었다. 피해자는 남학생인 3건을 제외

---
[40] 국가인권위원회, 『성희롱 시정권고 사례집』 9집의 부록(성희롱 진정사건 통계), 2020, 382면.
[41] 김엘림, "교수의 성희롱에 관한 법적 분쟁", 「법학논집」 제20권 제3호, 이화여자대학교 법학연구소, 2016, 292면.

Section 3. Basic Understanding of Sexual Harassment

three cases involving male students. All other victims were women.[42]

(2) Sexual harassment and human rights, labor and education

1) Violation of human rights

Sexual harassment violates human rights, such as the right to dignity, sexual self-determination, and equality. The right to dignity and value as a human being is the right to pursue happiness, as stipulated in Article 10 of the Constitution of the Republic of Korea, which states, "All citizens shall enjoy the basic rights inherent in human beings, and it shall be the duty of the State to confirm and guarantee the inviolable basic rights of individuals." Sexual self-determination refers to the right and freedom to make decisions and the right to act on matters related to sexuality without being objectified against one's own will. Although not explicitly stated as a fundamental right in the Constitution, the Constitutional Court and the Supreme Court recognize it as a basic right of citizens according to Article 10 and Article 17 of the Constitution. Sexual harassment violates the right to sexual self-determination, which is the right to decide on sexual matters without being subject to unwanted sexual behaviors. Furthermore, sexual harassment is a discriminatory action that violates the right to equality, particularly targeting one gender, especially women.

2) Workplace sexual harassment, labor and industrial accidents

Workplace sexual harassment leads to infringing on labor rights, deteriorating the working environment, and increasing the number of labor disputes, as well as issues related to industrial accidents.

Sexual harassment infringes rights that are related to work, by directing unwanted sexual behaviors at the victim in relation to work or using one's position to do so. The Constitution states, "All citizens have the right to work" (Article 32, paragraph 1). This right to work (labor right) includes not only the right to have employment opportunities, but also the right to be treated fairly and with dignity at work, and the right to work in a safe and pleasant environment. Sexual harassment unjustly and unreasonably affects the opportunities, treatment, and evaluation of victims in their work, thereby infringing on their right to be treated fairly and with dignity at work.

Sexual harassment causes physical, psychological, and mental suffering. It also

---

[42] Kim, Elim, "Legal Disputes on Sexual Harassment and Violence against University Students," Gender Law Journal, Vol. 3, No. 1 (Total No. 24), Korean Association of Gender Law, July 2021, p. 9.

하고는 모두 여성이었다.[42]

(2) 성희롱의 인권문제와 노동문제 · 산업재해문제

1) 성희롱의 인권침해 문제

성희롱은 상대방이 원하지 아니하는 성적 언동을 하여 인격권·성적 자기결정권·평등권 등의 인권을 침해하는 문제가 있다. 인격권이란 "모든 국민은 인간으로서의 존엄과 가치를 가지며, 행복을 추구할 권리를 가진다. 국가는 개인이 가지는 불가침의 기본적 인권을 확인하고 이를 보장할 의무를 가진다."라고 규정한 「헌법」 제10조에 따른 인간으로서의 존엄과 가치, 행복추구권을 말한다. 성적 자기결정권이란 성적(性的) 사항에 관하여 스스로 결정하고 행위할 수 있는 권리와 자기의 의사에 반해 성적 대상화가 되지 않을 권리와 자유를 말한다. 이 권리는 「헌법」에 명시된 기본권은 아니지만, 헌법재판소와 대법원은 이를 「헌법」 제10조의 인격권 또는 제17조의 사생활의 자유에 근거한 국민의 기본권으로 인정하고 있다. 또한 성희롱은 특정 성 특히 여성을 주된 대상으로 하는 점에서 평등권을 침해하는 차별행위에 해당된다.

2) 성희롱의 노동문제와 산업재해 문제

「헌법」은 "모든 국민은 근로의 권리를 가진다".(제32조제1항)라고 규정하고 있다. 근로권(노동권)에는 취업기회를 가질 권리 뿐 아니라 근로자가 정당하고 인격적 대우를 받으며 일할 권리, 근로자가 안전하고 쾌적한 환경에서 건강하게 일할 권리가 있다.

직장 내 성희롱은 피해자에게 행위자의 성적 언동의 수용 여부를 업무상의 기회와 대우, 평가를 받는 데 영향을 주게 하므로 부당하고 불합리하며, 근로자가 정당하고 인격적 대우를 받으며 일할 권리를 침해한다. 또한 직장 내 성희롱은 피해자에게 신체적·심리적·정신적 고통과 인권침해, 업무상의 스트레스를 발생시킨다. 성희롱 행위자가 해고당하거나 퇴사하거나 전근을 가지 않는 한, 피해자는 행위자와 사업장에서 마주치며 일을 해야 하므로 그 피해가 가중된다. 이로 인해 피해자는 직장에 가서 일할 의욕이 저하되고 생산성, 실적이 저하되는 문제를 겪게 된다. 성희롱은 피해자와 행위자 및 그 외의 업무

---

[42] 김엘림, "대학생의 성희롱·성폭력 사건과 관련 법적 분쟁," 「젠더법학」제3권 제1호(통권 제24호), 한국젠더법학회, 2021. 9면.

Section 3. Basic Understanding of Sexual Harassment

infringes on a victim's human rights and gives them work-related stress. Unless the perpetrator of sexual harassment is fired, resigns, or is transferred, the victim has to face the perpetrator and work in the same workplace, which aggravates the harm. As a result, the victim's motivation to work is reduced, and productivity and performance are compromised. In addition, sexual harassment creates a hostile and uncomfortable working environment and an increase in conflict between the victim, the perpetrator, and other parties involved in work. Furthermore, victims of sexual harassment often suffer mental and physical damage at the workplace, and as a result, their health deteriorates. This often leads to leaves of absence or resignation on the part of the victim. Therefore, sexual harassment can be viewed as equivalent to an industrial accident as it undermines the victims' labor rights and health rights.

Employers who hire workers for their business have a duty to create a safe, pleasant and human rights-friendly working environment in order to guarantee the labor rights and health rights of workers. If sexual harassment occurs in the workplace due to the employer's failure to take appropriate preventive measures, it becomes a violation of the employer's duty. On January 15, 2019, the Industrial Accident Compensation Insurance Act was amended to include mental stress over workplace harassment as a cause of "work-related illness" as defined in Article 76-2 of the Labor Standards Act. This recognizes that sexual harassment can cause work-related illnesses and should be addressed as an industrial issue.

In an actual case handled by the Seoul Regional Office of the Korea Workers' Welfare & Safety Agency, on July 7, 2019, a female employee who had previously served as a professor at SK University reported ongoing sexual harassment and violence from the university's graduate school dean. She raised awareness about the incidents both within the institution and externally, demanding action from the university. However, as a result, she faced secondary harm by being denied reappointment, which further deteriorated her mental and physical health. Consequently, she applied for industrial accident compensation insurance, citing work-related illness, and her claim was recognized.

Furthermore, when workplace sexual harassment occurs, the victim's affiliated autonomous organizations (labor unions, women's committees, etc.) collectively raise objections to the perpetrators and management. If the management fails to promptly and appropriately address the situation, labor-management disputes can arise. Moreover, disputes among workers (labor-labor conflicts) frequently arise due to differences in positions based on gender, job roles, or departments, as well as differing positions between individuals or organizations supporting the perpetrators

관련자 사이에 갈등을 발생시켜 적대적이고 불편한 근로환경을 조성한다. 직장 내에서 성희롱의 후유증으로 피해자는 건강이 악화되는 경우가 많다. 이로 인해 피해자 스스로 휴직, 퇴직하는 경우가 많이 발생한다. 그러므로 성희롱은 근로권(노동권)과 건강권을 해치는 산업재해 문제가 된다.

근로자를 고용하여 사업을 하는 사업주는 근로자의 근로권과 건강권을 보장하기 위해 안전·쾌적한 근로환경과 인권친화적 근로환경을 조성하여야 할 의무가 있다. 사업장에서 사업주가 적절한 예방 조치를 하지 않아 성희롱이 발생하여 근로자가 피해를 입는 것은 이러한 사업주의 의무를 위반한 결과이다. 「산업재해보상보험법」은 2019년 1월 15일, 「근로기준법」 제76조의2에 따른 직장 내 괴롭힘으로 인한 업무상 정신적 스트레스가 원인이 되어 발생한 질병을 산업재해보상보험급여가 지급되는 '업무상 질병'에 포함시켰다. 비록 직장 내 성희롱을 보험급여 사유로 명시하지 않았지만, 직장 내 성희롱도 직장 내 괴롭힘의 일종이므로 직장 내 성희롱으로 겪는 피해자의 고통이 법적으로 산업재해로 인정을 받을 가능성이 많아졌다. 예를 들면, 근로복지공단 서울지역본부는 SK대의 전임대우 교수였던 여성이 재직 중 대학원장으로부터 지속적으로 성희롱·성폭력을 당하였고 이 피해 사실을 학내 외에 알리고 대학에 조치를 요구했다가 재임용에서 탈락되는 2차 피해도 당하여 정신적·신체적 건강이 악화되었다며 산업재해보상보험을 신청한 사건에서 2019년 7월 7일, 업무상 질병으로 인한 보험급여를 인정하였다.

한편, 직장 내 성희롱이 발생하면 피해자가 속한 자치조직(노동조합, 여직원회 등)이 행위자와 사용자에게 집단적 항의를 한다. 이에 사용자가 신속 적절하게 대처하지 못하면 노·사간의 분쟁이 발생한다. 또한 종사자 사이의 성별이나 직군·부서의 차이에 따른 입장 차이, 행위자와 행위자를 옹호하거나 탄원을 요구하는 개인이나 조직과 피해자와 피해자를 옹호하는 개인이나 조직 사이의 입장 차이로 인해 근로자들 사이의 분쟁(노·노갈등)도 발생하는 경우가 많다.

(3) 성희롱 관련 분쟁의 문제
1) 성희롱 관련 분쟁의 증가와 장기화

우리나라 법은 1999년 7월부터 모든 일반 사업장과 공공기관에게 성희롱

Section 3. Basic Understanding of Sexual Harassment

or advocating for petitions and those supporting the victims.

(3) Disputes related to sexual harassment

1) Increase and prolongation of sexual harassment-related disputes

Despite the obligation imposed on all general businesses and public institutions in South Korea to annually conduct education to prevent sexual harassment since July 1999, disputes related to sexual harassment have increased, not decreased. This increase in reported incidents can be attributed to a higher awareness of issues related to sexual harassment, as well as improved conditions for reporting it. In recent years, the Ministry of Gender Equality and Family, the Ministry of Employment and Labor, the Ministry of Culture, Sports and Tourism, and others, have operated sexual harassment and violence reporting and counseling centers to allow victims to anonymously report incidents online. Anonymous reporting systems have also been introduced in universities as well, with the number of reports also increasing. Laws, regulations, and public institution guidelines are protecting victims and prohibiting retaliation against victims of sexual harassment and those who report it.

Sexual harassment disputes are often prolonged and recurring. For example, the first sexual harassment lawsuit in South Korea lasted for about 6 years, while the R Automobile sexual harassment lawsuit lasted for approximately 8 years. Sexual harassment disputes can recur when individuals who have been disciplined for sexual harassment fail to fully recognize the seriousness of their actions and their consequences. After they return to work or school, they eventually engage in sexual harassment again.

2) Collectivization and socialization of sexual harassment disputes

Sexual harassment disputes tend to be intensified through collective responses from organizations supporting victims. This trend has been further amplified by the #MeToo movement that started in 2018. The #MeToo movement refers to a victim bravely revealing that they have been a victim of sexual harassment, which in turn inspires others to disclose their experiences as victims. In addition, the "With You" movement, which seeks to support victims and stand in solidarity with them to resolve the issues related to sexual harassment and sexual assault, has led to the collectivization and intensification of disputes related to sexual harassment and sexual assault.

Sexual harassment disputes often become social issues when victims disclose the incidents to the public through the media or other means, with civic organizations intervening. Particularly, sexual harassment and sexual assault at universities are

예방교육을 매년 실시할 의무를 부과하고 있다. 그럼에도 성희롱 관련 분쟁은 감소되지 않고 오히려 증가하고 있다. 한편, 신고 사건의 증가는 성희롱에 관한 문제 인식이 높아진 데다가 성희롱 신고의 여건이 양호해진 상황도 요인이 된다고 볼 수 있다. 근래 여성가족부, 고용노동부, 문화관광부 등의 행정기관은 '성희롱·성폭력 신고·상담센터'를 운영하여 피해자가 인터넷을 통해 익명으로 신고할 수 있도록 하며, 대학도 인권센터에 익명 신고를 할 수 있게 하는 경우가 증가하고 있다. 법과 학칙, 공공기관 지침은 신고자와 피해자에 대한 보호와 불이익 조치를 금지하고 있다.

또한 성희롱 관련 분쟁은 장기화되는 경우가 많고 재발되는 경우가 종종 있다. 이 재발은 성희롱 혐의로 징계를 받은 사람들이 성희롱 문제와 피해의 중대성을 잘 인식하지 못한 채 직장이나 학교로 복귀하여 다시 성희롱을 하여 초래되는 경우들이 많다.

2) 성희롱 관련 분쟁의 집단화·사회문제화

성희롱 관련 분쟁은 피해자를 지원하는 조직의 집단적 대응으로 강경화되는 경향이 있다. 이러한 경향은 2018년부터 전개된 미투(Me Too)운동으로 더욱 증가하였다. '미투운동'이란 어느 피해자가 용기를 내어 피해 당한 사실을 공개하는 것에 자극을 받고 나도 피해를 당했다고 피해 사실을 공개하는 것을 지칭한다. 아울러 피해자를 지지하고 피해자와 연대하여 문제를 해결하려는 '위드유(With You) 운동'으로 성희롱·성폭력 사건에 관한 분쟁은 더욱 집단화되고 강경화되고 있다.

또한 성희롱 분쟁은 사업장 내, 학교 내에서 자율적으로 해결되는 경우보다 피해자가 피해 사실을 언론 등을 통해 외부에 알리고 시민사회단체들이 개입하여 사회문제화하는 경우가 많다. 특히 대학에서 발생한 성희롱·성폭력 사건에 관해서는 언론, 국정감사, 시민사회단체의 대책 촉구를 위한 공론화 등에 의해 사회문제로 비화되는 현상이 많다. 예를 들면, 최초의 성희롱 소송사건(S대 화학과 교수의 실험실 조교에 대한 성희롱 사건)에 S대 학생들과 인권변호사들, 여성단체 등의 시민사회단체들은 공동대책위원회를 조직하여 사건을 이슈화시키고 피해자의 법적 투쟁을 지원하였다. S대 서문과 교수의 대학원 여학생에 대한 성희롱 사건에서는 34개 시민사회단체가 개입하여 이 사건을 권력형

often sensationalized as social issues through mass media, parliamentary inspection of the institution, and public discussions initiated by civic organizations. For example, in the first sexual harassment lawsuit which involved students from S University, civil rights lawyers, women's organizations, and others actively participated in public discussions and demanded action to address the issue.

3) Legal disputes related to sexual harassment

There has been an increasing trend of legal disputes arising from sexual harassment cases, where the parties affected by sexual harassment don't go through internal dispute settlement processes at the workplace or school. Instead, they choose administrative or judicial agencies for resolution. Administrative dispute settlements can be initiated by appealing to the National Human Rights Commission, requesting a trial for an administrative ruling, appealing to local employment and labor administrations (labor inspectors), applying to the Labor Relations Commission for relief regarding unfair dismissal (disciplinary action) and correction of discriminatory treatment, appealing to the Appeals Committee to review the appeals of civil servants and public education officials. Judicial dispute settlements can be initiated by filing complaints with the police and prosecutors' office, filing lawsuits (civil, criminal, administrative) with the courts, or filing constitutional petitions or constitutional complaints with the Constitutional Court.

However, disputes tend to be prolonged until the Supreme Court makes a final ruling, once the victim of sexual harassment utilizes multiple legal dispute settlement systems. For example, the first sexual harassment lawsuit in South Korea, which was filed on October 18, 1993, took six years to conclude after going through five civil trials (first, second and third instance, retrial, and appellate review). The R Automotive sexual harassment lawsuit, which was filed on June 11, 2013, went through the same number of civil trials and lasted for approximately five years until July 23, 2018. Meanwhile, the victim reported that the company took unfair personnel management actions against her and her co-worker after she reported the sexual harassment, which is prohibited by the Equal Employment Act. She filed a complaint with the Ministry of Employment and Labor in February 2014, and filed a criminal complaint with the prosecutor's office in April 2014. The criminal trial in relation to this matter began approximately six years after the complaint was filed, and went through three trials (first, second and third instance) until the Supreme Court rendered a guilty verdict on July 21, 2021, after an 18-month trial. As a result, the R Automotive sexual harassment case lasted for approximately 8 years. In the case of the female professor who experienced sexual harassment and sexual assault by the dean of the graduate

성폭력 사건으로 이슈화시키고 조직적 항의를 하였다. R자동차 소속 연구소 팀장의 성희롱 사건에도 8개 시민단체, 노동단체, 여성단체 등이 'R자동차 직장 내 성희롱 사건 해결을 위한 공동대책위원회'를 결성하고 피해자를 지원하며 사건을 사회 이슈화시켰다.

3) 성희롱 관련 분쟁의 법적 분쟁화

성희롱 관련 분쟁이 법적 분쟁으로 비화되는 경우가 많아지고 있다. '성희롱 관련 법적 분쟁'이란 성희롱 사건의 당사자 또는 3자가 사업장 내 또는 학교 내 자율적 분쟁처리제도를 활용하지 않고 행정기관이나 사법기관에 의뢰해 분쟁이 처리되는 경우를 말한다. 행정적 분쟁처리는 국가인권위원회에 대한 진정, 지방고용노동관서(근로감독관)에 대한 통보·진정·고발, 노동위원회에 대한 부당해고(징계)구제신청과 차별적 처우의 시정신청, 공무원의 소청심사위원회에 대한 소청심사청구, 교원의 교원소청심사위원회에 대한 소청심사청구 등에 의해 개시된다. 사법적 분쟁처리는 경찰과 검찰에 대한 고소·고발, 법원에 대한 소송(민사소송, 형사소송, 행정소송) 제기, 헌법재판소에 대한 위헌법률심사제청과 헌법소원 등에 의해 개시되고 진행된다.

그런데 동일한 성희롱 사건의 당사자가 여러 개의 법적 분쟁처리제도를 활용하거나 대법원이 확정판결을 내릴 때까지 계속 분쟁처리절차를 진행하여 분쟁이 더욱 장기화 되는 경우가 많다. 예를 들면, 우리나라 최초의 성희롱소송 사건은 1993년 10월 18일에 소송이 제기된 후 5회의 민사재판(1심, 2심, 3심, 파기환송심과 재상고심)을 거쳐 1999년 11월 18일에 재판이 완결될 때까지 6년이 넘는 시간이 소요되었다. R자동차 성희롱 사건의 경우 2013년 6월 11일에 제기된 민사소송은 5회의 재판(1심, 2심, 3심, 파기환송심과 재상고심)을 거쳐 2018년 7월 23일의 대법원 확정 판결까지 5년여간 진행되었다. 한편, 피해자는 성희롱 피해를 신고한 후 자신과 조력자에 대하여 부당한 인사조치한 회사와 그 주역자들을 상대로 피해자 등에 대한 불리한 조치를 금지한 「남녀고용평등법」에 위반된다며 2014년 2월에 고용노동부에 진정하였고, 2014년 4월에 검찰에 고소를 하였다. 이에 관한 형사재판은 고소한 지 약 6년 후에 개시되어 3회의 재판(1심, 2심, 3심)을 거쳤는데 대법원이 2021년 7월 21일 유죄 판결을 할 때까지 약 1년 6개월의 시간이 소요되었다. 그리하여

Section 3. Basic Understanding of Sexual Harassment

school at S University in 2014, the victim pursued various legal actions for about 8 years: two civil and criminal lawsuits, filing a lawsuit for invalidation of dismissal due to failure to reappoint by the university and first and second instance of civil trials, filing a civil lawsuit for damages for defamation and first instance civil trial, applying for industrial accident compensation insurance benefits for illnesses caused by sexual harassment with the Korea Workers' Compensation and Welfare Service, and filing a reinstatement lawsuit against the school.

Long legal disputes often result in prolonged difficulties not only for the parties involved but also for those associated with the parties, such as business owners, because of the process of many investigations, prosecutions, and trials. In legal disputes, it is often the case that even if one party wins, it is still difficult to obtain real benefit because the emotions and conflicts escalate within the involved parties and organizations. For example, a female former adjunct professor at S University contributed to activation of the #MeToo movement in Korean universities by forming a National Association of Me-Too Survivors and winning all four lawsuits against the perpetrators. However, she was not reinstated by the university but instead simply received six years' salary after mediation by the court.

Sometimes, individuals or organizations who are accused of sexual harassment or misconduct sue for defamation, or file civil lawsuits against the victims and individuals or organizations that support the victims. Furthermore, when the accused individual or organization receives disciplinary action in the form of suspension or termination from the affiliated organization such as a university or workplace, there are often cases where they file an appeal for review of the disciplinary action or file civil or administrative lawsuits to nullify or invalidate the disciplinary action. This phenomenon, known as "counter-suing" or "counter-lawsuits," is on the rise. For example, Professor A was accused of sexual harassment against a female staff member at the university, and after he was dismissed from his position, he counter-sued the staff member for obstruction of business, only to be counter-sued for sexual harassment and non-criminal charges. The Supreme Court confirmed A's guilt by rejecting his appeal on November 25, 2018.

2. Harm to victims of sexual harassment

Sexual harassment affects not only the victims but also the accused individuals, perpetrators, the workplace where the harassment occurs, the employees within that workplace, and even society and the nation as a whole, causing harm and negative consequences.

R자동차 성희롱 사건의 법적 분쟁은 약 8년간 진행되었다. SK대 대학원 원장이 비전임대우 여성 교수를 성희롱·성폭력한 사건은 2014년에 발생하였는데 피해자는 강제추행과 성희롱으로 입은 피해에 대한 손해배상소송 제기와 1심 및 2심의 민사재판, 고소와 1심 및 2심의 형사재판, 대학의 재임용탈락에 대한 해고무효확인소송과 1심 및 2심의 민사재판, 명예훼손에 대한 손해배상소송과 1심의 민사재판, 근로복지공단에 성희롱으로 인한 질병에 대한 산업재해보상보험 급여 신청, 학교에 대한 복직소송 등 다양한 방법의 법적 투쟁을 약 8년간 하였다.

장기간의 법적 분쟁으로 당사자뿐 아니라 관련자, 사용자 모두가 조사와 수사, 재판을 받느라 장기간 곤경에 처하는 경우가 많다. 법적 분쟁은 당사자와 조직 내 감정과 대립의 악화를 발생시켜 당사자 중 어느 쪽이 이기더라도 실익을 얻기 힘든 경우가 발생하는 경우가 종종 있다. 예를 들면, SK대 비전임 여교수였던 여성은 성폭력 피해자들을 모아서 '전국미투생존자연대'를 결성하여 우리나라 대학 미투운동이 활성화되는데 기여하였고 가해자를 상대로 한 소송 4건에서 모두 이겼다. 그러나 대학이 복직을 거부해 복직은 결국 하지 못했고 대신 법원의 화해 권고에 따라 6년간의 급여를 받았다.

그런데 성희롱 혐의자나 행위자가 피해자와 피해자를 돕는 개인이나 조직에 대하여 명예훼손죄, 무고죄로 고소하거나 민사소송을 제기하는 경우가 있다. 또한 혐의자나 행위자가 대학이나 사업장 등의 소속 조직에서 징계를 받은 경우 징계의 취소나 무효를 구하는 소청심사청구나 민사소송, 행정소송을 제기하는 경우가 많다. 이러한 고소나 소송을 '역고소', '역소송'이라고 하는데 이 현상은 증가하고 있다. 예를 들면, 법대 학장이었던 K교수는 여성 직원을 추행한 혐의로 학교에 신고되고 보직해임 당하자 그 직원을 업무방해 혐의로 고소하였다가 강제추행죄와 무고죄로 되려 고소당했는데 대법원이 2018년 11월 25일, K교수의 상고를 기각함으로써 K교수의 유죄를 확정하였다.

2. 성희롱의 피해와 악영향

성희롱은 피해자뿐 아니라 혐의자와 행위자, 성희롱이 발생된 사업장과 그 소속 종사자, 사회와 국가에 까지 피해와 악영향을 미친다.

Section 3. Basic Understanding of Sexual Harassment

(1) Harm to the victim

1) Primary harm

"Primary harm" refers to the mental and emotional harm, infringement of human rights (such as to personal dignity, sexual self-determination, and equality), and harm in the workplace (such as infringement of labor rights, deterioration of working conditions, loss of motivation and performance, and industrial accidents) caused by sexual harassment by a perpetrator.

2) Secondary Victimization of Victims

"Secondary victimization of victims" refers to the harm that victims suffer from perpetrators, employers, and members of the workplace after reporting and demanding corrective actions for sexual harassment, as well as the harm they experience during counseling, investigation, legal proceedings, medical treatment, media coverage, and other processes. The "Act on the Prevention of Violence Against Women and the Protection of Victims" defines "secondary victimization" as one of the following harms that female victims of violence can experience (Article 3, Clause 3):

① Psychological, physical, and economic harm during the entire process of handling and recovering from violence against women, including investigation, trial, protection, medical treatment, and media coverage.
② Harassment, assault, verbal abuse, or other acts causing psychological or physical harm, including acts conducted through information and communication networks.
③ Adverse measures taken by users (employer or person in charge of business management, and others performing duties related to employees on behalf of the employer) due to reporting violence-related incidents, including:
   1. Dismissal, termination, or any other measures leading to loss of status.
   2. Disciplinary actions, demotion, salary reduction, promotion restriction, or any other unjust personnel measures.
   3. Transfer, reassignment, denial of job duties, or any other personnel measures contrary to the employee's intention.
   4. Discrimination in performance evaluation or peer evaluation, leading to unequal payment of wages or bonuses.
   5. Cancellation of self-development opportunities such as education or training, restriction or removal of available resources such as budget or personnel, suspension of security or confidential information usage, cancellation of handling qualifications, or any other discrimination or measures negatively affecting working conditions.
   6. Creation or public disclosure of a list of targeted individuals, harassment,

(1) 피해자의 피해

1) 피해자의 1차 피해

'피해자의 1차 피해'란 피해자가 행위자의 성희롱으로 인해 심신의 피해, 인권침해(인격권과 성적 자기결정권, 평등권 등), 업무상의 피해(근로권 침해, 근로환경 악화, 근로의 의욕과 실적 저하, 산업재해 등)를 받는 것을 말한다.

2) 피해자의 2차 피해

'피해자의 2차 피해'란 피해자가 성희롱 피해를 알리고 시정을 요구한 후에 행위자와 사용자, 사업장 구성원으로부터 받는 피해와 상담·조사 및 수사·사건 처리 등의 과정에서 담당자들로 부터 받는 피해를 말한다.

「여성폭력방지기본법」은 '2차 피해'를 여성피해자가 다음의 어느 하나에 해당하는 피해를 입는 것으로 정의하고 있다(제3조제3호).

"① 수사·재판·보호·진료·언론보도 등 여성폭력 사건처리 및 회복의 전 과정에서 입는 정신적·신체적·경제적 피해

② 집단 따돌림, 폭행 또는 폭언, 그 밖에 정신적·신체적 손상을 가져오는 행위로 인한 피해(정보통신망을 이용한 행위로 인한 피해를 포함한다)

③ 사용자(사업주 또는 사업경영담당자, 그 밖에 사업주를 위하여 근로자에 관한 사항에 대한 업무를 수행하는 자를 말한다)로부터 폭력 피해 신고 등을 이유로 입은 다음 어느 하나에 해당하는 불이익조치

1. 파면, 해임, 해고, 그 밖에 신분상실에 해당하는 신분상의 불이익조치
2. 징계, 정직, 감봉, 강등, 승진 제한, 그 밖에 부당한 인사조치
3. 전보, 전근, 직무 미부여, 직무 재배치, 그 밖에 본인의 의사에 반하는 인사조치
4. 성과평가 또는 동료평가 등에서의 차별과 그에 따른 임금 또는 상여금 등의 차별 지급
5. 교육 또는 훈련 등 자기계발 기회의 취소, 예산 또는 인력 등 가용 자원의 제한 또는 제거, 보안정보 또는 비밀정보 사용의 정지 또는 취급 자격의 취소, 그 밖에 근무조건 등에 부정적 영향을 미치는 차별 또는 조치
6. 주의 대상자 명단 작성 또는 그 명단의 공개, 집단 따돌림, 폭행 또는

Section 3. Basic Understanding of Sexual Harassment

assault, verbal abuse, or other acts causing psychological or physical harm.
7. Unjust auditing or investigation of job duties, or public disclosure of audit or investigation results.
8. Cancellation of licenses or permits, or any other administrative measures causing disadvantages.
9. Termination of contracts for goods or services, or any other measures causing economic disadvantages.

(2) Harm to suspects and perpetrators
1) Harm to the suspect

Even if the claims and reports of sexual harassment made by an accuser have not been confirmed as true during the investigation process, the reporter is referred to as a "victim" who needs protection. If an employer takes disadvantageous action against the victim or the reporter, the employer may face criminal punishment.

On the other hand, it is not easy for an individual accused of sexual harassment to clear the accusation without providing decisive evidence that can prove their innocence, even if they claim that they did not commit the harassment. Often times, individuals who have been accused of sexual harassment are later found not guilty, or were falsely accused. However, they have already suffered disciplinary action or faced difficulties at work or school, which caused them to suffer reputational damage, stigmatization and/or other disciplinary measures. Restoring their reputations, undoing disciplinary actions, and mitigating other damages caused in the course of duty are not easy. As a result, some individuals accused of sexual harassment may resort to extreme action such as committing suicide.

2) Harm to the perpetrator

Once an individual is determined to have perpetrated sexual harassment, they face moral condemnation and suffer significant damage to their trustworthiness, reputation, and social status. They may also face legal sanctions such as criminal punishment and compensatory damages. When the incident becomes publicly known through media coverage, it will also negatively affect the individual's family and create significant difficulties in their personal and social life. Finding employment or gaining admission or re-admission to educational institutions may become challenging, and recovering the reputation and undoing the stigma can be difficult even after a long time.

(3) Damage to the workplace and coworkers
1) Damages to the workplace

폭언, 그 밖에 정신적·신체적 손상을 가져오는 행위
7. 직무에 대한 부당한 감사 또는 조사나 그 결과의 공개
8. 인허가 등의 취소, 그 밖에 행정적 불이익을 주는 행위
9. 물품계약 또는 용역계약의 해지, 그 밖에 경제적 불이익을 주는 조치"

(2) 혐의자와 행위자의 피해

1) 혐의자의 피해

성희롱 피해를 당하였다고 주장하는 사람과 성희롱 발생 신고를 한 신고인은 아직 그 주장과 신고가 사실임이 확정되지 않더라도 현행법상 일단 "피해자", "피해자 등"으로 간주되고 조사과정에서 보호조치를 받는다. 사업주가 피해자와 신고자에 대하여 불이익한 처분을 하면 형사처벌을 받는다.

그런데 한편, 성희롱을 하였다는 혐의로 신고를 당한 혐의자는 극구 성희롱을 하지 않았다고 주장하더라도 결정적 반증을 제시하지 못하는 한 혐의를 벗기가 쉽지 않다. 혐의자가 되었다가 나중에 무혐의 처분이나 무죄 판결을 받는 경우와 허위의 신고로 성희롱 혐의자가 되어 직장이나 학교에서 징계를 받거나 재판을 받다가 무죄를 받는 경우도 종종 발생한다. 그렇더라도 이미 실추된 명예 회복과 징계 등의 업무상 피해나 낙인 등의 피해를 복구하기가 쉽지 않다. 그래서 성희롱 혐의자가 장기간 곤경에 처하거나 극단적 선택을 시도 또는 감행하는 사건도 발생한다.

2) 행위자에 대한 피해와 악영향

성희롱의 행위자가 되면 도덕적 비난을 받고 신뢰와 명예, 지위가 크게 손상되고 형사처벌이나 손해배상 등의 법적 제재를 받는다. 언론보도 등으로 사건이 알려지면 가족들에게 까지 악영향을 미치고 가정생활과 사회생활에 큰 어려움을 겪게 된다. 다른 곳에 취업하거나 입학, 재입학하는 것도 어렵게 될 수 있고 실추된 명예 회복과 낙인은 세월이 흘러도 복구하기가 어려운 경우가 많다.

(3) 성희롱 발생 사업장과 종사자의 피해

1) 성희롱 발생 사업장의 피해

Section 3. Basic Understanding of Sexual Harassment

When sexual harassment occurs, the individuals involved are not the only ones to suffer damage. The workplace where the incident occurred can suffer significant damage as well. The employer must invest a significant amount of manpower, money and time to investigate and handle the incident(s) of sexual harassment. The employer may also have to take disciplinary action and fill the vacancy left by dismissal or removal of the perpetrator and resolving labor-management conflict. These actions can lead to a deteriorating work environment and decline in productivity. Furthermore, the employer may bear administrative and legal responsibilities for failing to prevent sexual harassment as the employer of the perpetrator. Employers can also be involved in long-term legal disputes as defendants or co-defendants in cases before the National Human Rights Commission, labor relations commission and teacher petition review committees, as well as be caught up in civil or administrative lawsuits.

Finally, corporate image can suffer if the sexual harassment is repeated or there is extensive media coverage or extensive criticism from within the corporation regarding an incident or incidents. Financial damages can also result if civic organizations begin protesting or boycotting the company.

2) Damages to coworkers

When the workplace is troubled because of an incident of sexual harassment, the work environment can also deteriorate. Disputes between coworkers can increase if individuals are embroiled in conflict while in the process of writing petitions against the perpetrator. As a result, people who work in the same workplace may also endure mental suffering and violations of their labor rights and right to the pursuit of happiness.

3) Societal and National Harms and Negative Impact

The frequent occurrence of sexual harassment incidents and disputes has a detrimental effect on the protection of citizens' human rights, quality of life, personal development, and effective utilization of human resources. Consequently, it also negatively impacts the progress and development of society and the nation.

성희롱 사건이 발생하면 당사자뿐만 아니라 사건이 발생한 사업장도 상당한 피해를 입게 된다. 사용자는 성희롱 사건의 조사와 처리에 상당한 인력과 비용·시간을 투여해야 하고, 행위자에 대한 징계와 인사조치, 파면·해임된 행위자의 인력 보강, 노·노 갈등, 노·사 갈등 및 근로의 의욕과 실적의 저하, 근로환경 악화, 생산성 저하 등의 노동문제를 수습해야 한다. 또한 성희롱 행위자의 사용자와 관리자로서의 민사상 사용자의 책임과 성희롱을 방지해야 할 의무를 이행하지 못한 행정적 책임과 법적 책임을 져야 한다. 또한 당사자의 법적 분쟁 제기로 국가인권위원회의 피진정인, 노동위원회의 피신청인, 소청심사위원회와 교원소청심사위원회의 피소청심사기관, 민사소송과 행정소송의 피고 또는 피고보조참가인이 되어 법적 분쟁에 장기간 휘말리게 된다.

그리고 성희롱이 재발, 다발되거나 성희롱에 제대로 대처하지 못했다는 비판을 사업장 내부와 언론, 시민단체, 정부, 국회 또는 지방의회 등으로부터 받게 되면 사업장 내의 분쟁사태뿐 아니라 대외적 공신력, 이미지에 치명상을 당한다. 시민단체 주도로 항의시위나 불매운동이 전개되는 경우 경제적 타격도 받는다.

2) 성희롱 발생 사업장의 종사자 피해

성희롱 사건의 당사자와 사업장이 분쟁에 휘말리고 사업 운영이 원활치 않으면 업무환경도 악화된다. 행위자에 대한 탄원서 작성 여부로 구성원들 사이에 갈등이 심화되는 경우들도 발생한다. 이에 따라 당사자가 아닌 종사자들도 사업장 내 성희롱 사건의 발생으로 심신의 피해, 근로권과 행복추구권 등의 인권을 침해당하고 업무환경 악화로 피해를 입게 된다.

3) 사회와 국가의 피해와 악영향

성희롱 사건과 분쟁의 빈번한 발생은 국민의 인권 보장과 삶의 질, 능력 계발과 인력 활용에 악영향을 준다. 또한 성희롱의 문제와 피해를 경시하는 것과 현재 또는 장차 사회의 주역이거나 주역이 될 성희롱 행위자에 대한 지나친 관용은 피해자 뿐 아니라 사회와 국가의 발전에도 악영향을 준다.

Chapter 2 Workplace Harassment: Prevention and Response (Bongsoo Jung)

I. Workplace Harassment Resolved through Recognition of an Accident as Related to Work

II. A Case of Workplace Harassment and the Criteria for Recognizing Consequent Mental Illness as an Occupational Accident Related to Work

III. When Workplace Harassment Occurs, What Measures Should an Employer Take?

IV. A Case Study on Workplace Harassment against a New Employee

V. Cases of Workplace Bullying & Sexual Harassment and Disciplinary Committee Decisions

VI. Workplace Bullying and Sexual Harassment: A Case Analysis - Supreme Court ruling on November 25, 2021, 2020da270503

제2장 직장 내 괴롭힘 사건사례와 예방조치(정봉수)

Ⅰ. 직장 내 괴롭힘 원인제거를 통한 해결 사례
Ⅱ. 직장 내 괴롭힘 사례와 산재인정 요건
Ⅲ. 직장 내 괴롭힘 사건 사례를 통해서 본 사업주의 적절한 조치
Ⅳ. 직장 내 괴롭힘 처리 사례 (신입직원)
Ⅴ. 직장 내 괴롭힘, 성희롱 사건과 기각 결정 사례
Ⅵ. 직장 내 괴롭힘과 성희롱에 관한 판례 해석
 (대법원 2021.11.25. 선고, 2020다270503 판결)

Workplace Harassment Resolved through Recognition of an Accident as Related to Work

I. Introduction

Until recently, workplace harassment was resolved through workplace grievance handling, but if this did not work, the victim had no choice but to put up with such harassment or quit his or her job. However, since the procedures for remedy against harassment in the workplace were legislated on April 2021, now constituting a compulsory regulation that punishes employers if they do not comply with the required procedures, employers are much more involved in resolving things.[43]

According to a report by the Kyunghyang daily paper on June 29, 2022, one of every four office workers has experienced harassment at work, with 31% of that number saying the harassment had been serious, and 7.3% said they were contemplating the extreme response of suicide.[44] When someone is bullied for a long period of time, the mental strain can lead to depression and adjustment disorder, and finally to extreme choices.

This article will look at a case of harassment against an employee who had to avoid working overtime. This employee worked shifts at a production site and avoided working overtime due to a work-related injury and its long-term effects, and received psychiatric treatment over harassment from his colleagues. In this case, this labor attorney provided a reasonable solution through interviews with the victim.

II. Details of the Related Workplace Harassment

1. Harassment occurring after injury at work

"Hong Gil-dong" (hereinafter referred to as "Gil-dong") worked one of three shifts as a production worker for a large manufacturing company. At around 2:00

---

[43] On April 13, 2021, Article 76-3 of the Labor Standards Act (Measures in case of harassment at work) was introduced as an obligatory regulation for employers. Labor inspectors can impose fines for failures to comply.

[44] The Kyunghyang Daily Paper, "Harassment at work has resulted in the extreme choice to commit suicide...Industrial accident applications have almost doubled," June 19, 2022.

직장 내 괴롭힘 원인제거를 통한 해결 사례

I. 괴롭힘 사례 소개

직장 내 괴롭힘에 대해 기존까지는 직장 내 고충처리로 해결하였는데, 이를 통하여 해결되지 않으면 피해 근로자는 참고 생활하는 수밖에 없었다. 그러나 직장 내 괴롭힘에 대한 구제절차가 2021년 4월에 법제화되고, 사업주가 필요한 절차를 지키지 않으면, 사업주를 처벌하는 강행규정이 된 이후에는 사업주의 적극적인 조치가 이루어지고 있다.[43]

2022년 6월 29일에 경향신문 보도에 따르면, 직장인 4명 중 1명이 직장 내 괴롭힘을 당한 경험이 있고, 그 중 31%가 괴롭힘이 심각하다고 했고, 7.3%는 극단적 선택을 고민했다고 한다.[44] 피해자들이 장기간 괴롭힘을 당하게 되면, 정신적 고통이 우울증과 적응장애로 이어져 극단적인 선택을 할 수 있다.

이번 사례에서 소개하는 괴롭힘은 연장근로를 기피하는 동료에 대한 집단 따돌림에 대한 사례이다. 생산현장에서 교대근무를 하는 직원이 업무상 발생한 부상으로 인한 후유증 때문에 연장근로를 기피하게 되었고, 이로 인해 동료들로부터 집단 따돌림을 당해 정신과 치료를 받고 있었던 상황이었다. 이에 대해 본 노무사가 해당 피해 근로자와의 면담을 통해 합리적인 해결책을 제공해 준 사례를 소개하고자 한다.

II. 해당 직장 내 괴롭힘의 구체적 경위

1. 업무상 부상과 직장 내 괴롭힘의 원인

홍길동(이하 '길동')은 대형 제조업체에서 생산직으로 3교대 교대근무를 하고 있다. 2019년 6월 2일, 새벽 2시경 작업실에서 근무하던 중 노후화된 의자에

---

[43] 「근로기준법」 제76조의 3 (직장 내 괴롭힘 발생 시 조치) 규정이 2021년 4월 13일에 사업주의 의무규정으로 도입되어 이를 미준수 시 근로감독관은 과태료 처분을 할 수 있다.
[44] 경향신문, "직장 내 괴롭힘에 극단 선택까지...산재 신청도 2배 가까이 늘어", 2022.6.19.

I. Workplace Harassment Resolved through Recognition of an Accident as Related to Work

am on June 2, 2019 while working in the workroom, the old chair he was sitting on fell backwards, causing him to hit the handle of the chair with his back. Gil-dong had severe back pain, but he thought it was just a bruise from the bump and did nothing about it until his shift was over. He was barely able to get on the bus home from work due to the severe back pain he was enduring, and went to emergency and had an X-ray taken. The orthopedic surgeon in charge diagnosed that the 1st, 2nd, 3rd, and 4th transverse processes near the lumbar region (backbone) had been fractured.[45] However, he returned to work after a few days of treatment because the atmosphere at the workplace was chaotic due to personnel appointments between departments within the company. The severe pain continued, but he worked hard and simply took painkillers and wore an abdominal belt to support his back. He continued to receive treatment and work at the same time. On April 12, 2021, Gil-dong felt pain in his neck and shoulders, so he visited the hospital, where the doctor told him he needed surgery on his cervical disc after a thorough examination.

The harassment began on July 26, 2021, when one of the employees organized for the shift system was absent from work for a long time for personal reasons. Workers on the same shift had to fill in for the absent employee by working overtime. Gil-dong conveyed to the HR manager that he would not be able to work overtime as he was scheduled for back surgery. On August 3, he noticed on the shiftwork handover board a note saying, "Move Hong Gil-dong to another shift team." Gil-dong felt a deep sense of humiliation, as he had never seen a person's name written on the shiftwork handover board which was posted in a public place. It was the first time he would be moved in his 27 years working on that production line.

On September 7, 2021, Gildong experienced neck and shoulder spasms (pain) due to deterioration of the cervical disc, so he was hospitalized for surgery, and after 10 days of treatment, he returned to work. When he got back to work, his shift co-workers kept asking, "Why isn't he working overtime?" and began to harass him. However, as Gil-dong had back pain and thought it best not to engage in physical contact with his co-workers, he kept his distance from them as much as possible.

---

[45] Doctor Sujin Jang's Introduction to Spine, Naver Blog, Mar. 7, 2022. "Transverse process fractures: The transverse process is a bone that extends from the backbone horizontally on both sides. Its appearance resembles the side-wings extending to both sides of the official hat of the Joseon Dynasty. It is 1 cm long and wide, and 3-4 mm thick. The symptoms of a transverse process fracture are that even breathing or moving the body causes intense pain."

앉다가 이 의자가 뒤로 밀리면서 넘어졌고, 허리가 의자 손잡이에 세게 부딪치는 사고가 발생하였다. 길동은 허리의 고통이 심했지만 큰 사고가 아니고 부딪혀서 생긴 타박성에 의한 고통으로 생각하고 아침 교대근무시간까지 참았다. 퇴근 버스를 겨우 타고 퇴근하였지만, 허리의 통증이 심하여, 병원 응급실에 찾아가서 엑스레이 촬영을 하였다. 담당 정형외과 의사는 허리부근의 1, 2, 3, 4 번 횡돌기뼈가 골절되었다는 진단을 내렸다.[45] 당시 회사 내의 부서간 인사발령 등으로 어수선한 분위기라서 며칠 간 치료 후 근무에 복귀하였다. 당시 허리에 통증은 있었지만, 진통제와 복대 착용으로 통증을 이겨내면서 어렵게 근무하였다. 이후에도 길동은 골절된 부분에서 통증이 있었지만 계속된 치료와 근무를 병행하였다. 길동은 2021년 4월 12일 목부위와 어깨부분까지 통증이 있어 병원을 방문하여 정밀검진을 받은 결과 목디스크 수술이 필요하다는 의사의 소견서를 받았다.

집단 따돌림의 시작은 길동이 2021년 7월 26일 교대제에 편성된 직원 한 명이 개인사정으로 장기간 결근을 하면서 시작되었다. 이 결근한 직원을 대신하여 같은 근무조의 근로자들이 연장근로를 통해 공백을 메꾸어 주어야 했다. 이때 길동은 인사팀장과의 면담을 통해서 본인은 허리수술을 예정하고 있어 연장근로를 할 수 없다는 의사를 전달하였다. 8월 3일 교대제 근무 인수인계 상황판에 "홍길동을 다른 조로 이동시켜라"라는 기록을 확인하였다. 지금까지 근무 인수인계 상황판에 개인이름을 적시한 것은 한번도 보지 못했기 때문에 길동은 상당한 충격과 모멸감을 느꼈다. 길동은 27년간 현장직에서 근무하면서 이렇게 특정 개인신상을 공개된 장소에 기록하여 다른 조로 보내라고 한 사실은 처음이라 충격을 받았다.

2021년 9월 7일 길동은 목디스크가 악화되어 목과 어깨 경련이 일어나서 병원에 입원하여 수술을 했고, 10일간의 치료를 한 후 업무에 복귀 하였다. 업무에 복귀하자 교대제 근무조 동료들은 "왜 쟤는 연장근로를 하지 않는 거야?" 하면서 집단 따돌림을 하기 시작했다. 그러나 길동은 허리에 통증이 있고, 근무도 힘든 상황에서 동료 직원들과 부딪히지 않는 것이 상책이라 생각하고, 최대한 동료들과 거리를 두면서 지내게 되었다.

---

[45] "횡돌기뼈 골절: 가로 돌기는 척추체에서 양쪽으로 가로로 수평으로 나온 부분이다. 생김새는 조선시대 관모의 양쪽으로 뻗은 양각과 같이 생겼다. 길이와 폭은 1cm, 두께는 3-4 mm이다. 횡돌기 골절의 증상은 숨을 쉬거나 몸을 살짝 움직이는 행동조차도 통증을 강하게 유발한다." 장수진 원장의 척추학 개론 네이버 블로그, 2022.3.7. 게시글.

Ⅰ. Workplace Harassment Resolved through Recognition of an Accident as Related to Work

2. Persistent harassment

During a short break around 6:00 pm on November 15, 2021, Gil-dong told three colleagues who were complaining about him, "Don't swear at me behind my back." In response, colleague A began a tirade of abusive language: "Hey, you son of a b*tch! You aren't the only one having a hard time. I'm very sick too." "Aren't you the only one who isn't working overtime? You b*stard, you should say sorry to your seniors who have to work overtime because you won't." "Everyone knows how lazy you are!" This was followed by several curse words. In response, Gil-dong explained to colleague A that he couldn't work overtime because he had been injured and needed time to recover, but colleague A continued to insult him in the presence of several of his colleagues. Gil-dong then protested to Manager A, his senior, saying "Sir, you need to say something." Manager A apologized for the three other workers, to which Gil-dong also apologized to those three. However, the three workers continued to act very self-righteously, as if the insults had been justified. From that time, these three workers continued to harass and blame Gil-dong for their problems at work.

On November 19, 2021, Gil-dong left early because his head hurt and he felt so dizzy that he could not work. At the recommendation of a counselor, he saw a psychiatrist who prescribed him medication. Gil-dong used two weeks of his personal annual leave in lieu of sick leave from December 14, 2021 due to his back pain and extreme stress. On December 29th, Gil-dong returned to work with a strong sense of responsibility as a worker and as the head of a household. The harassment from his co-workers continued even though he was working hard. He had to continue taking painkillers and the psychiatrist's prescribed medications. Overheard statements included "That guy doesn't work overtime," and "There's something wrong with him mentally," which of course added to Gil-dong's work difficulties.

Ⅲ. Application for the Chair Accident to be Recognized as an Occupational Accident to Stop the Workplace Harassment

1. Fights between employees due to continued workplace harassment

From January 2022, Gil-dong continued to work even though it was difficult

2. 지속된 집단 따돌림

2021년 11월 15일 오후 6시경, 잠깐 휴식시간에 길동은 뒤에서 험담하는 동료 3명에게 "제 뒤에서 욕하고 다니지 마세요"라고 요구하였다. 이에 동료 A는 길동에게 갑작스럽게 욕설과 함께 폭언을 하였다. "임마 새끼야, 너만 힘든 지 아냐? 나도 많이 아프다." "너만 OT 안 하냐? 임마, OT한 선배들에게 사과부터 해라." "야, 너 인생 그렇게 사는 거 사람들이 다 알아?"라고 고함치면서 수차례 욕설을 하였다. 이에 길동은 동료 A에게 몸 아파서 OT에 못 들어 갔고, 병가도 냈다고 설명하였지만, 동료A는 동료들 여러 명이 있는데서 계속해서 모욕적인 폭언을 했다. 이에 길동도 대응하면서 "형이나 똑바로 살아라."라고 항의하였다. 이 상황에서 길동의 조장인 A매니저가 길동에게 사과하는 말로 위로해서, 길동도 자신을 비방했던 조원 3명에게 그 자리에서 사과하였다. 그러나 길동의 사과는 받아들여지지 않았고, 오히려 가해자들은 괴롭힘 행위가 합리화된 것처럼 기세 등등한 태도를 보였고, 그날 이후 그들은 지속적으로 길동에게 집단 따돌림과 비난을 계속하였다.

2021년 11월 19일 길동은 근무를 할 수 없을 정도로 머리가 아프고 어지러워 조퇴를 하고, 심리상담을 받았다. 심리상담사의 권유로 정신과 의사의 치료를 받고 약처방을 받았다. 길동은 허리의 고통과 정신적 고통으로 2021년 12월 14일부터 2주간 개인 연차를 이용하여 병가를 사용하였다. 12월 29일, 길동은 직장인으로서의 책임과 한가정의 가장으로서 책임감이 중요하다는 생각을 갖고 마음을 굳게 먹고 업무에 복귀하였다. 진통제와 정신과 약을 복용하면서 겨우 겨우 힘들게 근무하는 중에도 동료들의 집단적 따돌림은 계속되었다. "쟤는 OT를 하지 않는다". "쟤는 정신이 이상한 사람이다"라는 소문으로 길동은 더욱더 직장 내에서 근무하기가 힘들어지게 되었다.

Ⅲ. 해당 직장 내 괴롭힘에 대한 원인 제거를 위한 산재신청

1. 지속된 직장 내 괴롭힘으로 인한 직원 간의 싸움

2022년 1월부터, 길동은 집단 따돌림과 괴롭힘으로 힘들면서도 계속 근무

I. Workplace Harassment Resolved through Recognition of an Accident as Related to Work

due to the group harassing him. This included colleague B humming in front of Gil-dong (which is rude in Korea) continuously during handover meetings before the next shift started. Colleague B continued the noisy humming in front of Gil-dong for several months during every shift handover time. On May 5, 2022 at 6:45 am during another shift handover, colleague B began humming in a childish way to provoke Gil-dong, who found it too much on top of everything else over the past few months. When he shouted, "Quit humming like an idiot in front of me!" colleague B retorted, "What? Now you're hearing things too?"

Gil-dong was very angry at being treated like a psychopath in front of many people. He felt he had been harassed for no reason, resulting in him having to take psychiatric medication, counseling, and sick leave. In frustration and anger, he kicked colleague B and a fight ensued which had to be stopped by their colleagues. The company then ordered them to submit a report about their fight. Gil-dong then prepared and handed in a report on the harassment and contacted this labor attorney to ask for help.

2. Labor attorney's view and application for accident to be recognized as an occupational accident

On May 13, 2022, Gil-dong contacted this labor attorney to help him report the workplace harassment to the Ministry of Employment and Labor. This labor attorney said that in order to solve the problem of harassment at work, it must be officially acknowledged that the reason Gil-dong did not work overtime was simply due to the aftereffects of a work-related accident. This labor attorney explained that if Gil-dong's back pain were recognized as the result of an occupational accident, his colleagues would have to accept that he had to avoid overtime due to the pain and difficulties he had. In addition, it was explained that filing a complaint with the Ministry of Employment and Labor on the grounds of workplace harassment is done when the procedure in Article 76-3 of the Labor Standards Act has not been carried out properly or when the company has not investigated the report fairly nor put in place the remedy procedure for workplace harassment. Since Gil-dong's occupational accident occurred on June 2,

하고 있었는데, 동료 B는 교대근무시작 전 미팅에서 지속적으로 길동 앞에서 콧노래를 부르기 시작하였다. 길동은 동료 B의 콧노래 소리가 자신을 무시하고 놀리는 행위 같아 귀에 거슬렸다. 동료 B는 근무교대 시마다 지속적으로 몇 달 동안 길동의 귀에 거슬리는 콧노래를 지속하였다. 2022년 5월 5일 오전 6시 45분 근무교대 시도 동료 B가 의도적으로 콧노래를 지속적으로 하였고, 길동은 동료 B가 지난 몇 달 동안 수차례 본인 앞에서 콧노래를 부르면서 자신을 놀린다고 생각하니 더 이상 참기 어려웠다. 이에 "내 앞에서 날 놀리면서 노래하지 마" 하고 외치자, 동료 B는 "이젠 환청까지 들리냐?"면서 길동을 미친놈 취급하였다.

길동은 집단 괴롭힘으로 인해 정신과 치료, 심리 상담 치료, 병가 등의 치료를 받고 있는 것도 억울한데, 그런 자신을 보고 "환청이 들리냐?"는 소리로 여러 사람 앞에서 자신을 정신병 환자로 취급한다고 생각하였다. 길동은 이유 없이 괴롭힘 당하고 있는 것이 너무 억울하여 동료 B를 발로 차면서 서로 물리적 충돌이 발생하였다. 길동과 동료 B는 서로 간에 엉켜 싸웠고, 동료들이 말려서 곧 진정이 되었다. 회사는 직원 간 싸움에 대해 경위서 제출을 요구하였다. 여기서 길동은 회사측에 그동안 집단 따돌림과 괴롭힘에 대해 경위서를 작성하여 제출하였고, 본 노무사에게도 연락하여 도움을 요청하였다.

2. 공인노무사의 판단과 산재신청

2022년 5월 13일 길동은 고용노동부에 직장 내 괴롭힘으로 신고하려는 목적으로 본 노무사에게 연락을 해왔다. 노무사는 이번 직장 내 괴롭힘 문제를 해결하기 위해서는 길동이가 동료 직원들에게 연장근무(OT)를 하지 않는 이유가 꾀병이 아니라 업무상 발생한 사고로 인한 후유증 때문이라는 사실을 공식적으로 인정받아야만 된다고 생각했다. 노무사는 길동의 허리통증을 산재로 인정받으면, 회사와 동료 근로자들에게도 그동안 자신이 겪었던 통증과 어려움을 충분히 설명해줄 수 있을 것이고 또한 자신을 변호할 수 있다고 설명해주었다. 아울러 고용노동부에 직장 내 괴롭힘을 이유로 진정하는 것은 「근로기준법」 제76조3항의 절차가 제대로 이루어지지 않았거나, 직장 내

Ⅰ. Workplace Harassment Resolved through Recognition of an Accident as Related to Work

2019, there were only about 20 days left until expiration of the statute of limitations for the application. Even if Gil-dong's back injury was caused by a work-related accident, once the 3-year statute of limitations expired, there would be no way for his injuries to be recognized as from the occupational accident, so the labor attorney submitted the application right away.

On May 19, 2022, this labor attorney submitted an application for medical treatment stating that Gil-dong's back injury was caused by a work accident and submitted a report on the accident itself. This report described the details of what happened that day and the measures taken in the emergency room, with medical records, details of his application for sick leave, and eyewitness statements regarding the accident at the time as proof. The competent Labor Welfare Corporation office acknowledged the fact that Gil-dong's back injury was caused by a work-related accident through the related data and company verification procedures, and three months later, at the end of September 2022, Gil-dong's back injury was recognized as due to an occupational accident.

Ⅳ. Appropriate Actions and Lessons Learned

1. Actions taken by the company

The company acknowledged the physical violence between Gil-dong and colleague B on May 5, 2022 as due to temporary conditions, and the parties also showed an attitude of reflection and the incident was concluded with a written warning. On October 1, 2022, Gil-dong reported to the HR team in writing that he had been harassed at work by colleagues A and B and handed over an official confirmation letter from the Labor Welfare Corporation that the back injury that occurred three years ago was recognized as due to an occupational accident. In response, the company held its own personnel committee meeting, recognized that harassment at work had taken place, and admonished colleague A and colleague B with a disciplinary salary reduction. Judging that Gil-dong's current shift work was negatively impacting recovery from his back injury, the company transferred him to a new workplace in the quality control department, which is not physically demanding.

괴롭힘의 구제절차에 대해 회사가 공정하게 조사하는 것에 신뢰성이 없을 때 하는 것이라고 알려주었다. 이 시점은 길동의 산재사고가 2019년 6월 2일에 발생하였기 때문에 산재신청의 소멸시효 만료가 20일 정도 밖에 남아 있지 않은 상태였다. 길동의 허리부상이 업무상 사고로 인하여 발생하였다고 하더라도 3년의 소멸시효가 완성되면 더 이상 산재로 인정받을 길이 없었기 때문에 곧바로 산재신청에 들어갔다.

 2022년 5월 19일 본 노무사는 길동의 허리부상이 업무상 사고로 인하여 발생하였다는 내용의 요양신청서와 재해발생 경위서를 제출하였다. 당시 재해 당일 발생한 내용과 응급실에서의 조치 내용 등을 자세히 기술하였다. 이를 입증하는 의무기록, 병가신청 내역, 그리고 사고와 관련한 당시 목격자의 진술서를 첨부하였다. 관할 근로복지공단은 제출한 관련 자료와 함께 회사측에 확인절차를 거쳐 길동의 허리부상은 업무상 사고로 인하여 발생하였다는 사실을 인정하였고, 그로부터 3개월 후인 2022년 9월 말 길동의 허리부상에 대해 산업재해로 인정하였다.

Ⅳ. 회사의 적절한 조치와 시사점

1. 회사의 적절한 조치

 회사는 2022년 5월 5일에 발생한 길동과 직장동료 B와 육체적 폭력사태에 대해 일시적으로 발생한 싸움으로 인정하였고, 당사자들도 반성하는 태도를 보여 서면경고로 사건을 마무리하였다. 길동은 2022년 10월 1일에 3년 전에 발생한 허리부상을 산재로 인정받은 근로복지공단의 확인공문과 동료 A와 동료 B로부터 직장 내 괴롭힘을 당했다는 사실을 인사팀에 서면신고 하면서 적절한 조치를 공식으로 요구하였다. 이에 대해 회사는 자체적으로 인사위원회를 개최하여 본 사안에 대해 직장 내 괴롭힘 가해 사실을 인정하고 동료 A와 동료 B에 대해 감봉의 징계처분을 하면서 훈계하였다. 또한 현재 길동의 교대제 근무가 허리부상 회복에 부정적 영향을 준다고 판단하여 길동의 의견을 받아들여 육체적으로 무리가 없는 작업조인 품질관리부서 근무조로 재배치하는 등의 조치를 하였다.

II. A Case of Workplace Harassment and the Criteria for Recognizing Consequent Mental Illness as an Occupational Accident Related to Work

Under current law, workplace harassment is, in principle, resolved autonomously within a company through its internal procedures. Article 93 of the Labor Standards Act stipulates "matters concerning the prevention of workplace harassment and measures to be taken when it occurs" as mandatory items in the employment rules, allowing voluntary regulation. On the other hand, Article 76-3 of the Labor Standards Act specifies measures an employer must take in the event of workplace harassment, and includes a punishment clause if the employer fails to take such measures. As such, the current law requires that workplace harassment be reported to and dealt with by the employer, but in cases where it is difficult to expect fairness from the employer, the victim shall file a complaint with the Ministry of Employment and Labor.

2. Lessons from this workplace harassment

Employers have an obligation not only to provide a safe workplace, but also to prepare institutional devices for preventing workplace harassment and taking follow-up measures against it.[46] Therefore, employers need to regularly carry out activities to prevent harassment through the introduction of prevention and follow-up measures through their employment rules, periodic anti-harassment education, and a grievance-handling system.

A Case of Workplace Harassment and the Criteria for Recognizing Consequent Mental Illness as an Occupational Accident

I. Introduction

The most common consequences of bullying at work are mental illness such as depression, anxiety disorders, and adjustment disorders. As these mental disorders worsen, they are diagnosed by a psychiatrist, and if recognized as having a significant causal relationship to work, they can be recognized as occupational accidents and the person recognized as eligible for medical care

---

[46] 2019. 2. 91~99면. Ministry of Employment and Labor, "Manual on Judging and Preventing Workplace Harassment, Feb. 2019, pp. 91-99.

현행법상 직장 내 괴롭힘의 문제는 회사 내에서 사내절차를 통해 자율해결을 원칙으로 한다. 「근로기준법」 제93조에서 "직장 내 괴롭힘의 예방 및 발생 시 조치 등에 관한 사항"을 취업규칙 필수기재 사항으로 명시하여 자율적으로 규율하도록 하고 있다. 한편, 「근로기준법」 제76조의3은 직장 내 괴롭힘 발생시 사업주의 의무조치를 명시하고 있고, 사업주가 이러한 의무적 조치를 하지 않는 경우에는 처벌조항을 두고 있다. 이와 같이 현행법은 직장 내 괴롭힘이 발생하면 사용자에게 신고해서 처리해야 하지만, 사용자의 공정성을 기대하기 어려운 경우 피해자는 고용노동부에 진정을 제기한다.

2. 시사점

사용자는 직장 내 안전한 사업장을 제공해줘야 하는 의무 뿐만 아니라 직장 내 괴롭힘이 발생하지 않도록 직장 내 괴롭힘에 대한 예방과 사후조치에 대한 제도적 장치를 마련해야 하는 의무를 가지고 있다.[46] 따라서 사용자는 취업규칙을 통한 직장 내 괴롭힘 예방과 사후조치 시스템의 도입, 괴롭힘 예방 교육 실시, 괴롭힘에 대한 고충처리 시스템 도입 등을 통해서 직장 내 괴롭힘 발생을 예방하는 활동을 주기적으로 하여야 할 것이다.

직장 내 괴롭힘 사례와 산재인정 요건

Ⅰ. 사실관계

직장 내 괴롭힘의 결과로 가장 많이 발생하는 것이 우울증, 불안장애, 적응장애와 같은 정신질환이다. 이러한 정신질환이 악화됨에 따라 정신과 의사의 진단을 받게 되고 그러한 정신질환이 업무와 상당한 인과관계가 인정되는

---
[46] 고용노동부, "직장 내 괴롭힘 판단 및 예방과 대응 매뉴얼, 2019. 2. 91~99면.

benefits and suspension benefits under the Industrial Accident Compensation Insurance Act (IACI Act). In order to be recognized as an occupational accident, the mental disorders must be an illness recognized under the IACI Act, and the worker must prove that the illness occurred as a result of work. It is, in fact, difficult to prove this, but two methods make it easier: ① the company recognizes that workplace harassment has occurred, or ② the Labor Office recognizes that workplace harassment has occurred. However, it is not easy for someone to get the employer to recognize they have been the recipient of workplace harassment, even with a psychiatric diagnosis of mental illness, and it takes a considerable amount of time for the Labor Office to recognize that workplace bullying has occurred. Recently, the Korea Workers' Compensation and Welfare Corporation has significantly revised its Guidelines for Investigation of whether a Mental Illness is related to Work, suggesting a detailed method for investigation of whether a mental illness is the result of workplace bullying. The following describes a case in which a female employee developed a mental illness due to bullying by her workplace superior. In this case, I will review in detail the requirements for the worker's mental illness due to workplace bullying to be recognized as an occupational accident.

II. A Case of Mental Illness Caused by Workplace Bullying

1. Workplace bullying

Eun-joo Kim (hereinafter referred to as "Eunjoo") joined company A with about 100 employees on May 25, 2020, and was in charge of mechanical design in the machine team, and the team leader was a foreigner. The perpetrator was Mr. Kang (hereinafter referred to as "Manager Kang"), the head of the sales development team, who was intentionally involved in Eunjoo's work and constantly harassed her, even though he was not in her specific department. The harassment started on November 10, 2021. Manager Kang called Eunjoo at 08:54 before work started and asked, "Where are you?" She said that she was on the 1st floor. He said, "Why are you there now?" When she returned to her desk, he shook with his finger at her and e said, "Don't leave your seat empty." She had gone out to buy a coffee and was with several co-workers, but he scolded her only.

The second was on December 23, 2021, and a few employees on the same floor as Eunjoo worked overtime and had to eat dinner, but Manager Kang

경우에는 산업재해로 인정받아 산업재해보상보험법(산재보험법)에 따른 요양급여와 휴업급여를 지급 받을 수 있다. 하지만 이러한 부분을 산재로 인정받기 위해서는 정신질환이 산재보험법상 인정되는 질환이어야 하고, 그러한 질병이 업무로부터 발생했다는 사실을 해당 근로자가 입증을 해야 한다. 현실적으로 이러한 입증이 어렵기 때문에 우선적으로 ① 회사가 직장 내 괴롭힘으로 인정하거나 ② 노동청 조사에서 직장 내 괴롭힘으로 인정받는 절차가 필요하다. 그러나 정신과 진단을 받은 피해자가 회사로부터 직장 내 괴롭힘을 인정받는 것이 쉽지 않고, 노동청을 통해서 직장 내 괴롭힘을 인정받는 데에도 상당한 시간이 소요된다. 최근에 근로복지공단은 직장 내 괴롭힘에 관련된 '정신질병 업무관련성 조사 지침'을 대폭 개정하여 괴롭힘으로 인한 정신질병에 대해 구체적으로 조사방법을 제시하고 있다. 아래는 한 여직원이 직장 상사의 괴롭힘으로 인해 정신질병으로 이어지는 사례이다. 사례를 통해 그 피해근로자가 직장 내 괴롭힘으로 인한 정신질환을 산업재해로 인정받기 위한 요건에 대해 구체적으로 살펴보고자 한다.

Ⅱ. 직장 내 괴롭힘으로 인한 정신질환을 갖게 된 사례

1. 직장 내 괴롭힘 내용

사원 김은주는 100여명 규모의 A회사에 2020년 5월 25일에 입사하여 기계팀에서 기계설계를 담당하였고, 직속 팀장은 외국인이었다. 가해자는 영업개발팀의 강덕구 팀장 (이하 '강팀장')으로 관할 부서도 아니면서, 김은주의 업무에 관여하였고 지속적으로 괴롭혔다. 괴롭힘은 2021년 11월 10일부터 시작되었다. 강팀장은 업무가 시작하기 전인 08시 54분에 김은주에게 전화를 해서 "어디냐?"고 물어 1층이라고 했더니, "이 시간에 왜 거기에 있냐?"라고 해서 자리로 돌아왔더니 무슨 용건이 있는 것도 아니었는데, 삿대질하면서 "자리 비우지 말라"고 하였다. 사실상 커피를 사러 나가서 여러 동료들과 같이 있었는데도 불구하고 김은주에게만 야단을 쳤다.

두번째는 2021년 12월 23일 김은주와 같은 층에서 몇 명이 야근을 하면서 저녁을 시켜 먹여야 했는데, 강팀장은 "은주씨는 안 먹을 거죠?"라며 일방적

ordered a late-night meal for all employees excluding Eunjoo, saying, "Eunjoo will not eat." A few days later, Eunjoo was about to leave for the day when Manager Kang shouted to the managing director next to her, "Who's going to work overtime during this busy time? Who's leaving so early?" Eunjoo did not respond, but his critical remarks remained with her for a long time.

The third time was on January 5, 2022, while Eunjoo was talking to Section Chief Jin of the Electricity Team. Manager Kang interrupted their conversation and said, "Chief Jin, do you have any work for Eunjoo?" Eunjoo felt uncomfortable about Manager Kang trying to instruct Eunjoo on tasks even though he was not a senior in her department.

The fourth time was on May 23, 2022, when Eunjoo heard that Manager Kang called her team leader and asked, "This is urgent, but will Eunjoo work overtime?" She felt very uncomfortable when the team leader of another department essentially ordered her to work overtime.

The fifth incident was on July 20, 2022, when Eunjoo made a purchase request without a price quotation. Manager Kang called her to his desk and asked, "Where did the purchase order come from? If we pay that much, how are we going to eat? Will you be responsible, Eunjoo? Don't do these things without asking your superiors first." Manager Kang verbally mocked and rebuked her. After a while, Eunjoo sent another email to Manager Kang saying, "I checked the quotation and requested the purchase again." Then, Manager Kang sent a group email to employees who had no relation to the purchase, in the Technical Sales, Electrical Management, and Machine departments, mentioning that Eunjoo was not to make the same mistake and greatly exaggerated her error of failing to include a price quotation. It would have been enough for Manager Kang to scold her over the phone, but instead he humiliated and embarrassed her in front of many employees by email. Because of this, Eunjoo felt uncomfortable while working with people in other departments, and was under a lot of stress.

2. The company's poor investigation and secondary damage

After the email incident on July 20, 2022, Eunjoo suffered extreme mental anguish, and she received a flood of work assignments. On October 20, 2022, Eunjoo experienced severe anxiety and physical pain and found it difficult to endure any longer, so she consulted a psychiatrist and was diagnosed with an adjustment disorder, a kind of mental illness. The diagnosis stated that recuperation for the next three months was required. Eunjoo applied directly to

으로 김은주만 제외하고 야식을 주문하였다. 그리고 몇일 후 김은주가 맡은 일을 서둘러 마치고 퇴근하려고 하자, 강팀장은 마침 옆에 있던 00 상무한테 큰소리로, "누구는 시간이 남아돌아서 야근하냐, 가는 사람들은 뭐냐?"며 김은주를 쳐다보면서 귀에 거슬리는 말을 하였다.

세번째는 2022년 1월 5일 업무때문에 전기팀 진○○과장과 얘기를 하고 있었는데, 강팀장이 끼어들어, "진 과장, 김은주씨한테 일 줄거 없냐?"고 하였다. 해당부서 상급자도 아니면서 김은주에게 업무를 지시하려고 하는 것에 김은주는 불쾌감을 느꼈다.

네번째는 2022년 5월 23일 강팀장은 김은주의 부서팀장에 전화를 걸어 "이거 급한데 김은주는 야근하냐?"고 묻는 소리가 들렸다. 타 부서 팀장이 해당 팀장에게 김은주의 야근을 조장하는 게 무척 불쾌하게 느껴졌다.

다섯번째는 2022년 7월 20일 김은주는 물품구매를 하면서 견적서 없이 구매를 요청하였다. 이에 대해 강팀장은 김은주에게 전화를 해서 "발주서가 어디서 나간거야? 그 금액으로 구매하면 우린 뭐 먹고 사냐. 김은주씨가 책임질 거냐. 혼자 알아서 처리하지 말고 윗사람들에게 좀 물어보고 해라." 등의 말로 비꼬며 면박을 주었다. 얼마 후 강팀장에게 '견적서를 확인하니 오류가 있어 다시 구매를 요청한다'는 이메일을 다시 보냈다. 그런데, 강팀장은 김은주를 수신인으로 보내면서, 실제 업무와 상관도 없는 영업개발팀, 전기팀, 기계팀 전원에게 이메일 참조로 전달 하였다. 그 이메일에서 김은주의 실수를 크게 확대해석하면서, 같은 실수를 하지 말아야 한다는 내용으로 발송하였다. 강팀장이 전화로 면박줬으면 됐음에도 불구하고 이메일로 타 부서원들에게 까지 창피를 주는 행위를 하였다. 이 일로 인하여 김은주는 다른 부서 직원들과 일하는데도 불편한 상황이 되었고, 많은 스트레스를 받았다.

2. 회사의 부실한 조사와 2차 피해

2022년 7월 20일 이메일 사건 후 김은주는 극심한 정신적 고통을 받았으며, 내부적으로 김은주에게 더 많은 일들이 몰렸다. 김은주는 2022년 10월 20일에 정신적 신체적 고통이 심해서 더 이상 버티는 것이 힘이 들어 정신과 의사 상담을 받았고, 적응장애 판정을 받았다. 그 진단서에는 앞으로 3개월 동안의

II. A Case of Workplace Harassment and the Criteria for Recognizing Consequent Mental Illness as an Occupational Accident Related to Work

the company president, as the company had no HR head, for paid leave with a written opinion from a psychiatrist. In a meeting with the president on October 24, 2022, she stated her mental illness was due to Manager Kang's workplace harassment. She also requested a leave of absence with pay, as this case constituted an occupational accident. Regarding this, the president asked her to bring evidence, and so she submitted the email document that she received from Manager Kang and a psychiatric diagnosis as evidence. The president then told Eunjoo, "This is more like paranoia." He repeatedly asked, "Are you not normal?" When Eunjoo asked, "Shouldn't it be paid leave because (leave) is due to bullying at work?" the president said, "Go find a company that would give you paid vacation for this."

After the meeting with the president, Eunjoo submitted an additional statement related to Manager Kang on October 31, 2022. In response, the president called in the relevant witnesses to investigate. Eunjoo hoped that the bullying case would be resolved within the company quietly, without making the problem bigger, and only receiving an apology from Manager Kang and preventing recurrence. However, rumors spread to everyone in the office when the president summoned the employees for an investigation, and the summoned employees became uncomfortable with the president's attitude toward Eunjoo. For her part, Eunjoo found it more and more difficult to work and wondered why she was working so hard if this was going to be the result, feeling it was all unfair and futile.

On November 17, 2022, Eunjoo applied for two months of unpaid leave, and the next day the unpaid leave was approved. Eunjoo is about to file for an occupational accident claim for bullying at work. Hereby I would like to review what she needs to consider when doing this.

III. Mental Illness-related Occupational Labor Laws, Precedents, and Guidelines

We will review the standards of laws and precedents regarding the requirements for bullying-induced mental illness to be recognized as an occupational accident.

1. Criteria for recognition of mental illness as an occupational accident under the IACI Act

요양이 필요하다는 소견이 기재되어 있었다. 김은주는 정신과 의사의 소견서를 가지고, 회사에 인사부서장이 없어 사장에게 진단서를 첨부하여 유급휴직을 신청하였다. 2022년 10월 24일 사장과의 면담에서 강팀장의 직장 내 괴롭힘으로 신고하려고 하니 절차대로 진행해달라고 요청하였다. 또한 이런 경우에는 산재에 해당되므로 유급으로 휴직을 요청하였다. 이에 대해 사장은 증거를 갖고 오라고 해서, 강팀장이 보낸 이메일과 정신과 진단서를 증거자료로 제출하였다. 이에 대해 사장은 김은주에게 "피해망상증 같다." "네가 정상이 아니지 않느냐?"라는 발언을 반복해서 하였다. 김은주가 (휴직이) 직장 내 괴롭힘 때문이니 유급이어야 하지 않느냐는 말에, 사장은 "놀고먹는 직원에게 돈을 주는 회사는 없다. 유급휴가를 주는 회사를 찾아가라"고 하였다.

사장과의 면담 이후 김은주는 2022년 10월 31일 강팀장과 관련된 진술서를 추가로 사측에 제출하였다. 이에 사장은 관련 참고인들을 불러 조사를 하였다. 김은주는 문제를 더 크게 만들지 않고, 강팀장으로부터 사과 정도만 받고 재발 방지를 하는 정도에서, 이 괴롭힘 사건을 회사내에서 조용히 해결하기를 바랬다. 그러나 사장이 조사를 한다면서 직원들을 소환함으로써 사무실 내 모두에게 소문이 퍼졌고, 소환을 당했던 직원들이 김은주를 대하는 태도가 불편해짐으로 인해 김은주는 더 이상 회사를 다니기 어려운 상황까지 이르게 되었다. 열심히 일했던 결과가 이런 것인가 싶어 너무 억울하고 허무하다는 생각이 들었다.

2022년 11월 17일 김은주는 2개월 무급휴직을 신청하였고, 그 다음 날 무급휴직이 승인이 되었다. 김은주는 직장 내 괴롭힘으로 산재신청을 하려고 한다. 이에 대해 고려해야 할 내용을 살펴보고자 한다.

Ⅲ. 정신질병 업무관련성 관련 법, 판례, 지침 기준

괴롭힘이 업무상 정신질환으로 인정받기 위한 요건에 대해 법령과 판례의 기준을 살펴보자.

1. 산재보험법의 정신질병에 대한 인정기준

II. A Case of Workplace Harassment and the Criteria for Recognizing Consequent Mental Illness as an Occupational Accident Related to Work

On July 16, 2019, as the Workplace Harassment Prevention law was introduced pursuant to revision of the Labor Standards Act (Article 76-2), the IACI Act stipulates that "illnesses caused by work-related mental stress, such as bullying at work and verbal abuse by customers," are recognized as occupational accidents.[47] The specific criteria for mental illness are listed in Table 3 of the Enforcement Decree to the IACI Act, which are "(f) Post-traumatic stress disorder caused by an event that can cause mental shock in relation to work; (g) An incident that may cause psychological shock, such as violence or verbal abuse from customers in relation to work, or an adjustment disorder or depressive episode caused by stress directly related to work."[48]

2. Related precedents

A ruling in 2016 stated that an adjustment disorder caused by stress due to workplace bullying constitutes an occupational illness.[49] This court ruling stated the standard criteria for judging the case as follows. "Occupational accidents, as stipulated in Article 5, Item 1 of the IACI Act, refer to illnesses caused by work while a worker is performing his or her job, so there must be a substantial causal relationship between work and the illness. However, (i) even if the main cause of the illness is not directly related to work performance, at least if work-related overwork or stress overlaps with the main cause of the illness and causes or aggravates the illness, it must be seen that there is a causal relationship between them. (ii) The causal relationship does not necessarily have to be clearly proven medically or scientifically, and considering all circumstances, even if a substantial causal relationship can be presumed between the work and the illness, the proof must be admitted as verified. (iii) The presence or absence of a causal relationship between work and illness shall be judged based on the health and physical condition of the worker concerned, not of the average person."[50]

3. Types of mental illness

Occupational mental illness does not apply to illnesses caused by congenital

---

[47] Article 37 of the IACI Act (Criteria for Recognition of Occupational Accidents).
[48] Enforcement Decree (Table 3) of the IACI Act (Specific criteria for recognition of occupational illness) Art. 34, Para. 3.
[49] Seoul Administrative Court ruling on Mar. 30, 2016. 2014gudan 2112.
[50] Supreme Court ruling on July 25, 2013. 2011du10874.

2019년 7월 16일 직장 내 괴롭힘 방지법이 「근로기준법」 개정(제76조의2)에 따라 도입되면서, 산재보상법에서도 "직장 내 괴롭힘, 고객의 폭언 등 업무상 정신적 스트레스가 원인이 되어 발생한 질병"에 대해 산업재해로 인정하게 되었다.[47] 정신질환에 대한 구체적 기준은 시행령의 별표3에 "(바) 업무와 관련하여 정신적 충격을 유발할 수 있는 사건에 의해 발생한 외상후 스트레스장애. (사) 업무와 관련하여 고객 등으로부터 폭력 또는 폭언 등 정신적 충격을 유발할 수 있는 사건 또는 이와 직접 관련된 스트레스로 인하여 발생한 적응장애 또는 우울병 에피소드"를 기술하고 있다.[48]

2. 관련 판례

직장 내 괴롭힘 스트레스로 인해 생긴 적응장애는 업무상 질병에 해당된다[49]는 판결에서 인용한 기준판례는 다음과 같다. "산업재해보상보험법 제5조 제1호에 정한 업무상재해라고 함은 근로자의 업무수행 중 그 업무에 기인하여 발생한 질병을 의미하는 것이므로 업무와 질병 사이에 상당인과관계가 있어야 한다. 그러나 (ⅰ) 질병의 주된 발생원인이 업무수행과 직접적인 관계가 없더라도 적어도 업무상의 과로나 스트레스가 질병의 주된 발생원인에 겹쳐서 질병을 유발 또는 악화시켰다면 그 사이에 인과관계가 있다고 보아야 한다. (ⅱ) 그 인과관계는 반드시 의학적, 자연과학적으로 명백히 증명하여야 하는 것은 아니고 제반 사정을 고려할 때 업무와 질병 사이에 상당인과관계가 있다고 추단되는 경우에도 그 증명이 있다고 보아야 한다. (ⅲ) 업무와 질병과의 인과관계의 유무는 보통평균인이 아니라 당해 근로자의 건강과 신체조건을 기준으로 판단하여야 한다."[50]

3. 정신질병의 대상

업무상 정신질병은 선천적 신체의 장애로 인하여 발생하는 질병은 해당되지

---

47) 산재보험법 제37조 (업무상의 재해인정기준)
48) 산재보험법 시행령 별표3 (업무상 질병에 대한 구체적인 인정기준 – 시행령 제34조의 제3항)
49) 서울행정법원 2016.3.30. 선고 2014구단2112 판결.
50) 대법원 2013. 7. 25. 선고 2011두10874 판결 등

physical disorders, but refers to mental illnesses related to work-related psychological stress. Representative mental illnesses related to workplace bullying include (i) depressive episodes (depression), (ii) anxiety disorder, and (iii) adjustment disorder.[51]

① Workers with depression have reduced concentration, increased fatigue, and increased accident rates and absenteeism, which affects work efficiency. This depression impairs workers' social behavior, making them less likely to participate in conversation and less cooperative, affecting interpersonal relationships and even leading to suicide.

② Anxiety disorder refers to a mental illness that interferes with daily life due to various forms of abnormal or pathological anxiety and fear. Anxiety disorders include panic disorder and various phobias (fear of heights, agoraphobia, social phobia, etc.). Panic disorder has physical symptoms such as shortness of breath, a feeling of staggering, sweating, and choking. In particular, cognitive symptoms can include feeling like one is dying or going crazy and are characteristic of "panic attacks."

③ Adjustment disorder can be diagnosed as anxiety disorder or depression depending on the pattern of accompanying major symptoms. It is characterized by the presence of symptoms, either emotional or behavioral, in response to a recognizable stressor. Adjustment disorder appears within 3 months of the onset of an identifiable stressor and does not persist for more than 6 months once the stressor is resolved. Adjustment disorder is one of the most commonly used diagnoses in psychiatry, and tends to be given when the symptoms do not meet the diagnostic criteria for other mental disorders.

4. Work-related mental illness investigation procedure (Guideline No. 2021-05)

When the Korea Workers' Compensation and Welfare Corporation (hereafter referred to as "the Welfare Corporation") receives an occupational accident application for workplace harassment, it determines whether to recognize an incident as an occupational accident through the following procedure: ① Receipt of medical care benefit application → ② Confirmation of illness name and clinical psychological test result → ③ Incident investigation → ④ Preparation of incident investigation report → ⑤ Confirmation of medical opinion by a medical

---

[51] Korea Workers' Compensation and Welfare Service, "Guidelines for Investigation of whether a Mental Illness is related to Work," No. 2021-05, Jan. 13, 2021.

않고, 업무와 관련된 심리적 스트레스와 관련이 있는 정신질병을 대상으로 한다. 직장 내 괴롭힘과 관련된 대표적 정신질병으로 ① 우울에피소드(우울증), ② 불안장애, ③ 적응장애 등이 있다.[51]

① 우울증의 증상은 의욕저하와 우울감이 주요 증상으로 나타난다. 우울증이 있는 근로자는 집중력이 감소하고 피로감이 증가하며 사고율, 결근율 등이 증가하여 업무 효율에 영향을 준다. 이러한 우울증은 근로자의 사회적 행동에 손상을 보여, 대화에 덜 참여하고, 다른 사람과 협력하는 마음이 적어져 대인관계에 영향을 주게 되며, 우울증으로 인한 자살에 이르기도 한다.

② 불안장애는 다양한 형태의 비정상적, 병적인 불안과 공포로 인하여 일상생활에 장애를 일으키는 정신질병을 말한다. 불안장애에 해당하는 질병으로는 공황장애, 각종 공포증(고소 공포증, 광장 공포증, 사회 공포증 등)이 있다. 공황장애는 호흡곤란, 휘청거리는 느낌, 발한, 질식감 등의 신체증상을 가지고 있다. 특히, 죽을 것 같은 혹은 미칠 것 같은 느낌의 인지적 증상이 '공황발작'의 특징이다.

③ 적응장애는 동반하는 주요 증상의 양상에 따라 불안장애 또는 우울증 등으로 진단이 가능하다. 특징은 인식 가능한 스트레스 요인에 대한 반응으로 감정적 또는 행동적으로 증상이 존재하는 적응장애이다. 적응장애는 확인 가능한 스트레스 요인이 시작된 후 3개월 이내에 나타나고, 스트레스 요인이 해소되면 6개월 이상 지속되지 않는 특징이 있다. 적응장애는 정신과에서 흔하게 사용하는 진단 중 하나로 다른 정신질환의 진단기준에 미치지 못하는 경우에 진단하는 경향이 있다.

4. 근로복지공단 업무상 정신질환 조사 절차 (지침 2021-05호)

근로복지공단은 직장 내 괴롭힘에 대한 산재신청을 접수 받게 되면, 다음의 절차를 거쳐 산재인정 여부를 결정한다. ① 요양급여 신청 접수 → ② 질병명과 임상심리검사 결과 확인 → ③ 재해조사 → ④ 재해조사서 작성 → ⑤ 공단 전문의사의 의학적 소견 확인 → ⑥ 업무상 질병판정위원회 심의 의뢰

여기서 특히 주의할 점은 질병명과 임상심리검사 결과에 대해 신청인이 일반

---

[51] 근로복지공단, "정신질병 업무관련성 조사 지침", 제2021-05호, 2021.1.13.

doctor working for the Welfare Corporation → ⑥ Request for deliberation by the Occupational Illness Judgment Committee.

It needs to be noted here that the applicant's treatment in a psychiatric clinic is not enough for the name of the illness to be determined and the results of the clinical psychological test. A psychiatric diagnosis at a Welfare Corporation-affiliated occupational accident hospital or general hospitals must be submitted. The name of the illness must include depression, anxiety disorder, or adjustment disorder to be considered a mental illness.

During the incident investigation, the circumstances of the incident, work-related matters, confirmation of major work-related stress factors, and evidence must be collected. The circumstances of the incident are confirmed through statements from the applicant, the applicant's employer, and fellow workers. For work-related matters, the workplace should be observed and daily work stressors checked. "Daily work stressors" shall be checked according to a checklist of 11 items to determine the major work stress factors, with each item including answers to Who, What, Where, When, Why and How. The 11 items on the checklist are:

① Assess the severity of work-related incidents,
② Assess the severity of verbal abuse/violence/sexual harassment,
③ Assess the severity of changes in the quantity and quality of work,
④ Assess the severity of work mistakes/responsibility,
⑤ Assess the severity of complaints/conflicts with customers,
⑥ Assess the severity of conflict(s) with the company,
⑦ Assess the severity of placement change(s),
⑧ Assess the severity of conflict(s) in the workplace,
⑨ Assess the severity of maladjustment to work,
⑩ Assess the viewpoints of bullying and discrimination, and
⑪ Assess the severity of other work-related stressors.

Ⅳ. Conclusion

In order for Eunjoo's case mentioned above to be recognized as an occupational accident, evidence must be gathered in accordance with the Welfare Corporation's Guidelines for Investigation of whether a Mental Illness is related to Work. First, a recent diagnosis of mental illness must be issued for the specific illness by a general hospital. Second, a specific description of the incident(s) of bullying at the workplace must be made and answer Who, What, Where, When, Why and How. Particularly in this case, the company's

정신과에서 진료받은 내용으로는 충분치 않고, 근로복지공단의 산재판정병원이나 종합병원 급 이상의 정신과 진단서를 제출하여야 한다. 질병명은 정신질병으로 간주하는 우울증, 불안장애, 적응장애에 속해야 한다.

재해조사에서 있어서는 재해발생 경위, 업무관련 사항, 주요 업무상 스트레스 요인 확인, 증거자료를 수집하여야 한다. 재해발생 경위는 신청인, 신청인의 회사, 동료 근로자 등의 진술을 통해 재해 발생 경위를 확인한다. 업무관련 사항으로 사업장 개요와 일상적 업무상 스트레스 요인을 확인한다. 특히, 주요 업무상 스트레스 요인 11가지 기준을 가진 체크리스트로 확인한다. 그런 후 11가지 해당사항에 대하여 각각의 질문지에 대한 답변을 6하원칙에 따라 구체적으로 기술한다. 그 내용은 다음과 같다.

① 업무관련 사고의 심각도 파악
② 폭언-폭력-성희롱의 심각도 파악
③ 업무의 양과 질 변화 심각도 파악
④ 업무의 실수-책임 심각도 파악
⑤ 민원-고객과의 갈등 심각도 파악
⑥ 회사와의 갈등 심각도 파악
⑦ 배치전환의 심각도 파악
⑧ 직장 내 갈등 심각도 파악
⑨ 업무 부적응의 심각도 파악
⑩ 괴롭힘-차별의 심각도 파악
⑪ 기타 업무상 스트레스 요인의 심각도를 파악한다.

Ⅳ. 시사점

앞에서 언급한 김은주 씨가 산재로 인정받기 위해서는 근로복지공단의 '정신질병 업무 관련성 조사지침'에 따른 준비가 필요하다. 첫번째는 정신질병에 대한 진단서를 종합병원급에서 새로이 발급 받아야 한다. 둘째로 본인의 직장 내 괴롭힘에 대하여 6하 원칙에 따른 구체적인 기술이 필요하다. 특히, 이번 사건에 있어 직장 내 괴롭힘 신고에 대한 회사의 부적절한 조치와 이로 인한 2차 피해를 구체적으로 기술하여야 한다. 이로 인하여 정신질환이

inappropriate investigation into the report of workplace harassment and the resulting secondary damage must be described in detail. These occurrences worsened Eunjoo's mental state and made it difficult for her to continue working, so she had no choice but to take a leave of absence. In this way, if it is proven that her mental illness occurred from and was exacerbated by bullying at work, it will be recognized as an occupational accident.

The workplace not only provides a means of income for workers, but is also an important place where workers spend most of their time. Workers form interpersonal relationships through work and achieve self-realization through personal growth. In such an important place, workplace bullying is not only a violation of workers' personal rights, it can also cause a variety of mental disorders. Therefore, the employer must ensure a safe environment for workers in accordance with the principle of good faith accompanying the labor contract, and bear in mind that failure to uphold the duty to protect workers will incur liability for criminal[52] and civil[53] violations.

When Workplace Harassment Occurs, What Measures Should an Employer Take?

I. Introduction

Korea's workplace culture has a long tradition of top-down military-style hierarchies, but a new workplace culture is emerging as the workplace harassment prevention law is strictly applied, going in a desirable direction where individual personality is respected. A superior has the right to direct the work, and a subordinate has the duty to perform the work accordingly. However, if excessive work orders, abusive language, or threatening shouts are repeated, the moral rights of workers will be infringed.[54]

For this procedure to deal with workplace bullying, Article 93 of the Labor

---

[52] For violations of Article 76-2 of the Labor Standards Act, an administrative fine of up to KRW 10 million is charged.
[53] Supreme Court ruling on Feb. 23, 1999, 97da12082.
[54] Supreme Court ruling on Feb. 10, 1998: 95da39533: Whether the employer is liable for compensation for harassment in the workplace.

더욱 악화되었고 계속 근무하는 것이 어렵게 되어 휴직할 수 밖에 없었던 이유를 설명해야 한다. 이와 같이 본인의 정신 질병이 직장 내 괴롭힘에서 발생했다는 사실과 이로 인해 더욱 악화되었다는 사실을 입증하게 된다면 산업재해로 인정받을 수 있을 것이다.

직장은 근로자에게 생계수단을 제공할 뿐만 아니라 근로자가 대부분의 시간을 보내는 중요한 장소이다. 근로자는 직장생활을 통해서 인간관계를 형성하고 개인적 성장을 통해 자아실현을 하게 된다. 이렇게 중요한 장소인데, 이러한 사업장 내에서의 직장 내 괴롭힘은 근로자의 인격권을 침해하는 행위일 뿐만 아니라 근로자에게 각종 정신질환을 유발하게 한다. 따라서 사용자는 근로계약에 수반되는 신의성실원칙에 따라 근로자에게 안전한 환경을 보장하기 위하여 필요한 조치를 하여야 하고, 이를 위반하는 경우에는 근로자 보호의무 위반으로 인하여 형사책임[52]과 민사책임[53]을 져야 한다는 사실을 명심하여야 할 것이다.

직장 내 괴롭힘 사건 사례를 통해서 본 사용자의 적절한 조치

I. 사실관계

우리나라의 직장문화는 상명하복 군대식 위계질서의 오랜 전통을 가지고 있었으나, 최근에 직장 내 괴롭힘 방지법이 엄격하게 적용됨에 따라 새로운 직장 문화가 생기고 있다. 개인의 인격이 존중되는 바람직한 방향으로 가고 있다. 상급자는 업무지시권이 있고, 하급자는 이에 따라 업무를 수행해야 할 의무가 있다. 그러나 무리한 업무 지시, 폭언이나 위협적인 고성 등이 반복되는 경우에는 근로자의 인격권을 침해하게 된다.[54]

이러한 직장 내 괴롭힘 처리 절차를 위해서 「근로기준법」 제93조 (취업

---

[52] 「근로기준법」 제76조의2 위반시, 1천만 원 이하의 과태료 부과.
[53] 대법원 1999.2.23. 선고 97다12082 판결.
[54] 대법원 1998.2.10. 선고 95다39533 판결: 직장 내에서 성희롱 관련 사용자의 배상책임 여부.

Ⅲ. When Workplace Harassment Occurs, What Measures Should an Employer Take?

Standards Act (Preparation and Reporting of Employment Rules) No. 11 mandates that "the measures to be taken in cases of occurrence of workplace harassment" be stipulated in the rules of Employment Accordingly, all workplaces employing 10 or more people must act in accordance with the details of workplace harassment stipulated in those rules of employment. In other words, the employer must responsibly handle reports of harassment between workers in the workplace. Even when such harassment is reported to the Labor Office, the Labor Inspector's scope of investigation is limited to whether the employer has conducted an objective investigation into workplace harassment in accordance with Article 76-3 of the Labor Standards Act (Measures in the case of workplace harassment), whether appropriate measures have been taken according to the results of the investigation, and whether reasonable measures have been taken to protect the worker victim(s).[55]

Therefore, if an employer receives a report on workplace harassment or recognizes that workplace harassment has occurred, that employer shall, without delay, conduct an objective investigation to confirm the facts of such report or witnessed harassment. In this regard, I would like to review the desirable way to handle workplace harassment and look in detail at appropriate company actions.

Ⅱ. A Case of Workplace Harassment and Follow-up Measures by the Company

1. Facts

The company is a branch of a multinational corporation, and in Korea, it is managed by each department head for its own operation without a control center. The branch manager did not have authority to exercise personnel or business operation rights.

There were many cases where a certain female director (perpetrator) yelled at the branch manager or company executives and abused them. A number of employees complained about the abusive language, insulting words, and sexually harassing remarks, claiming they amounted to workplace harassment.

1) At around 10 a.m. on April 4, 2022, according to the statements of a number of witnesses, the perpetrator's raised voice was heard coming from a conference room where the perpetrator and the branch manager were alone. Even though the director did not outrank the branch manager, it is unacceptable for the perpetrator to use abusive language with the Korean

---

[55] Ministry of Employment and Labor, "Manual on Judgment, Prevention and Handling of Workplace Harassment," Feb. 2019.

규칙의 작성과 신고) 제11호에서는 "직장 내 괴롭힘의 예방 및 발생 시 조치 등에 관한 사항"을 취업규칙의 필수 기재사항으로 두고 있다. 이에 따라 10인 이상을 사용하는 모든 사업장은 취업규칙에 규정된 직장 내 괴롭힘에 대한 내용에 따라 필요한 조치를 해야 한다. 즉, 직장 내 발생한 근로자 간의 괴롭힘 문제에 대해서는 사업주가 전속적으로 책임을 갖고 처리해야 한다. 노동청에 신고된 경우에도 근로감독관은 사업장에서 발생한 직장 내 괴롭힘에 대해 사업주가 「근로기준법」 제76조의3(직장 내 괴롭힘 발생 시 조치)에 따라 객관적인 조사를 했는지, 조사결과에 따른 적절한 조치를 하였는지, 피해 근로자 보호에 대한 합당한 조치를 했는지 등에 대해서만 조사를 하게 된다.[55]

따라서 사용자는 직장 내 괴롭힘에 대한 신고가 접수되었거나 직장 내 괴롭힘 발생 사실을 인지한 경우에는 지체없이 당사자 등을 대상으로 그 사실관계를 확인하기 위하여 객관적인 조사를 실시하여야 한다. 이와 관련하여 최근 발생한 직장 내 괴롭힘 사건에 대한 회사의 대응을 통해 바람직한 처리방법을 살펴보고자 한다.

II. 직장 내 괴롭힘 사례와 처리내용

1. 사실관계

해당 사업장은 다국적 기업으로 한국에서는 부서장 체계로 관리가 되고 있어, 지사장은 직원들에 대한 인사권이나 업무집행권의 권한이 없었다.

여성 전무(행위자)가 지사장이나 회사 임원들에게 고성을 지르며 폭언을 하는 경우가 많았다. 다수의 직원들은 행위자의 폭언, 모욕감을 주는 행위, 남자 직원에 대한 성희롱 발언 등을 이유로 직장 내 괴롭힘 문제를 제기하였다.
1) 2022년 4월 4일 오전 10시경, 다수의 목격자들의 진술에 따르면, 행위자와 지사장이 단둘이 있는 회의실에서 행위자의 고성이 외부로 들렸다고 한다. 지사장이 행위자의 직속상사는 아니지만 경력이 많고 고령자임에도 불구하고 많은 직원들 앞에서 폭언과 고성을 한 행위는 용납될 수 없는 행위다.

---

[55] 고용노동부, "직장 내 괴롭힘 판단 및 예방과 대응 매뉴얼", 2019.2.

III. When Workplace Harassment Occurs, What Measures Should an Employer Take?

branch manager and shout at him where many junior employees could hear, considering his age and job experience.
2) Between March 3 and May 11, 2022, the perpetrator used sexually harassing language with the male sales manager four times. ① "You are pretty. You are working hard." ② "Our conclusion is that the pretty boy can brag about the company," ③ "With pretty boys, and ④ "The prettiest boy should do it."
3) On March 10, 2022, the perpetrator called manager A from another department on the phone and said, "You are the one who failed to meet the target," "How long do I have to waste my time writing emails like this to you," etc. The perpetrator's language was abusive and included insulting remarks while undermining the performance of this manager.
4) The perpetrator used abusive language or insulting words against a number of employees.
   ① The perpetrator wrote the following about a specific employee in an e-mail she sent to the head of the sales department and CC'd several employees. "Where else is there such a manager in his 30s who can't write emails properly or even introduce himself?"
   ② The perpetrator mentioned to assistant manager C in her marketing department: "Of the sales team members, Mr. Yoon and Mr. Han are surplus manpower."
   ③ The perpetrator spoke openly about the branch manager to other employees. "The branch manager has no influence, and he has no connections with head office executives. He's a country man from a poor background."

2. Details of the company's response actions

The company had difficulties determining on its own investigation because the perpetrator and employee victim were the managing director and the branch manager of this foreign company, so an external labor law firm was asked to investigate. The perpetrator was disciplined according to the results of this investigation.

This author's labor law firm, which received the request to investigate the reports of workplace harassment, confirmed prior information from the company, as well as the victims, perpetrator, and witnesses. In addition, prior to the investigation, investigators received a written confidentiality agreement from each related interviewee so that they could prevent secondary damage from occurring in the future.

This labor law firm first conducted interviews and written investigations with the employee victims. In addition, multiple witnesses were interviewed to confirm

2) 2022년 3월 3일부터 5월 11일 사이, 행위자는 영업부장을 4회에 걸쳐 성희롱을 하며 괴롭혔다. ① "우리 예쁜이가 고생하네", ② "예쁜 애가 회사 자랑하면 된다는 게 우리 결론", ③ "좀 예쁜 애들로", ④ "젤 예쁜 애가 해야 할 듯" 등 지속적으로 남자의 외모를 비하하는 메시지를 보냈다.
3) 2022년 3월 10일 행위자는 타 부서의 A상무와 전화하면서 "성과가 나오지 않는 것은 상무님 이시다", "제가 언제까지 상무님께 이 따위 이메일을 쓰는데 시간을 낭비해야 합니까?"라고 하는 등 A상무의 업무성과를 깎아내리면서 인격모독적 발언과 폭언을 하였다.
4) 행위자는 다수의 직원들에게 폭언이나 인격모독을 하였다.
   ① 행위자는 영업부서장과 몇 명의 직원을 참조로 발신한 이메일에서 특정 직원에 대하여 다음 같이 적었다. "이메일 하나 똑바로 못쓰고 자기소개도 못하는 30대가 어디 있어요?"
   ② 마케팅 부서의 C 대리에게는 다음과 같이 적었다. "영업팀원 중 윤○○, 한○○는 잉여인력이다."
   ③ 행위자는 다른 직원들에게 지사장에 대해 공공연하게 얘기했다. "지사장은 아무런 영향력이 없는 사람이고, 본사 임원진과의 인맥도 없으며, 지사장은 가난한 배경을 가진 시골 사람이다."

2. 회사의 조치 내용

회사는 행위자와 피해자가 외국기업의 전무이사와 지사장과 관련이 있어 자체적으로 판단이 어려워 외부의 노무법인에 맡겨 사실 조사를 하였다. 또한 그 결과에 따라 행위자를 징계하였다.

직장 내 괴롭힘 조사 의뢰를 받은 노무법인은 회사로부터 사전 정보를 파악하여 피해자, 행위자, 참고인을 확정하였다. 그리고 그 대상자들에게 조사에 앞서 비밀서약서를 받아 차후 발생할 수 있는 2차 피해를 예방하기 위한 조치를 하였다.

노무법인은 신고된 사건내용에 대해 신고자들과 면담과 서면 조사를 한 후, 복수의 참고인을 조사하여 사실관계를 확인하였다. 마지막으로 행위자와 면담을 통해 당시 상황에 대한 사실관계를 확인하고, 행위자에게 자신의

Ⅲ. When Workplace Harassment Occurs, What Measures Should an Employer Take?

the facts. Finally, through an interview with the perpetrator, it was able to confirm the facts of the situation at the time, and the perpetrator was given opportunity to explain her actions.

With these objective findings, the company held a disciplinary committee meeting in accordance with the rules of employment, and explained the facts to the perpetrator and gave her an opportunity to explain her actions in light of the confirmed facts. Finally, the disciplinary committee decided on a six-month salary reduction and a severe warning on the perpetrator's work record.

Ⅲ. Guidance on Employer Actions When Workplace Harassment Occurs

1. Guiding principle

When a report of workplace harassment is received, or such an incident is seen by the company's personnel manager, that manager shall conduct an objective investigation with related employees to confirm the facts without delay. Here, "related employees" refers to the alleged victim, the alleged perpetrator, and coworkers who witnessed the event(s). Prior to starting an investigation, it is necessary to ensure that the related employees sign a confidentiality agreement to prevent secondary damage from the investigation.[56]

2. Initiate investigation and take appropriate actions promptly

When a workplace harassment report is received, the employer shall investigate the persons concerned without delay. This is because, first, there is a need for the alleged victim(s) to receive prompt relief if the harassment actually occurred. Second, over time, memories of facts fade. Third, if a prompt investigation is not carried out, the employer may be deemed to have failed to take measures required by law.

When an investigation into a person is initiated, employer actions can include allowing the alleged victim(s) to work from work or go on paid leave if requested by the alleged victim(s) so that additional damage does not occur between the alleged victim and the alleged perpetrator.

---

[56] Lee, Sang-gon, "A Study on Improving the Workplace Harassment Law," Ajou Graduate School Ph.D. thesis, Aug. 2020, pp. 141-143.

행위에 대한 소명의 기회를 주었다.

이러한 객관적 결과물을 가지고 회사는 취업규칙에 근거하여 징계위원회를 열어 사실관계에 대해 설명하면서 행위자가 확정된 사실관계에 대해 소명 할 기회를 주었다. 최종적으로, 징계위원회는 행위자에 대해 6개월간의 감봉조치와 사내 괴롭힘에 대해 엄중히 경고하는 서면징계를 결정하였다.

III. 사용자의 직장 내 괴롭힘 발생과 처리 방향

1. 처리 원칙

직장 내 괴롭힘에 대한 사건이 접수되었거나 인지 된 경우 회사의 인사담당자는 지체 없이 당사자 대상으로 사실관계를 확인하기 위하여 객관적으로 조사를 실시하여야 한다. 여기서 당사자라고 하면 신고자인 피해근로자, 가해근로자(행위자), 관련 사항에 대한 목격을 한 직장 동료 등 참고인을 의미한다. 조사를 시작하기에 앞서 조사 당사자들에게 비밀준수 서약서를 작성하게 하여 해당 조사로 인한 2차 피해가 발생하지 않도록 유의해야 한다.[56]

2. 신속한 조사와 적절한 조치

직장 내 괴롭힘 사건이 접수되었거나 인지된 경우에는 사용자는 지체 없이 당사자를 조사해야 한다. 조사는 최대한 신속하게 이루어져야 한다. 그 이유는 첫째, 피해 근로자에 대한 신속한 구제가 필요하기 때문이다. 둘째로 시간이 지남에 따라 사실관계에 대한 당사자들의 기억이 희미해지기 때문이다. 따라서 빠른 시일 내에 사실관계를 확정하는 것이 필요하다. 셋째로, 신속한 조사가 이루어지지 않으면 사업주가 법에 의해 조치를 하지 않는 것으로 간주될 수 있기 때문이다.

사용자는 당사자에 대한 조사가 시작된 경우 피해자와 행위자 사이에 2차 피해가 발생하지 않도록 피해자의 요청이 있는 경우에는 재택근무, 유급휴가 등 적절한 조치를 해야 한다.

---

56) 이상곤, "직장 내 괴롭힘 법제의 개선방안 연구", 아주대학원 박사학위논문, 2020.8. 141-143면.

III. When Workplace Harassment Occurs, What Measures Should an Employer Take?

3. Ensure the investigation is objective

Investigations are conducted beginning with the alleged victim(s).

① As far as possible, the facts shall be clearly established according to the six basic outline of Who, What, Where, When, Why and How. Check if any concrete data exists such as cell phone voice recordings, KakaoTalk (or other messenger service) messages, and e-mails. When investigating an alleged victim, that person's psychological and emotional situation should be considered. Investigations are carried out by checking the facts from the alleged victim's point of view, and above all, the investigators need to listen for the immediate needs of the alleged victim.

② The second part of the investigation secures the statements of relevant persons who can confirm or reject the facts described in the alleged victim's statement. At this stage, it is necessary to focus on the facts, not the opinions of the alleged victim. It is also necessary, for simplicity, to interview only the essential persons. And for better objectivity, to interview two or more employees on each major aspect of the report to secure corroboration of statements.

③ The third part of the investigation is interviewing the alleged perpetrator. It is necessary to verify the accuracy of the claims made by the alleged victim(s) and related persons. During the investigation, the person in charge must avoid deciding for him or herself whether the alleged perpetrator is guilty or not. In addition, by looking at the situation for the perpetrator at the time of the alleged harassment, it is necessary to listen to the details of the reason(s) given for the act and to confirm whether the act is necessary for work. If possible, the perpetrator should be informed that the primary purpose of the investigation or disciplinary process is to improve the workplace atmosphere, not to punish.

In the process of investigating the related employees, there are many things that can be missed by written records alone. Therefore, it is necessary to supplement the investigation with recordings.

Investigations are conducted by the HR department within the company, but if the harassment is related to the HR department or the employer is the alleged direct perpetrator, entrusting the investigation to an external expert for a fair investigation of the facts can increase the trust of the related employees and ensure that the investigation is carried out objectively.

4. Judgment of facts and appropriate dispositions of the company

3. 객관적인 조사

조사는 피해자인 신고자(피해자) 부터 실시한다.
① 처음에 제출된 진술서의 사실관계를 확인하면서, 가급적 사실관계에 대해 육하원칙에 따라 명확히 사실관계를 확정한다. 핸드폰의 녹취록이나 카톡 메시지, 이메일 등 객관적인 자료가 있는지 확인한다. 피해자를 조사할 경우에는 피해자의 심리와 정서적 상황을 고려하여야 한다. 조사는 피해자의 입장에서 사실관계를 확인하고 피해자에 대한 긴급구제의 내용이 무엇인지 우선 청취하여 조치한다.
② 두번째 조사는 피해자의 진술서에 기술된 사실관계를 확인할 수 있는 관련인들에 대한 진술확보이다. 이 조사단계에서는 피해자의 판단이 아닌 사실관계의 여부를 중심으로 확인해야 한다. 가급적 소수의 인원을 조사대상으로 삼되, 한 사안에 대해 2인 이상을 조사하여 객관적 시각을 유지하는 것이 필요하다.
③ 세번째는 행위자 조사이다. 피해자와 관련자에 관하여 조사된 사실에 대한 진위여부를 확인해야 한다. 인사 담당자는 행위자 조사과정에서 사실관계를 확인하면서 그 사실에 대한 법률적 판단을 해서는 안된다. 그리고 가해자의 입장에 대한 조사를 통해 왜 그러한 행동을 했는지에 대한 내용을 청취하여 행위의 업무상 필요성 여부를 확인해야 한다. 가급적 가해자에게 조사과정이나 징계과정은 직장 문화의 개선에 위한 것이지, 처벌을 위한 것이 목적이 아님을 알려주어야 한다.

당사자들에 대한 조사 과정에서는 기록만으로는 놓칠 수 있는 것이 많다. 그래서 녹취를 통해 조사내용을 보완하는 것이 필요하다.

조사는 회사 내 인사부서에서 이루어지지만, 괴롭힘이 인사부와 관련되었거나 사용자가 직접적인 가해자인 경우에는 사실관계의 공정한 조사를 위해 외부 전문가에 맡겨서 조사를 하는 것이 당사자들의 신뢰감을 얻을 수 있고, 조사가 객관적으로 이루어질 수 있다.

4. 사실관계에 대한 판단과 적절한 회사의 처분

III. When Workplace Harassment Occurs, What Measures Should an Employer Take?

After confirming the facts in a report of workplace harassment, it is necessary to determine whether the relevant act(s) fall under what has been determined to be workplace harassment. In this regard, since the person in charge is not a legal expert, it is better to understand the legal view, based on the facts, through a request sent to the Ministry of Employment and Labor or seeking the opinion of a labor attorney with related experience.

If the facts of the case are confirmed and workplace harassment is recognized to have occurred according to a legal expert, a disciplinary committee shall be convened to determine the disciplinary action in accordance with the company's in-house rules of employment. Of particular note is that the disciplinary committee should check the facts and give the perpetrator an opportunity to explain, so that the reasons for disciplinary action remain clear.

Once a disciplinary committee decides on the type of disciplinary action, objective facts such as the degree of workplace harassment, the length of service and role of the perpetrator, and whether or not there has been a previous violation must be taken into consideration to prevent abuse of the authority to discipline. In this case, the employer can increase victim and perpetrator acceptability of disciplinary action only by explaining the disciplinary actions to the victim(s) and hearing their views beforehand.

If the alleged victim's report of workplace harassment is confirmed to be true during the investigation process, appropriate actions for the victim(s) can include a change of workplace, a change in job assignment, or a granting of paid leave, ideally in accordance with the victim's stated preference. Whether that is possible or not, the victim's preference should at least be heard.

Finally, the company must remind the perpetrator, victim(s), and employees involved in the investigation to strictly adhere to the confidentiality agreement they signed in relation to the investigation process. Revealing the investigation findings to the public may result in additional damage that may be undesirable for both sides.

IV. Conclusion

In calculating whether workplace harassment has occurred, the scope of actions that are appropriate to the performance of work can be ambiguous. If the workplace harassment leads to a court decision, this will result in damage to the alleged perpetrator, the alleged victim(s), and the company organization. Lawsuits over workplace harassment claims can also lead to undesirable consequences, so it is best to resolve such reports fairly and in accordance with the company's

피해자가 신고한 직장 내 괴롭힘에 대한 사실관계를 확정하고 나면, 해당 행위 등이 직장 내 괴롭힘에 해당되는지에 대한 판단을 해야 한다. 이 부분에 대해서 인사담당자는 법률전문가가 아니므로 법률적인 판단은 사실관계를 기초로 하여 노동부 질의회신을 통하거나 법률전문가인 공인노무사의 의견서를 받아 판단하는 것이 좋다.

사실관계가 대한 확정이 되고, 이에 대한 법률 전문가의 의견을 얻어 직장 내 괴롭힘으로 혐의가 인정되는 경우에는 회사의 사내 규정인 취업규칙에 따라 징계위원회를 열어 징계를 결정해야 한다. 특히, 징계위원회는 사실관계에 대한 확인과 가해자에게 소명의 기회를 주어 투명한 징계가 이루어 질 수 있도록 해야 한다.

징계위원회에서 양정을 결정할 때에는 직장 내 괴롭힘의 정도, 가해자의 근속 기간과 역할, 기존의 취업규칙 위반 여부 등 객관적인 사실을 함께 고려하여 징계권이 남용되지 않도록 해야 한다. 이 경우 사용자는 징계 등의 조치를 하기 전에 그 조치에 대하여 피해 근로자에게 설명을 해주고 의견을 들어야 피해자와 가해자로부터 징계의 수용성을 높일 수 있다.

조사과정에서 피해자의 직장 내 괴롭힘의 신고가 사실로 확인된 경우에는 피해자의 의견을 들어 근무장소의 변경, 배치전환, 유급휴가의 명령 등 적절한 조치를 해야 한다.

마지막으로 회사는 본 직장 내 괴롭힘 사건에 대해 가해자, 피해자, 관련 조사대상이 된 직원에게 조사과정에 대한 내용에 대해 비밀 준수를 엄격히 지키도록 안내해야 한다. 이를 위반한 경우에는 2차 피해를 일으킬 수 있기 때문이다.

Ⅳ. 시사점

직장 내 괴롭힘은 업무의 적정범위에 대한 판단이 애매모호하다. 이러한 직장 내 괴롭힘의 문제가 사법적 판단으로 이어지게 되면, 가해자, 피해자, 회사조직 모두에게 피해를 주게 된다. 또한 결과도 바람직하지 않은 방향으로 이어질 수 있기 때문에 직장 내 괴롭힘의 문제는 회사 내부의 처리 절차에 따라 종결되는 것이 바람직하다. 이를 위해서 인사담당자는 관련 사건에 대한 처리

A Case Study on Workplace Harassment against a New Employee

I. Introduction

Since the Workplace Harassment Prevention Act was introduced in the Labor Standards Act and enforced for employers in April 2021, many companies have experienced claims of workplace harassment. In the past, the general workplace atmosphere (in which new employees or lower-level employees accepted it as part of adapting to the existing workplace) is no longer placed on the individual alone, but the onus is now on organizations to improve. The employer's obligation introduced in April 2021 means an objective investigation must be conducted without delay if a worker reports workplace harassment to the company. If workplace harassment is confirmed, measures must be taken that are appropriate to the harassment of the victim, and disciplinary action must be taken against the perpetrator (offender). The claimant shall not be treated unfavorably because of the claim of workplace harassment. Of particular note is that all those involved in a claim of workplace harassment are obligated to maintain the confidentiality of the claim. If the employer fails to comply with these obligations, the fine for negligence shall be not more than 5 million won.[57]

A report was received that an employee recently hired by a foreign IT company had been harassed several times at the workplace by the team leader. Through the company's appropriate handling of this case, we can take a detailed look at how employers have dealt with such incidents. I would also like to take a look at what constitutes workplace bullying, the standard for determining whether workplace bullying has occurred and how the company's disciplinary

---

[57] However, unfavorable treatment of the complainant or the victimized worker by the employer shall be punished by imprisonment for not more than three years or by a fine not exceeding 30 million won (Labor Standards Act, Article 76-3 (6)).

능력을 키워야 하고, 근로자들도 직장 내 괴롭힘이 항상 발생할 수 있다는 사실을 인지하여 자신이 직장 내 괴롭힘의 가해자가 될 수도 있고 피해자가 될 수 있다는 사실에 대한 경각심이 필요하다.

직장 내 괴롭힘 처리 사례 (신입직원)

I. 사실관계

직장 내 괴롭힘 방지법이 2021년 4월부터 사업주에 대한 강행규정으로 도입되어 시행됨에 따라 많은 사업장에서 직장 내 괴롭힘에 대한 문제가 제기되고 있다. 기존에는 신입직원이나 하급직원들이 직장 내 적응과정으로 수용되었던 일반적인 직장 내 분위기가 더 이상 개인의 문제가 아닌 조직 개선의 문제로 대두되고 있다. 이번에 도입된 사업주의 의무는 근로자가 직장 내 괴롭힘에 대해 회사에 신고를 하는 경우 이에 대하여 회사는 지체없이 객관적인 조사를 실시하여야 한다. 그 밖에도 직장 내 괴롭힘으로 확인된 경우, 피해 근로자의 요구에 따른 적절한 조치가 이루어져야 하고, 가해 근로자에 대해서도 징계조치를 해야 한다. 그리고 직장 내 괴롭힘을 신고한 피해근로자에게 불리한 처우를 하여서는 아니된다. 특히, 해당 직장 내 고충 부서와 관련 사람들은 사건에 대한 비밀 준수의무가 있다. 이러한 과정에 대해 사업주가 절차를 위반한 경우 500만 원 이하의 과태료 처벌조항을 적용 받는다.[57]

최근, 한 외국계 IT회사에서는 입사한 신입직원이 해당 팀장으로부터 수차례에 걸쳐 직장 내 괴롭힘을 당했다는 신고가 접수되었다. 여기서 어떤 내용이 직장 내 괴롭힘이 되는지, 판단기준은 어디에 있는지, 그리고 직장 내 괴롭힘으로 인정된 경우 회사에서의 징계절차에 대한 처리방법을 사례를

---

[57] 다만, 신고자나 피해 근로자에 대한 불리한 처우를 한 경우 3년 이하의 징역 또는 3천만 원 이하의 벌금에 처한다 (「근로기준법」 제76조의 3 제6항).

IV. A Case Study on Workplace Harassment against a New Employee

procedures are to be conducted.

II. Criteria for Determining Workplace Harassment

"No employer or employee shall ① cause physical or mental suffering to other employees or deteriorate the work environment ② beyond the appropriate scope of work ③ by taking advantage of superiority in rank, relationship, etc. in the workplace." (The Labor Standards Act Article 76-2). Any judgment that workplace harassment (bullying) has occurred must be made only if the above three requirements are met.[58]

1. Taking advantage of one's position or relationship in the workplace

"Position in the workplace" refers to cases where the accused is of a higher position than the victim in the workplace organizational structure. Even if the employee is not higher, this component can be fulfilled if the accused perpetrator has taken advantage of his/her higher standing in terms of work performance (number of service years etc.) or is higher in the seniority ranking system.[59]

Dominance within workplace relations includes just about any relationship where advantage is deemed to exist for the accused perpetrator. The following can be used to judge advantage: ① stronger job competency, professional knowledge, or higher number of service years, ② Personal attributes such as age, academic background, gender, region of origin, race, ③ Influence in the workplace, such as working for the auditing or human resources department, ④ Employment status (full-time vs. part-time etc.), and ⑤ Influence within organizations such as labor unions or workplace councils. Workplace harassment has not occurred unless the act involved taking advantage of one's position or relationship at work.

2. Exceeding the appropriate scope of work

The relevance to work must be comprehensive. Even if the incident does not occur directly in the course of performing work, work relevance is recognized if it occurs while carrying out work duties and requires the claimant having to perform more than required by the job position, or under the guise of performing work.[60]

---

[58] Ministry of Employment and Labor, "Manual on Judgment, Prevention and Handling of Workplace Harassment," Feb. 2019, pp. 10-14.
[59] Supreme Court ruling on July 10, 2008, 2007du22498.

바탕으로 살펴보고자 한다.

Ⅱ. 직장 내 괴롭힘 판단기준

"사용자 또는 근로자는 ① 직장에서의 지위 또는 관계 등의 우위를 이용하여 ② 업무상 적정 범위를 넘어 ③ 다른 근로자에게 신체적·정신적 고통을 주거나 근무환경을 악화시키는 행위를 하여서는 아니 된다(「근로기준법」 제76조의2)." 직장 내 괴롭힘을 판단할 때, 위의 3가지 요건을 모두 갖추어야 직장 내 괴롭힘이 되므로, 그 행위에 대해 잘 살핀 후 종합적으로 판단하여야 한다.[58]

1. 직장 내 지위 또는 관계 등의 우위를 이용할 것

직장 내에서 지위란 행위자가 직장 내에서 지휘명령 관계에서 상위에 있는 경우를 말한다. 직접적인 지휘명령 관계에 놓여있지 않더라도 회사내 직위가 직급 체계상 상위에 있음을 이용하는 것도 여기에 속한다.[59]

직장 내에서 관계의 우위는 사실상 우위를 점하고 있다고 판단되는 모든 관계가 포함된다. ① 근속 연수나 전문지식 등의 업무역량, ② 연령, 학벌, 성별, 출신 지역, 인종 등 인적 속성, ③ 감사, 인사부서 등 같은 업무의 직장 내 영향력, ④ 정규직 여부, ⑤ 노동조합이나 직장 내 협의회 등 근로자의 조직 내 영향력 등이 문제가 될 수 있다. 따라서 직장에서의 지위나 관계 등의 우위를 이용하여 행위 한 것이 아니라면 직장 내 괴롭힘에 해당하지 않는다.

2. 업무상 적정 범위를 넘을 것

업무관련성은 포괄적인 업무관련성을 의미한다. 직접적인 업무수행 과정에서 발생한 경우가 아니더라도 업무수행에 편승하여 이루어졌거나 업무수행을 빙자하여 발생한 경우 업무 관련성이 인정된다.[60]

---

58) 고용노동부, "직장 내 괴롭힘 판단 및 예방과 대응 매뉴얼", 2019.2. 10-14면.
59) 대법원 2008.7.10 선고 2007두22498 판결.
60) 대법원 2006.12.21. 선고 2005두13414 판결.

IV. A Case Study on Workplace Harassment against a New Employee

In order to be recognized as exceeding the appropriate scope for work, it must be recognized that social norms would not see the incident as a business necessity, or that, even if business necessity is recognized, the behavior of the person in higher position would not, according to social norms, be deemed appropriate. Even if the employee is unhappy with some instructions, it is difficult to recognize it as workplace harassment if it is deemed that the act is necessary for work in accordance with social norms. However, if the instruction or command is accompanied by violence or verbal abuse, it can be deemed as exceeding the appropriate scope for work, and thus fall under workplace harassment. In addition, even if the act in question is recognized as necessary for work, if the target worker is designated without reasonable cause when compared to workers performing the same and similar work in the workplace, it can be considered as an inappropriate act in the conventional social sense.

3. Acts that inflict physical or mental pain or aggravate the working environment;

Inflicting physical or mental pain occurs from a variety of actions, such as:
① Assault or intimidation;
② Abusive language, profanity, gossip, particularly continuous and repeated violent or abusive language that could seriously impinge on the victim's personal rights and cause psychological pain;
③ Repeatedly requiring the employee to run personal errands;
④ Bullying in a group, intentionally ignoring or excluding the employee in the course of ordinary work;
⑤ Ordering the employee to do something repeatedly or over a considerable period of time that has no relation to the job description specified at the time the relevant labor contract was signed, and there is no justifiable reason for the instruction;
⑥ Requiring excessive amounts of work from the employee where no unavoidable circumstance to do so exists at the time the work is assigned;
⑦ Intentionally interfering with the employee's smooth business performance, such as not providing major equipment (computers, telephones, etc.) necessary for business or blocking access to the Internet or intranet.

"Aggravating the working environment" means that the act impedes the victim's ability to perform his or her work duties. Here, the intention of the accused perpetrator is not taken into account.

---

60) Supreme Court ruling on Dec. 21, 2006, 2005du13414.

업무상 적정범위를 넘는 것으로 인정되기 위해서는 그 행위가 사회 통념에 비추어 볼 때 업무상 필요성이 인정되지 않거나 필요성은 인정되더라도 그 행위 양태가 사회통념에 비추어 볼 때 상당하지 않다고 인정되어야 한다. 업무상 지시나 명령에 불만을 느끼는 경우라도 그 행위가 사회 통념상 업무적으로 필요성이 있다고 인정될 경우에는 직장 내 괴롭힘으로 인정하기는 곤란하다. 그러나 그 지시나 명령 행위의 양태가 폭행이나 과도한 폭언 등을 수반하는 경우에는 업무상 적정범위를 넘었다고 볼 수 있으므로 직장 내 괴롭힘에 해당된다. 또한 문제가 된 행위 자체는 업무상 필요성이 인정되더라도 사업장 내 동종 유사업무를 수행하는 근로자에 비하여 합리적인 이유 없이 대상 근로자에게 이루어진 것이라면 사회 통념적으로 상당하지 않은 행위라고 볼 수 있다.

3. 신체적 정신적 고통을 주거나 근무환경을 악화시키는 행위일 것

　신체적 정신적 고통을 주는 것은 다양한 행위로 다음의 예를 들 수 있다.
① 폭행행위나 협박하는 행위
② 폭언, 욕설, 험담 등 언어적 행위. 특히 지속 반복적인 폭언이나 욕설은 피해자의 인격권을 심각하게 해치며 정신적 고통을 유발 할 수 있다.
③ 반복적으로 개인적인 심부름을 시키는 행위
④ 집단 따돌림, 업무수행과정에서의 의도적 무시나 배제 등의 행위
⑤ 근로계약 체결 시 명시했던 업무와 무관한 일을 근로자의 의사에 반하여 지시하는 행위가 상당기간 반복되고 그 지시에 정당한 이유가 인정되지 않는 행위
⑥ 업무상 과도하게 부여하는 행위는 그렇게 하도록 지시하지 않으면 안 되는 업무상 불가피한 사정이 없는 경우를 말한다.
⑦ 업무상 필요한 주요 비품(컴퓨터, 전화 등)을 제공하지 않거나, 인터넷이나 사내 인트라넷 접속을 차단하는 등 원활한 업무수행을 방해하는 행위.
　근무환경을 악화시키는 것이란 그 행위로 인하여 피해자가 능력을 발휘하는데 지장을 주는 것을 말한다. 여기서 행위자의 의도 여부는 고려하지 않는다.

III. Facts of the Case

On May 15, 2022, at the end of a company dinner, a new employee (the claimant) approached the CEO and reported that he was being bullied in the workplace. Accordingly, the head of the personnel department conducted an interview with the claimant on May 17 and instructed him to submit the relevant details in writing with specific evidence. The new employee had been hired in December 2021 and had been assigned to the technical sales team. He submitted the facts in writing that he had been harassed at least 10 times by the team leader (the perpetrator) and provided the relevant body of evidence.

The details were as follows:

① On March 16, 2022, the team leader was having a serious conversation with another employee when the claimant went into the team leader's office and watered the flowerpots there. The team leader, who was angry, said to the claimant at lunchtime, "(Omitted) You have to run when others are walking, you have to climb three steps at a time when others are going up one at a time, and when others are running, you have to run faster. Understand? If you don't, we know you'll be a do-nothing later."

② On March 21, the victim had to give a PowerPoint presentation after completing the three-month probationary period. Here, as feedback, the team leader remarked, "This is not a place to consult with your psychiatrist," "Your English is not good enough, and your presentation was like what you presented in university. This is not school."

③ On April 1, the claimant was ordered to drive more than 5 hours round trip to and from a funeral for someone the team leader knew. During this trip in the car, the team leader scolded him, saying, "How many months have I been telling you about your clothes?"

④ On April 22, the claimant's team received an email from another department, complaining about the work of the technical sales team. In response, the team leader summoned everyone on the team and criticized the claimant in front of them for an hour for his incompetence in handling work. Here, thinking that the claimant had ignored the team leader's orders, the team leader stared at the claimant angrily, and slapped the victim's left thigh with his hand. In response, the victim apologized, "Team leader, I wasn't ignoring you, and I had no intention to do so. I'm sorry." The claimant stated in the

Ⅲ. 본 사건의 사실관계

2022년 5월 15일, 회사의 전체회식을 마친 후 신입사원(신고자)이 대표이사를 찾아와 본인이 직장 내 괴롭힘을 당하고 있다고 신고하였다. 이에 인사부서장은 5월 17일 그 신고자와 면담을 실시하고, 해당 내용을 구체적 증거자료를 가지고 서면으로 제출하라고 지시하였다. 신입사원 (피해근로자)은 작년 12월에 입사하여 기술영업팀에 배치되었고, 해당 팀장(가해자)으로부터 10회 이상의 괴롭힘을 당한 사실을 해당 근거자료를 가지고 제출하였다.

그 내용은 다음과 같았다.

① 3월 16일에 있었던 일이다. 팀장이 다른 직원과 진지하게 얘기할 때 팀장실 앞의 화분에 물을 주기 위해 안쪽으로 들어가 물을 주었다. 화가 났던 팀장은 점심시간에 피해 근로자에게 "(앞 생략) 너는 남 걸을 때 뛰어야 되고, 남들 계단 하나씩 오를 때 세 개씩 올라야 되고, 남들 뛸 때 너는 졸라 뛰어야 돼. 알아? 넌 그렇게 안 하면 진짜 아무것도 안 돼, 나중에~"라는 발언을 하여 피해 근로자에게 자책감과 비하감을 느끼게 했다.

② 3월 21일, 피해 근로자가 3개월간의 수습기간을 마치면서 PPT로 자신에 대해 발표하는 시간을 가졌다. 여기서 팀장은 피드백으로 "여기는 니 정신과 상담하는 곳이 아니야," "니 되지도 않는 영어와 무슨 대학교 발표하나? 여기는 학교가 아니야."라는 발언을 하였다.

③ 4월 1일 같은 팀원의 장례식장을 방문하면서, 왕복 5시간 이상을 피해 근로자에게 운전하게 하였다. 특히 이 자리에서 "내가 너 옷가지고 얘기한 게 대체 몇 달 째냐?"며 구박을 하였다.

④ 4월 22일, 회사의 다른 부서로부터 기술영업팀의 업무를 불평하는 메일을 수신하게 되었다. 이에 대해 팀장은 다른 팀원과 자신을 불러서 한 시간 내내 업무처리 미숙에 대해 질타를 하였다. 여기서 피해근로자가 팀장을 무시하였다고 여겨 굳은 표정으로 피해자를 심하게 노려 보았고, 이어 피해 근로자의 왼쪽 허벅지를 손뼉으로 내리쳤다. 이에 대해 피해 근로자는 "팀장님, 저는 정말 팀장님을 무시할 생각은 없었고, 그런 의도도 전혀 없었습니다. 죄송합니다." 라고 사과를 했다. 피해 근로자는 한 시간 동안 무슨 죄인인 것 마냥 숨이 막혔고, 팀장실에서 나왔을 때 머리가 아프고

Ⅳ. A Case Study on Workplace Harassment against a New Employee

claim, "For an hour I choked up, feeling as if I were a criminal, and after coming out of the team leader's office, my head hurt and I felt very dizzy."

⑤ On April 29, the team leader had a meeting with the team and took issue with the work attitude of the claimant. "I can't understand you guys born in the '90s these days. Work and life balance? Such a rotten thought. Isn't it really a rotten attitude?" "You work with the mindset that you will only give as much as you receive, all while the company has to pick up the slack from the new employee, who receives as much as 34 million won a year." The team leader looked at the claimant and said that the minds of kids born in the '90s are rotten and that he could not understand them. "If you don't take your work seriously, just leave. I still have a lot of people to work with. There's no need for you to start here. Right?"

⑥ On May 17, the claimant had a meal with three new employees and team members, but didn't say a word. In response, the team leader said, "If you don't feel good, is it okay to show your feelings here? Are you expressing your anger?" "Do what you want. If you're going to show your temper and not talk, fine. I'll have nothing to do with you anymore. Just get out of here!" After that, the team leader didn't respond to any greetings from the claimant. However, he called other employees from the department for a meeting over the claimant drinking too much the night before and coming late to work. The claimant had to write a letter of apology and submit it to the team leader.

The statements used to demean the claimant included:

⑦ "Dress properly. Don't you have any shirts? Buy some. Where is your salary going? When you have some money, buy some pants and new shoes.

⑧ "If you don't pass the OJT exam, you will be cut loose, you know that? If you're not serious about your work, you'll just be fired. If you don't come to your senses by the end of the three-month probation period, you'll be fired, you know?

⑨ "Your English skills aren't that good. Your language skills are very poor. You can't speak English anywhere. Your English skills are terrible."

⑩ During a team meeting, "Why are you wearing a mask? You bastard! You only care about yourself, about not getting infected."

⑪ The team leader never called the claimant by his title, instead calling the claimant by name directly (which is rude in Korea), or "Hey!" "You" and "Ni" (which are also rude in Korea).

어지러움을 크게 느꼈다'고 한다.

⑤ 4월 29일, 팀장이 팀원들과 회의를 하면서 피해 근로자의 업무태도에 대해 문제를 삼았다. "요즘 너네 90년생들 이해를 할 수 없어. 뭐 워라벨? 그딴 썩어 빠진 생각, 정말 그건 썩은 마인드 아니냐?" "너는 받은 만큼 일할 거라는 마인드로 일하는데, 반대로 회사는 신입에게 3,400만 원 주는 만큼 뽑아 먹어야 돼, 아니야?" 자신을 보면서 90년생 요즘 애들 마인드가 썩어 빠졌고 이해가 안 간다는 발언을 했다. "너 일 제대로 진지하게 안 할 거면 그냥 나가라. 그럼 돼. 난 일할 사람 수두룩해 많아. 아니 그냥 시작할 필요가 없잖아. 맞지? 그냥 너 보고 나가라 그럴 거야, 알겠어?"

⑥ 5월 17일. 신입사원 세 명과 팀원들이 함께 식사를 하는데, 피해 근로자가 한 마디도 하지 않자 이에 대해 팀장은 "회사가 꼬라지 부리고 싶으면 부리는 데냐? 니 성질 부리는 데냐?" "네 마음대로 해라. 인상쓰고 말 안할 거면 말하지 말고, 난 더 이상 너 한테 관여하지 않을 거야. 이 시간 이후로, 나가."라고 말했다. 이 날 이후 팀장은 인사를 해도 받지 않고 부서의 다른 직원을 불러 회의 하고, 피해 근로자가 처리하던 일들을 다른 팀원에 맡기고 업무에서 배제 시켰다. 사실 이 일은, 전날 피해 근로자가 과음을 하고 지각을 해서 반성문을 쓰게 한 것이 원인이 되었다.

평소에 자주 피해 근로자를 비하한 말은 다음과 같았다.

⑦ "니 옷 제대로 입어라. 셔츠 없냐, 이제 좀 사라. 너 월급이 얼마지? 돈 여유가 있을 때 바지도 좀 사고 구두는 없냐?

⑧ "OJT 시험 너 통과 못했으면 너 잘릴 뻔 했어 알아? 너 일 진지하게 안 할 거면 그냥 나가라 그럴거야. 너 이번 3개월 수습 때까지도 정신 못 차리면 너 짤린다고 알어.

⑨ "니 그깟 되지도 않는 영어 실력 진짜, 언어능력이 너무 떨어져 너는, 어디서 되지도 않는 그 따위 영어, 그 아무것도 아닌 니 영어실력"

⑩ 팀 회의 중에 "니 마스크 왜 끼냐? 이 새끼 지만 코로나 안 걸릴라고."

⑪ 행위자가 피해 근로자에게 ○○○ 주임이라 직함을 부르지 않고, "야" "너" "니" " ○○○"라고 이름을 직접 불렀다.

Ⅳ. Decisions on this Case and Actions Taken by the Company

1. Harassment in the workplace confirmed

The claimant was deemed a victim after the evidence was reviewed and all parties were interviewed. In fact, the team leader, who was the perpetrator, did not recognize the victim's personal rights in the process of performing his duties and concentrated only on the work process. Here, the superior (the team leader) used his superior position as the team leader to continue inflicting mental and physical pain on the new employee beyond the proper scope of work. Inappropriate terms and derogatory remarks were used repeatedly, and the victim was excluded from work and inflicted with psychological pain that was beyond acceptable. Therefore, protective measures were taken with the claimant, including a change of location to allow him to continue to work for the company, while disciplinary actions were taken against the team leader. The company is also working hard to prevent recurrence in the workplace where superiors infringe on the personal rights of their subordinates in the process of performing their duties.

2. Company actions upon receipt of claim

The company received a claim of workplace harassment on May 15. In response, the HR team leader realized harassment had likely taken place at work through interviews from May 17-19, and asked the claimant to provide additional evidence. On May 27, the company decided that an objective investigation into workplace harassment was necessary, to which it brought in an external expert: in this case, this author's firm, KangNam Labor Law Firm. After investigating the claimant, the related persons, and the perpetrator, the labor law firm reported its findings and determination of workplace harassment on July 10. Accordingly, as stipulated in the rules of employment, the company notified the perpetrator, seven days in advance, of a planned disciplinary committee meeting related to workplace harassment to be held on July 20, 2022. At the disciplinary meeting, the company notified the perpetrator of the facts that had been confirmed, and listened to the perpetrator's response. After that, the company imposed a six-month wage reduction in consideration of the severity, including excluding the

Ⅳ. 본사안의 판단과 회사의 조치

1. 사실관계를 통해서 본 직장 내 괴롭힘 여부

사실관계에서 가해자인 팀장은 업무수행 과정에서 근로자의 인격권을 인정하지 않고 오로지 업무처리에 대해서만 열중하고 있다. 여기서 팀장인 상급자가 직장 내의 팀장이라는 우월적 관계를 이용하여 업무의 적정 범위를 넘어 신입사원에게 정신적 육체적으로 고통을 주었다. 특히, 직장 내 괴롭힘과 관련하여 적절치 못한 용어나 비하하는 발언을 반복적으로 실시하였고, 피해 근로자를 업무에서 배제하여 정신적인 고통을 줌으로써, 그 수인 한계를 넘어 신입직원이 회사의 대표에게 괴롭힘에 대해 호소하는 상태까지 발전하였다. 본 직장 내 괴롭힘 사례에서 볼 때 회사 차원에서는, 신입사원이 제대로 회사에서 계속 근무를 할 수 있도록 부서 배치전환 등을 통해 보호조치를 하고, 팀장은 업무수행 과정에서 부하직원들의 인격권을 침해하지 않도록 특별한 징계 조치와 더불어 관련 교육 이수 등 재발방지의 노력이 필요하다.

2. 회사의 조치

회사는 5월 15일 직장 내 괴롭힘에 대한 신고를 접수하였다. 관련하여 인사팀장은 5월 17일부터 19일까지의 피해직원과의 면담을 통해 직장 내 괴롭힘 내용에 대해 인지하였고, 관련 증거자료를 보충하도록 요구하였다. 그리고 회사는 5월 27일 직장 내 괴롭힘에 대하여 객관적인 조사가 필요하다는 판단으로 노무법인에 직장 내 괴롭힘 내용에 대한 조사를 의뢰하였다. 노무법인은 피해자, 이해 관계자, 가해자 등을 조사한 후, 7월 10일 직장 내 괴롭힘 사실관계에 대해 조사 내용과 판단 내용을 보고하였다. 이에 따라 회사는 취업규칙에 정하는 바(징계위7일전 해당자에게 사전통보)에 따라 가해자에게 직장 내 괴롭힘에 관련하여 징계계획 통지를 하고, 2022년 7월 20일에 징계위원회를 개최하였다. 징계위원회에서 회사는 확인된 사실관계에 대해 근로자에게 통보하고, 주어진 변명의 기회를 통해 가해 근로자의 의견을 청취하였다. 그 후 회사는 징계 양정을 고려하여 6개월간 당사자의 감봉징계를

offender from pay-for-performance for one year and suspending promotion for one year. In addition, after listening to the claimant, it was decided to assign the victimized worker to the development team where he would perform similar tasks as he had for the technical sales team.

V. Conclusion

The Workplace Harassment Prevention Act was introduced to bolster the personal rights of employees. It was enacted due to the conviction that Korea's long tradition of seniority-based personnel management was deeply rooted and that abuses could not be prevented by the introduction of voluntary rules of employment alone. Therefore, as in the case we've looked at here, acts that exceed the appropriate scope of work violate the company's duty to protect workers, and companies need to be aware that they may find themselves compensating recipients of workplace harassment in the future. The case herein looked at the most frequent type of workplace harassment, bullying, which involved a new employee and that employee's superior. The resulting consequences show the significant implications of such bullying, even if done with the intent to "mentor."

Cases of Workplace Bullying & Sexual Harassment and Disciplinary Committee Decisions

I. Summary

Last month, I received a request from a public institution (hereinafter referred to as the "Company") to participate as a member of their disciplinary committee. A female fixed-term worker (applicant) submitted a grievance counseling application stating that the male team leader (defendant) had repeatedly engaged in workplace harassment, sexually harassed her, and abused his authority, all of which led to her resignation. On August 16, 2022, the Company received the

하고, 1년간 성과급 지급 제외와 승진에서 제외시키는 처분을 하였다. 피해 근로자에 대해서는 본인 의견을 반영하여 기술영업팀과 유사한 업무를 수행하는 개발팀으로 인사발령 내기로 결정하였다.

V. 시사점

직장 내 괴롭힘 방지법은 회사의 직원들 간에 서로 존중하고 근로자의 인격권을 보호하자는 취지에서 도입되었다. 이러한 직장 내 괴롭힘이 강행법으로 도입된 것은 우리나라의 오랜 전통의 연공서열식 인사관리가 뿌리 박혀 있기 때문에 회사의 자율적인 취업규칙의 도입만으로는 이를 예방할 수 없다는 확신으로 인해 법제화가 된 것이다. 따라서 앞에서 언급한 사례와 같이, 업무의 적정 범위를 넘은 행위는 근로자에 대한 회사의 보호의무를 위반하므로 회사가 차후 피해근로자에 대한 정신적 손해 배상도 할 수 있다는 사실을 인식하여야 할 것이다. 기업에서 가장 빈번하게 발생하는 신입근로자와 기존의 선임자나 상급자 사이에 업무를 가르친다는 명목으로 발생하는 직장 내 괴롭힘에 대한 사례에 대해 살펴보았다. 이와 유사한 사례가 많이 발생하는 현 시점에서 시사하는 바가 크다고 할 수 있을 것이다.

직장 내 괴롭힘, 성희롱 사건과 기각 결정 사례

I. 경위

지난달 한 공공기관(이하 '회사')으로부터 징계위원회 징계위원으로 참석해 달라는 요청을 받았다. 기간제 여성근로자(신청인)가 남성 팀장(피신청인)으로부터 수차례의 직장 내 괴롭힘, 직장 내 성희롱과 갑질을 받았다고 하면서, 본인 퇴사의 계기가 되었다는 내용을 담은 고충상담 신청서가 접수되었다.

grievance counseling application, formed a grievance handling committee, and investigated the applicant's workplace harassment and sexual harassment claims. They investigated the applicant, the witness, and the alleged perpetrator, in that order. On September 15, 2022, the grievance handling committee requested convening of a disciplinary committee after determining that the allegations were indeed workplace harassment and sexual harassment. On October 18, 2022, the company convened a disciplinary committee consisting of two internal and three external members according to the procedures in Company disciplinary regulations. The disciplinary committee dismissed the case, judging that while the defendant's actions were inappropriate, they could not be regarded as workplace harassment or workplace sexual harassment as stipulated in labor law.

Most disciplinary committees lead to a process for disciplinary action, but in this case, the details presented by the applicant alone could not be regarded as workplace harassment beyond the appropriate scope of work, and although the alleged sexually harassing words and actions were inappropriate, a third party could not feel sexual shame. Accordingly, the committee dismissed the claim. The facts and criteria are described in the following.

II. Workplace Bullying & Sexual Harassment

1. Workplace bullying and sexual harassment described by the applicant

The applicant is a team member who was hired by the Company as a two-year contract intern, and the defendant is the leader of the team where the applicant was placed. The details of the claims of harassment and sexual harassment in the workplace by the applicant were as follows.

(1) Bullying at work
1) During working hours on March 22, 2022, the defendant said to the applicant, "In the second-half evaluation of 2021, your evaluation was the lowest among your co-workers who were hired during the same period. If you wish to receive a full-time position, you will need to smile and otherwise be cheerful at work and greet people well. Then the senior executives will give you a good evaluation." The applicant claimed that the team leader, who has the right to decide on contract extensions, made unnecessary comments under the guise of performance evaluation, which caused her a lot of stress.

회사는 2022년 8월 16일 고충 상담 신청서를 접수받고, 고충처리위원회를 구성하여, 신청인의 직장 내 괴롭힘과 직장 내 성희롱 사건에 대해 조사를 실시하였다. 조사는 신청인, 참고인, 그리고 가해자 순으로 진행되었다. 2022년 9월 15일 고충처리위원회는 본 직장 내 괴롭힘과 직장 내 성희롱 신청사건에 대해 모두 혐의가 인정된다고 판단하여 징계위원회 소집을 요청하였다. 회사는 2022년 10월 18일 징계규정의 절차에 따라 징계위원을 내부 인원 2명과 외부 인원 3명으로 구성하는 징계위원회를 소집하였다. 징계위원회에서는 피신청인의 행위들은 부적절한 면이 있지만, 노동법에서 정한 직장 내 괴롭힘이나 직장 내 성희롱이라고 볼 수는 없다고 판단하여 사건을 기각하였다.

대부분의 징계위원회는 징계를 위한 과정으로 이어지지만, 이번 사건은 신청인이 제시한 내용만으로는 업무의 적정 범위를 넘는 직장 내 괴롭힘으로 볼 수 없었고, 성희롱 발언도 부적절한 언행은 맞지만, 제3자가 성적 수치심을 느낄 사안은 아니기에 징계를 기각하는 결정을 하였다. 이러한 판단에 이르게 된 사실관계와 판단기준에 대해 구체적으로 살펴보고자 한다.

Ⅱ. 직장 내 괴롭힘 및 직장 내 성희롱 내용

1. 신청인이 기술한 직장 내 괴롭힘과 성희롱 내용

신청인은 2년 계약직 인턴으로 입사한 팀원이고, 피신청인은 신청인이 소속된 팀의 팀장이다. 신청인이 느꼈다는 직장 내 괴롭힘과 성희롱의 내용은 다음과 같다.

(1) 직장 내 괴롭힘
1) 2022년 3월 22일 근무시간 중 피신청인이 신청인에게 "21년 하반기 평가에서 입사 동기들 중 제 평가가 하위권이며, 정규직으로 전환되려면 회사 내에서 웃는 등 밝은 모습을 보이고, 인사를 잘 해야 상위 보직자들에게 좋은 평가를 받을 수 있다"는 이야기를 하였다. 이에 대해 계약연장 결정권을 가지고 있는 팀장이 근무평가를 빌미로 불필요한 지적을 하여 스트레스를 받았다.

2) Between May and July 2022, the defendant took the applicant and other team members to a place where he went to smoke on the roof of the office building. The applicant did not want to go to the place, but she had to because the defendant made announcements or wanted to discuss work-related things there. Later, the frequency decreased after some co-workers resisted going to the rooftop together. However, these meetings on the rooftop continued on occasion, where the defendant smoked.

(2) Sexual harassment in the workplace
1) On April 29, 2022, when visiting an eel restaurant with team members for lunch, the defendant remarked to the team, "Let's get some [sexual] stamina from eating eel today!" His remarks made me feel uncomfortable.
2) On July 14, 2022, during a business trip to the city, the applicant and the defendant visited the old downtown of Yongsan. While driving, the defendant made the statement, "Ajumma wouldn't be able to get here," in the sense that it would be difficult for inexperienced female drivers to drive the area due to its geographical characteristics. The applicant was offended by the defendant's "blatant stereotyping sexism."
3) During lunch at the Company cafeteria on August 5, 2022, the applicant said that she would not drink the omija tea on the menu. In response, the defendant asked, "Isn't omija tea good for women?" which the applicant claimed made her feel uncomfortable.

During the face-to-face investigation by the Company's grievance handling committee members, the applicant explained that the reason for her resignation was due to the bullying and sexual harassment by her superior at work. The applicant resigned on August 21.

2. Actions taken by the company

On August 16, 2022, after receiving an application for grievance counseling from the applicant for the related case, the Company immediately investigated things face-to-face, looking with the applicant at the claims she raised as well as interviewing three references, and then supplementing with other information. After further investigation, the Company reported the results to the Grievance Deliberation Committee on September 15. On September 29, the Grievance Deliberation Committee reviewed the case and determined that it amounted to harassment and sexual harassment at work, and asked the Disciplinary Committee to take disciplinary action.

2) 2022년 5월에서 7월 중에, 피신청인이 사옥 건물 옥상에 담배를 피우러 가는 자리에 신청인을 포함한 팀원들을 데려갔으며, 그 자리에서 업무와 관련한 공지나 논의를 진행하여 그 자리에 가고 싶지 않아도 가야만 하는 분위기를 조성하였다. 그 후 옥상에 다 같이 가자는 제안을 거절한 이후로 빈도는 줄었으나, 간혹 논의 사항이 있는 경우에도 담배를 피우는 자리에서 회의가 진행되었다.

(2) 직장 내 성희롱

1) 2022년 4월 29일 팀원들과 장어 음식점에 점심식사를 위해 방문하였을 때, 피신청인은 팀원들에게 "오늘 장어 먹고 힘써야지"라는 발언을 하여 불쾌감을 느꼈다.
2) 2022년 7월 14일 시내 출장 중에, 용산의 구도심을 방문했다. 피신청인이 운전을 하면서 지리적 특성 때문에 운전이 미숙한 사람은 차로 방문하기 어렵겠다는 의미에서 "아줌마들은 못 오겠다"라는 발언을 하였다. 신청인은 피신청인이 성차별적 고정관념을 노골적으로 드러내어 불쾌감을 느꼈다.
3) 2022년 8월 5일 사내식당에서 점심식사 중 메뉴에 나온 오미자 차를 신청인이 안 먹겠다고 했다. 이에 피신청인은 "오미자가 여자한테 좋은 거 아니야?"라는 발언을 하여 불쾌감을 느끼게 했다.

신청인은 회사의 고충처리위원들의 대면조사를 받으면서, 퇴직사유가 상급자의 직장 내 괴롭힘과 성희롱 때문이라고 설명하였다. 신청인은 8월 21일 퇴직하였다.

2. 회사의 조치

회사는 2022년 8월 16일 신청인으로 관련 사건에 대해 고충상담 신청서를 받은 후, 곧바로 신청인을 대면조사 하였다. 신청인이 제기한 내용에 대해 참고인 3명을 추가적으로 조사한 후 사실관계를 보강하였다. 신청인을 추가조사한 뒤에 9월 15일에 조사 결과를 고충심의 위원회에 보고하였다. 9월 29일 고충처리심의 위원회는 본 사건을 심의한 결과 이는 충분히 직장 내 괴롭힘과 직장 내 성희롱에 해당된다고 판단하여 징계위원회에 징계를 의뢰하였다.

III. Criteria for Determining Workplace and Sexual Harassment in Related Cases

1. Criteria

(1) Bullying at work

"No employer or employee shall ① cause physical or mental suffering to other employees or deteriorate the work environment ② beyond the appropriate scope of work ③ by taking advantage of superiority in rank, relationship, etc. in the workplace" (Labor Standards Act, Article 76-2). Only if these three requirements are met can a judgment be made that workplace harassment (bullying) has occurred.[61]

The factors and criteria suggested by the court can be used to determine whether workplace harassment has occurred. This shall be decided by considering and evaluating the following collectively: "

① the relationship between the alleged offender and alleged victim,

② the motive and intention of the act,

③ the timing, place, and situation,

④ the details of the alleged victim's explicit or presumed reaction,

⑤ the content and extent of the act, and

⑥ the repetition or continuity of the act."[62]

Simply put, it is possible for an employer to infringe on human and personal rights or worsen the employment environment with position (power relations), related work (work relations), or other actions unwanted by the receiving party that are outside the scope of the relevant work (harassment, abusive language, etc.).[63]

(2) Sexual harassment in the workplace

"Sexual harassment in the workplace refers to the deterioration of the employment environment by employers, superiors, and workers using their

---

[61] Ministry of Employment and Labor, "Manual on Judgment, Prevention and Handling of Workplace Harassment," Feb. 2019, pp. 10-14.
[62] Supreme Court ruling on Feb. 10, 1998: 95da39533.
[63] Kim, Elim, "Gender Equality and Law," Korea National Open University Press and Culture Center, 2013, p. 242.

Ⅲ. 사례에 대한 판단 기준과 사례에 대한 적용

1. 사례에 대한 판단기준

(1) 직장 내 괴롭힘

"사용자 또는 근로자는 ① 직장에서의 지위 또는 관계 등의 우위를 이용하여 ② 업무상 적정범위를 넘어 ③ 다른 근로자에게 신체적·정신적 고통을 주거나 근무환경을 악화시키는 행위를 하여서는 아니 된다(「근로기준법」 제76조의2)." 직장 내 괴롭힘을 판단할 때, 위의 3가지 요건을 모두 갖추어야 직장 내 괴롭힘이 되므로, 그 행위에 대해 잘 살핀 후 종합적으로 판단하여야 한다.[61]

법원이 제시한 위법성 판단기준은 직장 내 괴롭힘 여부를 판단하는 잣대로 삼을 수 있다. 괴롭힘 행위인지의 여부는 "
① 위법행위와 관련한 행위자와 피해자의 관계
② 행위의 동기와 의도
③ 시기와 장소 및 상황
④ 피해자의 명시적 또는 추정적 반응의 내용
⑤ 행위의 내용과 정도
⑥ 행위의 반복성이나 지속성 등을 종합하여 노동인격의 침해여부를 가려야 할 것이다.[62]"

이를 단순히 정리하면, 사용자가 지위를 이용하여(권력관계), 업무와 관련하여(업무관련성), 상대방이 원하지 않는 행동(괴롭힘, 언동 등)을 함으로써, 인권 및 인격권을 침해하거나 고용환경을 악화시키는지 여부를 판단하는 것이다.[63]

(2) 직장 내 성희롱

"직장 내 성희롱이란 사업주, 상급자, 근로자가 직장 내의 지위를 이용하거나 업무와 관련하여 다른 근로자에게 성적인 언어나 행동 또는 이를 조건으로 고용상의 불이익을 주거나 성적 굴욕감을 유발하게 하여 고용환경을 악화

---

[61] 고용노동부, "직장 내 괴롭힘 판단 및 예방과 대응 매뉴얼", 2019.2. 10-14면.
[62] 대법원 1998.2.10. 선고 95다39533 판결
[63] 김엘림, "남녀평등과 법", 한국방송통신대학교 출판문화원, 2013, 242면.

positions in the workplace or by expressing towards other workers sexual language or behavior in relation to work, or by giving employment disadvantages or causing sexual humiliation as a condition thereof" (Article 2 of the Equal Employment Act). Sexual harassment in the workplace has the potential to occur anywhere inside or outside the workplace, and occurs when a superior uses his/her position or the actions/words are related to work. For example, sexual harassment that occurs in a car while on a business trip or at a business-related meeting is also sexual harassment in the workplace.

The decisive criteria for judging sexual harassment in the workplace:

① Whether the alleged victim felt sexual humiliation or disgust due to the act is the main fact. It is considered sexual harassment if the alleged victim felt sexual humiliation and disgust due to the act.

② At this time, whether or not the alleged perpetrator intended to sexually harass cannot affect the criteria for judgment.

③ A normal and average person must be able to feel sexual humiliation or disgust on the part of the alleged victim.[64]

2. Application to case

(1) Judgment on claims of workplace bullying

1) The defendant said to the applicant, "In the second-half evaluation of 2021, your evaluation was the lowest among your co-workers who were hired during the same period. If you wish to receive a full-time position, you will need to smile and otherwise be cheerful at work and greet people well. Then the senior executives will give you a good evaluation."

Regarding this part, the applicant argued that it was equivalent to abuse of authority or harassment in the workplace. The applicant was about to switch to a full-time position just before the end of the two-year labor contract period. The defendant stated that, as her team leader, his words were supposed to help the applicant improve her working relations by correcting her negative attitude as a team leader, and that such remarks did not constitute an abuse of power. When judging the background to and purpose for the defendant's remarks and whether they were repetitively stated, it cannot be regarded as harassment in the workplace, as it is judged that the senior gave advice in the process of leading the junior to a full-time job.[65]

---

[64] Supreme Court ruling on June 14, 2007: 2005du6461.

시키는 것을 말한다 (「남녀고용평등법」 제2조)." 직장 내 성희롱은 사업장 안이나 밖 어디서나 발생할 가능성이 있으며, 상급자가 그 지위를 이용하거나 업무와 관련이 있다면 성립된다. 예를 들어 출장 중인 차 안이나 업무와 관련이 있는 전체회식 장소 등에서 발생하는 성희롱도 직장 내 성희롱이다.

직장 내 성희롱 여부를 판단하는 결정적인 기준은
① 그 행위로 인해 피해자가 성적인 굴욕감이나 혐오감을 느꼈는지의 문제이다. 피해자가 성적인 굴욕감이나 혐오감을 느꼈다면 성희롱이 성립될 수 있다.
② 이때 행위자가 성희롱을 할 의도가 있었는지 없었는지의 여부는 판단 기준에 영향을 줄 수 없다.
③ 일반적이고도 평균적인 사람이 피해자의 입장에서 성적 굴욕감이나 혐오감을 느낄 수 있어야 한다.[64]

2. 사례에 대한 적용

(1) 직장 내 괴롭힘 사례에 대한 판단

1) "21년 하반기 평가에서 입사 동기들 중 제 평가가 하위권이며, 정규직으로 전환되려면 회사 내에서 웃는 등 밝은 모습을 보이고, 인사를 잘 해야 상위 보직자들에게 좋은 평가를 받을 수 있다"는 이야기를 하였다.

이 부분에 대해 신청인은 직장 내 갑질 내지 직장 내 괴롭힘에 해당한다고 주장하였다. 직장 내 괴롭힘에 대한 판단기준으로 볼 때, 2년이 지나면 정규직으로 전환을 코 앞에 두고 있었다. 담당 팀장으로 생활태도 개선을 위해서 부족한 부분을 개선하도록 도와 준 것이지, 이를 갑질로 볼 수 있는 성질이 되지 않는다. 피신청인이 이 발언을 하게 된 배경, 취지, 반복성 여부에 대해 논점을 두고 판단할 때, 이는 선배가 후배를 정규직으로 이끌기 위한 과정에서 조언을 해준 것이라 판단하여 직장 내 괴롭힘으로 볼 수 없다.[65]

---

[64] 대법원 판례 2007. 6. 14. 선고 2005두6461 판결.
[65] 유사판결: 대법원 2003.7.22. 선고 2002도7225 판결.

V. Cases of Workplace Bullying & Sexual Harassment and Disciplinary Committee Decisions

2) "From May to July 2022, the defendant took me to a place on the roof of the office building where the defendant could smoke and talk about work. As work-related announcements were given or group discussion took place there, I felt peer pressure to go too." As a non-smoker, the applicant must have felt uncomfortable attending a meeting while a senior and other team members smoked on the roof of the office building. However, judging from the grounds such as the continuity of the rooftop meetings, coercion using power relations, and the subordinate's intention to reject, the defendant's behavior was undesirable, but doesn't lend well to a definition of workplace harassment. Because these rooftop meetings did not last, and considering that they were to change the mood, it is difficult to see it as bullying in the workplace.[66]

(2) Criteria for judging claims of sexual harassment in the workplace

1) When the team members visited an eel restaurant for lunch, the team leader said to the team members, "Let's get some [sexual] stamina by eating eel today!" His remarks made the applicant feel disgust. Regarding this, the criteria for determining sexual harassment in the workplace is based upon the feelings felt by the victim. Also, if a person with common sense feels sexual humiliation from the victim's point of view, it can be called sexual harassment. However, in this case, going to an eel restaurant during lunchtime cannot be seen as sexual harassment from a general point of view, considering that it is to rejuvenate the body through a special health food.[67]

2) On a business trip to the city, the applicant and the defendant visited the old downtown of Yongsan. While driving, the defendant made the statement, "Ajumma wouldn't be able to get here," during their conversation, meaning it would be difficult for inexperienced drivers to drive there due to the geographical characteristics. Ajumma refers to full-time housewives and middle-aged women.[68] The defendant's words mean, generally speaking, that the average woman drives too cautiously, but it is difficult to say that women would reasonably feel sexual humiliation in response.

---

[65] Similar case: Supreme Court ruling on July 22, 2003: 200do7225.
[66] Similar case: Supreme Court ruling on Feb. 10, 1998: 95da39533.
[67] Similar case: Supreme Court ruling on June 14, 2007: 2005doo6461.
[68] Internet encyclopedia 'Namu Wiki' keyword search for "Ajumma." Ajumma refers to middle-aged women. In everyday life, if a woman looks middle-aged, people often call her ajumma.

2) "신청인은 2022년 5월에서 7월 중에, 사옥 건물 옥상에 담배를 피우러 가는 자리에 데려갔으며, 그 자리에서 업무와 관련한 공지나 논의를 진행하여 그 자리에 가고 싶지 않아도 가야하는 분위기를 조성하였다." 이 사옥 건물 옥상에서 상급자가 담배를 피우면서 회의를 진행한 것은 비흡연자로서 참기 어려운 부분이 있었을 것이라 볼 수 있다. 그러나 이에 대한 판단은 옥상 회의 지속성, 권력관계 이용하여 강요한 것, 하급자의 거부의사 등의 근거로 판단해 볼 때, 바람직하지 않은 피신청인의 행위는 맞지만, 이를 직장 내 괴롭힘으로 판단하기는 어렵다. 왜냐하면 이러한 옥상 회의가 지속되지 않았고, 기분전환 차원에서 1회성으로 진행되었다고 볼 때, 이를 직장 내 괴롭힘으로 보기가 어렵다.[66]

(2) 직장 내 성희롱 사례 판단 기준

1) 팀원들과 장어 음식점에서 점심식사를 위해 방문하였을 때, 팀장은 팀원들에게 "오늘 장어 먹고 힘써야지"라는 발언을 하여 불쾌감을 느꼈다고 한다. 이에 대해 직장 내 성희롱에 대한 판단기준이 피해자의 느꼈던 감정이 중요하다. 또한 일반적인 상식을 가진 사람이 그 피해자의 입장에서 성적 굴욕감을 느꼈다면 이를 성희롱이라 할 수 있다. 그러나 본 사안에 있어서는 점심시간에 장어집에 간다는 것은 특별한 보양식을 통해 몸을 원기를 찾기 위한 것으로 간주해 볼 때, 일반적인 입장에서 성희롱으로 볼 수 없다.[67]

2) 시내 출장 중에, 용산의 구도심을 방문했다. 팀장이 운전을 하면서 지리적 특성 때문에 운전이 미숙한 사람은 차로 방문하기 어렵겠다는 대화 도중에 "아줌마들은 모 오겠다"라는 발언을 하였다. 아줌마라고 하면 전업주부를 일컫는 말로 중년여성을 말한다고 할 수 있다.[68] 일반적인 여성이 조심스럽게 운전한다는 뜻이지, 이 설명을 통해 성적인 수취심이나 성적 굴욕감을 느꼈다고 보기 어렵다.

---

66) 유사한 판례 참조: 대법원 1998.2.10. 선고 95다39533 판결
67) 유사한 판례 참조: 대법원 2007.6.14. 선고, 2005두6461 판결
68) 인터넷 백과사전 '나무위키' 키워드 "아줌마" 검색. 아줌마는 중년여성을 통칭한다. 일상에서 그냥 딱 봐서 아줌마스러우면 아줌마라고 부르는 경우가 생긴다.

3) During lunch at the in-house cafeteria, the applicant said that she would not drink omija tea on the menu. In response, the team leader remarked, "Isn't omija tea good for women?" This part is generally based on the fact that omija is good for women.[69] This remark does not fall under workplace bullying, as it was merely recommending omija tea for the purpose of drinking together.

IV. Disciplinary Committee's Decision to Dismiss

1. Main details of the Disciplinary Committee's decision meeting

On October 25, 2022, the Company Disciplinary Committee held a hearing according to the Company's disciplinary regulations. The committee consisted of 5 members: 2 internal and 3 external. As internal members, the employee representative of the labor-management council and the head of the Company's Audit Office attended, and as external members, the head of the audit office of an external public company and two certified labor attorneys attended. This labor attorney was appointed as the chairman. The chairman made a statement that disciplinary action should be aimed at punishing workers who violate the company's regulations, thereby preventing recurrence and restoring order in the company.[70] In addition, I suggested to the committee that they should decide whether the defendant's actions amounted to workplace harassment and workplace sexual harassment. The head of the Audit Office, an in-house disciplinary committee member, also gave the opinion that this case could not be viewed as bullying because it did not meet the requirements for workplace bullying, and that it could not be thought that an ordinary person would have felt sexual humiliation. Regarding this, some disciplinary committee members said that the defendant's actions amounted to sexual harassment in the workplace and bullying in the workplace. In this regard, there was sufficient discussion among the committee, which reached the view that the defendant's actions were not to the extent of bullying in the workplace and sexual harassment in the workplace as a whole.

The disciplinary committee gave the defendant an opportunity to explain himself at the hearing before a final decision was made. The defendant took an attitude of

---

[69] Reporter Jang In-seon, "Omija Tea Instead of Ice Coffee – A Wise Summer for Menopausal Women," Health Trend, July 8, 2019, and many other related materials.
[70] Jung, Bong-soo, "Lawful Dismissal Manual", 2nd ed., K-Labor Press, June 2022, p. 39.

3) 사내식당에서 점심식사 중 메뉴에 나온 오미자 차를 신청인이 안 먹겠다고 했다. 이에 팀장은 "오미자가 여자한테 좋은 거 아니야?"라는 발언을 하였다. 이 부분에 대해 일반적으로 오미차가 여자한테 좋다는 사실에 근거하고 있다.[69] 이 발언은 같이 마시자는 취지에서 오미자 차를 권했을 뿐이므로 직장 내 괴롭힘에 해당되지 않는다.

Ⅳ. 징계위원회의 결정과 결정배경

1. 징계위원회의 주요 내용

2022년 10월 25일 회사의 징계규정에 따라 징계위원회가 개최되었다. 징계위원회는 내부위원 2명과 외부위원 3명 총 5명으로 구성하였다. 내부위원으로 노사협의회의 근로자위원과 회사의 감사실장이 참석했고, 외부인원으로 외부 공기업의 감사실장과 공인노무사 2명이 참석했다. 본 노무사를 위원장으로 선임하였다. 위원장은 징계는 회사의 사규를 위반한 근로자에 대해 벌칙을 가하고 이를 통해 재발방지와 사내질서 회복에 목적으로 두어야 발언을 하였다.[70] 그리고 피신청인의 행위가 직장 내 괴롭힘과 직장 내 성희롱에 해당되는지에 대해 법률적 검토가 필요하다고 문제 제기를 하였다. 사내의 징계위원인 감사실장도 본 직장 내 괴롭힘 사례에 대해 직장 내 괴롭힘 구성요건에 맞지 않아 괴롭힘으로 볼 수 없고, 직장 내 성희롱에 대해서도 일반인으로 성적 수치감을 느낄 수 있었을 것이라 생각할 수 없다고 의견을 주었다. 이에 대해 피신청인의 행위는 직장 내 성희롱과 직장 내 괴롭힘에 해당된다는 징계위원도 있었다. 이와 관련하여 징계위원들 간에 충분한 토론이 있었고, 전체적으로 직장 내 괴롭힘과 직장 내 성희롱이라 볼 정도의 것은 아니다 라는 의견이 모아졌다.

징계위원회는 피신청인을 징계위원회에 출석시켜 징계에 앞서 소명할 기회를 주었다. 피신청인은 신청인에 바람직하지 않은 행위로 인해 정신적 피해를 입혔기 때문에 어떠한 처벌도 달게 받겠다고 하면서, 반성하는 태도를

---
[69] 장인선 기자, "아이스 커피 대신 오미차 – 갱년기 여성의 현명한 여름나기" 헬스경향, 2019. 7. 8. 등 다수 관련 자료.
[70] 정봉수, "실무자를 위한 해고 매뉴얼", 2판, K-Labor Press, 2022.6. 39면.

VI. Workplace Bullying and Sexual Harassment: A Case Analysis

self-reflection, saying that he would gladly accept any decision because he had caused psychological injury to the applicant due to his undesirable behavior.

The defendant was asked about the reasons for her resignation. He replied that the applicant had said many times that she wanted to be hired by a large company that paid a lot more because this public institution didn't pay enough, and that he had heard that she'd passed the entrance exam and would be hired by a large company.

2. Background to Decision

The Company's rules of employment cover dismissal, suspension, demotion, salary reduction, and reprimand as appropriate disciplinary actions. And if disciplined, the employee wouldn't be able to resume team leadership for 1 year, nor be eligible for promotion during that period. In this case, any disciplinary action would result in the defendant losing his position and eligibility for promotion for one year, during which his salary would be frozen. While the defendant's conduct could not be regarded as desirable, the level of punishment in the Company's disciplinary regulations were seen as excessive in this case.

The Disciplinary Committee decided on the fundamental content of whether the conduct actually corresponded to workplace harassment or sexual harassment in the workplace. Of the 5 disciplinary committee members, 3 concluded that the defendant's actions were not workplace bullying or workplace sexual harassment, while the remaining 2 members were of the view that the inappropriate behavior was not serious, but reason for minor disciplinary action. In the end, the disciplinary committee decided that this case was not worthy of disciplinary action with a 3:2 opinion, and dismissed the call for disciplinary action.

Workplace Bullying and Sexual Harassment: A Case Analysis

- Supreme Court ruling on November 25, 2021, 2020da270503 -

취하였다.

피신청인에게 신청인의 퇴직사유에 대해 물었다. 이에 대해 신청인은 공공기관이 급여가 적기 때문에 급여를 많이 주는 대기업에 입사하고 싶었다고 여러 번 얘기 한적이 있었고, 이번 대기업에 입사시험에 합격하여 이직을 하게 되었다고 들었다고 답변하였다.

2. 결정 배경

당해 공공기관은 징계의 종류를 해고, 정직, 강등, 감봉, 견책으로 구성하고 있다. 그리고 징계를 받게 되면, 1년간 보직을 맡을 수 없었고, 승진도 배제되었다. 징계규정에 따라 징계를 할 경우에는 피신청인은 현재의 팀장 직책을 잃게 되고 1년 동안 임금과 승진이 동결된다는 후속조치가 예정되어 있었다. 본 사안에 피신청인의 행위가 바람직한 행위로 볼 수 없었지만, 징계규정에 명시된 징계를 줄 경우 실제로 피신청인에 대한 처벌수준이 너무 높았기 때문에 징계의 성립여부 자체를 따질 수밖에 없었다.

징계위원회는 본 위반의 내용이 실질적으로 직장 내 괴롭힘에 해당되는지, 직장 내 성희롱에 해당되는지에 대한 근본적인 내용에 대해 결정을 하기로 하였다. 징계위원 5명 중, 3명은 피신청인은 직장 내 괴롭힘이나 직장 내 성희롱에 해당되지 않는다는 결론을 내렸고, 나머지 징계위원 2명은 위반의 내용이 그렇게 크지는 않지만, 경징계 사유에 해당된다는 의견을 주었다. 결국, 징계를 인용할 것인지 기각할 것인지 여부에 대해 의견이 모아졌고, 징계위원들은 2/3의 의견으로 본 사안은 징계 대상에 해당되지 않는다는 결정하고, 징계에 대해 기각하는 처분을 내렸다.

직장 내 괴롭힘과 성희롱에 관한 판례 해석

대법원 2021. 11. 25. 선고 2020다270503 판결

VI. Workplace Bullying and Sexual Harassment: A Case Analysis

I. Facts

1. Parties and Relevant Circumstances

The Plaintiff (P) was a contract employee for C Children's Hospital Sponsorship Association (hereinafter referred to as the "Association") from around March 2014. P was responsible for selecting and determining the scope of support for child patients to receive support from the Association. The Defendant (D) was an outpatient professor at C Hospital and an Association director. D planned and conducted events for the Association and sometimes directly instructed or severely reprimanded Association employees in relation to their work.

On October 15, 2015, the day of a charity golf event hosted by the Association, P rode in a passenger car driven by D near D's home and traveled with D to the golf course, located in Icheon City. Afterwards, P assisted D with his duties in the VIP room provided at the golf course clubhouse for the event. After the event ended that evening, P sat in the back seat of D's passenger car, driven by a substitute driver, along with D for the ride back to D's home.

On the following day, October 16, 2015, P visited the manager (E) of the Association's office, and reported that she had been sexually assaulted by D on three occasions: (1) in the VIP room the day before, (2) inside D's car after the event ended, and (3) repeatedly over time in the workplace. On the same day, at E's direction, P prepared a list of incidents when D had harassed her and submitted it to E in an Excel file. On October 27, 2015, P filed a criminal complaint with the police regarding the sexual assault incidents. Although the prosecutor indicted D, he was later found not guilty.

2. Plaintiff (P)'s Claim

A. On October 15, 2015, at 2:05 PM, while in the golf course's VIP room, D ordered P to bring a tree branch to hit P with as punishment. P did so, and D proceeded to break it and then used it to strike P's buttocks, causing physical pain. Furthermore, at the same time and place, D sexually harassed

I. 사실관계

1. 당사자와 당시 정황

원고(P)는 2014년 3월경부터 C 어린이병원 후원회(이하 '후원회'라고 한다)의 계약직 직원으로 후원회에서 지원할 어린이 환자의 선정과 지원범위 결정 등의 업무를 맡아왔다. 피고(D)는 C병원의 외래진료교수이자 후원회의 이사로, 후원회의 행사를 스스로 기획 진행하면서 후원회 직원들에게 직접 업무 지시를 하거나 그와 관련하여 후원회 직원들을 심하게 질책하기도 하였다.

P는 후원회가 주최하는 자선골프행사 당일인 2015년 10월 15일 아침에 D의 집 주변에서 D가 운전하는 승용차에 탑승하여 행사장소인 이천시 소재 D골프장까지 동행하였다. 이후 행사 진행을 위하여 제공된 위 골프장 클럽하우스 내 VIP룸에서 D의 업무를 보조하였다. 당일 저녁 행사 종료 후 D의 집 주변까지 대리기사가 운전하는 D의 승용차 뒷자리에 D와 나란히 동승하였다.

P는 위 행사 다음날인 2015년 10월 16일 오전에 후원회 사무국장인 E를 찾아가 '① 전날 위 VIP룸에서, ② 행사 종료 후 D의 승용차 안에서 추행을 당한 것을 비롯하여 ③ 그동안 D에게 성폭력 피해를 입었다'는 취지로 말하였고, 같은 날 오후에는 E의 지시에 따라 그동안 D로부터 입었다는 피해 내용을 정리한 표를 엑셀 파일로 작성하여 E에게 전송하였다. P는 2015년 10월 27일 경찰에 위 각 성추행 피해사실 등에 관한 고소장을 제출하였다. P가 경찰에 제기한 강제추행 사건은 검사가 공소제기를 하였으나, 무죄판결을 받았다.

2. 원고(P)의 주장

가. D는 2015년 10월 15일에 D 골프장 VIP룸 안에서 2015년 10월 15일 14시05분에 P에게 회초리를 맞아야 한다며 P로 하여금 P를 칠 회초리로 쓸 나뭇가지를 구해오도록 하고, P가 구해온 나뭇가지를 부러뜨려 부러진 나뭇가지로 P의 엉덩이를 폭행하였다. 또한 같은 일시와 장소에서 P의 몸을 위아래로 훑어보며 P에게 "너는 피부가 하얗다. 몸매가 빼빼 말랐었는데,

P with remarks such as "Your skin is so white. You used to be skinny, but now you've put on weight." "Your legs are so thin and white. Are you using whitening cream? Do you shave your body hair?" and "Do you have a boyfriend? Why have you gained weight? You don't work properly and your mind is elsewhere."

B. On the same day, while in the car on the way back, D verbally reprimanded P and sexually harassed her by inserting his finger into her right ear and using an empty plastic water bottle to poke her on her chest.

C. From April 3, 2015, to October 2015, D called P to the examination room at C Hospital, where he worked as an outpatient medical practitioner, and asked her to sit on a wheelchair and pulled her closer and tapped on her thighs.

D. D accused P, office manager E of the Association, a former employee, and P's lawyer who testified against him for sexual harassment, of submitting falsified evidence to the court by manipulating the facts. P claimed that it was an illegal act of secondary harm against P that abused the legal procedures.

3. Defendant (D)'s Claim

D denied the sexual harassment allegations leveled by P in the relevant criminal case and stated the following regarding what had occurred in the VIP room on October 15, 2015: D asked P to bring a tree branch to use as a punishing cane to hit her, saying that she had ruined the charity event. P brought a large branch that was over one meter long to the VIP room. When D asked her how many times she wanted to be hit, P said three times, and D broke the branch. P appeared to be crying, and D apologized to her for making her cry. P continued to fake cry, so D put his hand on her shoulder to stop her from lowering her head further and getting closer to her face to find out if she was really crying or not. When he saw that she was smiling, D grabbed P by the upper part of his elbow and pushed her away. During this process, D found out that P had a fat body, so D told P something to the effect of gaining weight On the same day and in the same place, D made remarks to P about P's calves, asked whether P had a boyfriend, and

요즘은 살이쪘다.", "네 다리가 가늘고 새하얗다. 화이트닝 크림을 바르냐? 몸에 잔털을 쉐이빙하냐?", "너 요즘 남자친구가 생겼냐? 왜 이렇게 살이 쪘냐? 일도 제대로 안하고 정신은 다른 데 팔려있지?"라는 등으로 말한 언어적 성희롱을 하였다.

나. D는 2015년 10월 15일 저녁 돌아오는 차량 안에서 P를 질책하면서 오른쪽 귓구멍에 손가락을 집어넣고, 이어 빈 플라스틱 물병을 이용하여 P의 가슴 부위를 찌르는 등 신체적 성희롱을 하였다.

다. D는 2015년 4월 3일부터 2015년 10월 말 사이에 C병원에 외래진료 업무를 하러 온 날 종종 P를 진료실로 불러 바퀴가 달린 환자진료의자에 앉도록 한 후 당겨 가까이 앉도록 하거나 P의 허벅지를 툭툭 건드렸다.

라. D는 P를 포함하여, 업무상위력에 의한 강제추행 혐의와 관련하여 증언하였던 후원회의 사무국장, 전직 직원, 그리고 P의 변호사를 상대로 증거를 변조하여 재판부에 제출하는 방법으로 행사했다면서 이들을 고소하였다. 이는 무고이자 P에 대한 법적절차를 악용한 2차 가해로서 명백히 위법한 불법행위이다.

3. 피고(D)의 주장

D는 관련 형사사건에서 P에 대한 추행 사실을 부인하면서, 2015년 10월 15일 위 VIP룸에서의 상황에 관하여 다음과 같이 구체적으로 진술하였다.

P에게 'P가 자선만찬행사를 망쳤으니 회초리를 맞아야 한다'며 회초리감으로 쓸 나무를 구해오라고 한 사실이 있다. 그러자 P가 VIP룸을 나가 길이가 1m가 넘는 커다란 나뭇가지를 구해왔다. 나뭇가지를 들고 VIP룸으로 돌아온 P에게 '몇 대 맞겠냐'고 묻자 P가 '3대만 맞겠다'고 하여, D가 그 나뭇가지를 부러뜨렸다. 이때 P가 우는 듯한 모습을 보여서 P에게 '울려서 미안하다'며 사과하였다. 그 후로도 P가 계속 우는 듯한 시늉을 하며 고개를 숙이기에 더 이상 고개를 숙이지 못하도록 손으로 P의 어깨를 막으면서 고개를 숙여 P 얼굴에 가까이 대고 보니, P가 웃고 있는 것 같아, P의 팔꿈치 윗부분을 잡아 밀쳐버렸다. 이 과정에서 P에게 살집이 있는 것을 알게 되어 P에게 '살이 쪘다'는 취지로 말하였다. 같은 날, 같은 장소에서

remarked about P's skin and use of skin-related products. At the above golf course, D once recommended that P use hot spring water to bathe.

4. Summary of the First Court Ruling[71]

P claimed that D had sexually harassed her and reported the people who had witnessed the actions to the police, both of which amounted to illegal actions against P. P claimed compensation for mental suffering under the tort liability of Article 750 of the Civil Code. However, the court dismissed P's claim due to insufficient evidence.

5. Appeal (Original trial)[72]

P appealed the decision, arguing that even if D's conduct mentioned in one of P's claims did not constitute "coercive sexual assault through the abuse of power," additional actions that D had intentionally committed against P during the investigation and trial constituted "illegal and inappropriate behavior equivalent to physical or verbal sexual harassment and bullying or harassment within the workplace" or "secondary acts of harm towards a victim of assault, insult, or sexual violence." Therefore, D had an obligation to compensate for damages caused by those illegal acts against P. However, the appellate court found that the evidence submitted by P in the first trial and additional evidence submitted remained insufficient to back up P's claims.

II. Details of Supreme Court Ruling[73]

The Supreme Court cited labor laws regarding workplace harassment and sexual harassment to make a decision in this case. Sexual harassment refers to behavior by a civil servant, employee of a public entity such as a state agency, local government or school, or employee, employer or superior at a workplace, or related

---

[71] Seoul Central District Court ruling on Aug. 27, 2019, 2018gadan5252208 (Compensation for damage).
[72] Seoul Regional District Court ruling on Sept. 18, 2020, 2019na54179 (Compensation for damage).
[73] Supreme Court ruling on Nov. 25, 2021, 2020da270503.

P에게 P의 종아리 부위, P의 남자친구 유무, P의 피부와 피부 관련 제품 사용에 관한 발언을 한 적이 있고, 위 골프장에서 온천수를 사용하여 목욕을 하도록 권유한 적이 있다.

4. 제1심 판결의 요지[71]

P는 D가 P에 대하여 신체적 성희롱을 하고, P와 관련 증인 등을 경찰에 고소하였는데, 이는 모두 P에 대한 위법한 가해행위이다. 이에 민법 제750조의 불법행위 책임에 따라 P가 입은 정신적 피해에 대하여 손해배상을 청구하였다. 그러나 법원은 증거가 부족하다며 P의 주장은 받아들이기 어렵다는 판결을 하였다.

5. 항소의 제기 (원심)[72]

P는 제1심에서 P가 한 주장에서 거론된 D의 행위들이 '업무상 위력에 의한 강제추행'에 해당하지 않더라도, 위 행위들과 D가 그 이후 D에 대한 수사 및 형사재판 과정에서 P를 상대로 추가적으로 한 언행들은 D가 고의적으로 저지른 '직장 등에서 발생하는 신체적 또는 언어적 성희롱 및 갑질 또는 직장 내 괴롭힘에 해당하는 수준의 위법하고 부적절한 행동' 또는 '폭행, 폭언 등 모욕, 성폭력 피해자에 대한 2차 가해행위'에 해당하므로 D가 P에 대하여 불법행위로 인한 손해배상의무를 부담한다고 항소하였다. 그러나 항소법원은 P의 주장에 대하여 P가 제1심에서 제출한 증거들과 추가로 제출한 증거자료를 가지고 P의 위 주장을 인정하기에 부족하다고 판단하였다.

Ⅱ. 대상판결의 내용[73]

대법원은 본 사건에 대해 노동법의 직장 내 괴롭힘과 성희롱에 대한 법리를 인용하여 판단하였다. 성희롱이란 업무, 고용, 그 밖의 관계에서 국가기관

---

[71] 서울중앙지방법원 2019. 8. 27. 선고 2018가단5252208 판결 (손해배상)
[72] 서울중앙지방법원 2020. 9. 18. 선고 2019나54179 판결 (손해배상)
[73] 대법원 2021. 11. 25. 선고 2020다270503 판결

VI. Workplace Bullying and Sexual Harassment: A Case Analysis

to employment, using one's position or related to sexual conduct or sexual demands, etc., to make the other party feel sexually humiliated or disgusted, or to impose disadvantage or condition benefits on them. Here, the unwanted "sexual conduct" refers to physical, verbal, and visual acts related to physical relationships between men and women or physical characteristics of men or women that can objectively cause an average person in the same position to feel sexually humiliated or disgusted according to sound common sense and practices of the community. Furthermore, if a person in a higher position exceeds the proper scope of work and causes physical or mental pain to other employees or worsens the work environment through the use of his or her position or relationship in the workplace, this amounts to illegal "harassment at the workplace" and the cause of civil liability against the defendant for illegal acts against the victimized employee.[74]

The Supreme Court acknowledged the consistent statements of the plaintiff and the defendant regarding workplace harassment and sexual harassment, which had been dismissed in the lower court due to a lack of evidence. "The claims that harassment in the workplace had occurred on the day of the voluntary event in the VIP room is mostly not disputed by D, and a significant portion of it was actively admitted by D in the related criminal case. In addition, considering the specificity and consistency of P's statement and the details of the victim statement summary sheet, as well as the timing and process of P reporting the damage to the support group and reporting to the investigative agency that she was suing D, and D's response in the related criminal case, there is ample room to find that P's claims about verbal sexual harassment in the same time and place are highly likely to be true."

The Supreme Court rejected the decision of the lower court and introduced the labor law definition of workplace harassment and sexual harassment in this case, rather than sexual assault by the employer. The Supreme Court stated, "Furthermore, D's behavior, which has been claimed to constitute harassment in the workplace or verbal sexual harassment, is conduct that exceeds the proper scope of work by D, a superior at the workplace, in an employment relationship, using his or her position to harass or treat other employees unfairly or to create a hostile

---

[74] Supreme Court ruling on Apr. 12, 2018, 2017doo74702; Sept. 16, 2021da219529.

지방자치단체, 각급 학교, 공직유관단체 등 공공단체의 종사자, 직장의 사업주 상급자 또는 근로자가 지위를 이용하거나 업무 등과 관련하여 성적 언동 또는 성적 요구 등으로 상대방에게 성적 굴욕감이나 혐오감을 느끼게 하는 행위 또는 상대방이 성적 언동 또는 요구 등에 따르지 아니한다는 이유로 불이익을 주는 행위를 하는 것을 말한다. 여기에서 '성적 언동'이란, 남녀 간의 육체적 관계나 남성 또는 여성의 신체적 특징과 관련된 육체적, 언어적, 시각적 행위로써 사회공동체의 건전한 상식과 관행에 비추어 볼 때, 객관적으로 상대방과 같은 처지에 있는 일반적이고도 평균적인 사람으로 하여금 성적 굴욕감이나 혐오감을 느끼게 할 수 있는 행위를 의미한다. 또 이러한 지위에 있는 사람이 직장에서의 지위 또는 관계 등의 우월적 지위를 이용하여 업무상 적정범위를 넘어 다른 근로자에게 신체적 정신적 고통을 주거나 근무환경을 악화시켰다면, 이는 위법한 '직장 내 괴롭힘'으로써 피해 근로자에 대한 민사상 불법행위책임의 원인이 된다.[74]

대법원은 원심에서 증거부족으로 기각하였던 직장 내 괴롭힘과 성희롱을 원고의 일관성이 있는 진술과 피고의 진술을 가지고 인정하였다. 자선행사 당일 VIP룸에서의 직장 내 괴롭힘으로 주장된 사실관계는 D도 대부분 다투지 않는 것으로 보이고, 그 중 상당부분은 D가 관련 형사사건에서 적극적으로 인정하기까지 하였다. 또 P의 진술 및 피해내용 정리표 기재 내용상의 구체성 및 일관성, P가 후원회에 피해사실을 신고하고 수사기관에 D를 고소한 시점과 경위 및 관련 형사사건에서 진술을 비롯한 D의 대응을 종합하면, 같은 일시 및 같은 장소에서의 언어적 성희롱에 관한 P의 주장도 그 주장 내용이 사실일 고도의 개연성이 증명되었다고 볼 여지가 충분하다.

대법원은 본 사안에 대해 직장상사의 추행이 아닌 직장 내 괴롭힘과 직장 내 성희롱의 노동법적 논리를 도입하여 원심 판결을 배척하였다. 대법원은 나아가 직장 내 괴롭힘이나 언어적 성희롱에 해당한다고 주장된 D의 행위는, 고용 관계에서 직장의 상급자인 D가 그 지위를 이용하여 업무상 적정 범위를 넘어 근로자인 P에게 신체적 정신적 고통을 준 '직장 내 괴롭힘'이자 그 우월적 지위를 이용하여 여성인 P의 신체적 특징이나 남녀 간의 육체적 관계와 관련된 육체적 언어적 행위로써 P에게 성적 굴욕감이나 혐오감을 느끼게 하는

---

[74] 대법원 2018. 4. 12. 선고 2017두74702 판결, 2021. 9. 16. 선고 2021다219529 판결

working environment, and constitutes a violation of the Labor Standards Act."

III. Commentary

1. Difference between Sexual Assault and Sexual Harassment

P accused D of sexual harassment and forced sexual contact through the use of work-related power in a VIP room and in a vehicle on October 15, 2015. However, D was found not guilty of the criminal charges, as this case fell under the category of workplace harassment and sexual harassment according to the Labor Standards Act, which should have been reported to the Ministry of Employment and Labor. P reported the case to the police as sexual assault, but the judgment was based on the difference between sexual assault and sexual harassment. Article 10 of the Sexual Violence Crimes Prevention Act defines forced sexual contact through the use of work-related power as "the use of hierarchical or authoritative power to engage in unwanted sexual contact against a person who is under one's protection or supervision in relation to work, employment, or other relationships." The Supreme Court defines sexual assault as "an act that objectively violates sexual morality and would cause sexual shame or disgust for an ordinary person, infringing upon the victim's sexual freedom.[75] In other words, for sexual assault to be a criminal offense under the law, there must be violence or coercion that violates the victim's sexual freedom." In contrast, Article 2 of the Equal Employment Act defines workplace sexual harassment as "the use of one's position as an employer, superior, or worker to sexually harass another worker by making sexual advances or engaging in sexual behavior that causes sexual humiliation or disgust." Therefore, sexual harassment does not violate the victim's sexual freedom, but rather refers to behavior in which a superior or a worker harasses another worker through the use of their position or work-related language or actions. The current law imposes imprisonment or a fine for forced sexual contact through work-related power, and administrative fines for workplace or sexual harassment.

2. Burden of Proof

---

[75] Supreme Court ruling on Dec. 24, 2014, 2014do6416; Sept. 26, 2013, 2013do5856.

성희롱에 해당하고, 이는 P에 대한 민사상 불법행위책임의 원인이 될 수 있다고 판시하였다.

Ⅲ. 해설

1. 성추행과 성희롱의 구분

P는 D가 2015년 10월 15일 VIP룸과 차량에서 한 성희롱에 대해 경찰에 '업무상 위력에 의한 강제추행'으로 고소를 제기하였으나 형사처벌은 무죄가 확정되었다. 그 이유는 본 사건은 「근로기준법」상 직장 내 괴롭힘과 성희롱에 해당되므로 노동청에 진정이나 고소를 제기해야 했는데, P는 본 사건을 경찰로 신고하여 성추행으로 형사처벌을 요구하였다. 성추행과 성희롱의 차이를 가지고 판단한 사안이라고 할 수 있다. 성폭력처벌법 제10조 업무상 위력 등에 의한 추행은 업무, 고용이나 그 밖의 관계로 인하여 자기의 보호, 감독을 받는 사람에 대하여 위계 또는 위력으로 추행한 사람을 말한다. 이에 대해 대법원은 성추행이란 객관적으로 일반인에게 성적 수치심이나 혐오감을 일으키게 하는 선량한 성적 도덕관념에 반하는 행위로써 피해자의 성적 자유를 침해하는 것이다고 판시하고 있다.[75] 즉, '성추행'이 형법상 범죄가 되기 위해서는 피해자의 성적 자유를 침해하는 '폭력이나 협박'이 있어야 한다는 것이다. 이에 반해 「남녀고용평등법」 제2조의 직장 내 성희롱 개념은 "직장 내 성희롱"이란 사업주·상급자 또는 근로자가 직장 내의 지위를 이용하거나 업무와 관련하여 다른 근로자에게 성적 언동 등으로 성적 굴욕감 또는 혐오감을 느끼게 하는 것을 말한다.라고 명시하고 있다. 즉, 성희롱은 피해자의 성적 자유를 침해하는 것이 아니라 상급자나 근로자가 직장 내의 지위를 이용하거나 업무와 관련하여 성적인 언어, 행동 등으로 다른 근로자를 괴롭히는 행동을 말한다. 현행법은 업무상 위력에 의한 추행은 징역이나 벌금형의 처분이 있고, 직장 내 성희롱이나 괴롭힘은 행정벌인 과태료 처분 대상이 된다.

2. 입증책임

---

[75] 대법원 2014. 12. 24. 선고 2014도6416 판결, 대법원 2013. 9. 26. 선고 2013도5856 판결.

In cases of workplace harassment or sexual harassment, the burden of proof is crucial. Generally, it lies with the person making the claim, and if they fail to prove it, they lose the case. However, according to Article 30 (Burden of Proof) of the Equal Employment Act, "the burden of proof in disputes related to this Act shall be borne by the employer." Therefore, in matters related to this law, if an employee claims they have a grievance or have suffered damage, they only need to provide evidence that could lead judges or members of the labor commission to reasonably infer that the problems are related to the law.[76] In this particular case, even though the employer and the victim provided different explanations for the occurrence of harassment and sexual misconduct, the Supreme Court recognized P's claims of workplace harassment and sexual harassment as true, as it was reasonable to assume that such events had occurred.

3. Implications of the Ruling

The lower court ruling was dismissed as it mistakenly classified the case as falling under "sexual assault through coercion in the workplace" and failed to address the actual issue of "workplace harassment and sexual harassment." However, the Supreme Court ruled that the harassment and sexual misconduct committed by the superior in this case were not a result of work-related power dynamics but rather stemmed from the use of superior position or relationship in violation of labor standards, causing physical and mental pain to employee P. As a result, the Supreme Court overturned the lower court's ruling and acknowledged the workplace harassment and sexual harassment. Furthermore, the Supreme Court ruled that D's actions constituted "workplace harassment" and went beyond the acceptable boundaries of work, resulting in physical and mental pain for P, as well as "sexual harassment," which caused P to feel sexually humiliated or disgusted, both of which fall under the category of illegal acts under Article 750 of the Civil Code. Therefore, D was ordered to compensate P for the mental damages caused by his illegal actions.

---

[76] Kim, El-lim, "Employer's Responsibility for Sexual Harassment in the Workplace - Supreme Court Decision 95da39533, February 10, 1998," in Labor Case Law: 100 Cases, First Edition, Korean Labor Law Association, Parkyoungsa, 2014.

직장 내 괴롭힘이나 성희롱 사건은 입증책임이 중요하다. 일반적으로 입증책임은 이를 주장하는 사람이 이를 입증해야 하고 입증하지 않으면 패소한다. 그러나 「남녀고용평등법」 제30조(입증책임)에서는 이 법과 관련한 분쟁해결에서 입증책임은 사업주가 부담한다. 이에 따라 이 법과 관련된 문제에 관하여 근로자는 고충과 피해를 받았음을 법관, 노동위원회 위원 등 판단자들이 추측할 수 있을 정도의 실증을 주거나 증거를 제출하면 된다.[76] 이번 대상 판결에서도 상사와 피해자 사이에서 발생한 성희롱이나 괴롭힘에 대해서는 근로자가 일관되게 경찰조사나 법원, 그리고 회사에 이의제기하는 내용이 동일하고, 피고도 그러한 정황을 다른 각도에서 설명했지만 전체적으로 그러한 사실이 일어났을 것이라 추측할 수 있는 상황에서 대법원은 P가 진술한 직장 내 괴롭힘과 성희롱을 모두 사실로 인정하였다.

3. 판결의 시사점

원심 판결은 본 사안을 '업무상 위력 등에 의한 추행'에 관한 사건으로 오해하여, 실질 사례인 '직장 내 괴롭힘과 성희롱'에 관한 필요한 심리를 하지 않음으로써 기각 판결을 하였다. 그러나 대법원은 본 사안에 대해 '업무상 위력으로 인한 추행'이 아니라 「근로기준법」상의 상급자가 직장 내 지위나 관계 등의 우위를 이용한 괴롭힘과 성적 혐오감이나 성적 수치심을 일으킨 내용으로 판단하였다. 이러한 이유로 대법원은 원심의 판결을 취소하고 본 사건에 대해 직장 내 괴롭힘과 성희롱을 인정하였다.

또한 대법원은 D의 직장 내 괴롭힘과 성희롱의 행위는 고용관계에서 직장 내에서의 지위를 이용하여 업무상 적정 범위를 넘어 근로자 P에게 신체적, 정신적으로 고통을 준 '직장 내 괴롭힘'이자 그 지위를 이용하여 여성인 P에게 성적인 굴욕감이나 혐오감을 느끼게 하는 성희롱에 해당된다고 판단하였다. 이는 P에게 D에 대한 명백한 가해 행위이므로 민법 제750조의 불법행위 책임에 따라 P가 입은 정신적 피해에 대해 손해배상 책임을 인정하였다.

---

[76] 김엘림, 직장 내 성희롱 사용자 책임 대법원 1998. 2. 10. 선고 95다39533 판결, 「노동판례백선 초판」, 한국노동법학회 편, 박영사, 2014.

Chapter 3. Workplace Sexual Harassment: Prevention and Response (El-lim Kim)

Section 1. **Measures to Prevent Workplace Sexual Harassment**
  I. Prohibiting Workplace Sexual Harassment
  II. Preventing Workplace Sexual Harassment

Section 2. **Responding to Reported Incidents of Workplace Sexual Harassment**
  I. Responding Inside the Workplace
  II. Handling of Incidents by the Labor Relations Commission
  III. Handling of Incidents by the Minister of Employment and Labor
  IV. Handling of Incidents by the National Human Rights Commission of Korea
  V. Handling of Incidents by Investigative Agencies and the Courts

Section 3. **Issues and Related Cases in Handling Workplace Sexual Harassment Incidents**
  I. The criteria for Judgment by Courts and National Human Rights Commissions
  II. Precedents and Decisions related to Workplace Sexual Harassment
  III. Court Rulings and Decisions related to Sexual Harassment by Superiors
  IV. Court Rulings and Decisions related to Sexual Harassment of Employees

제3장 직장 내 성희롱의 예방과 발생시 조치 및 사건처리사례(김엘림)

제1절 직장 내 성희롱 금지와 예방조치
 Ⅰ. 직장 내 성희롱의 금지
 Ⅱ. 직장 내 성희롱의 예방조치

제2절 직장 내 성희롱 발생 시 조치와 사건처리
 Ⅰ. 사업장 내 발생시 조치와 사건처리
 Ⅱ. 노동위원회의 사건 처리
 Ⅲ. 고용노동부장관의 사건 처리
 Ⅳ. 국가인권위원회의 사건 처리
 Ⅴ. 수사기관과 법원의 사건 처리

제3절 직장 내 성희롱 사건 처리 사례
 Ⅰ. 법원과 국가인권위원회의 판단기준 등
 Ⅱ. 사업주의 성희롱 사건과 관련 판례·결정례
 Ⅲ. 상급자의 성희롱 사건과 관련 판례·결정례
 Ⅳ. 근로자의 성희롱 사건과 관련 판례·결정례

Section 1: Measures to Prevent Workplace Sexual Harassment[77]

I. Prohibiting Workplace Sexual Harassment

1. Prohibiting sexual harassment in the workplace

The Equal Employment Act stipulates in Article 12 (Prohibition of Sexual Harassment in the Workplace) that "employers, superiors, or employees must not engage in sexual harassment in the workplace." Therefore, the scope of those prohibited from engaging in sexual harassment in the workplace under this law are "employers, superiors [and] employees."

2. Legal sanctions against perpetrators of sexual harassment in the workplace

The Equal Employment Act also stipulates that if an employer violates Article 12 and allows sexual harassment in the workplace, the Minister of Employment and Labor may impose a fine of up to KRW 10 million (Article 39, Paragraph 2). The Enforcement Decree to this law specifies the fines as follows in its "Criteria for Imposing Fines for Violations" (Annex 1 to Article 22): (1) KRW 10 million for employers who have received a fine for a violation related to sexual harassment in the workplace within the past 3 years and allow sexual harassment to occur again, (2) KRW 5 million for employers who allow sexual harassment to occur in the workplace against two or more employees multiple times, and (3) KRW 3 million for other cases of sexual harassment in the workplace.

However, this Act does not specifically regulate sanctions other than a fine for negligence, against superiors or employees who engage in sexual harassment in the workplace. If the sexual harassment behavior of employers, superiors, or employees corresponds to disciplinary measures stipulated in employment regulations or workplace collective agreements, they will be subject to sanctions according to such regulations. If it falls under sexual assault crimes within the Act on the Punishment of Sexual Assault, they will be subject to criminal punishment according to that law.

---

[77] Kim El-lim, "Sexual Harassment: Law and Dispute Resolution Cases," Episteme, 2023, pp. 189-192.

제1절 직장 내 성희롱 금지와 예방조치[77]

I. 직장 내 성희롱의 금지

1. 직장 내 성희롱의 금지 대상

「남녀고용평등법」은 제12조(직장 내 성희롱의 금지)에서 "사업주, 상급자 또는 근로자는 직장 내 성희롱을 하여서는 아니 된다."라고 규정하고 있다. 그러므로 이 법의 직장 내 성희롱의 금지 대상은 "사업주, 상급자 또는 근로자"이다.

2. 직장 내 성희롱 행위자에 대한 법적제재

그런데 「남녀고용평등법」은 제12조를 위반하여 사업주가 직장 내 성희롱을 한 경우에는 고용노동부장관이 1천만 원 이하의 과태료를 부과한다는 것을 규정하고 있다(제39조제2항). 그런데 이 법의 시행령은 [과태료 부과기준](제22조 별표 1)에서 ① 직장 내 성희롱과 관련하여 최근 3년 이내에 과태료 처분을 받은 사실이 있는 사업주가 다시 직장 내 성희롱을 한 경우에는 1천만 원, ② 사업주가 한 사람에게 수차례 직장 내 성희롱을 하거나 2명 이상에게 직장 내 성희롱을 한 경우에는 500만 원, ③ 그 밖의 직장 내 성희롱의 경우에는 300만 원으로 정하고 있다.

한편, 이 법은 사업주가 아닌 상급자 또는 근로자의 직장 내 성희롱에 대해서는 사업주에게 징계, 근무장소의 변경, 배치전환, 유급휴가 명령 등 적절한 조치를 하여야 한다고 규정하고 있지만(제14조제5항), 벌칙 조항은 두고 있지 않다. 그러나 사업주, 상급자 또는 근로자의 직장 내 성희롱 행태가 「성폭력처벌법」 상의 성폭력범죄에 해당되면 이 법에 따른 형사처벌을 받게 된다.

---

[77] 김엘림, 「성희롱: 법과 분쟁처리사례」, 에피스테매, 2023, 189~192면.

II. Preventing Workplace Sexual Harassment

1. Implementing sexual harassment prevention education and posting education materials in the workplace

The prevention measures for sexual harassment, including sexual harassment prevention education, are regulated in the Framework Act on Gender Equality and the Equal Employment Act. However, the Enforcement Decree to the Framework Act on Gender Equality stipulates that "The head of national government agencies, local government agencies, and public agencies defined in Article 2 (hereinafter referred to as "national government agencies") shall take the following measures towards preventing sexual harassment in accordance with Article 31(1) of the Act; the employers of businesses or workplaces that are not national government agencies, but are subject to Article 3(1) of the Equal Employment Act shall also take measures towards preventing sexual harassment in accordance with the same Act" (Article 20(1)). Accordingly, education towards preventing workplace sexual harassment in workplaces other than national government agencies, including government agencies, local government agencies, and schools, shall be subject to provisions in the Equal Employment Act regarding sexual harassment prevention education in the workplace.

(1) Obligation to conduct education towards preventing sexual harassment and delegating to an outside institution

1) Persons obligated to provide sexual harassment prevention education

The Equal Employment Act stipulates in Article 13 (1) (Sexual Harassment Prevention Education in the Workplace, etc.) that "Employers shall conduct education on the prevention of sexual harassment (hereinafter referred to as 'sexual harassment prevention education') every year in order to prevent sexual harassment in the workplace and create conditions for employees to work in a safe work environment." Therefore, employers are obligated to conduct sexual harassment prevention education. This does not apply to employers of workplaces where only cohabiting relatives are employed.

However, this Act stipulates that "When applying Article 13, paragraph 1 to workplaces where dispatch workers are dispatched according to the Act on the Protection, etc. of Dispatched Workers, the 'using employer' as defined in Article 2, subparagraph 4 of that Act shall be considered the employer under this law" (Article 34). In the Act on the Protection, etc. of Dispatched Workers, the term "using employer" refers to "a person who uses dispatched workers under a dispatch labor contract" (Article 2, subparagraph 4). "Worker dispatch" refers to "a system in which a sending employer, while maintaining employment relations with a worker after hiring, has the worker work for a using employer under the direction and order of the using employer in accordance with a worker dispatch contract" (Article 2, subparagraph 1).

Ⅱ. 직장 내 성희롱의 예방조치

1. 직장 내 성희롱의 예방을 위한 교육 실시와 자료 게시

성희롱 예방교육 등 방지조치에 관해서는 「양성평등기본법」과 「남녀고용평등법」에서 각각 규정하고 있다. 그런데 「양성평등기본법 시행령」은 "국가기관, 지방자치단체 및 제2조에 따른 공공단체(이하 "국가기관등"이라 한다)의 장은 법 제31조제1항에 따라 성희롱 방지를 위하여 다음 각 호의 조치를 하여야 하며, 「남녀고용평등법」 제3조제1항에 따른 사업 또는 사업장 중 국가기관 등이 아닌 사업 또는 사업장의 사업주는 같은 법에 따라 성희롱 방지조치를 하여야 한다."(제20조제1항)라고 규정하고 있다. 이에 따라 국가기관, 지방자치단체, 각급 학교, 공직유관단체가 아닌 일반사업장의 예방교육은 「남녀고용평등법」의 직장 내 성희롱 예방조치에 관한 규정(제13조, 제13조의2)을 적용받는다.

(1) 예방교육 실시 의무와 교육 위탁
1) 예방 교육의 실시 의무자

「남녀고용평등법」은 제13조(직장 내 성희롱 예방 교육 등)에서 "사업주는 직장 내 성희롱을 예방하고 근로자가 안전한 근로환경에서 일할 수 있는 여건을 조성하기 위하여 직장 내 성희롱의 예방을 위한 교육(이하 "성희롱 예방 교육"이라 한다)을 매년 실시하여야 한다."(제1항)라고 규정하고 있다. 그러므로 예방교육의 실시의무자는 사업주이다. 다만, 시행령 제2조제1항에 따라 이 법의 적용대상이 되지 않는 '동거하는 친족만으로 이루어지는 사업 또는 사업장'의 사업주는 이 법에 따른 예방교육 실시의무자에서 제외된다.

그런데 이 법은 "「파견근로자 보호 등에 관한 법률」(약칭: 파견법)에 따라 파견근로가 이루어지는 사업장에 제13조제1항을 적용할 때에는 「파견법」 제2조제4호에 따른 사용사업주를 이 법에 따른 사업주로 본다."(제34조)라고 규정하고 있다. 「파견법」에서 '사용사업주'란 "근로자파견계약에 따라 파견근로자를 사용하는 자"(제2조제4호)를 말한다. '근로자파견'이란 "파견사업주가 근로자를 고용한 후 그 고용관계를 유지하면서 근로자파견계약의

Section I. Measures to Prevent Workplace Sexual Harassment

"Dispatched worker" refers to "a worker who is employed by a sending employer and subject to worker dispatch" (Article 2, subparagraph 5). Therefore, if a using employer has dispatched workers to a using employer's workplace, the using employer must conduct sexual harassment prevention education for them.

2) Those obligated to attend sexual harassment prevention education

The Equal Employment Act stipulates that "Employers and employees shall receive education on the prevention of sexual harassment in the workplace" (Article 13, paragraph 2). Therefore, employers, supervisors of workplaces and all types of employees, including dispatched workers, are subject to sexual harassment prevention education, but especially employers and employees. and

3) Sexual harassment prevention education in the workplace: Content & methods

The necessary matters regarding the content, methods, and frequency of sexual harassment prevention education in the workplace are stipulated in Article 3 of the Enforcement Decree to the Equal Employment Act, and the details can be seen in Table 5.

<Table 5> Sexual Harassment Prevention Education in the Workplace: Content & Methods

Content	▪ Laws and regulations related to the prevention of workplace sexual harassment ▪ Procedures and criteria for handling workplace sexual harassment ▪ Grievance counseling and relief procedures for employees who experience workplace sexual harassment ▪ Other matters necessary for the prevention of workplace sexual harassment
Frequency	▪ At least once a year
Methods	▪ Employee training, consultations, meetings, or cyber education using information and communication networks such as the Internet, taking into consideration the size and characteristics of the business (However, the preventive education may not be recognized if it is difficult to confirm whether the content was properly delivered to employees because educational materials were simply distributed or posted, or sent via email, or announced on bulletin boards.) ▪ If the business employs fewer than 10 employees at all times and is composed of only one gender (male or female), the preventive education can be conducted by posting or distributing educational materials or promotional materials so that employees can learn the content.

내용에 따라 사용사업주의 지휘·명령을 받아 사용사업주를 위한 근로에 종사하게 하는 것"(제2조제1호)을 말하며, '파견근로자'란 "파견사업주가 고용한 근로자로서 근로자파견의 대상이 되는 사람"(제2조제5호)를 말한다. 그러므로 사용사업주는 사업장에서 파견근로자를 사용하고 있는 경우에는 그 파견근로자에 대한 성희롱 예방교육을 실시해야 한다.

2) 예방 교육의 실시 대상과 수강의무자

「남녀고용평등법」은 "사업주 및 근로자는 직장 내 성희롱 예방 교육을 받아야 한다."(제13조제2항)라고 규정하고 있다. 그러므로 사업장의 사업주, 사용자, 상급자, 파견근로자를 포함한 모든 고용형태의 근로자는 예방교육의 대상이 되며 그 중 사업주 및 근로자는 수강의무자가 된다.

3) 예방 교육의 내용과 방법

직장 내 성희롱 예방 교육의 내용·방법 및 횟수 등에 관하여 필요한 사항은 시행령 제3조가 규정하고 있는데 그 내용은 다음 <표 5>와 같다.

<표 5> 직장 내 성희롱 예방 교육의 내용과 방법

내용	■ 직장 내 성희롱 예방에 관한 법령 ■ 해당 사업장의 직장 내 성희롱 발생 시의 처리절차와 조치기준 ■ 해당 사업장의 직장 내 성희롱 피해 근로자의 고충상담 및 구제절차 ■ 그 밖에 직장 내 성희롱 예방에 필요한 사항
횟수	■ 연 1회 이상
방법	■ 사업의 규모나 특성 등을 고려하여 직원연수·조회·회의, 인터넷 등 정보통신망을 이용한 사이버 교육 등(다만, 단순히 교육자료 등을 배포·게시하거나 전자우편을 보내거나 게시판에 공지하는 데 그치는 등 근로자에게 교육내용이 제대로 전달되었는지 확인하기 곤란한 경우에는 예방교육 실시는 불인정)

Section I. Measures to Prevent Workplace Sexual Harassment

4) Delegating sexual harassment prevention education to an external institution

The Equal Employment Act stipulates in Article 13-2 (Entrustment of Preventive Education of Sexual Harassment) that "Employers may delegate the implementation of sexual harassment prevention education to an institution designated by the Minister of Employment and Labor (hereinafter referred to as the 'Sexual Harassment Prevention Education Institution')" (paragraph 1). The designated Sexual Harassment Prevention Education Institution shall be from among the institutions designated by the Minister of Employment and Labor according to the Enforcement Decree to this Act, and shall have at least one instructor designated by the Enforcement Decree to this Act (Paragraph 3).

In accordance with this, the Enforcement Rules of this Act stipulate the delegation of prevention education as follows. The Minister of Employment and Labor shall designate the Sexual Harassment Prevention Education Institution from among the following: ① Employer organizations, ② Labor law firms under Article 7-2 of the Certified Public Labor Attorney Act, ③ Private organizations (Equal Employment Counseling Offices) that receive support for expenses under Article 23 of this Act, ④ Training and education facilities operated by business groups under Article 2(2) of the Monopoly Regulation and Fair Trade Act(Paragraph 2 of Article 6). The term "instructor designated by the Enforcement Decree to this Act" referred to in Paragraph 3 of Article 13-2 of this Act means "an instructor who has completed the training program directly conducted by the Minister of Employment and Labor, or approved by the Minister of Employment and Labor, and who has also completed instructor training with full or partial support of expenses" (Article 6 (3)). If an employer delegates the sexual harassment prevention education to the head of a sexual harassment prevention education institution, the institution shall organize a training course of at least one hour in accordance with paragraph 3 of Article 13-2 of this Act and ensure that the instructor designated under paragraph 3 of Article 6 conducts the education (Article 8).

(2) Posting of sexual harassment prevention education materials

According to the law, "Employers are required to always make available by posting and distributing the materials on sexual harassment prevention education in a place where workers can freely access" (Article 13, paragraph 3).

However, employers of workplaces with fewer than 10 employees and employers of businesses consisting entirely of the same gender (either male or female), may conduct sexual harassment prevention education by posting or distributing educational/promotional materials that allow workers to know the contents of sexual harassment prevention education, including ① relevant laws and regulations on sexual harassment in the workplace, ② procedures and criteria for handling incidents of sexual harassment in the workplace, ③ grievance counseling and relief procedures for employees who have experienced workplace sexual harassment and ④ other necessary matters for preventing sexual harassment in the workplace" (Article 3, paragraph 4).[78]

4) 예방교육의 위탁

「남녀고용평등법」은 제13조의2(성희롱 예방 교육의 위탁)에서 "사업주는 성희롱 예방 교육을 고용노동부장관이 지정하는 기관(이하 "성희롱 예방 교육기관"이라 한다)에 위탁하여 실시할 수 있다."(제1항)라고 규정하고 있다. 성희롱 예방 교육기관은 고용노동부령으로 정하는 기관 중에서 지정하되, 고용노동부령으로 정하는 강사를 1명 이상 두어야 한다(제3항).

이 법의 시행규칙에 따라 고용노동부장관은 ① 사업주단체, ② 「공인노무사법」 제7조의2에 따른 노무법인, ③ 법 제23조에 따라 비용을 지원받는 민간단체(고용평등상담실), ④ 「독점규제 및 공정거래에 관한 법률」 제2조제2호에 따른 기업집단이 운영하는 연수·교육 시설 중에서 성희롱 예방교육기관을 지정하여야 한다(제6조제2항).

법 제13조의2제3항에서 '고용노동부령으로 정하는 강사'란 "고용노동부장관이 직접 실시하는 강사양성교육 또는 고용노동부장관이 교육과정을 승인하거나 비용의 전부 또는 일부를 지원하는 강사양성교육을 수료한 강사"(제6조제3항)를 말한다. 성희롱 예방 교육기관의 장은 사업주에게 위탁받아 성희롱 예방 교육을 하는 경우에는 법 제13조의2 제3항에 따라 1시간 이상의 교육과정을 편성하여야 하고 제6조제3항에 따른 강사가 교육을 하도록 하여야 한다(제8조).

(2) 예방교육 내용의 자료 게시

"사업주는 성희롱 예방 교육의 내용을 근로자가 자유롭게 열람할 수 있는 장소에 항상 게시하거나 갖추어 두어 근로자에게 널리 알려야 한다."(제13조제3항)

그리고 '상시 10명 미만의 근로자를 고용하는 사업'과 '사업주 및 근로자 모두가 남성 또는 여성 중 어느 한 성(性)으로 구성된 사업'의 사업주는 성희롱 예방교육의 내용을 근로자가 알 수 있도록 교육자료 또는 홍보물을 게시하거나 배포하는 방법으로 직장 내 성희롱 예방 교육을 할 수 있다."(시행령 제3조제4항)[78]

---

[78] 그런데 이러한 사업에도 직장 내 성희롱이 발생할 수 있으므로 교육자료 또는 홍보물을 게시하거나 배포하는 방법으로만 직장 내 성희롱 예방 교육을 할 수 있게 한 시행령의 규정은 재검토가 필요하다고 본다.

Section I. Measures to Prevent Workplace Sexual Harassment

(3) Sanctions for violating of regulations on sexual harassment prevention education

The Equal Employment Act stipulates that the Minister of Employment and Labor may impose a fine of up to KRW 5 million for each violation, 1) if an employer fails to provide sexual harassment prevention education in violation of Article 13, paragraph 1, 2) or fails to always post or make available the contents of sexual harassment prevention education in a place where workers can freely access in violation of Article 13, Paragraph 3 (Article 39, Paragraph 3, Item 2 and Item 3).

2. Composing and posting guidelines for the prevention of workplace sexual harassment

The Equal Employment Act stipulates that "employers must take measures to prevent and prohibit sexual harassment in the workplace in accordance with the standards set by the Minister of Employment and Labor" (Article 13, paragraph 4). In accordance with this provision, the Enforcement Rules to this Act state in Article 5-2 (Measures for the Prevention and Prohibition of Sexual Harassment) that "employers must establish guidelines for the prevention of sexual harassment in the workplace in accordance with Article 13, Paragraph 4 of the Act, and must always post or provide them in a place where employees can freely access them" (Paragraph 1). These sexual harassment prevention guidelines should include: ① Matters related to counseling and handling of complaints regarding sexual harassment in the workplace, ② Procedures for investigating sexual harassment in the workplace, ③ Procedures for protecting victims of sexual harassment in the workplace, ④ Procedures and levels of disciplinary action against perpetrators of sexual harassment in the workplace, ⑤ Any other matters necessary for the prevention and prohibition of sexual harassment in the workplace (Paragraph 2)."

3. Utilizing an "honorary supervisor for employment equality"

The Equal Employment Act allows employers to appoint an honorary supervisor for employment equality. This honorary supervisor shall perform the following tasks: ① Provide counseling and advice to victims of discrimination and sexual harassment in the workplace, ② Participate in voluntary self-assessments and give guidance on the implementation of employment equality policies in the workplace, ③ Provide improvement plans to employers about violation of laws, and report to supervisory agencies, ④ Promote and raise awareness about the equal employment systems between men and women, and ⑤ Perform other tasks designated by the

---

[78] However, considering that sexual harassment can also occur in such workplaces, the measures that allow sexual harassment prevention education to be conducted only by posting or distributing educational materials or promotional materials shall be reconsidered.

(3) 예방 교육 관련 법규정 위반에 대한 제재

「남녀고용평등법」은 사업주가 "제13조제1항을 위반하여 성희롱 예방 교육을 하지 아니한 경우", "제13조제3항을 위반하여 성희롱 예방 교육의 내용을 근로자가 자유롭게 열람할 수 있는 장소에 항상 게시하거나 갖추어 두지 아니한 경우"에는 각각 500만 원의 과태료를 고용노동부장관이 부과한다는 것을 규정하고 있다(제39조제3항의 제1호의2,와 제1호의3, 시행령의 [과태료의 부과기준]).

2. 직장 내 성희롱 예방지침의 작성과 게시

「남녀고용평등법」은 "사업주는 고용노동부령으로 정하는 기준에 따라 직장 내 성희롱 예방 및 금지를 위한 조치를 하여야 한다."라고 규정한 조항(제13조제4항)을 두고 있다.

이에 따라 이 법의 시행규칙은 제5조의2(성희롱 예방 및 금지를 위한 조치)에서 "사업주는 법 제13조제4항에 따라 직장 내 성희롱 예방 및 금지를 위하여 성희롱 예방지침을 마련하고 사업장 내 근로자가 자유롭게 열람할 수 있는 장소에 항상 게시하거나 갖추어 두어야 한다."(제1항)라고 규정하고 있다. 이 성희롱 예방지침에는 ① 직장 내 성희롱 관련 상담 및 고충 처리에 필요한 사항, ② 직장 내 성희롱 조사절차, ③ 직장 내 성희롱 발생 시 피해자 보호절차, ④ 직장 내 성희롱 행위자 징계절차 및 징계 수준, ⑤ 그 밖에 직장 내 성희롱 예방 및 금지를 위하여 필요한 사항이 포함되어야 한다(제2항).

3. 명예고용평등감독관의 활용

「남녀고용평등법」은 사업주에게 명예고용평등감독관(이하 "명예감독관"이라 한다)을 둘 수 있도록 하고 있다. 명예감독관은 " ① 해당 사업장의 차별 및 직장 내 성희롱 발생 시 피해 근로자에 대한 상담·조언 ② 해당 사업장의 고용평등 이행상태 자율점검 및 지도 시 참여 ③ 법령위반 사실이 있는 사항에 대하여 사업주에 대한 개선 건의 및 감독기관에 대한 신고 ④ 남녀고용평등 제도에 대한 홍보·계몽 ⑤ 그 밖에 남녀고용평등의 실현을 위하여 고용노동부장관이 정하는 업무"를 수행한다(제24조제2항). 그러므로 이 명예감독관의 업무

Section I. Measures to Prevent Workplace Sexual Harassment

Minister of Employment and Labor for the realization of equal employment between men and women (Article 24, paragraph 2).

Therefore, employers can take measures to prevent the occurrence of sexual harassment in the workplace through voluntary self-assessments and other tasks performed by the honorary supervisor for employment equality.

The honorary supervisor for employment equality can resolve matters through consultation between labor and management or referring the matter to labor-management council for discussion (Enforcement Rules to the Act, Article 16 (3)). In principle, when the honorary supervisor for employment equality performs these tasks, it shall be done on a non-regular and unpaid basis (Article 16, paragraph 5 of the Enforcement Rules).

The Minister of Employment and Labor can appoint an honorary supervisor for employment equality from among those recommended by labor and management in the workplace, in order to promote the implementation of equal employment between men and women in the workplace (Article 24, paragraph 1). The persons eligible for such appointment are as follows: ① Members of the labor-management council or grievance handling committee under the Act on the Promotion of Employees' Participation and Cooperation, ② Managers of labor unions or HR departments, and ③ Other persons who are considered suitable to realize equal employment between men and women in the workplace (Article 16, paragraph 1 of the Enforcement Rules).

Employers are prohibited from taking unfavorable actions, such as personnel disadvantages, against workers who have performed their duties as honorary supervisor for employment equality (Article 24, paragraph 3). If an employer violates Article 24, paragraph 3 and takes unfavorable actions against such a worker, they can be fined up to KRW 5 million (Article 37, paragraph 4, item 6).

4. Labor-Management consultation on prevention of sexual harassment in the workplace

The Act on the Promotion of Employees' Participation and Cooperationaims to promote industrial peace and contribute to the development of the national economy by enhancing mutual participation and cooperation between workers and employers to promote the welfare of workers and sound development of enterprises (Article 1).

This law defines a labor-management council (LMC) as a consultative body established to promote the welfare of workers and the sound development of enterprises through the participation and cooperation of workers and employers (Article 3, clause 1). It also mandates the installation of such council in businesses or workplaces that employ 30 or more workers on a regular basis and have decision-making authority over working conditions (Article 4, clause 1). Anyone who refuses or obstructs the establishment of an LMC without justifiable reason may be subject to a fine of up to KRW 10 million (Article 30, clause 1). The council is composed of an equal number of representatives from workers and employers, with

수행을 통해 사업주는 직장 내 성희롱의 발생 예방을 도모할 수 있다.

명예감독관은 법 제24조제2항에 따른 업무를 수행하는 경우에 노사의 협의를 통하여 해결할 필요가 있다고 판단되는 사안은 노사협의회의 토의에 부쳐 처리하게 할 수 있다(시행규칙 제16조제3항). 업무 수행은 비상근, 무보수로 함을 원칙으로 한다(시행규칙 제16조제5항).

고용노동부장관은 명예감독관을 사업장의 남녀고용평등 이행을 촉진하기 위하여 그 사업장 소속 근로자 중 노사가 추천하는 사람으로 위촉할 수 있다(제24조제1항). 명예감독관으로 위촉될 수 있는 사람은 "① 「근로자참여 및 협력증진에 관한 법률」에 따른 노사협의회의 위원 또는 고충처리위원, ② 노동조합의 임원 또는 인사·노무 담당부서의 관리자, ③ 그 밖에 해당 사업의 남녀고용평등을 실현하기 위하여 활동하기에 적합하다고 인정하는 사람"(시행규칙 제16조제1항)이다.

사업주는 명예감독관으로서 정당한 임무 수행을 한 것을 이유로 해당 근로자에게 인사상 불이익 등의 불리한 조치를 하여서는 아니 된다(제24조제3항). 사업주가 이를 위반하면 500만 원 이하의 벌금에 처한다(제37조제4항제6호).

4. 직장 내 성희롱 예방에 관한 노사협의

「근로자참여 및 협력증진에 관한 법률」(약칭: 근로자참여법)은 "근로자와 사용자 쌍방이 참여와 협력을 통하여 노사 공동의 이익을 증진함으로써 산업평화를 도모하고 국민경제 발전에 이바지함을 목적으로 한다."(제1조)

이 법은 '노사협의회'를 "근로자와 사용자가 참여와 협력을 통하여 근로자의 복지증진과 기업의 건전한 발전을 도모하기 위하여 구성하는 협의기구"(제3조제1호)로 규정하고, 상시(常時) 30명 이상의 근로자를 사용하고 근로조건에 대한 결정권이 있는 사업이나 사업장에 그 설치를 의무화하고 있다(제4조제1항). 이 협의회의 설치를 정당한 사유 없이 거부하거나 방해한 자는 1천만 원 이하의 벌금에 처한다(제30조제1호). 협의회는 근로자와 사용자를 대표하는 같은 수의 위원으로 구성하되, 각 3명 이상 10명 이하로 한다(제6조제1항). 협의회는 3개월마다 정기적으로 회의를 개최하여야 하고(제12조제1항), 필요에 따라 임시회의를 개최할 수 있다(제12조제2항). 사용자가 제12조제

a minimum of 3 and a maximum of 10 members each (Article 6, clause 1). The council must hold regular meetings every 3 months (Article 12, clause 1), and may also hold temporary meetings if needed (Article 12, clause 2). If the employer violates Article 12, clause 1 by failing to hold regular LMC meetings, they may be subject to a fine of up to KRW 2 million (Article 32). The duties of the council are classified into matters for consultation (Article 20), matters for decision (Article 21), matters for reporting (Article 22), and handling of grievances (Article 28).

However, on April 16, 2019, the Act included "matters related to the prevention of sexual harassment in the workplace as stipulated in Article 2, clause 2 of the Equal Employment Act(Article 20, clause 1, item 16)" in the matters for consultation. The decisions of the council are made with the attendance of a majority of worker members and employer members, and require the approval of two-thirds or more of the attending members (Article 20, clause 2). The council must promptly inform workers of the decisions made (Article 23). Workers and employers are required to faithfully implement the decisions made by the council (Article 24). Anyone who fails to implement the decisions made by the council in violation of Article 24 without justifiable reason may be subject to a fine of up to KRW 10 million (Article 30, clause 2).

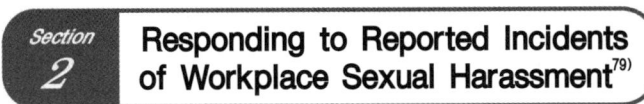

Ⅰ. Responding Inside the Workplace

1. Reporting and filing of reports

(1) Reporting

1) Reporting of grievances related to sexual harassment

Article 25 of the Equal Employment Act stipulates that "employees may report grievances to employers regarding matters related to Article 12 (Prohibition of Sexual Harassment in the Workplace), Article 13 (Prevention Education on Sexual Harassment in the Workplace), Article 13-2 (Outsourcing of Sexual Harassment Prevention Education), Article 14 (Measures to be Taken in the Event of Sexual Harassment in the Workplace), Article 14-2 (Prevention of Sexual Harassment by

---

79) Kim El-lim, "Sexual Harassment: Law and Dispute Resolution Cases," Episteme, 2023, pp. 193~214, pp. 253~282

1항을 위반하여 협의회를 정기적으로 개최하지 아니하면 200만 원 이하의 벌금에 처한다(제32조). 협의회의 임무는 협의사항(제20조), 의결사항(제21조), 보고사항(제22조), 고충처리(제28조) 등으로 구분된다.

그런데 이 법은 2019년 4월 16일, 노사협의회가 협의하여야 할 사항에 "「남녀고용평등법」 제2조제2호에 따른 직장 내 성희롱 및 고객 등에 의한 성희롱 예방에 관한 사항"을 신설하였다(제20조제1항제16호). 협의회의 협의사항은 근로자위원과 사용자위원 각 과반수의 출석으로 개최하고 출석위원 3분의 2 이상의 찬성으로 의결할 수 있다(제20조제2항). 협의회는 의결된 사항을 신속히 근로자에게 널리 알려야 한다(제23조). 근로자와 사용자는 협의회에서 의결된 사항을 성실하게 이행하여야 한다(제24조). 제24조를 위반하여 협의회에서 의결된 사항을 정당한 사유 없이 이행하지 아니한 자는 1천만 원 이하의 벌금에 처한다(제30조제2호).

제2절 직장 내 성희롱 발생 시 조치와 사건처리[79]

I. 사업장 내 발생시 조치와 사건처리

1. 신고와 신고 접수

(1) 신고
1) 성희롱 관련 규정에 관한 고충의 신고
「남녀고용평등법」은 제25조(분쟁의 자율적 해결)에서 "제12조(직장 내 성희롱의 금지), 제13조(직장 내 성희롱 예방 교육 등), 제13조의2(성희롱 예방 교육의 위탁), 제14조(직장 내 성희롱 발생 시 조치), 제14조의2(고객

---
[79] 김엘림, 「성희롱: 법과 분쟁처리사례」, 에피스테메, 2023, 193~214면, 253~282면

Section 2. Responding to Reported Incidents of Workplace Sexual Harassment

Customers or Others) and anti-discrimination provisions,[80] maternity protection provisions,[81] and provisions on support for reconciliation of work and family life."[82] Such grievances shall be reported verbally, in writing, by mail, by phone, by fax, or through the Internet, etc., according to Article 18, paragraph 1 of the Enforcement Rules.

2) Reporting sexual harassment incidents

The Equal Employment Act stipulates in Article 14 (Measures in Case of Sexual Harassment in the Workplace) that "anyone who comes to realize the occurrence of sexual harassment in the workplace may report such fact to the employer" (paragraph 1). Accordingly, not only victims but also third parties such as colleagues or labor unions can report incidents of sexual harassment.

However, this law does not have provisions regarding measures in cases where the victim does not wish to report. The National Human Rights Commission of Korea Act stipulates in Article 32 (Resolution of Disputes, etc.) that "if it is clear that a person other than the victim does not wish to undergo an investigation in a dispute, the National Human Rights Commission may dismiss such dispute" (paragraph 3 of Article 1). If a dismissal is made, no investigation shall take place.

3) Reporting on sexual harassment by customers, etc.

The Equal Employment Act stipulates in Article 14-2 (Prevention of Sexual Harassment by Customers, etc.) that "if a person who is closely related to the performance of duties, such as customers, engages in sexual behavior or other actions that cause sexual humiliation or disgust to a worker during the course of that worker performing duties, and the worker requests resolution of the resulting grievance, the employer shall take appropriate measures, such as changing the place

---

[80] Provisions on Prohibition of Gender Discrimination according to Article 7 (Recruitment and Hiring), Article 9 (Gifts or Benefits other than Wages), Article 10 (Education, Placement, and Promotion), Article 11 (Retirement Age, Retirement, and Dismissal), Equal Pay for Equal Work within the same value labor in the same business according to Article 8 (Wages), Prohibition of Conclusion of Employment Contracts based on Marriage, Pregnancy, or Childbirth as a Reason for Terminating Employment of Female Workers according to paragraph 2 of Article 11

[81] Cooperation in all procedures, including the preparation and verification of relevant documents, for workers to receive maternity leave and benefits, etc., in accordance with paragraph 4 of Article 18 (Support for Maternity Leave, etc.), Article 18-2 (Spousal Childbirth Leave)

[82] Article 19 (Parental Leave), Article 19-2 (Reduction of Working Hours during Childcare Period), Article 19-3 (Working Conditions during Childcare Period), Article 19-4 (Forms of Utilization of Parental Leave and Reduction of Working Hours during Childcare Period), Article 19-5 (Other Measures for Childcare Support), Article 19-6 (Employer's Support for Returning to Work), Article 21 (Establishment and Support of Workplace Childcare Centers, etc.), Article 22-2 (Support for Family Care by Workers)

등에 의한 성희롱 방지)와 차별금지 규정[80], 모성보호 규정[81] 및 일·가정양립 지원 규정[82]에 따른 사항에 관하여 근로자가 사업주에게 고충을 신고할 수 있다."라고 규정하고 있다. 이 고충 신고는 구두, 서면, 우편, 전화, 팩스 또는 인터넷 등의 방법으로 하여야 한다(시행규칙 제18조제1항).

2) 성희롱 발생의 신고

「남녀고용평등법」은 제14조(직장 내 성희롱 발생 시 조치)에서 "누구든지 직장 내 성희롱 발생 사실을 알게 된 경우 그 사실을 해당 사업주에게 신고할 수 있다."(제1항)라고 규정하고 있다. 이에 따라 피해자가 아닌 동료, 노동조합 등 제3자도 성희롱 발생의 신고를 할 수 있다.

그런데 이 법은 피해자가 신고하기를 원하지 아니한 경우의 조치에 관한 규정을 두고 있지 않다. 「국가인권위원회법」은 제32조(진정의 각하 등)에서 "피해자가 아닌 사람이 한 진정에서 피해자가 조사를 원하지 아니하는 것이 명백한 경우"에는 국가인권위원회가 그 진정을 각하한다는 것을 규정하고 있다(제1항제3호). 각하가 되면 조사가 실시되지 않는다.

3) 고객 등의 성적 언동에 대한 고충 신고

「남녀고용평등법」은 제14조의2(고객 등에 의한 성희롱 방지)에서 "사업주는 고객 등 업무와 밀접한 관련이 있는 사람이 업무수행 과정에서 성적인 언동 등을 통하여 근로자에게 성적 굴욕감 또는 혐오감 등을 느끼게 하여 해당 근로자가 그로 인한 고충 해소를 요청할 경우 근무 장소 변경, 배치전환, 유급휴가의 명령 등 적절한 조치를 하여야 한다."(제1항)라고 규정하고 있다. 금융관계법들은 고객의 성적 언동으로부터 고객응대근로자를 보호하는 규정을 두고 있다.

그러므로 사업주, 상급자, 근로자가 아닌 고객 등의 성적 언동에 의한 피해

---

[80] 제7조(모집과 채용), 제9조(임금 외의 금품 등), 제10조(교육·배치 및 승진), 제11조(정년·퇴직 및 해고)에 따른 남녀차별금지규정, 제8조(임금)에 따른 동일한 사업 내의 동일 가치 노동에 대한 동일한 임금 지급, 제11조제2항에 따른 여성 근로자의 혼인, 임신 또는 출산을 퇴직 사유로 예정하는 근로계약 체결 금지

[81] 제18조(출산전후휴가 등에 대한 지원)) 제4항에 따른 근로자가 출산전후휴가급여 등을 받으려는 경우 관계 서류의 작성·확인 등 모든 절차에의 적극 협력, 제18조의2(배우자 출산휴가)

[82] 제19조(육아휴직), 제19조의2(육아기 근로시간 단축), 제19조의3(육아기 근로시간 단축 중 근로조건 등), 제19조의4(육아휴직과 육아기 근로시간 단축의 사용형태), 제19조의5(육아지원을 위한 그 밖의 조치), 제19조의6(직장복귀를 위한 사업주의 지원), 제21조(직장어린이집 설치 및 지원 등), 제22조의2(근로자의 가족 돌봄 등을 위한 지원)

Section 2. Responding to Reported Incidents of Workplace Sexual Harassment

of work, reassigning duties, or ordering paid leave" (paragraph 1). Finance-related Acts also have provisions to protect customer service workers who are subjected to sexual harassment by customers, etc.

Therefore, victims of sexual harassment by customers or employers, supervisors, or non-worker individuals, can also report grievances.

(2) Recognition of reporting

Complaints that are related to sexual harassment and its regulations, sexual harassment by customers or others, must be made to the employer. The employer must clearly and specifically outline the methods, department in charge and procedures regarding recognizing complaints and the handling process. This can be done when composing the rules of employment, collective agreements, or labor-management consultation agreements.

2. Investigation

(1) Prompt investigation to verify facts

According to Article 14 (2) proviso of the Equal Employment Act, the employer must promptly conduct an investigation to verify the facts when receiving a report or becoming aware of sexual harassment in the workplace, otherwise the employer is subject to a fine for negligence of up to KRW 5 million Korean (Article 39(3), subparagraph 1-4).

(2) Protective measures for alleged victims during the investigation process

1) Prohibiting actions that cause sexual embarrassment for the victim during the investigation

According to this law, when conducting an investigation to verify the facts as per the Article 14(2) proviso, "the employer must take necessary measures to ensure that the victim employee or the employee who claims to be a victim (hereinafter referred to as 'victim employee, etc.') does not experience sexual embarrassment or similar emotions during the investigation process" (Article 14(2), latter part).

2) Interim measures for alleged victims

This law stipulates that "during the investigation period pursuant to paragraph 2,

근로자도 고충을 신고할 수 있다.

(2) 신고의 접수

성희롱 관련 규정에 관한 고충신고, 성희롱 발생의 신고, 고객 등의 성적 언동에 대한 고충 신고는 사업주에 대하여 해야 한다. 그러므로 사업주는 취업규칙, 단체협약, 노사협의서 등으로 신고의 방법과 접수처, 접수 절차와 처리 등에 관하여 명확하고 구체적으로 규정하여야 한다.

2. 조사

(1) 신속한 사실확인 조사

「남녀고용평등법」은 제14조(직장 내 성희롱 발생 시 조치)에서 "사업주는 제1항에 따른 신고를 받거나 직장 내 성희롱 발생 사실을 알게 된 경우에는 지체 없이 그 사실 확인을 위한 조사를 하여야 한다."(제2항 전단)라고 규정하고 있다.

사업주가 제14조제2항 전단을 위반하여 직장 내 성희롱 발생 사실 확인을 위한 조사를 하지 아니한 경우에는 500만원의 과태료를 고용노동부장관이 부과한다(제39조제3항제1호의4, 시행령의 [과태료 부과기준]).

(2) 조사 과정에서 피해자 등에 대한 보호조치

1) 피해자 등에 대한 성적 수치심의 유발금지

「남녀고용평등법」은 제14조제2항 전단에 따라 "사업주가 사실 확인을 위한 조사를 하는 경우 직장 내 성희롱과 관련하여 피해를 입은 근로자 또는 피해를 입었다고 주장하는 근로자(이하 "피해근로자등"이라 한다)가 조사 과정에서 성적 수치심 등을 느끼지 아니하도록 하여야 한다."(제14조제2항 후단)라고 규정하고 있다.

2) 피해자 등에 대한 임시조치

이 법은 "사업주는 제2항에 따른 조사기간 동안 피해근로자등을 보호하기 위하여 필요한 경우 해당 피해근로자등에 대하여 근무장소의 변경, 유급휴가

Section 2. Responding to Reported Incidents of Workplace Sexual Harassment

the employer must take appropriate measures; such as changing the workplace or granting paid leave to protect the victim employee, etc., and in doing so, the employer must not take measures is against the will of the victim employee, etc." (Article 14(3)).

(3) Prohibiting disclosure of confidential information by participants in the investigation

This law stipulates that "those 1) who have investigated the occurrence of sexual harassment in the workplace, 2) received reports regarding the investigation, or 3) otherwise participated in the investigation process, shall not disclose the confidential information they have learned during the investigation to others contrary to the will of the victim employee, etc. However, this does not apply to reporting the information related to the employer or providing necessary information upon request from relevant offices" (Article 14, paragraph 7).

If an employer violates Article 14, paragraph 7 by disclosing the confidential information to others, he or she is subject to a fine for negligence of up to KRW 5 million imposed by the Minister of Employment and Labor (Article 39, paragraph 3, clause 1-7). The Enforcement Decree sets KRW 5 million as the standard.

(4) Burden of proof

This law stipulates in Article 30 (Burden of Proof) that "in resolving disputes related to this law (including Article 26 to Article 29-7), the burden of proof shall be borne by the employer." Accordingly, in issues related to the Equal Employment Act, workers shall present or submit circumstantial evidence that allows the judges, labor relations commission members, and other decision-makers to reasonably infer the existence of grievances and damages. The burden of proof that there was no occurrence of sexual harassment or that personnel and management actions that have caused the dispute are not related to sexual harassment, shall be borne by the employer.

Generally, the burden of proof rests on the party who makes the claim. However, in employment discrimination disputes, it is often difficult for workers to prove their claims as companies do not usually disclose personnel and management information that could serve as evidence. Taking such circumstances into consideration, Article 30 of the Equal Employment Act is a legislative measure designed to facilitate workers reporting discrimination and illegal acts such as sexual harassment.

명령 등 적절한 조치를 하여야 한다. 이 경우 사업주는 피해근로자등의 의사에 반하는 조치를 하여서는 아니 된다."(제14조제3항)라고 규정하고 있다.

(3) 조사 관여자의 비밀누설금지

이 법은 "직장 내 성희롱 발생 사실을 조사한 사람, 조사 내용을 보고 받은 사람 또는 그 밖에 조사 과정에 참여한 사람은 해당 조사 과정에서 알게 된 비밀을 피해근로자 등의 의사에 반하여 다른 사람에게 누설하여서는 아니 된다. 다만, 조사와 관련된 내용을 사업주에게 보고하거나 관계 기관의 요청에 따라 필요한 정보를 제공하는 경우는 제외한다."(제14조제7항)라고 규정하고 있다.

사업주가 제14조제7항을 위반하여 직장 내 성희롱 발생 사실 조사 과정에서 알게 된 비밀을 다른 사람에게 누설한 경우에는 500만 원의 과태료를 고용노동부장관으로부터 부과 받는다(제39조제3항제1호의7, 시행령의 [과태료 부과 기준]).

(4) 입증책임의 부담

「남녀고용평등법」은 제30조(입증책임)에서 "이 법과 관련한 분쟁해결 (제26조부터 제29조까지) 및 제29조의2부터 제29조의7까지를 포함한다)은 사업주가 부담한다."라고 규정하고 있다. 이에 따라 「남녀고용평등법」과 관련된 문제에 관하여 근로자는 고충과 피해를 받았음을 법관, 노동위원회 위원 등 판단자들이 추측할 수 있을 정도의 심증을 주거나 증거를 제출하는 소명(疎明)을 하면 된다. 직장 내 성희롱의 발생 사실이 없다거나 분쟁의 원인이 된 인사 및 경영상의 조치가 성희롱과 관련된 것이 아니며 정당한 조치임을 증명할 책임은 사업주가 부담한다.

통상 분쟁에서 입증책임은 권리를 주장하는 자가 부담하는 것이 원칙이다. 그런데 고용차별과 관련한 분쟁에서는 그 판단자료가 될 수 있는 인사 및 경영자료 등을 일반적으로 기업이 공개하지 않으므로 근로자가 입증하기 매우 어렵다. 이 법의 제30조는 이러한 상황을 감안하여 근로자가 성차별과 성희롱 등 위법행위에 대한 신고를 용이하게 할 수 있도록 마련된 입법조치이다.

Section 2. Responding to Reported Incidents of Workplace Sexual Harassment

3. Handling of incidents

(1) Handling of incidents by the employer

When an employer receives a report of sexual harassment, the employer must promptly conduct an investigation to confirm whether sexual harassment indeed occurred in the workplace, and take protective measures for the alleged victim and, in the event sexual harassment did occur, take disciplinary measures against the perpetrator in accordance with Article 14(3) to (5). In addition, unless there are special reasons otherwise, if the employer receives a complaint from an employee in accordance with Article 25 (Voluntary Resolution of Disputes), the employer must make efforts to handle the reported complaint directly, or delegate it to the labor-management council established under the Act on Promotion of Employees' Participation and Cooperation within 10 days from the date of complaint to reach an autonomous resolution. If the employer handles the complaint directly, the employee must be notified of the outcome. If the complaint is delegated to the labor-management council for handling, the employee must be notified of such (Article 18(2) of the Enforcement Decree).

(2) Handling of incidents by the labor-management council

If the employer has delegated the handling of the incident to the labor-management council, the council may appoint a grievance handling member or committee to handle the incident. The Act on The Promotion of Employees' Participation And Cooperation stipulates that "every business or workplace must establish a complaint handling committee to listen to and handle workers' complaints. However, this does not apply to businesses or workplaces with fewer than 30 regular employees at all times" (Article 26).

The complaint handling committee shall consist of no more than 3 members each, representing both labor and management. In workplaces where there is a labor-management council, the council shall appoint the member(s). However, if there is no labor-management council, the employer shall appoint the member(s) (Article 27). The complaint handling committee must notify the relevant employee of the measures taken and the outcome within 10 days after listening to the complaint (Article 28(1)). If it is difficult for the complaint handling committee to handle the matter, it shall be referred to the labor-management council for deliberation (Article 28(2)).

3. 사건처리

(1) 사업주의 사건처리

사업주는 「남녀고용평등법」 제14조(직장 내 성희롱 발생 시 조치)에 따라 직장 내 성희롱의 발생 신고를 받은 때에는 지체 없이 그 사실 확인을 위한 조사를 하여야 하며(제2항), 직장 내 성희롱의 발생 사실을 확인한 후 제3항부터 제6항에 따른 피해자에 대한 보호조치와 행위자에 대한 제재 조치를 하여야 한다.

그리고 사업주는 제25조(분쟁의 자율적 해결)에 따라 근로자로부터 고충신고를 받은 경우 특별한 사유가 없으면 신고 접수일부터 10일 이내에 신고된 고충을 직접 처리하거나 「근로자참여법」에 따라 설치된 노사협의회에 위임하여 처리하게 하는 등 자율적 처리를 위하여 노력하여야 한다. 이 경우 사업주가 직접 처리한 경우에는 처리 결과를, 노사협의회에 위임하여 처리하게 한 경우에는 위임 사실을 해당 근로자에게 알려야 한다(시행령 제18조제2항).

(2) 노사협의회의 사건처리

노사협의회가 사업주로부터 성희롱과 관련한 근로자의 고충 처리를 위임받은 경우 「근로자참여법」에 따라 노사협의회 내에 설치된 고충처리위원으로 하여금 고충을 처리하게 할 수 있다. 「근로자참여법」은 "모든 사업 또는 사업장에는 근로자의 고충을 청취하고 이를 처리하기 위하여 고충처리위원을 두어야 한다. 다만, 상시 30명 미만의 근로자를 사용하는 사업이나 사업장은 그러하지 아니하다."(제26조)라고 규정하고 있다. 고충처리위원은 노사를 대표하는 3명 이내의 위원으로 구성하되, 노사협의회가 설치되어 있는 사업이나 사업장의 경우에는 협의회가 그 위원 중에서 선임하고, 협의회가 설치되어 있지 아니한 사업이나 사업장의 경우에는 사용자가 위촉한다(제27조).

고충처리위원은 근로자로부터 고충사항을 청취한 경우에는 10일 이내에 조치사항과 그 밖의 처리결과를 해당 근로자에게 통보하여야 한다(제28조제1항). 고충처리위원이 처리하기 곤란한 사항은 협의회의 회의에 부쳐 협의 처리한다(제28조제2항).

Section 2. Responding to Reported Incidents of Workplace Sexual Harassment

(3) Measures to protect victims of sexual harassment

1) Personnel measures for victims

The Equal Employment Act stipulates that "if the occurrence of sexual harassment in the workplace is confirmed as a result of the investigation under paragraph 2, the employer shall take appropriate measures, such as changing the place of work, reassignment, or granting paid leave, at the request of the victim worker" (paragraph 4). If the employer violates this, a penalty of up to KRW 5 million may be imposed by the Minister of Employment and Labor (Article 39, paragraph 3, item 1-5). The Enforcement Decree to the Act sets the penalty amount at KRW 5 million.

2) Prohibition of disadvantageous measures (secondary victimization) against the (alleged) victim

Article 14, paragraph 6 of the Act stipulates that "the employer shall not disadvantage workers or victims who have reported the occurrence of sexual harassment in the workplace, falling under any of the following:

① Dismissal, discharge, termination, or other actions equivalent to loss of status;
② Disciplinary action, demotion, reduction of wages, demotion, or restrictions on promotion, or other unfair personnel measures;
③ Failure to assign job duties, reassignment of job duties, or other personnel measures contrary to the employee's intention;
④ Pay discrimination regarding wages, bonuses, or other benefits based on discriminatory performance evaluation or peer evaluation;
⑤ Limitation of opportunities regarding vocational training and development;
⑥ Acts of bullying, assault, or verbal abuse that can cause mental or physical harm, or acts of neglecting the occurrence of such acts;
⑦ Other disadvantages that go against the will of the workers or victims who have reported the occurrence of sexual harassment.

If an employer takes adverse measures against workers or victims who have reported the occurrence of sexual harassment in the workplace, the employer may be subject to imprisonment for up to 3 years or a fine up to KRW 30 million (Article 37, paragraph 2, item 2).

(3) 직장 내 성희롱의 피해자 등에 대한 보호조치

1) 피해근로자의 요청에 따른 적절한 인사조치

「남녀고용평등법」은 "사업주는 제2항에 따른 조사 결과 직장 내 성희롱 발생 사실이 확인된 때에는 피해근로자가 요청하면 근무장소의 변경, 배치전환, 유급휴가 명령 등 적절한 조치를 하여야 한다."(제4항)라고 규정하고 있다.

사업주가 제14조제4항을 위반하여 피해자 근무장소의 변경 등 적절한 조치를 하지 아니한 경우에는 500만 원의 과태료를 고용노동부장관으로부터 부과받는다(제39조제3항제1호의5, 시행령의 [과태료 부과기준]).

2) 피해자 등에 대한 불이익(2차 가해)금지조치

「남녀고용평등법」은 "사업주는 성희롱 발생 사실을 신고한 근로자 및 피해근로자등에게 다음 각 호의 어느 하나에 해당하는 불리한 처우를 하여서는 아니 된다."(제14조제6항)라고 규정하고 있다. 여기서 "피해 근로자등"이란 "피해를 입은 근로자 또는 피해를 입었다고 주장하는 근로자"이다. 이 법이 제시한 불리한 처우에 해당되는 조치는 다음과 같다. 이것은 「여성폭력방지기본법」이 규정한 "2차 피해"에 해당된다.(제3조제3호)

① 파면, 해임, 해고, 그 밖에 신분상실에 해당하는 불이익 조치
② 징계, 정직, 감봉, 강등, 승진 제한 등 부당한 인사조치
③ 직무 미부여, 직무 재배치, 그 밖에 본인의 의사에 반하는 인사조치
④ 성과평가 또는 동료평가 등에서 차별이나 그에 따른 임금 또는 상여금 등의 차별 지급
⑤ 직업능력 개발 및 향상을 위한 교육훈련 기회의 제한
⑥ 집단 따돌림, 폭행 또는 폭언 등 정신적·신체적 손상을 가져오는 행위를 하거나 그 행위의 발생을 방치하는 행위
⑦ 그 밖에 신고를 한 근로자 및 피해근로자 등의 의사에 반하는 불리한 처우

사업주가 제14조제6항을 위반한 경우에는 3년 이하의 징역 또는 3천만 원 이하의 벌금에 처한다(제37조제2항제2호).

그런데 이 법은 제38조(양벌규정)을 두고 "법인의 대표자나 법인 또는 개인의 대리인, 사용인, 그 밖의 종업원이 그 법인 또는 개인의 업무에 관하여

However, this law also stipulates in Article 38 (Dual Punishment) that "the corporation or individual shall also be subject to the fine prescribed in the said provision, in addition to the punishment of the person who committed the act, if a representative or the legal representative of a corporation, or employer, or other employee related to the business of the corporation or individual violates Article 37. However, the fine shall not be imposed if the corporation or individual has not neglected to exercise due care and supervision to prevent the violation of such act in relation to the business." Accordingly, if an employer other than the corporation or individual takes disadvantageous actions against workers or victims who have reported the occurrence of sexual harassment in the workplace, the employer may also be subject to punishment (imprisonment for up to 3 years or a fine of up to KRW 30 million).

(4) Sanctions against perpetrators who are not employers

According to this Act, "When an employer confirms the occurrence of sexual harassment in the workplace based on the investigation pursuant to paragraph 2, the employer must take necessary measures such as disciplinary action and change of workplace against the person who committed the sexual harassment in the workplace without delay. In this case, the employer must listen to the opinion of the victim of sexual harassment in the workplace before taking measures such as disciplinary action" (Article 14, paragraph 5).

If an employer fails to take necessary measures such as disciplinary action and change of workplace against the perpetrator, the employer shall be subject to a fine of up to KRW 5 million imposed by the Minister of Employment and Labor (Article 39, paragraph 3, subparagraph 1-6). The Enforcement Decree sets the fine to a maximum KRW 5 million.

(5) Handling employee complaints due to sexual harassment by customers or others

1) Handling complaints according to the Equal Employment Act

Article 14-2 of the Equal Employment Act has been titled "Preventing Sexual Harassment by Customers or Others" since its addition on December 21, 2007. However, this provision corresponds to the protection of victims of sexual harassment by customers or others through the handling of complaints (paragraph 1) and prohibition of disadvantageous actions (paragraph 2) against (alleged) victims.

According to Article 14-2 (1), employers must take appropriate measures, such as changing the workplace, reassigning duties, or granting paid leaves, when a worker requests the resolution of complaints caused by sexual gestures or other actions that cause the worker to feel sexual humiliation or disgust during performance of duties. If the employer violates Article 14-2 paragraph 1, a fine up to KRW 3 million

제37조의 위반행위를 하면 그 행위자를 벌하는 외에 그 법인 또는 개인에게도 해당 조문의 벌금형을 과(科)한다. 다만, 법인 또는 개인이 그 위반행위를 방지하기 위하여 해당 업무에 관하여 상당한 주의와 감독을 게을리하지 아니한 경우에는 그러하지 아니하다."라고 규정하고 있다. 이에 따라 사업주(법인, 개인)가 아닌 사용자가 직장 내 성희롱 발생 사실을 신고한 근로자 및 피해 근로자 등에게 불리한 처우를 한 경우에 처벌(3년 이하의 징역 또는 3천만 원 이하의 벌금)받고 사업주도 3천만 원 이하의 벌금에 처할 수 있게 된다.

(4) 사업주가 아닌 성희롱 행위자에 대한 제재

「남녀고용평등법」은 "사업주는 제2항에 따른 조사 결과 직장 내 성희롱 발생 사실이 확인된 때에는 지체 없이 직장 내 성희롱 행위를 한 사람에 대하여 징계, 근무장소의 변경 등 필요한 조치를 하여야 한다. 이 경우 사업주는 징계 등의 조치를 하기 전에 그 조치에 대하여 직장 내 성희롱 피해를 입은 근로자의 의견을 들어야 한다."(제14조제5항)라고 규정하고 있다.

사업주가 법 제14조제5항 전단을 위반하여 징계, 근무장소의 변경 등 필요한 조치를 하지 않은 경우에는 500만 원의 과태료를 고용노동부장관으로부터 부과받는다(제39조제3항제1호의6, 시행령의 [과태료 부과기준]).

(5) 고객 등의 성적 언동으로 인한 근로자의 고충처리

1) 「남녀고용평등법」에 의한 고충처리

「남녀고용평등법」은 2007년 12월 21일, 제14조의2 조항을 신설하여 고객 등의 성적 언동에 의한 피해근로자를 보호하고 있다.

사업주는 제14조의2(고객 등에 의한 성희롱 방지) 제1항에 따라 "고객 등 업무와 밀접한 관련이 있는 사람이 업무수행 과정에서 성적인 언동 등을 통하여 근로자에게 성적 굴욕감 또는 혐오감 등을 느끼게 하여 해당 근로자가 그로 인한 고충 해소를 요청할 경우 근무 장소 변경, 배치전환, 유급휴가의 명령 등 적절한 조치를 하여야 한다." 사업주가 법 제14조의2제1항을 위반하면 300만 원의 과태료를 고용노동부장관로 부터 부과받는다(제39조제4항제1의2호, 시행령의 [과태료 부과기준]).

또한 사업주는 제14조의2(고객 등에 의한 성희롱 방지) 제2항에 따라

may be imposed by the Minister of Employment and Labor (Article 39 paragraph 4, item 2). The standards for imposing the fine is set in the Enforcement Decree as 3 KRW million.

In addition, according to Article 14-2 (2), employers must not dismiss or take other disadvantageous actions against workers who claim damages under paragraph 1 or who refuse to comply with sexual demands from customers or others. If the employer violates Article 14-2, paragraph 2, a fine up to KRW 5 million may be imposed (Article 39, paragraph 3, item 2). The standard for the fine is set in the Enforcement Decree as KRW 5 million.

2) Handling complaints under finance-related acts

The Banking Act, Insurance Business Act, Mutual Savings Bank Act, and Credit Unions Act each have provisions that require "the protection of customer service employees." The details of these obligation provisions are similar.

For example, the Banking Act added Article 52-4 (Obligation to Take Protective Actions for Customer Service Employees) on March 29, 2016. This provision states that "(1). In operating business under this Act, a bank must take the following measures to protect employees who directly serve customers from customer verbal abuse, sexual harassment, assault, etc., when requested by the employee; 1) Separation from the customer involved and replacement of the person in charge at the request of the employee involved, 2) Assistance to employees in medical treatment and counseling, 3) Establishment of a permanent ombudsman organization for employees who provide direct customer services: Provided, That, if a bank shall have ombudsmen pursuant to Article 26 of the Act on the Promotion of Workers' Participation and Cooperation, ombudsmen shall be appointed or commissioned for employees who provide direct customer services, 4) Other measures prescribed by Presidential Decree, including legal measures necessary for protecting employees. (2) Employees of a bank may demand that the bank take the measures specified in paragraph (1). (3) No bank shall disadvantage an employee on the grounds of the employee's demand referred to in paragraph (2)."

Article 52-4 (1) 4 of the Banking Act, "Other measures prescribed by Presidential Decree," refers to Article 24-7 of the Enforcement Decree to the Banking Act, which is as follows: ① Where it is considered that a customer has used abusive language or engaged in sexual harassment, physical violence, or any similar offense (hereinafter referred to as "abusive language, etc.") in violation of any provision concerning criminal punishment in a relevant Act and the employee who sustains damage by such act requests that measures be taken, including: Filing a criminal complaint with the relevant investigative authority, ② Where a customer's words or actions do not violate any provision concerning criminal punishment in a relevant Act but it is considered necessary to take action, taking into consideration the degree of damage to an employee from such actions, the

"근로자가 제1항에 따른 피해를 주장하거나 고객 등으로부터의 성적 요구 등에 따르지 아니하였다는 것을 이유로 해고나 그 밖의 불이익한 조치를 하여서는 아니 된다." 사업주가 법 제14조의2제2항을 위반하여 근로자가 고객 등에 의한 성희롱 피해를 주장하거나 고객 등으로부터의 성적 요구 등에 따르지 않았다는 이유로 해고나 그 밖의 불이익한 조치를 한 경우에는 500만 원의 과태료를 부과 받는다(제39조제3항제2호, 시행령의 [과태료 부과기준]).

2) 금융관계법에 의한 고충처리

「은행법」, 「보험업법」, 「상호저축은행법」, 「신용협동조합법」은 공통적으로 "고객응대직원에 대한 보호조치 의무"라는 제목의 규정을 각각 두고 있다. 그 내용은 유사하다.

그 중 「은행법」은 2016년 3월 29일. 제52조의4(고객응대직원에 대한 보호조치 의무)를 신설하였다. 이 조항은 " ① 은행은 이 법에 따른 업무를 운영할 때 고객을 직접 응대하는 직원을 고객의 폭언이나 성희롱, 폭행 등으로부터 보호하기 위하여 다음 각 호의 조치를 하여야 한다. 1. 직원이 요청하는 경우 해당 고객으로부터의 분리 및 업무담당자 교체 2. 직원에 대한 치료 및 상담 지원 3. 고객을 직접 응대하는 직원을 위한 상시적 고충처리 기구 마련. 다만, 「근로자참여 및 협력증진에 관한 법률」 제26조에 따라 고충처리위원을 두는 경우에는 고객을 직접 응대하는 직원을 위한 고충처리위원의 선임 또는 위촉 4. 그 밖에 직원의 보호를 위하여 필요한 법적 조치 등 대통령령으로 정하는 조치 ② 직원은 은행에 대하여 제1항 각 호의 조치를 요구할 수 있다. ③ 은행은 제2항에 따른 직원의 요구를 이유로 직원에게 불이익을 주어서는 아니 된다."라고 규정하고 있다.

이 법의 시행령 제24조의7(고객응대직원의 보호를 위한 조치)은 " 법 제52조의4제1항제4호에서 "법적 조치 등 대통령령으로 정하는 조치"란 다음 각 호의 조치를 말한다. 1. 고객의 폭언이나 성희롱, 폭행 등(이하 "폭언등"이라 한다)이 관계 법률의 형사처벌규정에 위반된다고 판단되고 그 행위로 피해를 입은 직원이 요청하는 경우: 관할 수사기관 등에 고발 2. 고객의 폭언 등이 관계 법률의 형사처벌규정에 위반되지는 아니하나 그 행위로 피해를 입은 직원의 피해정도 및 그 직원과 다른 직원에 대한 장래 피해발생 가능성 등을

possibility of any damage to the employee and other employees in the future, etc. responses can include: Requesting the relevant investigative authority to take action, ③ Rendering administrative and procedural assistance to employees in taking action personally against a customer who uses abusive language, etc., such as filing a criminal complaint or charges with the relevant investigative authority and pursuing damages, ④ Conducting educational programs with regard to the code of conduct of employees, etc. to prevent or respond to customer abusive language, etc., ⑤ Other measures determined and publicly notified by the Financial Services Commission as necessary for protecting employees from such abusive language, etc.

If the bank fails to take the necessary protective measures for the employees as required under Article 52-4, paragraph 1, a fine of KRW 3 million may be imposed (Article 111, paragraph 2, item 2) by the Financial Supervisory Commission. The standard for imposing the fine is set as KRW 3 million in the Enforcement Decree.

II. Handling of Incidents by the Labor Relations Commission

1. Overview of the Labor Relations Commission

The Labor Relations Commission (LRC) is a specialized administrative agency responsible for prompt, fair adjudication and adjustment of labor-related matters in accordance with the Labor Relations Commission Act.

The LRC consists of the Central Labor Relations Commission under the jurisdiction of the Minister of Employment and Labor, 13 regional labor relations commissions, and special labor relations commissions (Seafarer Labor Relations Commission, Teacher Labor Relations Adjustment Committee, Civil Servant Labor Relations Adjustment Committee). The Central Labor Relations Commission and regional labor relations commissions are under the jurisdiction of the Minister of Employment and Labor. Regional labor relations commissions are responsible for incidents occurring in their respective jurisdictions. The Central Labor Relations Commission is responsible for ① reviewing appeals against decisions of regional labor relations commissions and special labor relations commissions, ② mediating labor disputes over which two or more regional labor relations commissions have jurisdiction, and ③ cases which fall under its jurisdiction in accordance with any other Act (Article 3).

There are two main characteristics of the LRC. First, the adjudication is conducted by "public interest members" who represent workers, employers, and the public interest. Public interest members mainly include professors, legal professionals, and former high-ranking civil servants. Secondly, despite being an administrative agency, the LRC has the authority to adjudicate on the legality of

고려하여 필요하다고 판단되는 경우: 관할 수사기관 등에 필요한 조치 요구 3. 직원이 직접 폭언등의 행위를 한 고객에 대한 관할 수사기관 등에 고소, 고발, 손해배상 청구 등의 조치를 하는 데 필요한 행정적, 절차적 지원 4. 고객의 폭언등을 예방하거나 이에 대응하기 위한 직원의 행동요령 등에 대한 교육 실시 5. 그 밖에 고객의 폭언등으로부터 직원을 보호하기 위하여 필요한 사항으로서 금융위원회가 정하여 고시하는 조치"라고 규정하고 있다.

법 제52조의4를 위반하여 직원의 보호를 위한 조치를 하지 아니하거나 직원에게 불이익을 준 은행은 금융위원회로부터 3천만 원 이하(1800만원)의 과태료를 부과받는다(제69조제3항, 시행령의 [과태료 부과기준]).

Ⅱ. 노동위원회의 사건처리

1. 노동위원회의 개요

노동위원회는 「노동위원회법」에 근거하여 노동관계에 관한 판정 및 조정(調整) 업무를 신속·공정하게 수행하기 위한 전문행정기관이다.

노동위원회는 고용노동부장관 소속의 중앙노동위원회와 13개소의 지방노동위원회, 특별노동위원회(선원노동위원회, 교원노동관계조정위원회, 공무원노동관계조정위원회)로 구분된다. 지방노동위원회는 해당 관할구역에서 발생하는 사건을 관장한다. 중앙노동위원회는 ① 지방노동위원회 및 특별노동위원회의 처분에 대한 재심사건, ② 둘 이상의 지방노동위원회의 관할구역에 걸친 노동쟁의의 조정(調整)사건, ③ 다른 법률에서 그 권한에 속하는 것으로 규정된 사건을 관장한다(제3조).

노동위원회의 특성은 2가지이다. 하나는 근로자를 대표하는 위원(근로자위원)과 사용자를 대표하는 위원(사용자위원) 및 공익을 대표하는 위원(공익위원)들이 심판에 참여하는 것과 판정은 공익위원들이 하는 것이다. 공익위원은 주로 교수, 법조인, 전직 고위 공무원들로 구성된다. 또 하나의 특성은 행정위원회임에도 위법 여부를 판정하고 위법자에게 원상회복적 시정명령을 할 수 있는 권한을 가지는 것이다.

노동위원회는 부당해고(징계) 구제신청 사건, 비정규직에 대한 차별적 처우의

Section 2. Responding to Reported Incidents of Workplace Sexual Harassment

actions and issue corrective orders for restoration to the original state against those found to have acted illegally.

2. Dispute resolution Related to workplace sexual harassment by the Labor Relations Commission

The LRC can also be utilized in sexual harassment-related dispute settlements in the following cases: where 1) a person accused of engaging in sexual harassment in the workplace has been disciplined, such as through dismissal, on the grounds of committing sexual harassment, or 2) where an alleged victim of workplace sexual harassment has been disciplined, such as dismissal, for falsely stating or exaggerating to the outside the events leading to accusations of sexual harassment, causing damage to the reputation of the workplace. In such cases, the procedures for remedying unjust dismissal (discipline) are conducted in accordance with the Labor Standards Act and other relevant laws.

On May 18, 2021, the Equal Employment Act came to include provisions that prohibit employers from violating the gender discrimination prohibitions stipulated by this law, and require employers to take actions as specified therein in cases where employees experience sexual harassment in the workplace, including in relation to (alleged) victims and reporters of workplace sexual harassment, and workers who suffer from sexual advances by customers or clients. The amended provisions also establish dispute settlements provisions (Articles 26 to 29-7) by the Labor Relations Commission and the Minister of Employment and Labor for cases of discriminatory treatment. Furthermore, the scope of application of Article 30 (Burden of Proof) was expanded to include matters related to discriminatory treatment under this law. These amended provisions have been in effect since May 19, 2022.

(1) Actions to be handled in relation to claims of sexual harassment (Discriminatory Treatment)

The Equal Employment Act stipulates that the following actions by employers shall be regarded as "discriminatory treatment" (Article 1, main text).

1) Acts violating any provision of Articles 7 through 11 (hereinafter referred to as "discriminatory treatment"[83]) (clause 1)

2) Failure to take appropriate measures pursuant to Article 14, paragraph 4[84] or

---

[83] Article 7 (Recruitment and Hiring), Article 9 (Non-Monetary Benefits), Article 10 (Education, Assignment, and Promotion), and Article 11 (Prohibition of Discrimination Based on Gender) prohibit discrimination between men and women. Article 8 (Wages) requires equal payment for equal work of equal value within the same business. According to Article 11, paragraph 2, it is prohibited to terminate an employment contract based on marriage, pregnancy, or childbirth of a female worker.

[84] Article 14 (Measures in Case of Sexual Harassment in the Workplace), paragraph 4: When it is confirmed that sexual harassment has occurred in the workplace according to an investigation as stated in paragraph 2, the employer must take appropriate measures, such as changing the place of work, transferring to another position, or granting paid leave, at the request of the victim employee.

시정신청 사건, 집단적 노사분쟁에 대한 조정과 중재 신청 사건 등을 처리하여 왔다.

2. 노동위원회의 직장 내 성희롱 관련 분쟁처리

노동위원회가 직장 내 성희롱 관련 분쟁처리에서 활용되는 경우에는 혐의자와 행위자가 성희롱을 한 것을 이유로 해고 등의 징계를 당한 경우와 피해자가 성희롱의 발생을 허위 또는 과장되게 외부에 알려 사업장의 명예를 실추하였다는 이유로 해고 등의 징계를 당한 경우이다. 이 경우 「근로기준법」 등에 따라 부당해고(징계) 구제절차가 진행된다.

그런데 「남녀고용평등법」은 2021년 5월 18일에 개정될 때, 사업주가 이 법이 규정한 남녀차별금지규정들을 위반하는 경우와 직장 내 성희롱의 피해자와 신고자, 고객 등의 성적 언동으로 고충을 가진 근로자 등에 대하여 이 법이 규정한 적절한 조치를 하지 않거나 이 법이 금지한 불리한 조치를 한 경우를 '차별적 처우'로 규정하였다. 그리고 이에 대한 노동위원회와 고용노동부장관에 의한 분쟁처리 규정들(제26조부터 제29조의7까지)을 신설하였다. 이러한 신설 규정들은 2022년 5월 19일부터 시행되고 있다.

(1) 직장 내 성희롱 관련 사건처리 대상(차별적 처우)

「남녀고용평등법」은 사업주가 다음의 조치를 한 경우를 '차별적 처우'로 규정하고 있다(제1항 본문).
1) 남녀차별금지규정(제7조부터 제11조까지[83]))중 어느 하나를 위반한 행위를 한 경우(제1호)
2) 제14조제4항[84] 또는 제14조의2제1항[85]에 따른 적절한 조치를 하지 아니한

---

[83] 제7조(모집과 채용), 제9조(임금 외의 금품 등), 제10조(교육·배치 및 승진), 제11조(정년·퇴직 및 해고)에 따른 남녀차별금지규정, 제8조(임금)에 따른 동일한 사업 내의 동일 가치 노동에 대한 동일한 임금 지급, 제11조제2항에 따른 여성 근로자의 혼인, 임신 또는 출산을 퇴직 사유로 예정하는 근로계약 체결 금지.

[84] 제14조(직장 내 성희롱 발생 시 조치) ④ 사업주는 제2항에 따른 조사 결과 직장 내 성희롱 발생 사실이 확인된 때에는 피해근로자가 요청하면 근무장소의 변경, 배치전환, 유급휴가 명령 등 적절한 조치를 하여야 한다.

[85] 제14조의2(고객 등에 의한 성희롱 방지) ①사업주는 고객 등 업무와 밀접한 관련이 있는 사람이 업무 수행 과정에서 성적인 언동 등을 통하여 근로자에게 성적 굴욕감 또는 혐오감 등을 느끼게 하여 해당 근로자가 그로 인한 고충 해소를 요청할 경우 근무 장소 변경, 배치전환, 유급휴가의 명령 등 적절한 조치를 하여야 한다.

Section 2. Responding to Reported Incidents of Workplace Sexual Harassment

Article 14-2, paragraph 1[85] : Failure to take appropriate corrective measures in response to requests from victims of sexual harassment and sexual advances by customers or other persons related to the business (clause 2).

① When it is confirmed that workplace sexual harassment has occurred in violation of Article 14, Paragraph 4, and despite the request made by the affected worker, the employer fails to take appropriate measures such as changing the work location, reassignment, or granting paid leave.

② When it is confirmed that the employer, in violation of Article 14-2, Paragraph 1, fails to take appropriate measures such as changing the work location, reassignment, or issuing orders for paid leave, despite the worker's request for relief from the sexual humiliation or disgust experienced by the worker as a result of sexually suggestive behavior by individuals closely involved in business activities, such as customers.

3) Unfavorable treatment in violation of Article 14, paragraph 6[86] or dismissal or other disadvantageous measures in violation of Article 14-2, paragraph 2[87] : Disadvantages given to the victims of sexual harassment and sexual advances by customers or other persons related to the business (Article 3).

① When the employer, in violation of Article 14, Paragraph 6, subjects a worker who reported the occurrence of sexual harassment, a worker who suffered from it, or a worker claiming to have been victimized to unfavorable treatment.

② When the employer, in violation of Article 14-2, Paragraph 2, dismisses or takes other detrimental actions against a worker who felt sexual humiliation or disgust due to sexually suggestive behavior by individuals closely involved in business activities, such as customers, or who refused to comply with sexual demands from customers or others.

(2) Employee's request for correction of discriminatory treatment and support from the LRC

---

[85] Article 14-2 (Preventing Sexual Harassment by Customers or Other Related Persons), paragraph 1: If a customer or any person closely related to the job causes a female worker to feel sexual humiliation or disgust through sexual advances or other sexual behaviors during the performance of duties, the employer must take appropriate measures, such as changing the place of work, transferring to another position, or granting paid leave, at the request of the employee for resolving the resulting grievance.

[86] Article 14 (Measures in Case of Sexual Harassment in the Workplace), paragraph 6: The employer must not impose any unfavorable measures on employees who report the occurrence of sexual harassment or on employees who suffered from it, such as dismissal, removal from office, demotion, promotion restriction, denial of job assignments, or other unfair personnel measures; discriminatory payment of wages, bonuses, or other benefits based on performance evaluation or peer evaluation; restriction of opportunities for occupational skill development and improvement; or acts of psychological or physical harm, such as group bullying, assault, or verbal abuse, or neglecting the occurrence of such acts, against the employees who reported or suffered from sexual harassment or other unfavorable measures that are against the intentions of the employees.

[87] Article 14-2 (Prevention of Sexual Harassment by Customers or Other Related Persons), paragraph 2: The employer must not dismiss or take any other unfavorable measures against an employee based on the employee's claim of damages under paragraph 1 or the employee's refusal to comply with sexual demands from customers or others.

행위 (제2호)

① 사업주가 제14조제4항을 위반하여 직장 내 성희롱 발생 사실이 확인된 때에 피해근로자가 요청하였는데도 근무장소의 변경, 배치전환, 유급휴가 명령 등 적절한 조치를 하지 않은 경우

② 사업주가 제14조의2제1항을 위반하여 고객 등 업무와 밀접한 관련이 있는 사람이 업무수행 과정에서 성적인 언동 등을 통하여 근로자에게 성적 굴욕감 또는 혐오감 등을 느끼게 하여 해당 근로자가 그로 인한 고충 해소를 요청하였는데도 근무 장소 변경, 배치전환, 유급휴가의 명령 등 적절한 조치를 하지 않은 경우

3) 제14조제6항[86]을 위반한 불리한 처우 또는 제14조의2 제2항[87]을 위반한 해고나 그 밖의 불이익한 조치(제3조)

① 사업주가 제14조제6항을 위반하여 성희롱 발생 사실을 신고한 근로자, 피해를 입은 근로자, 피해를 주장하였다고 주장하는 근로자에 대하여 불리한 처우를 한 경우

② 사업주가 제14조의2 제2항을 위반하여 고객 등 업무와 밀접한 관련이 있는 사람이 업무수행 과정에서 행한 성적인 언동 등을 통하여 성적 굴욕감 또는 혐오감 등을 느낀 근로자가 피해를 주장하거나 고객 등으로부터의 성적 요구 등에 따르지 아니하였다는 것을 이유로 해고나 그 밖의 불이익한 조치를 한 경우

(2) 근로자의 '차별적 처우'에 대한 시정 신청

1) 차별적 처우의 신청방법

근로자는 「남녀고용평등법」에 따라 노동위원회에 성희롱 관련 차별적

---

[86] 제14조(직장 내 성희롱 발생 시 조치) ⑥사업주는 성희롱 발생 사실을 신고한 근로자 및 피해 근로자 등에게 다음 각 호의 어느 하나에 해당하는 불리한 처우를 하여서는 아니 된다.
  1. 파면, 해임, 해고, 그 밖에 신분상실에 해당하는 불이익 조치
  2. 징계, 정직, 감봉, 강등, 승진 제한 등 부당한 인사조치
  3. 직무 미부여, 직무 재배치, 그 밖에 본인의 의사에 반하는 인사조치
  4. 성과평가 또는 동료평가 등에서 차별이나 그에 따른 임금 또는 상여금 등의 차별 지급
  5. 직업능력 개발 및 향상을 위한 교육훈련 기회의 제한
  6. 집단 따돌림, 폭행 또는 폭언 등 정신적·신체적 손상을 가져오는 행위를 하거나 그 행위의 발생을 방치하는 행위
  7. 그 밖에 신고를 한 근로자 및 피해근로자 등의 의사에 반하는 불리한 처우

[87] 제14조의2(고객 등에 의한 성희롱 방지) ②사업주는 근로자가 제1항에 따른 피해를 주장하거나 고객 등으로부터의 성적 요구 등에 따르지 아니하였다는 것을 이유로 해고나 그 밖의 불이익한 조치를 하여서는 아니 된다.

Section 2. Responding to Reported Incidents of Workplace Sexual Harassment

1) Employee's request for correction of discriminatory treatment

According to the Equal Employment Act, if a worker wishes to apply to the LRC for the correction of discriminatory treatment related to sexual harassment, such application must be made to the LRC having jurisdiction over the workplace and within 6 months from the date the discriminatory treatment was committed by the employer (or the final date of discrimination in case of "continuous discriminatory treatment" according to Article 3). In this case, the applicant must specify the details of the discriminatory treatment, etc. (Article 26, paragraph 2).

The procedures and methods for the request shall be separately prescribed and announced by the National Labor Relations Commission in accordance with Article 2, paragraph 1 of the Labor Relations Commission Act (Article 26, paragraph 3).

2) Support from the Labor Relations Commission

In cases related to the correction of discriminatory treatment, the LRC may appoint an attorney or a certified public labor attorney represent the rights of members of socially vulnerable groups (Article 6-2 of the Labor Relations Commission Act).

Those eligible to apply for a representative for rights relief shall be a person whose average monthly wage is less than the amount (KRW 3 million) specified by the Minister of Employment and Labor (Article 4 of the Enforcement Decree).

(3) Investigations and inquiries by the Labor Relations Commission

When the LRC receives a request for corrective action under Article 26, it must promptly conduct the necessary investigation and interviews with the relevant parties (paragraph 1).

According to Article 23 of the Labor Relations Commission Act, if necessary, the LRC may request the attendance, reporting, testimony, or submission of necessary documents from workers, labor unions, employers, employer organizations, relevant parties, appointed members or investigators designated by the LRC chairman or chairman of the relevant subcommittee to investigate the business or workplace situation, documents, and other items (paragraph 1). The LRC must send a copy of the request for corrective action submitted by the applicant in an adjudication case or discriminatory treatment case to the other parties and require them to submit a response (Article 4). It must also promptly send a copy of the response submitted by the other parties to the applicant (paragraph 5).

처우에 대한 시정 처리를 의뢰하려면 사업주로부터 차별적 처우를 받은 날(제3호에 따른 차별적 처우등이 계속되는 경우에는 그 종료일)부터 6개월 이내에 사업장을 관할하는 지방노동위원회에 신청하여야 한다(제26조제1항). 이 경우 신청자는 차별적 처우 등의 내용을 구체적으로 명시하여야 한다(제26조제2항).

시정신청의 절차·방법 등에 관하여 필요한 사항은 「노동위원회법」 제2조제1항에 따른 중앙노동위원회가 따로 정하여 고시한다(제26조제3항).

2) 노동위원회의 저소득 신청자에 대한 지원

「노동위원회법」 제6조의2(사회취약계층에 대한 권리구제 대리)에 따라 노동위원회는 차별적 처우 시정 등에 관한 사건에서 사회취약계층을 위하여 변호사나 공인노무사로 하여금 권리구제업무를 대리하게 할 수 있다.

시정 신청을 할 때 권리구제업무 대리인 선임을 신청할 수 있는 사람은 월평균임금이 고용노동부장관이 고시하는 금액(2023년 현재 300만 원) 미만인 사람으로 한다(시행규칙 제4조).

(3) 노동위원회의 조사

노동위원회는 제26조에 따른 시정신청을 받은 때에는 지체 없이 필요한 조사와 관계 당사자에 대한 심문을 하여야 한다(제1항).

「노동위원회법」은 제23조(위원회의 조사권 등)에서 "노동위원회는 소관 사무와 관련하여 사실관계를 확인하는 등 그 사무집행을 위하여 필요하다고 인정할 때에는 근로자, 노동조합, 사용자, 사용자단체, 그 밖의 관계인에 대하여 출석·보고·진술 또는 필요한 서류의 제출을 요구하거나 위원장 또는 부문별 위원회의 위원장이 지명한 위원 또는 조사관으로 하여금 사업 또는 사업장의 업무상황, 서류, 그 밖의 물건을 조사하게 할 수 있다."(제1항)라고 규정하고 있다.

노동위원회는 심판사건과 차별적 처우 시정사건의 신청인이 제출한 신청서 부본을 다른 당사자에게 송달하고 이에 대한 답변서를 제출하도록 하여야 한다(제4조). 노동위원회는 다른 당사자(사업주)가 제출한 답변서의 부본을 지체 없이 신청인에게 송달하여야 한다(제5항).

Section 2. Responding to Reported Incidents of Workplace Sexual Harassment

(4) Inquiries by the LRC

When conducting an inquiry pursuant to Article 27, paragraph 1 of the Equal Employment Act, the LRC may summon witnesses to appear either upon request of the relevant parties or at its own discretion and may question them on relevant matters (Article 27, paragraph 2). When conducting an inquiry, the it must provide the relevant parties with sufficient opportunities to submit evidence and to cross-examine a witness (Article 27, paragraph 3).

(5) Burden of proof

With amendment of the Equal Employment Acton May 18, 2021, the application of Article 30 (Burden of Proof) has been expanded to 1) the disputes settled by the Labor Relations Commission (from Article 26 to Article 29), and 2) the disputes settled by the Minister of Employment and Labor (from Article 29-2 to Article 29-7) under this law. Therefore, employers bear the burden of proof in investigations and dispute settlements.

(6) Exclusion, challenge, and refrainment of parties

According to Article 21 of the Labor Relations Commission Act, the chairperson of the Labor Relations Commission shall inform the involved parties of their right to request exclusion etc. under paragraph 2 and paragraph 3, immediately upon filing of the case (paragraph 5).

1) Exclusion of committee members

If a reason described in paragraph (1) applies, the relevant LRC member shall be excluded from performing their duties related to the relevant case (paragraph 1). In such cases, the chairperson shall make a decision to exclude the member by virtue of his/her authority or at the request of the parties (paragraph 2).

① Where the member or his/her spouse or ex-spouse is a party to the case or holds rights or liabilities jointly with a party to the case.
② Where a member is a current or former relative of any party to the relevant case.
③ Where a member has made a statement or given an expert opinion with regard to the relevant case.
④ Where a member is or was involved in any affairs as an agent of any party.
⑤ Where a corporation, organization, or law office to which a member belongs was

(4) 노동위원회의 심문

노동위원회는 「남녀고용평등법」 제27조제1항에 따른 심문을 하는 때에는 관계 당사자의 신청 또는 직권으로 증인을 출석하게 하여 필요한 사항을 질문할 수 있다(제27조제2항). 노동위원회는 심문을 할 때에는 관계 당사자에게 증거의 제출과 증인에 대한 반대심문을 할 수 있는 충분한 기회를 주어야 한다(제27조제3항).

(5) 입증책임 부담

「남녀고용평등법」은 2021년 5월 18일 개정될 때 제30조(입증책임)의 적용을 이 법에 따른 노동위원회의 분쟁해결(제26조부터 제29조까지) 및 고용노동부장관의 분쟁해결(제29조의2부터 제29조의7까지)에로 확대하였다. 이에 따라 노동위원회의 조사와 분쟁처리에서 사업주는 차별적 처우가 아님을 입증할 책임을 부담한다.

(6) 위원의 제척·기피·회피 등

「노동위원회법」 제21조(위원의 제척·기피·회피 등)에 따라 노동위원회 위원장은 사건이 접수되는 즉시 제2항에 따른 제척신청과 제3항에 따른 기피신청을 할 수 있음을 사건 당사자에게 알려야 한다(제5항).

1) 위원의 제척

노동의원회 위원은 다음의 어느 하나에 해당하는 경우에 해당 사건에 관한 직무집행에서 제척(除斥)된다(제1항). 위원장은 제척 사유가 있는 경우에 관계 당사자의 신청을 받아 또는 직권으로 제척의 결정을 하여야 한다(제2항).

① 위원 또는 위원의 배우자이거나 배우자였던 사람이 해당 사건의 당사자가 되거나 해당 사건의 당사자와 공동권리자 또는 공동의무자의 관계에 있는 경우
② 위원이 해당 사건의 당사자와 친족이거나 친족이었던 경우
③ 위원이 해당 사건에 관하여 진술이나 감정을 한 경우
④ 위원이 당사자의 대리인으로서 업무에 관여하거나 관여하였던 경우
⑤ 위원이 속한 법인, 단체 또는 법률사무소가 해당 사건에 관하여 당사자의

Section 2. Responding to Reported Incidents of Workplace Sexual Harassment

involved in the relevant case as an agent of any party.
⑥ Where a member or a corporation, organization, or law office to which a member belongs took part in a disposition or omission which has caused the relevant case.

2) Challenge of committee members

Any party may challenge a member from whom impartiality and independence during deliberation, resolution, or conciliation are deemed difficult to expect, by sending a written statement of the reason(s) to the chairperson of the relevant Labor Relations Commission (Article 28, paragraph 3). The chairperson shall decide whether the request for exclusion under paragraph (3) is reasonable (Article 28, paragraph 4).

3) Refrainment of committee members

If any of the causes prescribed in paragraph (1) or (3) apply to an LRC member, the relevant member shall voluntarily abstain from performing their duties in relation to the case. In this case, the member shall expound to the chairperson (Article 28, paragraph 6).

(7) Mediation and arbitration by the Labor Relations Commission
1) Commencement of mediation and arbitration

In accordance with Article 28 of the Equal Employment Act, the LRC can initiate mediation procedures upon request of either or both parties during the hearing process under Article 27 (paragraph 1). The request for mediation must be made within 14 days from the date the request for corrective action was filed under Article 26. However, if the LRC recognizes that there was a justifiable reason for not being able to file the request within that period, the request may still be made after 14 days (paragraph 2). Mediation procedures can also be initiated by the Labor Relations Commission.

The Labor Relations Commission may engage in arbitration if the interested parties have agreed to follow an arbitration award by the LRC in advance, and filed for arbitration (paragraph 2). An application for arbitration must be made within 14 days from the date of filing a request for corrective action (Paragraph 2).

2) Methods of medication and arbitration

The LRC must thoroughly consider the opinions of the parties involved when conducting mediation or arbitration (paragraph 3). Unless there are special reasons

대리인으로서 관여하거나 관여하였던 경우
⑥ 위원 또는 위원이 속한 법인, 단체 또는 법률사무소가 해당 사건의 원인이 된 처분 또는 부작위에 관여한 경우

2) 위원의 기피
 당사자는 공정한 심의·의결 또는 조정 등을 기대하기 어려운 노동위원회 위원이 있는 경우에 그 사유를 적어 위원장에게 기피신청을 할 수 있다(제28조제3항). 위원장은 기피신청이 이유 있다고 인정되는 경우에 기피의 결정을 하여야 한다(제28조제4항).

3) 위원의 회피
 노동위원회 위원 위원은 제척 사유와 기피 신청이 있는 경우에는 스스로 그 사건에 관한 직무집행에서 회피할 수 있다. 이 경우 해당 위원은 위원장에게 그 사유를 소명하여야 한다(제28조제6항).

(7) 노동위원회의 조정·중재
1) 조정과 중재의 개시
 노동위원회는 「남녀고용평등법」제28조(조정·중재)에 따라 심문 과정에서 관계 당사자 쌍방 또는 일방의 신청이나 직권으로 조정(調停)절차를 개시할 수 있다(제1항). 조정의 신청은 시정신청을 한 날부터 14일 이내에 하여야 한다. 다만, 노동위원회가 정당한 사유로 그 기간에 신청할 수 없었다고 인정하는 경우에는 14일 후에도 신청할 수 있다(제2항). 조정이란 상반된 주장을 하는 당사자로 하여금 상호 이해와 양보로 절충안에 합의하게 하여 분쟁을 해결하는 분쟁해결방법이다.
 한편, 관계 당사자가 미리 노동위원회의 중재(仲裁)결정에 따르기로 합의하여 중재를 신청한 경우에는 중재를 할 수 있다(제2항). 중재의 신청은 시정신청을 한 날부터 14일 이내에 하여야 한다(제2항).

2) 조정과 중재의 방법
 노동위원회는 조정과 중재를 하는 경우 관계 당사자의 의견을 충분히 들어야

Section 2. Responding to Reported Incidents of Workplace Sexual Harassment

to do otherwise, it must present a mediation proposal or make an arbitration decision within 60 days from the date the mediation process was initiated or the request for arbitration was received (paragraph 4).

If both parties accept the mediation proposal, the LRC must prepare a mediation report (paragraph 4). The mediation report must be signed or sealed by all LRC personnel who were involved in the mediation. The same follows for arbitration decisions (paragraph 5).

Mediation decisions have the same legal effect as a judicial compromise in a civil lawsuit, pursuant to the Civil Procedure Act(paragraph 7).

(8) Dismissals and corrective orders from the Labor Relations Commission

1) Dismissals

According to Article 29 (Corrective Orders, etc.) of the Equal Employment Act, if the LRC determines that there is no discrimination in wages or other treatment after completing an investigation and hearing under Article 27, it must reject the application for correction (paragraph 1). The rejection decision must be made in writing, and the reasons for the rejection clearly stated and the relevant parties notified (paragraph 2).

2) Decision and details of corrective orders

According to Article 29 (Corrective Orders, etc.) of the Equal Employment Act, if the LRC determines that there has been discrimination in wages or other treatment after completing an investigation and hearing under Article 27, it must issue a corrective order to the employer concerned (paragraph 1). Any determination, corrective order, or decision of dismissal under paragraph (1) shall be made in writing and the respective interested parties notified together with the detailed reasons therefor. When issuing a corrective order in such cases, the details (compliance period, etc.) shall be specified (paragraph 2).

Article 29-2 of the Equal Employment Act stipulates that "the details of mediation, arbitration, or corrective orders under Article 28 or Article 29 may include measures to stop the discriminatory treatment, improve working conditions such as wages (including improve the rules of employment, collective agreements, etc.), or provide adequate compensation, or take other corrective actions (paragraph 1). The amount of "adequate compensation" from paragraph 1 shall be based on the amount of damages suffered by the employee due to discriminatory treatment. However, where the employer's explicit intention to discriminate is recognized or if the discriminatory treatment, etc. is repeated, the Labor Relations Commission may

한다(제3항). 노동위원회는 특별한 사유가 없으면 조정절차를 개시하거나 중재신청을 받은 날부터 60일 이내에 조정안을 제시하거나 중재결정을 하여야 한다(제4항).

노동위원회는 관계 당사자 쌍방이 조정안을 받아들이기로 한 경우에는 조정조서를 작성하여야 한다(제4항). 조정조서에는 관계 당사자와 조정에 관여한 위원 전원이 서명 또는 날인을 하여야 하고, 중재결정서에는 관여한 위원 전원이 서명 또는 날인을 하여야 한다(제5항).

조정과 중재의 결정은 「민사소송법」에 따른 재판상 화해와 동일한 효력을 가진다(제7항).

(8) 노동위원회의 판정

1) 기각결정

「남녀고용평등법」 제29조(시정명령 등)에 따라 노동위원회는 제27조에 따른 조사·심문을 끝내고 차별적 처우 등에 해당하지 아니한다고 판정한 때에는 그 시정신청을 기각하는 결정을 하여야 한다(제1항). 기각결정은 서면으로 하되, 그 이유를 구체적으로 명시하여 관계 당사자에게 각각 통보하여야 한다(제2항).

2) 시정명령

「남녀고용평등법」 제29조(시정명령 등)에 따라 노동위원회는 제27조에 따른 조사·심문을 끝내고 차별적 처우등에 해당된다고 판정한 때에는 해당 사업주에게 시정명령을 하여야 한다(제1항). 제1항에 따른 판정, 시정명령은 서면으로 하되, 그 이유를 구체적으로 명시하여 관계 당사자에게 각각 통보하여야 한다. 이 경우 시정명령을 하는 때에는 시정명령의 내용 및 이행기한 등을 구체적으로 적어야 한다(제2항).

이 법은 제29조의2(조정·중재 또는 시정명령의 내용)에서 "① 제28조에 따른 조정·중재 또는 제29조에 따른 시정명령의 내용에는 차별적 처우등의 중지, 임금 등 근로조건의 개선(취업규칙, 단체협약 등의 제도개선 명령을 포함한다) 또는 적절한 배상 등의 시정조치 등을 포함할 수 있다. ② 제1항에 따라 배상을 하도록 한 경우 그 배상액은 차별적 처우등으로 근로자에게 발생한

issue an order to provide compensation not exceeding three times the amount of damage (paragraph 2).

(9) Appeals against decisions and orders of the Labor Relations Commission

Any party dissatisfied by a corrective order from or dismissal by a regional labor relations commission may file an appeal to the National Labor Relations Commission within 10 days of receiving the written corrective order or the written decision of dismissal (Article 29-3, paragraph 1). Any party dissatisfied by the decision on review by the National Labor Relations Commission may file an administrative lawsuit within 15 days from the date the written decision of dismissal was received (Article 29-3, paragraph 2). Where no request for review is filed within the period prescribed in paragraph 1 above or no administrative litigation is instituted within the period prescribed in paragraph 2 above, the relevant corrective order, decision of dismissal, or decision on review shall become final and conclusive (Article 29-3, paragraph 3).

(10) Finalization and implementation of decisions of and orders from the Labor Relations Commission

If an employer fails to comply with a corrective order that has been finalized in accordance with Article 29-3 (including cases where Article 29-5, paragraph 4 or Article 29-6, paragraph 3 apply), a fine for negligence of up to KRW 100 million may be imposed (Article 39, paragraph 1).

However, the Enforcement Decree to the Act stipulates the following penalty criteria: KRW 50 million won for the first violation of failing to comply with a corrective order involving compensation as its content, KRW 100 million for the second violation, and KRW 200 million won for the third and subsequent failures to comply with a corrective order involving measures such as ceasing discriminatory treatment or improving working conditions, including wages (KRW 500 million, KRW 1 billion, and KRW 2 billion, respectively).

3. Prohibition against adverse treatment of workers for filing remedial requests

An employer shall not dismiss or give any other unfavorable treatment to an employee for any of the following acts (Article 29-7): Filing a request for corrective action for discriminatory treatment under Article 26, attending and making statements at a Labor Relations Commission meeting under Article 27, filing a request for re-examination under Article 29-3, or filing an administrative lawsuit; Reporting an employer for not complying with the corrective order under

손해액을 기준으로 정한다. 다만, 노동위원회는 사업주의 차별적 처우등에 명백한 고의가 인정되거나 차별적 처우등이 반복되는 경우에는 그 손해액을 기준으로 3배를 넘지 아니하는 범위에서 배상을 명령할 수 있다."라고 규정하고 있다.

(9) 노동위원회의 기각결정과 시정명령에 대한 불복

지방노동위원회의 시정명령 또는 기각결정에 불복하는 관계 당사자는 시정명령서 또는 기각결정서를 송달받은 날부터 10일 이내에 중앙노동위원회에 재심을 신청할 수 있다(제29조의3제1항).

중앙노동위원회의 재심결정에 불복하는 관계 당사자는 재심결정서를 송달받은 날부터 15일 이내에 행정소송을 제기할 수 있다(제29조의3제2항).

이 기간에 재심을 신청하지 아니하거나 행정소송을 제기하지 아니한 때에는 그 시정명령, 기각결정 또는 재심결정은 확정된다(제29조의3제3항).

(10) 노동위원회의 결정과 명령의 확정과 이행

사업주가 법 제29조의3(법 제29조의5제4항 및 제29조의6제3항에 따라 준용되는 경우를 포함한다)에 따라 확정된 시정명령을 정당한 이유 없이 이행하지 않은 경우에는 1억원 이하의 과태료가 부과된다(제39조제1항). 그런데 시행령의 [과태료 부과기준]은 1억원의 범위에서 1차 위반의 경우 500만 원, 2차 위반의 경우 1천만 원, 3차 이상 위반의 경우 2천만 원으로 과태료 금액을 정하고 있다.

3. 시정신청 근로자 등에 대한 불리한 처우 금지

사업주는 근로자가 제26조에 따른 차별적 처우등의 시정 신청, 제27조에 따른 노동위원회에의 참석 및 진술, 제29조의3에 따른 재심신청 또는 행정소송의 제기 또는 제29조의4 제2항에 따른 시정명령 불이행의 신고를 한 것을 이유로 해고나 그 밖의 불리한 처우를 하지 못한다(제29조의7).

사업주가 제29조의7를 위반하여 근로자에게 해고나 그 밖의 불리한 처우를 한 경우는 3년 이하의 징역 또는 3천만 원 이하의 벌금에 처한다(제37조제2항제9호).

Section 2. Responding to Reported Incidents of Workplace Sexual Harassment

Article 29-4, paragraph 2.

If an employer violates Article 29-7 and dismisses or takes other disadvantageous measures against a worker, the employer shall be subject to imprisonment for up to 3 years or a fine of up to KRW 30 million (Article 37, paragraph 2, item 9).

In addition to the penalties imposed on the individual who committed the violation under Article 37, the same penalty may also be imposed on the representative director of a corporation, the agent of a corporation or individual, the employer, or other employees who committed the violation in relation to the business of the corporation or individual. However, if the corporation or individual has exercised reasonable care and supervision to prevent such violation in relation to the business, the penalty may not be imposed (Article 38).

III. Handling of Incidents by the Minister of Employment and Labor

Article 29-4, Article 29-5, Article 29-6, and Article 30 state that the handling of cases by the Minister of Employment and Labor is carried out by the local organizations of the Ministry of Employment and Labor (6 regional employment and labor offices, 40 local employment and labor offices, and 2 branch offices) and the labor inspectors under their jurisdiction.

1. Demand to submit compliance status reports about corrective orders

The Minister of Employment and Labor may demand that an employer submit a status report on compliance with finalized corrective orders (Article 29-4, paragraph 1).

If an employer fails to comply with a demand from the Minister of Employment and Labor to submit a report on the status of compliance with corrective orders without justifiable reasons, including cases where Article 29-4, paragraph 1 of the Act (including cases where Article 29-5, paragraph 4 and Article 29-6, paragraph 3 apply) is violated, a fine of up to KRW 5 million may be imposed (Article 39, paragraph 3, subparagraph 9). However, the Enforcement Decree sets different fine amounts of KRW 2 million for the first violation, KRW 4 million for the second violation, and KRW 5 million for the third and subsequent violations (Article 29-4, paragraph 2).

2. Notification to the labor commission regarding the request for corrective action to the employer and their non-compliance

(1) **Demands from the Minister of Employment and Labor for the correction of discriminatory treatment**

The Minister of Employment and Labor may demand correction from any

법인의 대표자나 법인 또는 개인의 대리인, 사용인, 그 밖의 종업원이 그 법인 또는 개인의 업무에 관하여 제37조의 위반행위를 하면 그 행위자를 벌하는 외에 그 법인 또는 개인에게도 해당 조문의 벌금형을 과(科)한다. 다만, 법인 또는 개인이 그 위반행위를 방지하기 위하여 해당 업무에 관하여 상당한 주의와 감독을 게을리하지 아니한 경우에는 그러하지 아니하다(제38조).

Ⅲ. 고용노동부장관의 사건처리

「남녀고용평등법」은 고용노동부장관의 직장 내 성희롱 관련 분쟁 처리에 관하여 제29조의4(시정명령 이행상황의 제출요구 등), 제29조의5(고용노동부장관의 차별적 처우 시정 요구 등), 제29조의6(확정된 시정명령의 효력 확대), 제30조(입증책임)에서 규정하고 있다.

고용노동부장관의 사건처리는 고용노동부의 지방 조직(6개의 지방고용노동청, 40개 지방고용노동지청, 2개의 출장소)과 소속 근로감독관에 의해 수행된다.

1. 사업주에게 시정명령 이행상황의 제출 요구

고용노동부장관은 확정된 시정명령에 대하여 사업주에게 이행상황을 제출할 것을 요구할 수 있다(제29조의4 제1항).

사업주가 법 제29조의4제1항(법 제29조의5제4항 및 제29조의6제3항에 따라 준용되는 경우를 포함한다)을 위반하여 정당한 이유 없이 고용노동부장관의 시정명령에 대한 이행상황의 제출요구에 따르지 않은 경우에는 500만 원 이하의 과태료를 부과 받는다(제39조제3항제9호). 그런데 시행령의 [과태료 부과기준]은 1차 위반(200만 원), 2차 위반(400만 원), 3차 이상 위반(500만 원)과 같이 차등적으로 과태료 금액을 정하고 있다(제29조의4제2항).

2. 사업주에게 시정 요구와 그 불응에 관한 노동위원회에의 통보

(1) 사업주에게 차별적 처우의 시정요구

고용노동부장관은 사업주가 차별적 처우를 한 경우에는 그 시정을 요구할

Section 2. Responding to Reported Incidents of Workplace Sexual Harassment

employer engaging in discriminatory treatment (Article 29-5, paragraph 1).

(2) Notification to the Labor Relations Commission

Should an employer fail to comply with a demand for correction under paragraph 1 above, the Minister of Employment and Labor shall notify the LRC of the details of the relevant discriminatory treatment. In such cases, the Minister of Employment and Labor shall notify the relevant employer and employee of such facts (Article 29-5, paragraph 2).

(3) The decision and handling by the Labor Commission

① Upon receiving notification from the Minister of Employment and Labor under paragraph 2 above, the relevant LRC shall, without delay, examine whether the discriminatory treatment has occurred. In such cases, the commission shall provide the relevant employer and employee with an opportunity to present their opinions (Article 29-5, paragraph 3).

② Articles 26~29 and 29-2~29-4 shall apply correspondingly to the following procedures and effects of LRC for its decision under paragraph 3 above. In such cases, the "date the request for correction was filed" shall be understood as the "date notification was received," "decision of dismissal" as "decision that there has been no discriminatory treatment," "interested parties" as "relevant employer and employee(s)," and "employee who has filed a request for correction" as "relevant employee" (Article 29-5, paragraph 4).

3. Expanding the effect of a finalized corrective order

(1) Filing a Complaint by the Worker

A worker who has requested corrective action for discriminatory treatment may report to the Minister of Employment and Labor if the employer fails to comply with the finalized corrective order (Article 29-4, Paragraph 2).

(2) Expansion of the effectiveness of finalized corrective orders

① The Minister of Employment and Labor may investigate whether discriminatory treatment has occurred in the workplace of an employer who has the obligation to comply with a finalized corrective order under Article 29-3 (including cases applied mutatis mutandis under Article 29-5 (4)) against other employees who are subject to the effect of the relevant corrective order. If further discriminatory treatment is found, the Minister of

수 있다(제29조의5제1항).

(2) 사업주의 불응시 노동위원회에게 통보
고용노동부장관은 사업주가 제1항에 따른 시정요구에 따르지 아니할 경우에는 차별적 처우의 내용을 구체적으로 명시하여 노동위원회에 통보하여야 한다. 이 경우 고용노동부장관은 해당 사업주 및 근로자에게 그 사실을 알려야 한다(제29조의5제2항).

(3) 노동위원회의 심리와 처리
① 노동위원회는 제2항에 따라 고용노동부장관의 통보를 받은 때에는 지체 없이 차별적 처우가 있는지 여부를 심리하여야 한다. 이 경우 노동위원회는 해당 사업주 및 근로자에게 의견을 진술할 수 있는 기회를 주어야 한다(제29조의5제3항).
② 제3항에 따른 노동위원회의 심리, 시정절차 및 노동위원회 결정에 대한 효력 등에 관하여는 제26조부터 제29조까지 및 제29조의2부터 제29조의4까지를 준용한다. 이 경우 "시정신청을 한 날"은 "통보를 받은 날"로, "기각결정"은 "차별적 처우가 없다는 결정"으로, "관계 당사자"는 "해당 사업주 또는 근로자"로, "시정신청을 한 근로자"는 "해당 근로자"로 본다(제29조의5제4항).

3. 사업주의 시정명령 불이행에 대한 대처

(1) 근로자의 신고 접수
차별적 처우의 시정 신청을 한 근로자는 사업주가 확정된 시정명령을 이행하지 아니하는 경우 이를 고용노동부장관에게 신고할 수 있다(제29조의4제2항).

(2) 확정된 시정명령의 효력 확대
① 고용노동부장관은 제29조의3(제29조의5제4항에 따라 준용되는 경우를 포함한다)에 따라 확정된 시정명령을 이행할 의무가 있는 사업주의 사업 또는 사업장에서 해당 시정명령의 효력이 미치는 근로자 외의 근로자에

Section 2. Responding to Reported Incidents of Workplace Sexual Harassment

Employment and Labor may demand further correction (Article 29-6, paragraph 1).

② Where an employer fails to comply with a demand for correction under paragraph 1 above, the Minister of Employment and Labor shall notify the relevant Labor Relations Commission of such failure. The LRC shall, without delay, examine whether or not discriminatory treatment is given (Article 29-6, paragraph 2).

Ⅳ. Handling of Incidents by the National Human Rights Commission of Korea

1. Overview of the National Human Rights Commission

The National Human Rights Commission (hereinafter referred to as the "NHRC") performs tasks related to the protection and improvement of human rights, such as formulating policy, educating, investigating and conducting research, providing remedy for rights violations, and exchanging and cooperating with domestic and international human rights organizations and groups, based on the National Human Rights Commission of Korea Act(Article 19).

The Commission's remedies for rights violations target acts of discrimination that infringe upon human rights and equal rights, in accordance with Chapter 4 of the Act (Article 30, paragraph 1). The Act includes harassment as a type of discrimination that infringes upon equal rights. However, on January 4, 2022, a new article, 4-2, was added and titled, Military Human Rights Protection Officer, Military Human Rights Protection Committee, and Investigation and Remedy of Military Human Rights Violations. "Human rights violations against military personnel" refers to acts of violation or discrimination that occur during the performance of duties or military life (as defined in subparagraph 5 of Article 2 of the Framework Act on Military Status and Service) of military personnel (Article 2, paragraph 7). Therefore, the Human Rights Commission can also receive and address cases of sexual harassment within the military.

The tasks of the Commission are performed by the commissioners and the secretariat. The Commission consists of 11 commissioners, including one chairperson and three standing commissioners, with one gender (sex) not exceeding 60% of the total commissioners. The appointments are as follows: ① Four commissioners are elected by the National Assembly, including two standing commissioners; ② Four commissioners are appointed by the President, including one standing commissioner;

대해서도 차별적 처우가 있는지를 조사하여 차별적 처우가 있는 경우에는 그 시정을 요구할 수 있다(제29조의6제1항).
② 고용노동부장관은 사업주가 제1항에 따른 시정요구에 따르지 아니하는 경우 노동위원회에 통보하여야 하고, 노동위원회는 지체 없이 차별적 처우가 있는지 여부를 심리하여야 한다. 제2항에 따른 통보 및 심리에 관하여는 제29조의5제2항부터 제5항까지를 준용한다(제29조의6제2항).

Ⅳ. 국가인권위원회의 사건처리

1. 국가인권위원회의 개요

국가인권위원회(이하 "인권위"라 한다)는 「국가인권위원회법」을 근거로 인권의 보호와 향상을 위하여 정책, 교육, 실태조사와 연구, 권리구제, 국내외 인권기구 및 단체와의 교류·협력 등에 관한 업무를 수행한다(제19조).

인권위의 권리구제는 「국가인권위원회법」의 [제4장 인권침해 및 차별행위의 조사와 구제]에 따라 '인권침해행위'와 '평등권 침해의 차별행위'를 대상으로 한다(제30조제1항), 그런데 이 법은 '평등권을 침해한 차별행위'의 유형에 '성희롱'을 포함하고 있다.

그런데 이 법은 2022년 1월 4일, [제4장의2 군인권보호관·군인권보호위원회 및 군인권침해의 조사·구제]를 신설하였다. '군인권침해'란 "제30조제1항에 따른 인권침해나 차별행위에 해당하는 경우로서 군인등의 복무 중 업무 수행 과정 또는 병영생활(「군인의 지위 및 복무에 관한 기본법」제2조제5호에 따른 병영생활을 말한다)에서 발생하는 인권침해나 차별행위를 말한다."(제2조제7호). 그러므로 군대 내 성희롱 사건도 인권위가 진정받고 처리할 수 있다.

인권위의 업무는 인권위원들과 사무처가 수행한다. 인권위원은 위원장 1명과 상임위원 3명을 포함한 11명의 인권위원으로 구성되어 있는데 특정 성(性)이 10분의 6을 초과하지 못한다. 인권문제에 관하여 전문적인 지식과 경험이 있고 인권의 보장과 향상을 위한 업무를 공정하고 독립적으로 수행할 수 있다고 인정되는 사람으로서 ① 국회가 선출하는 4명(상임위원 2명을 포함한다), ② 대통령이 지명하는 4명(상임위원 1명을 포함한다), ③ 대법원장이 지명하는

Section 2. Responding to Reported Incidents of Workplace Sexual Harassment

and ③ Three commissioners are appointed by the Chief Justice of the Supreme Court, upon recommendation by the President (Article 5). The Secretariat consists of the Operational Support Division, the Human Rights Counseling and Mediation Center, the Policy and Education Bureau, the Investigation and Remedy Division, the Discrimination Rectification Bureau, and the Military Human Rights Protection Division.

The Commission has subcommittees that include the Standing Committee, the Remedy Committee, and the Correction of Discrimination Committee, as well as the plenary committee. Deliberations on cases related to sexual harassment are mainly conducted by the Discrimination Rectification Committee, which is composed of three to five commissioners, and sometimes by the plenary committee. There is also a Professional Correction of Discrimination Committee that conducts prior research on and reviews matters related to the Correction of Discrimination Committee.

2. Methods and procedures for handling sexual harassment cases by the National Human Rights Commission

(1) Petitions and response to petitions

1) Filing a petition

Those who have experienced sexual harassment or those who are aware of such incidents can file a petition directly to the Human Rights Commission by visiting in person or through mail, fax, email, through the website, or by phone. If a third party (such as the victim's family, relatives, or labor union) files the petition on behalf of the victim, and if it is clear that the victim does not desire an investigation, the Human Rights Commission may dismiss the petition (Article 32, clause 3). Statistics show that 83.3% of the petitions were filed by the victims themselves, while others were filed by third parties.[88]

Petition related to sexual harassment can be filed with the Human Rights Counseling and Mediation Center, its official website or local Human Rights Offices. Currently, there are Human Rights Offices in Busan, Gwangju, Daegu, and Daejeon, and a branch office in Jeju, so those residing in these areas can utilize these locations. According to the Investigation and Resolution Rules, if the content of the petition which is to be received by the Center Director, Human Rights Office Director, or Branch Office Director is not specified, and the main point of the mediation cannot be clearly identified, they must notify the petitioner within 10 days of receipt of the specific details that must be added. If the petitioner does not

---

[88] National Human Rights Commission, July 2020, "Guidelines for Mediation in Sexual Harassment Cases" (Appendix), Vol. 9, p. 381.

3명을 대통령이 임명한다(제5조). 사무처에는 운영지원과, 인권상담조정센터, 정책교육국, 침해조사국, 차별시정국 및 군인권보호국이 있다.

인권위의 조직에는 상임위원회와 침해구제위원회, 차별시정위원회 등의 소위원회와 전체 위원회가 있는데 성희롱 사건의 심의는 주로 인권위원 3명 이상 5명 이하로 구성된 차별시정위원회에서 하고 때로는 전체 위원회에서 하는 경우도 있다. 차별시정위원회의 사안에 관하여 미리 연구·검토하는 차별시정 전문위원회가 조직되어 있다.

2. 국가인권위원회의 성희롱 관련 사건 진정

(1) 진정

1) 진정인과 진정 방법

성희롱의 피해자 또는 피해 사실을 알고 있는 사람은 인권위를 방문하여 직접 진정하거나 우편, 팩시밀리, 전자우편 및 홈페이지, 전화 등을 통해 진정할 수 있다. 성희롱 피해자가 아닌 제3자(피해자의 가족, 친지, 노동조합 등)가 진정하는 경우에는 피해자가 조사를 원하지 아니하는 것이 명백하면 인권위는 진정을 각하할 수 있다(제32조제3호).[88]

성희롱의 진정은 인권위의 인권상담조정센터 또는 홈페이지, 인권사무소에 할 수 있다. 현재 부산, 광주, 대구, 대전에 인권사무소가 있고, 광주인권 사무소에 제주출장소가 있으므로 이 지역에 거주하는 사람은 이곳에 진정할 수 있다.

인권위가 제정한 「인권침해 및 차별행위 조사구제규칙」 (이하 "조사구제규칙" 이라 한다)에 따라 인권상담조정센터장과 인권사무소장 및 출장소장은 접수 하려는 진정의 내용이 특정되어 있지 아니하여 진정의 요지를 알 수 없을 때에는 진정인에게 해당 진정을 접수하지 아니할 수 있음을 설명하고 보완 하여야 할 사항을 구체적으로 제시하여 10일 이내에 이를 보완할 것을 요구 하여야 한다. 진정인이 이 기간 내에 진정내용을 보완하지 아니할 경우에 센터장과 인권사무소장 및 출장소장은 해당 진정을 접수하지 아니하고 종결 처리할 수 있다(제8조). 진정은 이를 접수한 날로부터 3개월 이내에 처리하는

---
[88] 인권위의 진정사건에서 피해자 본인이 진정인이 된 경우는 83.3%이며 그 외는 제3자가 진정인이 되었다 (국가인권위원회,「성희롱 시정권고사례집」제9집의 부록(성희롱 진정사건 통계), 2020.7, 381면.)

Section 2. Responding to Reported Incidents of Workplace Sexual Harassment

revise the content within this period, the Center Director, Human Rights Office Director, or Branch Office Director may refuse the petition and may conclude the case (Article 8). In principle, mediation should be processed within 3 months from the date of receipt of the petition (Article 4, clause 1). If it is not possible to process within this period due to unavoidable circumstances, the reasons must be explained to the petitioner in writing. However, if the explanation is provided through methods such as face-to-face interviews or phone calls and a record kept, the written submission may be unnecessary (Article 4, clause 2).

2) Respondent

The term "respondent" refers to "a national agency, its affiliated public officials and employees, or private individuals according to Article 30, Paragraph 1 of the Act, who have been specified by the victim for violating human rights or discriminating " (Article 2, Clause 3) as defined in the Investigation and Resolution Rules.

When filing a petition, the petitioner must specify the respondent. This may include the perpetrator of sexual harassment (including civil servants and employees, employers, and workers of national agencies, local governments, schools at all levels, and public organizations), as well as the head of the affiliated organization or workplace, as sexual harassment is not just one individual's sexual misconduct, but also involves the responsibility of the organization's management or employer, who must work to prevent sexual harassment and improve the work and educational environment to prevent recurrence.

3) Dismissal of petition

The NHRC shall not proceed with an investigation if any of the following apply to a complaint, and shall dismiss the complaint (Article 32, paragraphs 1 and 3). The dismissal shall be made by the head of the investigation department in accordance with the Investigation and Resolution Rules. If one or more of the reasons listed below for dismissal exists, the head of the relevant subcommittee shall report to the subcommittee chairperson, who shall review it and make a decision (Article 14):

① The content of the petition does not fall within the scope of investigation by the Commission;
② The content of the petition is clearly false or groundless;
③ It is evident that the alleged victim does not wish to proceed with an investigation;
④ The petition is filed more than one year after the occurrence of the facts that caused the filing. However, this shall not apply if the NHRC decides otherwise because the

것을 원칙으로 한다(제4조제1항). 부득이한 사정으로 이 기한 내에 처리하지 못하는 경우 진정인에게 그 사유를 문서로 설명하여야 한다. 다만, 진정인에게 면담 또는 전화통화 등의 방법으로 설명하고 그 기록을 남긴 경우 문서 송부를 생략할 수 있다(제4조제2항).

2) 피진정인

「조사구제규칙」에서 '피진정인'이란 "피해자에게 인권침해 또는 차별행위를 하였다고 진정인에 의하여 특정된 법 제30조제1항에 따른 국가기관 등과 그 소속 공무원 및 직원 또는 사인(개인)"(제2조제3호)을 말한다.

진정인은 진정할 때 피진정인을 특정해야 하는데 성희롱의 행위자(국가기관, 지방자치단체, 각급학교, 공직유관단체의 소속 공무원 및 직원 또는 사용자, 근로자) 뿐 아니라 소속기관이나 사업장의 장도 피진정인으로 할 수 있다. 성희롱이 개인의 성적 일탈 문제가 아니라 조직 내에서 업무와 관련하거나 지위를 이용하여 행해진 성적 언동으로서 기관장이나 사업주가 성희롱 발생에 대한 책임을 져야 하고 재발을 방지하기 위해 업무환경, 교육환경을 개선할 책임을 있다고 보기 때문이다.

3) 진정의 각하

인권위는 접수하거나 조사를 시작한 진정이 다음의 어느 하나에 해당하는 경우에는 그 진정을 각하(却下)하여 조사를 진행하지 아니한다(제32조제1항, 제3항). 이 각하는 「조사구제규칙」에 따라 조사부서의 장이 예비조사를 실시하고, 해당사유가 있는 경우에는 소관 소위원장에게 보고하고 소위원장이 이를 검토하여 결정한다(제14조).

① 진정의 내용이 위원회의 조사대상에 해당하지 아니하는 경우
② 진정의 내용이 명백히 거짓이거나 이유 없다고 인정되는 경우
③ 피해자가 아닌 사람이 한 진정에서 피해자가 조사를 원하지 아니하는 것이 명백한 경우
④ 진정의 원인이 된 사실이 발생한 날부터 1년 이상 지나서 진정한 경우(다만, 진정의 원인이 된 사실에 관하여 공소시효 또는 민사상 시효가 완성되지 아니한 사건으로서 위원회가 조사하기로 결정한 경우에는

Section 2. Responding to Reported Incidents of Workplace Sexual Harassment

statute of limitations or prescription under the Civil Act has not expired;
⑤ Other legal procedures regarding the facts that caused the filing of the petition—such as a court trial, constitutional trial, or an investigation by a law enforcement agency—are in progress or haven't been concluded;
⑥ The petition is submitted anonymously or under a pseudonym;
⑦ It is determined to be inappropriate for the Commission to investigate the petition;
⑧ The petitioner withdraws the petition;
⑨ The petition contains the same details of a petition dismissed by the NHRC;
⑩ The petitioner's intention is contrary to the final ruling of a court or the Constitutional Court regarding the facts that caused the petition.

3. Investigation and Handling of Sexual Harassment Cases by the National Human Rights Commission

The reporting, investigation, and resolution of sexual harassment cases by the National Human Rights Commission (NHRC) are conducted in accordance with the "National Human Rights Commission Act" and the "Investigation and Remedial Measures for Human Rights Violations and Discriminatory Acts Regulations" (referred to as the "Investigation and Remedial Measures Regulations") established by the NHRC.

(1) Investigation
1) Investigations based on the petition
If the National Human Rights Commission determines that a complaint does not fall under any of the reasons for dismissal, it shall conduct an investigation, which may be conducted in the following ways (Article 36, paragraph 1):
① Request the attendance, statement or submission of written statements from the parties involved, including the petitioner, victim(s), or respondent(s) (hereinafter referred to as "the parties");
② Demand the submission of data, etc., deemed relevant to the investigation, from the parties, related parties, or relevant organizations;
③ Engage in onsite investigation or inspection of places, facilities, or data deemed relevant to the investigation;
④ Inquire into facts or information deemed relevant to the investigation from the parties, related parties, or relevant organizations.

2) Investigation by Authority

그러하지 아니하다.)
⑤ 진정이 제기될 당시 진정의 원인이 된 사실에 관하여 법원 또는 헌법재판소의 재판, 수사기관의 수사 또는 그 밖의 법률에 따른 권리구제 절차가 진행 중이거나 종결된 경우
⑥ 진정이 익명이나 가명으로 제출된 경우
⑦ 진정이 위원회가 조사하는 것이 적절하지 아니하다고 인정되는 경우
⑧ 진정인이 진정을 취하한 경우
⑨ 위원회가 기각한 진정과 같은 사실에 대하여 다시 진정한 경우
⑩ 진정의 취지가 그 진정의 원인이 된 사실에 관한 법원의 확정판결이나 헌법재판소의 결정에 반하는 경우

3. 국가인권위원회의 성희롱 관련 사건의 조사와 처리

인권위는 「국가인권위원회」과 「조사구제규칙」에 따라 성희롱 관련 사건을 조사하고 처리한다.

(1) 조사
1) 진정에 의한 조사

인권위는 접수한 진정이 각하 사유에 해당되지 않는다고 인정되면 조사를 실시한다. 조사는 다음의 방법으로 할 수 있다(제36조제1항).
① 진정인·피해자·피진정인(이하 "당사자"라 한다) 또는 관계인에 대한 출석 요구, 진술 청취 또는 진술서 제출 요구
② 당사자, 관계인 또는 관계 기관 등에 대하여 조사 사항과 관련이 있다고 인정되는 자료 등의 제출 요구
③ 조사 사항과 관련이 있다고 인정되는 장소, 시설 또는 자료 등에 대한 현장조사 또는 감정(鑑定)
④ 당사자, 관계인 또는 관계 기관 등에 대하여 조사 사항과 관련이 있다고 인정되는 사실 또는 정보의 조회

2) 직권조사

Section 2. Responding to Reported Incidents of Workplace Sexual Harassment

Even without a petition, the National Human Rights Commission may initiate an investigation if there are reasonable grounds to believe that a significant violation of human rights or discrimination has taken place (Article 30, paragraph 3).

(2) Exclusion, challenge, refrainment of commissioners

The National Human Rights Commission has established a system of excluding, challenging, and refraining commissioners in order to ensure fairness in handling each case (Article 38).

1) Exclusion

Any commissioner for whom any of the following subparagraphs apply shall be excluded from deliberation and resolution on a petition:

① Where the commissioner or any person who is or was his or her spouse is a party to the relevant petition or the joint holder of any rights or joint obligor of any duties with the said party in regard to the relevant petition;

② Where the commissioner is or was a blood relative of a party to the relevant petition;

③ Where the commissioner has previously testified or appraised on the relevant petition;

④ Where the commissioner has participated or is participating in the relevant petition as an agent of a party;

⑤ Where the commissioner has participated in any investigation, trial or relief procedures related to the petition under any other Act.

2) Challenge

Where there exist circumstances causing the participation of a commissioner to be prejudiced and therefore may compromise the fairness of deliberation and resolution, the party may file an application with the Commission chairperson to challenge the inclusion of such commissioner. The Commission chairperson shall make the decision him or herself, without referring the decision to the Committee. However, if it is inappropriate for the Commission chairperson to make the decision, then it shall be referred to the committee.

3) Refrainment

If sufficient grounds exist to challenge or exclude a commissioner, that commissioner may voluntarily avoid participating in the deliberation and decision-making for the relevant case (paragraph 3).

인권위는 진정이 없어도 인권침해나 차별행위가 있다고 믿을 만한 상당한 근거가 있고 그 내용이 중대하다고 인정할 때에는 직권으로 조사할 수 있다(제30조제3항).

(2) 위원의 제척·기피·회피
인권위는 사건처리의 공정성을 위해 인권위원의 제척·기피·회피 제도를 두고 있다(제38조).

1) 위원의 제척
위원(제41조에 따른 조정위원을 포함한다.)은 다음의 어느 하나에 해당하는 경우에는 진정의 심의·의결에서 제척된다(제1항).
① 위원이나 그 배우자 또는 그 배우자이었던 사람이 해당 진정의 당사자이거나 그 진정에 관하여 당사자와 공동권리자 또는 공동의무자인 경우
② 위원이 해당 진정의 당사자와 친족이거나 친족이었던 경우
③ 위원이 해당 진정에 관하여 증언이나 감정을 한 경우
④ 위원이 해당 진정에 관하여 당사자의 대리인으로 관여하거나 관여하였던 경우
⑤ 위원이 해당 진정에 관하여 수사, 재판 또는 다른 법률에 따른 구제절차에 관여하였던 경우

2) 위원의 기피
당사자는 위원에게 심의·의결의 공정을 기대하기 어려운 사정이 있는 경우에는 위원장에게 기피신청을 할 수 있으며 위원장은 당사자의 기피신청에 대하여 위원회의 의결을 거치지 아니하고 결정한다. 다만, 위원장이 결정하기에 타당하지 아니하는 경우에는 위원회의 의결로 결정한다(제2항).

3) 위원의 회피
위원이 제척 또는 기피 사유에 해당하는 경우에는 스스로 그 진정의 심의·의결을 회피할 수 있다(제3항).

Section 2. Responding to Reported Incidents of Workplace Sexual Harassment

(3) Handling of sexual harassment cases by the National Human Rights Commission

The National Human Rights Commission has various ways to handle sexual harassment cases, including dismissing the petition, recommending conciliation or mediation or corrective measures, expressing opinions, recommending disciplinary action, filing a complaint, requesting legal structure for the benefit of victims, and recommending emergency relief. According to data[89] published by the Commission, the most common decision made regarding sexual harassment claims is dismissal due to not eligible application, which accounts for 66.3%, followed by dismissal of complaints (12.5%), recommending conciliation (8.7%), settlement (8.6%), conciliation during investigation (1.2%), suspension of the investigation (2.0%), and transfer to other legal channels (0.7%).

1) Dismissal

The Commission dismisses a petition as a result of the investigation if any of the following apply (Article 39, paragraph 1):
① It is clear that the content of the petition is untrue, or there is no objective evidence to verify the truth;
② The facts uncovered do not constitute a human rights violation or discrimination;
③ When it is determined that separate remedial measures are not necessary, such as when the victim has already received compensation for damages.

2) Recommending conciliation

The Commission may recommend conciliation to the parties involved in an ongoing or concluded investigation in order to achieve a fair resolution of the case (Article 40).

3) Mediation

Mediation is a process in which parties resolve disputes through mutual understanding and compromise. The National Human Rights Commission of Korea establishes a mediation committee composed of commission members and experts to ensure prompt and fair handling of mediations (Article 41). This committee may initiate mediation procedures upon request from one of the parties to the dispute or on its own authority for cases referred to it that involve human rights violations or discrimination (Article 42, paragraph 1). Mediation is deemed to be established when the parties sign a mediation agreement, which is then confirmed by the mediation committee (Article 42, paragraph 2).

If no agreement is reached between the parties during the mediation process, the mediation committee may decide to go beyond mediation in the interest of a fair

---
[89] National Human Rights Commission, July 2020, Casebook Appendix (Statistics on Sexual Harassment Cases), p. 380.

(3) 국가인권위원회의 사건처리 방법

인권위의 성희롱 사건의 처리방법에는 진정의 기각, 합의의 권고, 조정, 시정권고, 의견표명, 징계권고, 고발, 피해자를 위한 법률구조 요청, 긴급구제조치 권고가 있다.

인권위가 발간한 자료[89]를 보면, 인권위가 성희롱 진정 사건에 관하여 가장 많이 처리한 방법은 "각하"로서 66.3%에 이른다. 다음은 "기각"(12.5%), "권고"(8.7%), "합의종결"(8.6%), "조사 중 해결조정"(1.2%), "조사중지"(2.0%), "이송"(0.7%)의 순이다.

1) 기각 결정

인권위는 진정을 조사한 결과 진정의 내용이 다음 어느 하나에 해당하는 경우에는 그 진정을 기각한다(제39조제1항).
① 진정의 내용이 사실이 아님이 명백하거나 사실이라고 인정할 만한 객관적인 증거가 없는 경우.
② 조사 결과 인권침해나 차별행위에 해당하지 아니하는 경우.
③ 이미 피해 회복이 이루어지는 등 별도의 구제 조치가 필요하지 아니하다고 인정되는 경우.

2) 합의의 권고

인권위는 조사 중이거나 조사가 끝난 진정에 대하여 사건의 공정한 해결을 위하여 필요한 구제 조치를 당사자에게 제시하고 합의를 권고할 수 있다(제40조).

3) 조정

인권위는 조정의 신속하고 공정한 처리를 위하여 인권위원과 전문가로 구성된 조정위원회를 둔다(제41조). 조정위원회는 인권침해나 차별행위와 관련하여 당사자의 신청이나 위원회의 직권으로 조정위원회에 회부된 진정에 대하여 조정 절차를 시작할 수 있다(제42조제1항). 조정은 조정 절차가 시작된 이후 당사자가 합의한 사항을 조정서에 적은 후 당사자가 기명날인하고 조정위원회가 이를 확인함으로써 성립한다(제42조제2항).

---

[89] 국가인권위원회, 앞의 사례집의 부록(성희롱 진정사건 통계), 2020.7.,380면.

Section 2. Responding to Reported Incidents of Workplace Sexual Harassment

resolution of the case (Article 42, paragraph 3), and may include one or more of the following measures: 1. Ordering cessation of the human rights violations or discrimination against the claimant(s); 2. Ordering the employer to reinstate the claimant, compensate the claimant for damages, or other similar remedies; 3. Ordering action towards preventing the recurrence of the same or similar violations of human rights or discriminatory acts (Article 42, paragraph 4). If a party does not file an objection within 14 days from the date the decision is received, the decision is considered accepted (Article 42, paragraph 5).

4) Recommending remedies and expressing opinion

When the National Human Rights Commission determines that human rights violations or discriminatory acts have occurred as a result of its investigation, it may recommend to the head of the relevant agency, organization, or supervisory agency (hereinafter referred to as the "affiliated agency, etc.") the implementation of corrective measures as stipulated in Article 42, paragraph 4 (① Ordering cessation of the human rights violations or discrimination against the claimant(s); ② Ordering the employer to reinstate the claimant, compensate the claimant for damages, or other similar remedies; ③ Ordering action towards preventing the recurrence of the same or similar violations of human rights or discriminatory acts, 4. Revising/improving laws, regulations, policies, or practices (Article 44, paragraph 1). The heads of relevant agencies, etc., who receive a recommendation under Article 44, paragraph 1 shall notify the Commission of plans to implement it within 90 days of the date on which the recommendation is received (Article 25, paragraph 3). If the heads of relevant agencies, etc., fail to comply with such recommendation, they shall notify the Commission of the reasons (Article 25, paragraph 4).

The Commission may verify and inspect the status of implementing the recommendation(s) or opinion(s) (Article 25, paragraph 5), and may disclose the recommendations and opinions, with the details notified by the heads of relevant agencies, etc., the results of verification and the status of implementation if necessary (Article 25, paragraph 5).

In cases where the Commission recommends corrective measures related to sexual harassment, the most common is to take special human rights education conducted by the Commission (44.5%). The most common recommendation to heads of organizations is to establish measures to prevent recurrence (22.2%). Other recommendations include personnel measures (disciplinary action, transfers, warnings, etc.) at 16.0%, pay compensation for damages at 14.1%, and others at 3.2%.[90]

5) Recommending disciplinary action

---

[90] National Human Rights Commission, July 2020, Casebook Appendix (Statistics on Sexual Harassment Cases), p. 381.

조정위원회는 조정 절차 중에 당사자 사이에 합의가 이루어지지 아니하는 경우 사건의 공정한 해결을 위하여 조정을 갈음하는 결정을 할 수 있다(제42조제3항). 조정을 갈음하는 결정에 ① 조사대상 인권침해나 차별행위의 중지, ② 원상회복, 손해배상, 그 밖에 필요한 구제조치, ③ 동일하거나 유사한 인권침해 또는 차별행위의 재발을 방지하기 위하여 필요한 조치의 어느 하나의 사항을 포함시킬 수 있다(제42조제4항).

당사자가 결정서를 송달받은 날부터 14일 이내에 이의를 신청하지 아니하면 조정을 수락한 것으로 본다(제42조제5항).

4) 시정조치의 권고와 의견표명

인권위가 진정을 조사한 결과 인권침해나 차별행위가 일어났다고 판단할 때에는 피진정인, 그 소속 기관·단체 또는 감독기관(이하 "소속기관 등"이라 한다)의 장에게 제42조제4항에서 규정한 구제조치(① 인권침해나 차별행위의 중지, ② 원상회복, 손해배상, 그 밖에 필요한 구제조치, ③ 동일하거나 유사한 인권침해 또는 차별행위의 재발을 방지하기 위하여 필요한 조치)의 이행 또는 법령·제도·정책·관행의 시정 또는 개선을 권고할 수 있다(제44조제1항).

권고를 받은 소속기관 등의 장은 권고를 받은 날부터 90일 이내에 그 권고사항의 이행계획을 인권위에 통지하여야 한다(제25조제3항). 그 권고의 내용을 이행하지 아니할 경우에는 그 이유를 인권위에 통지하여야 한다(제25조제4항).

인권위는 권고 또는 의견의 이행실태를 확인·점검할 수 있고(제25조제5항), 필요하다고 인정하면 위원회의 권고와 의견 표명, 권고를 받은 관계기관 등의 장이 통지한 내용 및 이행실태의 확인·점검 결과를 공표할 수 있다(제25조제6항).

인권위가 성희롱 사건의 시정권고에서 피진정인에게 가장 많이 권고하는 것은 "인권위가 실시하는 특별인권교육을 받을 것"(44.5%)이다. 기관장에게 하는 권고에는 "재발방지대책 수립"(22.2%)이다. 그 외 "인사조치(징계, 전보, 경고, 주의 등)권고"가 16.0%, "손해배상 권고"(14.1%), 기타(3.2%)가 있다.[90]

5) 징계의 권고

인권위는 진정을 조사한 결과 피진정인이 성희롱 행위를 하였다고 인정되면

---

[90] 국가인권위원회, 앞의 사례집의 부록(성희롱 진정사건 통계), 2020, 381면.

Section 2. Responding to Reported Incidents of Workplace Sexual Harassment

If it is determined through an investigation that sexual harassment has occurred, the National Human Rights Commission may recommend that the head of the relevant organization or agency discipline the alleged perpetrator and other persons responsible for the human rights violation (Article 45, paragraph 2). The head of the organization or agency that receives the disciplinary recommendation shall carry out the recommendation and notify the National Human Rights Commission of the outcome (Article 45, paragraph 4).

6) Accusation

If it is determined through an investigation that the content of the allegation constitutes a criminal act (such as sexual assault) and requires criminal prosecution, the National Human Rights Commission may file a criminal complaint with the Prosecutor General. However, in cases when the alleged perpetrator is military personnel, etc., the complaint may be filed with the Chief of the General Staff of the military or the Minister of National Defense (Article 45, paragraph 1). The Prosecutor General, the Chief of the General Staff of the military, or the Minister of National Defense shall complete the investigation and notify the Commission of the results within 3 months from the date the complaint is received. However, if the investigation cannot be completed within 3 months, the reasons for the delay shall be disclosed (Article 45, paragraph 2).

7) Request for legal assistance

If the National Human Rights Commission determines that it is necessary for the investigation, collection of evidence, or remedy of the rights of the victim, it may request legal assistance for the victim from the Legal Aid Corporation or other relevant agencies. Such request for legal assistance cannot be made against the explicit consent of the victim (Article 47).

8) Emergency relief

After receiving a petition, the Human Rights Commission can determine if there is a considerable probability that the sexual harassment under investigation is still ongoing. If there is a risk of damage that is difficult to recover because of being unattended, by the petitioner or victim's request or by authority, recommendations can be made to the head of the affiliated agency or respondent to take necessary measures, such as to provide medical care, meals, clothing, etc. (Article 48).

4. Appealing a decision by the National Human Rights Commission

(1) Administrative appeals

피진정인 또는 인권침해에 책임이 있는 사람을 징계할 것을 소속기관 등의 장에게 권고할 수 있다(제45조제2항). 징계권고를 받은 소속기관 등의 장은 권고를 존중하여야 하며 그 결과를 인권위에 통지하여야 한다(제45조제4항).

6) 고발

인권위는 진정을 조사한 결과 진정의 내용이 범죄행위(성폭력범죄 등)에 해당하고 이에 대하여 형사처벌이 필요하다고 인정되면 검찰총장에게 그 내용을 고발할 수 있다. 다만, 피고발인이 군인 등인 경우에는 소속 군 참모총장 또는 국방부장관에게 고발할 수 있다(제45조제1항).

검찰총장, 군 참모총장 또는 국방부장관은 고발을 받은 날부터 3개월 이내에 수사를 마치고 그 결과를 인권위에 통지하여야 한다. 다만, 3개월 이내에 수사를 마치지 못할 때에는 그 사유를 밝혀야 한다(제45조제2항).

7) 법률구조 요청

인권위는 진정에 관한 조사, 증거의 확보 또는 피해자의 권리 구제를 위하여 필요하다고 인정하면 피해자를 위하여 대한법률구조공단 또는 그 밖의 기관에 법률구조를 요청할 수 있다. 이 법률구조 요청은 피해자의 명시한 의사에 반하여 할 수 없다(제47조).

8) 긴급구제 조치

인권위는 진정을 접수한 후 조사대상 성희롱 행위가 계속 중에 있다는 상당한 개연성이 있고, 이를 방치할 경우 회복하기 어려운 피해 발생의 우려가 있다고 인정할 때에는 그 진정에 대한 결정 이전에 진정인이나 피해자의 신청에 의하여 또는 직권으로 피진정인, 그 소속기관 등의 장에게 의료·급식·의복 등의 제공, 행위의 중지, 행위자의 직무배제 등의 필요한 조치를 하도록 권고할 수 있다(제48조).

4. 국가인권위원회의 결정에 대한 불복

(1) 행정심판

Section 2. Responding to Reported Incidents of Workplace Sexual Harassment

An administrative appeal allows people who have suffered a violation of their rights or interests due to unfair decisions by administrative agencies or the exercise or failure to exercise public power to seek remedies quickly and easily. As the National Human Rights Commission is also a type of administrative agency, appeals against its decisions can be made through the Administrative Appeals Committee established within the National Human Rights Commission in accordance with the "Rules of the Administrative Appeals Committee of the National Human Rights Commission." Appeals to the Administrative Appeals Committee can be made online or in writing within 90 days from the date of the relevant National Human Rights Commission decision (or 180 days with justifiable reasons).

(2) Administrative lawsuits

Appeals against decisions of the National Human Rights Commission can also be made by filing an administrative lawsuit with a court without going through the process of administrative appeal.

V. Handling of Incidents by Investigative Agencies and the Courts

1. Investigative agencies

(1) Handling of incidents by the police

Police handle disputes related to sexual harassment when an incident falls under the category of sexual assault crimes or crimes equivalent to sexual assault, according to the Act on Special Cases concerning the Punishment, etc. of Sexual Crimes. The Commissioner General of the National Police Agency designates a specialized police officer for sexual assault crimes at each police station and instructs them to investigate a victim's claims unless special circumstances preclude such investigation (Article 26, paragraph 2).

(2) Handling of incidents by prosecutors

Prosecutors handle disputes related to sexual harassment in cases where an employer disadvantages workers or victims who have reported incidents of sexual harassment (Article 14, paragraph 6 of the Equal Employment Act) Also, when the case falls under the category of sexual assault crimes of the Act on Special Cases concerning the Punishment, etc. of Sexual Crimes or crimes under the Criminal Act.

The Labor Standards Act stipulates that "investigation of the site, submission of documents, interrogation, and other investigations according to this Act or other labor-related laws shall be carried out by labor supervisors belonging to the

'행정심판'이란 행정청의 부당한 처분 또는 그 밖의 공권력의 행사·불행사 등으로 권리나 이익을 침해받은 국민이 신속하고 간편하게 권익을 구제받을 수 있도록 한 제도를 말한다. 인권위도 행정기관의 일종이므로 그 결정에 대한 불복은 「국가인권위원회행정심판위원회규칙」에 따라 인권위에 설치된 행정심판위원회를 통해 할 수 있다. 행정심판은 인권위의 처분이 있음을 안 날로부터 90일 이내(정당한 사유가 있는 경우에는 180일 이내)에 온라인 또는 서면으로 청구할 수 있다.

(2) 행정소송

인권위의 결정에 대한 불복은 행정심판을 거치지 아니하고 법원에 행정소송을 제기하여 할 수 있다.

V. 수사기관과 법원의 사건처리

1. 수사기관의 사건처리

(1) 경찰의 사건처리

경찰이 성희롱 사건의 분쟁처리를 하는 경우는 그 사건이 성폭력범죄와 그와 관련된 범죄(명예훼손죄, 무고죄, 모욕죄, 스토킹범죄 등)에 해당되는 경우이다. 성폭력범죄에 있어서 경찰은 「성폭력범죄처벌법」에 따라 수사한다. 경찰청장은 각 경찰서장으로 하여금 성폭력범죄 전담 사법경찰관을 지정하도록 하여 특별한 사정이 없으면 이들로 하여금 피해자를 조사하게 하여야 한다(제26조제2항).

(2) 검찰의 사건처리

검찰이 성희롱 사건의 분쟁처리를 하는 경우는 「남녀고용평등법」에서 사업주가 제14조제6항을 위반하여 직장 내 성희롱 발생 사실을 신고한 근로자 및 피해근로자등에게 불리한 처우를 한 경우와 「성폭력처벌법」에 따른 성폭력범죄와 그와 관련된 범죄에 해당되는 경우이다.

「근로기준법」은 "이 법 또는 그 밖의 노동관계 법령에 따른 현장조사, 서류의

Section 2. Responding to Reported Incidents of Workplace Sexual Harassment

prosecutor's office and the Ministry of Employment and Labor" (Article 105). The Act on Special Cases concerning the Punishment, etc. of Sexual Crimes stipulates that "the Prosecutor General shall designate a prosecutor in charge of sexual assault crimes at each local prosecutor's office and instruct them to investigate a victim's claim, unless special circumstances preclude such investigation" (Article 26, paragraph 1).

If, upon investigation, the prosecutor finds that there is evidence of a crime occurring, the prosecutor shall file criminal charges with the court. If there is no evidence of a crime, the prosecutor may decide not to indict. Types of non-indictment decisions include suspensions of indictment, cleared of suspicion, no crime, no authority to prosecute, dismissal of the case, and suspension of prosecution.

Prosecutors may also make summary indictments, which are requests for a written order for a fine without holding a trial.

2. Handling of lawsuits by the courts

The Constitution of the Republic of Korea stipulates that "Judicial power shall be vested in courts composed of judges" (Article 101, paragraph 1) and that "The courts shall be composed of the Supreme Court [⋯] and other courts at specified levels" (Article 101, paragraph 2). In accordance with the Court Organization Act, courts have jurisdiction over all legal disputes, except for cases where the Constitution provides special provisions, and they have authority as prescribed by that Act and other Acts (Article 2, paragraph ① There are seven types of courts: 1) Supreme Court, ② High Court, ③ Patent Court, ④ District Court, ⑤ Family Court, ⑥ Administrative Court, and ⑦ Bankruptcy Court (Article 3, paragraph 1). The Supreme Court primarily conducts legal reviews of the interpretation and application of laws by the courts. The judgment of a higher court binds lower courts with respect to case in question (Article 8).

(1) Processing of criminal lawsuits

When a prosecutor investigates a sexual assault crime or a related crime and decides to indict (file charges) against the accused, a criminal trial is held in criminal court. If the accused turns out to be guilty, a penalty is imposed. The Act on Special Cases concerning the Punishment, etc. of Sexual Crimes stipulates that "the president of the district court or of a higher court shall designate a trial division in exclusive charge of sexual crimes to render judgment on such crimes, except in exceptional circumstances" (Article 28).

제출, 심문 등의 수사는 검사와 고용노동부 소속의 근로감독관이 전담하여 수행한다."(제105조)라고 규정하고 있다. 「성폭력처벌법」은 "검찰총장은 각 지방검찰청 검사장으로 하여금 성폭력범죄 전담 검사를 지정하도록 하여 특별한 사정이 없으면 이들로 하여금 피해자를 조사하게 하여야 한다."(제26조 제1항)라고 규정하고 있다.

검찰이 이러한 범죄사건을 수사하고 범죄사실이 있다고 인정되면 법원에 재판을 청구하는 기소를 한다. 범죄사실이 있다고 인정되면 불기소한다. 불기소 처분의 종류에는 기소유예, 혐의 없음, 죄가 안 됨, 공소권 없음, 각하, 공소 보류가 있다. 검사는 약식기소도 할 수 있다. 이것은 공판을 열지 않고 서면 심리로 재판하여 벌금형에 처해 달라는 뜻의 약식명령을 청구하는 것이다.

2. 법원의 소송사건 처리

「헌법」은 "사법권(司法權)은 법관으로 구성된 법원에 속한다."(제101조제1항), "법원은 최고법원인 대법원과 각급 법원으로 조직된다."(제101조제2항)라고 규정하고 있다.

「법원조직법」에 따라 법원은 「헌법」에 특별한 규정이 있는 경우를 제외한 모든 법률상의 쟁송(爭訟)을 심판하고, 이 법과 다른 법률에 따라 법원에 속하는 권한을 가진다(제2조제1항). 법원의 종류에는 7가지(① 대법원, ② 고등법원, ③ 특허법원, ④ 지방법원, ⑤ 가정법원, ⑥ 행정법원, ⑦ 회생법원)가 있다(제3조제1항). 대법원은 원칙적으로 법원의 법의 해석·적용에 관하여 잘못 여부만을 판단하는 법률심(法律審)을 한다. 상급법원 재판에서의 판단은 해당 사건에 관하여 하급심을 기속(羈束)한다(제8조).

(1) 형사소송 사건의 처리

검찰이 성폭력범죄와 그와 관련된 범죄 사건을 수사하고 범죄사실이 있다고 기소(공소 제기)를 하면, 형사법원에서 형사재판이 열려 기소된 피고인에 대하여 유·무죄를 가리고 유죄가 인정되면 형벌을 부과한다. 「성폭력처벌법」은 "지방법원장 또는 고등법원장은 특별한 사정이 없으면 성폭력범죄 전담재판부를 지정하여 성폭력범죄에 대하여 재판하게 하여야 한다."(제28조)라고 규정하고

Section 2. Responding to Reported Incidents of Workplace Sexual Harassment

The court may impose fines or order the accused to provide restitution through a simplified order without going through a public trial. When the court pronounces a guilty verdict (excluding suspended sentences) or issues a simplified order for sexual crimes, it must also issue an order for completion of a program to prevent recurrence or a sexual offender treatment program of up to 500 hours, as necessary (Article 16, paragraph 2).

In some cases, individuals or groups who are accused of sexual harassment or sexual assault may enter a charge of defamation or false accusation against the alleged victim and/or the person or group assisting the alleged victim, and criminal trials may proceed.

(2) Processing of civil lawsuits

In cases related to sexual harassment, civil lawsuits are filed when a victim is seeking compensation from the perpetrator for damages suffered such as mental distress or medical expenses. Civil lawsuits can also be filed against employers, school corporations, presidents, or the Republic of Korea if the victim claims damages for joint and several liability for the illegal acts of the perpetrator as their employer or supervisor. Additionally, there are lawsuits where the victim seeks compensation for damages for defamation against the perpetrator and related parties. On the other hand, civil lawsuits can also be filed by alleged perpetrators of sexual harassment, who seek invalidation of personnel measures or confirmation of their status against employers or universities in response to the disciplinary measures they have received. Civil lawsuits can also be filed in cases where the alleged victims or those who support the alleged victims are sued for defamation by alleged perpetrators of sexual harassment or related parties.

(3) Processing of administrative lawsuits

The Administrative Court deals with administrative lawsuits filed against the National Labor Relations Commission, the National Human Rights Commission, and other administrative agencies, when there is dissatisfaction with their handling of disputes related to sexual harassment and remedies for rights.

For instance, when national universities impose disciplinary actions against professors and employees who have been accused of sexual harassment, those professor or employees may file administrative lawsuits after going through the appeal process of the Appeal Commission for Educators or the Appeals Commission.

있다.

  법원은 공판절차를 거치지 아니하고 원칙적으로 서면심리만으로 피고인에게 벌금·과료를 부과하는 약식명령을 할 수 있다. 법원이 성폭력범죄를 범한 사람에 대하여 유죄판결(선고유예는 제외한다)을 선고하거나 약식명령을 고지하는 경우에는 500시간의 범위에서 재범예방에 필요한 수강명령 또는 성폭력 치료프로그램의 이수명령을 병과하여야 한다(제16조제2항).

  한편, 성희롱·성폭력의 혐의자와 행위자가 피해자나 피해를 주장하는 사람, 피해자에 조력하는 사람이나 단체를 대상으로 명예훼손죄, 무고죄로 고소하여 형사재판이 진행되는 경우가 있다.

(2) 민사소송 사건의 처리

  성희롱 관련 분쟁에 있어 민사소송은 피해자가 성희롱이란 불법행위로 입은 정신적 고통이나 치료비 부담 등의 손해에 대한 배상을 행위자에게 청구하는 경우와 사업주, 학교 법인, 총장, 대한민국에게 행위자의 사용자 또는 관리감독자로서 행위자와 공동불법행위의 손해배상을 청구하는 경우에 제기된다. 또한 피해자가 행위자와 관계자에 대하여 명예를 훼손당한 것에 대한 손해배상을 청구하는 소송도 있다.

  한편, 성희롱 행위자가 사업주나 대학으로부터 성희롱 행위로 인한 인사조치를 받고 이에 대하여 무효소송을 제기하거나 지위확인 소송을 제기하여 민사재판이 진행되는 경우도 있다. 또한 민사재판은 성희롱·성폭력의 혐의자와 행위자가 피해자나 피해를 주장하는 사람, 피해자에 조력하는 사람이나 단체를 대상으로 명예훼손에 대한 손해배상을 청구하는 경우에도 진행된다.

(3) 행정소송 사건의 처리

  행정법원은 중앙노동위원회, 국가인권위원회가 성희롱 분쟁에 관한 사건처리와 권리구제조치에 불복이 있는 경우와 그 밖의 행정기관의 행정처분에 대하여 제기되는 행정소송을 처리한다.

  국립대학이 성희롱 행위자인 교수와 직원을 징계 또는 불이익 처분을 한 경우에 이들은 교원소청심사위원회 또는 소청심사위원회의 심사 절차를 거쳐 행정소송을 제기할 수 있다.

Section 3. Issues and Related Cases in Handling Workplace Sexual Harassment Incidents

I. The criteria for Judgment by Courts and National Human Rights Commissions[91]

1. Criteria for determining whether sexual harassment has occurred

(1) Elements of judgment

The first sexual harassment lawsuit in South Korea was a civil case where a female teaching assistant at a university claimed to have been wrongfully terminated after refusing the sexual advances of a male professor. At that time, South Korea did not have specific laws or guidelines regarding sexual harassment.

In the first sexual harassment lawsuit in South Korea, the Supreme Court (Supreme Court ruling on Feb. 10. 1998, 95Da39533) indicated that in determining the legality of a certain sexual conduct, "the age and relationship of both parties, the place and situation where the conduct occurred, the presence or absence of sexual motive or intent, the explicit or presumed reactions of the other party, the content and degree of the conduct, whether the behavior was a one-time occurrence or ongoing, and other specific circumstances" should be considered comprehensively. These elements of judgment have also been cited in subsequent court rulings and decisions of the National Human Rights Commission of Korea.

However, in this particular ruling, the main point of contention was whether the defendant professor's conduct towards his female assistant constituted illegal conduct under the Civil Act. Also, the ruling was made before the enactment of laws regarding sexual harassment. The law states that the elements of an illegal action include intent or gross negligence, illegality, and damage, and were presented as criteria for judgment. Particularly, the issue of "the presence or absence of sexual motive or intention" was debated. In a subsequent ruling by the Supreme Court (Supreme Court ruling on June 14, 2007, 2005Du6461), it was stated that "it is not necessary for the perpetrator to have sexual motive or intent for sexual harassment to be established, but rather, it should be judged comprehensively based

---

[91] Kim El-lim, "Sexual Harassment: Law and Dispute Resolution Cases," Episteme, 2023, pp. 429~435.

제3절 직장 내 성희롱 사건처리 사례

I. 법원과 국가인권위원회의 판단기준 등[91]

1. 성희롱 여부의 판단기준

(1) 판단의 요소

우리나라 최초의 성희롱 소송사건은 대학의 실험실에서 조교로 근무한 여성이 실험실 관리 책임자인 남성 교수의 성적 언동을 거부한 후 계약 종료 전에 해임당하자 성희롱이라고 주장하며 손해배상을 청구한 민사소송 사건이다. 당시 우리나라에는 성희롱 관련 법이나 판단 지침이 없었다.

그런데 이 소송에 대한 대법원(1998. 2. 10. 선고 95다39533 판결 [손해배상(기)]은 "어떤 성적 표현행위의 위법성 여부를 판단할 때 쌍방 당사자의 연령이나 관계, 행위가 행해진 장소 및 상황, 성적 동기나 의도의 유무, 행위에 대한 상대방의 명시적 또는 추정적인 반응의 내용, 행위의 내용 및 정도, 행위가 일회적 또는 단기간의 것인지 아니면 계속적인 것인지 여부 등의 구체적 사정을 종합하여 판단하여야 한다."라고 판시하였다. 이러한 판단의 요소 중 "성적 동기나 의도의 유무"를 제외한 것은 현재에도 성희롱에 관한 판결들과 국가인권위원회의 결정에서도 인용되고 있다.

그런데 "성적 동기나 의도의 유무"는 논란이 많이 되었는데 행위자가 성적 동기나 의도가 없었다고 주장하면 성희롱이 성립되지 않는 것인지가 쟁점이 되었다. 이에 관해 국가인권위원회(2003.9.13. 결정 05진차470)는 "행위자의 성적 의도가 없었더라도 행위의 상대방이 그러한 행위를 원치 않았고 불쾌감을 느꼈는지, 일반여성의 합리적 관점에서 볼 때 성적 함의가 있는 불쾌감을 주는 행위였는지에 의해 결정되어야 한다."라고 하였다. 대법원(2007. 6. 14. 선고 2005두6461 판결 [성희롱결정처분취소])도 "성희롱이 성립하기 위해서는 행위자에게 반드시 성적 동기나 의도가 있어야 하는 것은 아니지만,

---

[91] 김엘림, 「성희롱: 법과 분쟁처리사례」, 에피스테매, 2023, 429~435면.

on the specific circumstances, such as the relationship between the parties, the place and situation where the conduct occurred, the explicit or presumed reactions of the other party, the content and degree of the conduct, and whether the conduct was a one-time occurrence or ongoing." The National Human Rights Commission of Korea (Decision No. 05JinCha470, issued on Sept. 13, 2003) stated that "Even if the perpetrator did not have any sexual intent, [sexual harassment] should be determined based on whether the conduct was unwanted by the other party and caused discomfort from the perspective of a reasonable woman."

(2) Perspective of judgment

1) Perspective of the court ruling

The Supreme Court first introduced the perspective of "sound common sense of the social community (reasonable person)" in the first sexual harassment case. In a dispute related to sexual harassment by a male professor against a female teaching assistant, this judgment stated, "Whether an act of sexual expression is illegal or not should be determined by comprehensively considering specific circumstances such as the ages and relationship of the parties involved, the place and situation where the act was committed, the presence or absence of sexual motives or intentions, the explicit or implicit reactions of the other party, the content and degree of the act, and whether the act is a one-time or continuous occurrence, in the eyes of sound common sense and customs of the social community." These criteria are also known as the "reasonable person perspective."

2) The perspective of an objective, average person in a similar situation as the other party.

However, in Korea, the laws related to sexual harassment specifically mention "actions that cause sexual humiliation or disgust" as the legal concept of sexual harassment. Accordingly, the contentious issue becomes whether sexual harassment is established or not, when only one person claims to have felt sexual humiliation or disgust, regardless of the perpetrator's sexual intentions or the circumstances at the time of the incident. Regarding this contention, the Supreme Court (ruling on June 14, 2007, 2005Du6461) introduced the perspective of the "general and average person who is objectively in the same position as the other party." In a dispute related to sexual harassment by a male principal against female teachers, this

당사자의 관계, 행위가 행해진 장소 및 상황, 행위에 대한 상대방의 명시적 또는 추정적인 반응의 내용, 행위의 내용 및 정도, 행위가 일회적 또는 단기간의 것인지 아니면 계속적인 것인지 여부 등의 구체적 사정을 종합하여 판단하여야 한다."라고 판시하였다.

(2) 법원의 판단 관점
1) '사회공동체의 건전한 상식(합리적 인간)의 관점
　대법원(1998.2.10. 선고 95다39533 판결)은 최초의 성희롱 소송 사건에서 "어떤 성적 표현행위의 위법성 여부는 앞에서 언급한 판단 요소들을 종합적으로 고려하여 사회공동체의 건전한 상식과 관행에 비추어 볼 때 용인될 수 있는 정도의 것인지 여부, 즉 선량한 풍속 또는 사회질서에 위반되는 것인지 여부에 따라 결정되어야 할 것이다."라고 판시하였다. 이러한 판단기준을 '합리적 인간'의 관점이라고도 한다.

2) 객관적으로 상대방과 같은 처지에 있는 일반적이고도 평균적인 사람의 관점
　그런데 우리나라 성희롱 관련법은 성희롱의 법적 개념에서 공통적으로 "성적 굴욕감이나 혐오감을 느끼게 하는 것"을 명시하고 있다. 성적 굴욕감이나 혐오감을 느꼈는지 여부는 상대방의 주관적 감정에 좌우된다. 그리하여 여러 명이 참석한 회식자리 등에서 행위자의 언동에 대하여 1명만이 "성적 굴욕감이나 혐오감을 느꼈다"라고 주장하면 성희롱이 성립되는 것인지가 쟁점이 된다.
　대법원(2007. 6. 14. 선고 2005두6461 판결 [성희롱결정처분취소])은 남성 교감이 회식자리에서 여성 교사들에게 술을 남성교장에게 따라 주라고 한 발언이 성희롱인지 여부가 쟁점이 된 사건에서 교장이 여교사를 배려하여 소주잔에 맥주를 따라 준 점, 교감이 여교사들에게 술을 먼저 따라 준 교장에 대한 답례로 술을 따라 드리라고 두어차례 말한 점, 3명의 여교사들 중 2명은 교감의 발언에 성적 굴욕감을 느끼지는 않았다고 진술한 점, 회식자리의 대화가 주로 학생지도에 관련한 것이었던 점을 중시하였다. 그리하여 이 판결은 '어떠한 언동이 상대방 뿐 아니라 객관적으로 상대방과 같은 처지에 있는 일반적이고도 평균적인 사람(이 사건에서는 진정인을 제외한 다른 2명의

judgment stated, "In order to recognize that there was an act that would make a general and average person who is objectively in the same position as the other party feel sexual humiliation or disgust, it must be shown that the act was such that it would make a general and average person who is objectively in the same position as the other party feel sexual humiliation or disgust. Therefore, it is not sufficient to establish sexual harassment solely based on the fact that the other party felt sexual humiliation or disgust, unless there was an act that would make a general and average person who is objectively in the same position as the other party feel sexual humiliation or disgust." This ruling has been widely cited in sexual harassment-related judgments.

3) The perspective of gender sensitivity and perceptions.

However, the Supreme Court (ruling on Apr. 12, 2018, 2017Du74702) presented a new criterion, "gender sensitivity," in a dispute related to sexual harassment by male professors against female students. The main point of this judgment is as follows:

"When a court handles litigation related to sexual harassment, it should understand the issue of gender discrimination in the context in which the incident occurred and maintain 'gender sensitivity' in order to realize gender equality. Therefore, it should be noted that victims may suffer from so-called 'secondary victimization' such as negative reactions, public opinion, disadvantages, or psychological harm in the process of disclosing sexual harassment facts and addressing the issue due to the culture and perception in our society that are mainly of the perpetrators'. Victims may continue to maintain their relationship with the perpetrators even after suffering from such secondary harm, because of the anxiety or fear they feel about the perpetrator. Also, they may report the incident only when another victim or a third party raises the issue or encourages them to do so. There are also cases where victims show a passive attitude towards statements related to the incident even after reporting it to investigative agencies or courts. Therefore, dismissing the probative value of victim statements without fully considering the special circumstances faced by sexual harassment victims seems inconsistent with the principles of justice and fairness. Also, it cannot be considered as evidence-based judgment according to logic and experience."

"It must be taken into consideration that the perpetrator is a professor and the

여교사)으로 하여금 성적 굴욕감이나 혐오감을 느낄 수 있게 하는 행위이어야 성희롱에 해당된다. 따라서 객관적으로 상대방과 같은 처지에 있는 일반적이고도 평균적인 사람으로 하여금 성적 굴욕감이나 혐오감을 느끼게 하는 행위가 아닌 이상 상대방이 성적 굴욕감이나 혐오감을 느꼈다는 이유만으로 성희롱이 성립할 수는 없다."라고 판시하였다. 이러한 판단 관점은 현재에도 성희롱 판결에서 많이 인용되고 있다.

3) 성인지 감수성의 관점

대법원(2018. 4. 12. 선고 2017두74702 판결 [교원소청심사위원회결정취소])은 남성 교수가 취업추천서를 요청하는 여학생들에 대하여 "뽀뽀해 주면 추천서 써 주겠다" "나랑 사귀자"는 등의 언동을 한 것이 성희롱에 해당되는지 여부가 문제가 된 사건에서 '성인직 감수성의 관점'이란 새로운 판단 관점을 '객관적으로 상대방과 같은 처지에 있는 일반적이고도 평균적인 사람의 관점'에 추가로 제시하면서 교수의 성희롱과 대학의 해임 조치의 정당성을 인정하였다. 이 판결의 판단기준은 다음과 같다.

"법원이 성희롱 관련 소송의 심리를 할 때에는 그 사건이 발생한 맥락에서 성차별 문제를 이해하고 양성평등을 실현할 수 있도록 '성인지 감수성'을 잃지 않아야 한다. 그리하여 우리 사회의 가해자 중심적인 문화와 인식, 구조 등으로 인하여 피해자가 성희롱 사실을 알리고 문제를 삼는 과정에서 오히려 부정적 반응이나 여론, 불이익한 처우 또는 그로 인한 정신적 피해 등에 노출되는 이른바 '2차 피해'를 입을 수 있다는 점을 유념하여야 한다. 피해자는 이러한 2차 피해에 대한 불안감이나 두려움으로 인하여 피해를 당한 후에도 가해자와 종전의 관계를 계속 유지하는 경우도 있고, 피해사실을 즉시 신고하지 못하다가 다른 피해자 등 제3자가 문제를 제기하거나 신고를 권유한 것을 계기로 비로소 신고를 하는 경우도 있으며, 피해사실을 신고한 후에도 수사기관이나 법원에서 그에 관한 진술에 소극적인 태도를 보이는 경우도 적지 않다. 이와 같은 성희롱 피해자가 처하여 있는 특별한 사정을 충분히 고려하지 않은 채 피해자 진술의 증명력을 가볍게 배척하는 것은 정의와 형평의 이념에 입각하여 논리와 경험의 법칙에 따른 증거판단이라고 볼 수 없다."

"원고의 행위가 성희롱에 해당하는지 여부는 가해자가 교수이고 피해자가

Section 3. Issues and Related Cases in Handling Workplace Sexual Harassment Incidents

victim is a student, and that the sexual harassment occurred in a laboratory or research room where lectures were conducted. Also, the sexual advances were made as a pretext for the students in receiving their recommendation letters from the professor, which are important for students' employment. Nevertheless, such conduct occurred continuously, not as a one-time incident. Whether the plaintiff's conduct constitutes sexual harassment should be assessed from the perspective of an average person in a similar position as the victims."

(3) Perspectives on decisions of the National Human Rights Commission of Korea

The National Human Rights Commission of Korea (Sept. 14, 2005, 05JinCha470) has provided the following criteria to determine "the reasonable perspective of a general woman," in disputes related to sexual harassment by male professors against female students. These criteria and perspectives are frequently cited in decisions of the National Human Rights Commission when the victim is a woman. They can be considered as gender sensitive criteria, considering that the individuals may perceive and judge sexual conduct differently depending on their gender during socialization.

① Is there any work-relatedness with the following? - Relationship between the parties involved, the process and content of the problematic behavior, and the place and situation where the behavior occurred

② Does the problematic sexual conduct imply sexual connotations?

③ Considering the specific circumstances of the explicit or implied reactions of the victim, did the other party not want such behavior, and feel sexual humiliation or disgust because of the sexual conduct?

④ From the perspective of a reasonable woman (or the perspective of a general woman), did the victim feel sexual humiliation or disgust from the problematic sexual conduct?

On the other hand, in cases where the victim is a man or a sexual minority, the National Human Rights Commission often cites the perspective of "reasonable perspective of the victim" or "perspective of a reasonable person" in its decisions.

2. Recognizing the reliability of victim's statements and the notion of "victimhood"

학생이라는 점, 성희롱 행위가 학교 수업이 이루어지는 실습실이나 교수의 연구실 등에서 발생하였고, 학생들의 취업 등에 중요한 교수의 추천서 작성 등을 빌미로 성적 언동이 이루어지기도 한 점, 이러한 행위가 일회적인 것이 아니라 계속적으로 이루어져 온 정황이 있는 점 등을 충분히 고려하여 우리 사회 전체의 일반적이고 평균적인 사람이 아니라 피해자들과 같은 객관적으로 같은 처지에 있는 평균적인 사람의 입장에서 성적 굴욕감이나 혐오감을 느낄 수 있는 정도였는지를 기준으로 심리·판단하였어야 옳았다."

이러한 판단기준은 현재 성희롱·성폭력 사건에 관한 판결에서 가장 많이 인용되고 있다.

(3) 국가인권위원회의 판단관점

국가인권위원회(2005. 9. 13. 결정 05진차470)는 남성 교수가 강의실에서 "요즈음 여학생들이 돈을 벌기 위하여 난자를 판다."고 하면서 특정 여학생(진정인)을 지적하며 "너 정도면 난자 값이 비싸겠다."고 한 언행등이 성희롱인지 여부가 문제가 된 사건에서 다음과 같은 판단기준을 제시하면서 '일반여성의 합리적 관점'이란 판단관점을 제시하였다. 이 판단기준은 진정인(피해자)이 여성인 경우에 국가인권위원회 결정에서 많이 인용되고 있다. 성적 언동에 관하여 사회화하는 과정에서 성별에 따라 다르게 감응, 판단하는 경우가 있는 사실을 고려한 성인지적 판단기준이라 할 수 있다.

① 당사자의 관계, 문제가 된 언동을 하게 된 경위 및 내용, 언동이 행해진 장소 및 상황 등에 업무관련성이 있는지?
② 문제가 된 언동이 성적 함의가 있는 성적 언동인지?
③ 상대방의 명시적 또는 추정적인 반응 등의 구체적 사정을 종합하여 볼 때, 상대방이 그러한 언동을 원치 않았고 성적 굴욕감이나 혐오감을 느꼈는지?
④ 합리적 여성의 관점(또는 일반여성의 합리적 관점)에서 볼 때, 문제가 된 성적 언동에 성적 굴욕감이나 혐오감을 느꼈는지?

한편, 인권위는 진정인(피해자)가 남성이나 성소수자인 경우에는 '합리적 피해자의 관점'이란 판단 관점을 제시하는 경우가 있다.

2. 피해자 진술의 신뢰성 인정과 '피해자다움'의 통념

Section 3. Issues and Related Cases in Handling Workplace Sexual Harassment Incidents

(1) Criteria for recognizing the reliability of a victim's statement

Sexual harassment and sexual assault often occur in situations where there are only two parties involved: the perpetrator and the victim. However, disputes often arise when the parties provide conflicting statements about the situation. For example, in situations such as work-related dinners where multiple people are present, there may be different memories and statements from the attendees. Moreover, the victim's statement may change or deviate from the facts during the investigation process. In such cases, the legal issue becomes the criteria for determining whether to trust the victim's statement and reject the claims of the accused.

The court often cites the above criteria when evaluating the credibility of a victim's statement which is: "Unless there is a special reason to reject its credibility, the victim's statement should not be rejected merely because there are inconsistencies in minor details due to differences in expression. As long as the main content of the statement is consistent, rational, not contradicting itself, and there is no clear motive or reason for the victim to make false statements that would disadvantage the accused, the victim's statement shall be accepted." (Supreme Court ruling on Nov. 23, 2006, 2006do5407)

(2) Common perception of "victimhood"

The concept of "victimhood" refers to the belief that if someone is a victim, they should behave or react in a certain way in accordance with common sense or societal norms. This notion of "victimhood" has been a contentious issue in disputes related to sexual harassment and sexual assault. Sometimes, it is considered reasonable, but other times it may result in unfair dismissal of a victim's statement due to biased or preconceived ideas about how a victim should behave in a specific situation.

For example, in a dispute between a male provincial governor and a female secretary which involved claims of "rape through abuse of occupational authority" and "victimhood," a lower court (Seoul Western District Court, ruling on Aug. 14, 2018, 2018 GoHap 75) acquitted the governor, stating that the victim's statement was not credible as she did not behave like a victim. The court pointed out that she continued search for his favorite tofu stew restaurant even after being sexually

(1) 피해자 진술의 신뢰성 인정 기준

성희롱과 성폭력은 행위자와 피해자가 단 둘이 있는 상황에서 많이 발생하는데 당사자가 그 상황에 대해 매우 상반된 진술을 하는 경우가 많아 분쟁이 발생한다. 여러 명이 참석한 회식자리에서의 상황에 대해서도 참석자들 마다 다른 기억과 진술을 하는 경우들이 있다. 또한 피해자의 진술이 조사과정에서 다소 변경되거나 사실과 다른 경우도 발생한다. 이 경우 피해자의 피해 진술을 신뢰하고 혐의자의 주장을 배척하는 판단기준이 법적 쟁점이 된다.

법원은 "피해자 등의 진술은 그 진술 내용의 주요한 부분이 일관되며, 경험칙에 비추어 비합리적이거나 진술 자체로 모순되는 부분이 없고, 또한 허위로 피고인에게 불리한 진술을 할 만한 동기나 이유가 분명하게 드러나지 않는 이상, 표현상의 차이로 인하여 사소한 부분에 일관성이 없는 것처럼 보이는 부분이 있거나 최초의 단정적인 진술이 다소 불명확한 진술로 바뀌었다고 하여 그 진술의 신빙성을 특별한 이유 없이 함부로 배척해서는 안 될 것이다."라는 대법원 (2006. 11. 23. 선고 2006도5407 판결 등 참조)의 판시를 많이 인용한다.

(2) '피해자다움'의 통념

'피해자다움'이란 피해자라면 마땅히, 통상적으로, 상식적으로 어떠한 행동이나 반응을 해야 할 것이라는 통념을 말한다. 이 '피해자다움'은 성희롱·성폭력 관련 분쟁에서 쟁점이 많이 되고 있다. 때로는 이 통념이 합리적 판단으로 여겨지는 경우가 있지만, 때로는 피해자다움이란 편견, 고정관념으로 특정 사건에서 피해자의 피해 진술을 불합리하게 배척하는 경우가 발생하기도 한다.

예를 들면, 남성 도지사의 여성 비서에 대한 언동이 '업무상 위력에 의한 간음과 추행'에 해당되는 지 여부가 된 소송 사건에서 1심 법원(서울서부지방법원 2018.8.14. 선고 2018고합 75 판결)은 피해자라면 도지사의 성적 언동이나 요구를 피해야 할 텐데 해외에서 피해를 입은 뒤에도 도지사가 좋아하는 순두부 식당을 찾는 등 수행을 계속하였고 담배를 사오라는 지시를 받고 담배를 문 앞에 두지 않고 호텔방에 들어가 주려다 다시 성폭력을 당하였다는 진술 등은 피해자답지 못하여 신뢰할 수 없다며 피고인에 대하여 무죄 판결을 하였다.

그러나 이 사건에 대한 2심 법원(서울고등법원 2019.2.1.선고 2018노2354

harassed and also failed to leave cigarettes outside the hotel room as instructed, which led to another sexual assault. However, the appellate court (Seoul High Court ruling on Feb. 1, 2019, 2018No2354) overturned the lower court's decision by applying the gender sensitivity criteria (Supreme Court ruling on Apr. 12, 2018, 2017Du74702). Upon further appeal, the Supreme Court (Supreme Court ruling on Sept. 9, 2019, 2019Do2562) confirmed that the governor was guilty as charged.

3. Scope of "sexual behavior"

With the legal concept of sexual harassment, there are differences in interpreting the meaning of " sexual behavior or demands" which is considered a measure of sexual harassment. Supreme Court ruling on June 14, 2017, 2005Du6461 A frequently-cited Supreme Court ruling states "'Sexual behavior or demands,' which must exist for sexual harassment to occur, refer to conduct that can make the other party feel sexual humiliation or disgust. There is physical, linguistic and visual conduct related to physical relationship between the sexes or the characteristics of males or females that can be harmful when considered by the sound common sense and societal norm of an ordinary and average person in the same position as the other party."

However, in the R Automobile sexual harassment lawsuit, the appellate court (Seoul High Court ruling on Dec. 18, 2015, 2015Na2003264) interpreted sexual harassment more broadly. It included not only actions of a sexual nature, but also discriminatory remarks based on gender such as "doing housework at home," and insults based on gender, among others. The appellate court's view on sexual behavior is as follows.

The term "sexual behavior, etc." is not limited to the level of behavior exemplified in Annex 1 of Article 2 of the Enforcement Decree of the Equal Employment Act. Specific circumstances should be taken into consideration, such as ① the relationship between the parties, ② the place and situation where the behavior occurred, ③ the explicit or presumed reaction of the other party, ④ the content and extent of the behavior, and ⑤ whether the behavior was done only once or has been continuous.

판결)은 대법원 (2018. 4. 12. 선고 2017두74702 판결 [교원소청심사위원회 결정취소])의 성인지적 감수성 판단 관점을 적용하여 도지사의 언동을 업무상 위력에 의한 간음과 추행임을 인정하고 '피해자다움' 통념에 기초한 1심 판결을 취소하였다. 대법원(2019. 9. 9. 선고 2019도2562 판결 [강제추행, 피감독자간음, 성폭력범죄의 처벌등에 관한 특례법 위반(업무상위력등에의한 추행)])도 원심판단을 인정하였다.

3. 성적 언동의 범위

성희롱의 법적 개념에서 성희롱의 수단이 된 "성적 언동 등", "성적 언동이나 요구"의 의미에 관한 견해 차이가 있다.

이에 관하여 우리나라 법원 판결에서 많이 인용되고 있는 것은 대법원 판결 (2007. 6. 14. 선고 2005두6461 판결 [성희롱결정처분취소])이다. 이 판결은 "성희롱의 전제 요건인 '성적 언동 등'이란 남녀 간의 육체적 관계나 남성 또는 여성의 신체적 특징과 관련된 육체적, 언어적, 시각적 행위로서 사회공동체의 건전한 상식과 관행에 비추어 볼 때 객관적으로 상대방과 같은 처지에 있는 일반적이고도 평균적인 사람으로 하여금 성적 굴욕감이나 혐오감을 느끼게 할 수 있는 행위를 의미한다."라고 판시하였다.

그런데 R자동차 성희롱 소송사건에서 2심 법원(서울고등법원 2015.12.18. 선고 2015나2003264 판결(손해배상(기)))은 성희롱을 성적인 성질을 가지는 언동뿐 아니라 여성 근로자에게 "집에서 살림이나 하지" 등의 성차별적 발언을 하거나 성별에 기반한 비하 등을 하는 것을 포함하여 폭넓게 해석하였다. 2심 법원의 성적 언동에 관한 견해는 다음과 같다.

"'성적인 언동 등'이라 함은 반드시 「남녀고용평등법 시행규칙」 제2조 별표1이 예시한 수준의 행위에 국한되는 것이 아니고, ① 당사자의 관계 ② 행위가 행해진 장소 및 상황 ③ 행위에 대한 상대방의 명시적 또는 추정적인 반응의 내용 ④ 행위의 내용 및 정도 ⑤ 행위가 일회적 또는 단기간의 것인지 아니면 계속적인 것인지 여부 등의 구체적 사정을 참작하여 볼 때, 객관적으로 보아 상대방과 같은 처지에 있는 일반적이고도 평균적인 사람에게 성적 굴욕감 내지 혐오감을 느낄 정도로, 상대방이 원하지 않음에도 불구하고 상대방

Section 3. Issues and Related Cases in Handling Workplace Sexual Harassment Incidents

Therefore, it is valid to interpret that all behaviors, such as making unwanted sexual advances or harassing the other party, requesting sexual favors, making discriminatory remarks based on sex, and other words and actions that treat the other party as a sexual object or subject them to sexual discrimination despite the other party's unwillingness that would make an objectively reasonable and average person of the same position feel sexual humiliation or disgust, are "sexual behaviors."

This is because a narrow interpretation of "sexual behavior, etc." is not fair when the reality of sexual harassment in the workplace is considered. If only physical behaviors or language related to physical characteristics or characteristics of the human body in sexual or non-sexual relationships are considered "sexual behavior," demanding conversations or meetings of a personal nature that the other party does not want in an oppressive or persistent manner, looking at the other party's certain body parts for a long time with one's eyes, and making discriminatory remarks such as "do household chores at home" especially towards female workers, may be excluded from the definition of "sexual behavior, etc."

Considering the reality that female workers often experience sexual humiliation or disgust and are hindered in performing their duties due to such behavior in the workplace, it is not valid to exclude such behavior from the definition of "sexual behavior, etc." In order to uproot the problem of sexual harassment in our society's workplaces, it is reasonable to consider that even if the behavior was carried out with the pretext of being a light joke or playful banter that could be a source of vitality in the workplace, assuming that the female worker is someone's mother, sister, younger sister, or daughter, it would still be considered "sexual behavior, etc." unless circumstances indicate otherwise.

However, the manual on sexual harassment published by the Ministry of Gender Equality and Family and the Ministry of Employment and Labor defines "sexual gestures" as gestures that are of a sexual nature. Speech that denigrates women or actions that assign exclusively women to demeaning or menial tasks does not constitute sexual harassment along this line of thought. The Convention concerning the Elimination of Violence and Harassment in the World of Work (No. 190) adopted by the International Labour Organization (ILO) on June 21, 2019 defines

에게 성적인 접근 내지 구애를 하는 것, 성적인 호의를 요청하는 것, 성차별적인 발언을 하는 것, 그 밖에 상대방을 성적인 대상으로 삼거나 성적인 차별의 대상으로 삼아 말과 행동을 하는 것 일체를 가리킨다고 해석함이 타당하다.

왜냐하면 이와 달리 해석하여 '성적 언동 등'을 이성 또는 동성 간의 육체적 관계나 사람의 신체적 특징과 관련된 육체적, 언어적, 시각적 행위로 한정할 경우, 상대방에게 원하지 않는 개인적인 교제 차원의 대화나 만남을 강압적 내지 지속적으로 요구하는 행위, 눈으로 상대방의 신체를 훑어보는 행위, 특히 여성 근로자에게 "집에서 살림이나 하지" 등의 성차별적 발언을 하는 행위 등이 성적 언동 등에서 자칫 제외될 가능성이 있는데, 이는 특히 여성 근로자들이 직장 내에서 위와 같은 언동 등으로 인하여 성적 굴욕감 또는 혐오감을 느끼고 그로 인하여 업무수행에 방해를 받는 경우가 적지 않은 현실을 감안할 때 타당하다고 볼 수 없기 때문이다.

우리 사회의 직장 내 성희롱 문제를 뿌리째 들어내기 위해서는 특히 여성 근로자에 대하여 그 여성 근로자가 내 어머니나 누나, 여동생, 딸이라고 가정할 경우 차마 쉽게 하지 못할 행위를 하였다면 설령 행위자가 직장생활의 활력소가 될 만한 가벼운 농담 내지 장난 차원에서 행하였다는 명분을 내세우더라도 다른 특별한 사정이 없는 한 이는 '성적 언동 등'에 해당한다고 보아도 틀림이 없다 할 것이다."

그런데 우리나라 여성가족부, 고용노동부가 발간한 성희롱에 관한 매뉴얼은 "성적 언동"을 성적 성질을 가지는 언동으로 규정하고 여성을 비하하는 발언 혹은 여성에게만 차 또는 복사 심부름을 시키는 행위는 성희롱에 해당되지 않는다고 해석하였다.

ILO가 2019년 6월 21일에 채택한 「일의 세계에서의 폭력과 괴롭힘 철폐에 관한 협약」(제190호)은 '젠더에 기반한 폭력과 괴롭힘(gender-based violence and harassment)'을 "성별과 젠더를 이유로 인간에게 향하는, 혹은 특정 성 혹은 젠더에 편중되게 영향을 주는 폭력과 괴롭힘으로서 sexual harassment를 포함한다."라고 정의하였다. 이것은 '젠더에 기반한 폭력과 괴롭힘'은 남성, 여성 등 성별에 관한 인식(gender)에 기반한 다양한 유형의 폭력과 괴롭힘이며 'sexual harassment'는 성적 성질을 가지는 폭력과 괴롭힘으로서 '젠더에 기반한 폭력과 괴롭힘'의 일종임을 표명한 것이다. 이러한 관점에서 성차별적 발언을 하거나

Section 3. Issues and Related Cases in Handling Workplace Sexual Harassment Incidents

"gender-based violence and harassment" as "violence and harassment directed against persons because of their sex or gender, or that disproportionately affects persons of a particular sex or gender, including sexual harassment." This signifies that "gender-based violence and harassment" encompasses various forms of violence and harassment based on perceptions of gender, including men and women. Also that "sexual harassment" is a type of violence and harassment of a sexual nature within the scope of "gender-based violence and harassment." From this perspective, while discriminatory speech based on gender or gender-based insults may fall under "gender-based violence and harassment," they do not constitute sexual harassment as they are not of a sexual nature.

4. Burden of proof

The Equal Employment Act has had a provision (Article 30) in effect since April 1989 which states that the burden of proof in disputes related to this law rests with the employer. The amended law on May 18, 2021, expanded application of this provision not only to settlement of internal disputes by employers but also to settlements of disputes by labor relations commissions and the Minister of Employment and Labor.

However, the second ruling in the R Automobile (Seoul High Court ruling on Dec. 18, 2015, 2015Na2003264) sexual harassment case, sparked controversy by stating that "it is not reasonable or fair to impose all burden of proof on the employer, and the victim must at least prove that there was unfavorable treatment. The employer has the burden of proof to prove that there were other legitimate reasons for such unfavorable treatment." However, the Supreme Court ruling in this case (Supreme Court ruling on Dec. 22, 2017, 2016Da202947) stated that the burden of proof provision of the Equal Employment Act applies to sexual harassment cases, and that "the employer must prove that there was no relevant connection between the unfavorable treatment of the victim and the sexual harassment, or that there were legitimate reasons for such unfavorable treatment."

5. Responsibility of employers

성별에 기반한 비하는 '젠더에 기반한 폭력과 괴롭힘'에 해당되지만 성적 성질의 언동은 아니므로 성희롱에 해당되지 않는다고 본다.

4. 입증책임의 부담

「남녀고용평등법」은 "이 법과 관련한 분쟁해결에서 입증책임은 사업주가 부담한다."는 조항(제30조)을 1989년 4월부터 시행하고 있다. 2021년 5월 18일에 개정된 법은 이 조항의 적용범위를 사업주의 사건처리 뿐 아니라 노동위원회와 고용노동부장관의 사건처리에서도 적용되도록 확대하였다.

그런데 R자동차 성희롱 사건의 제2심 판결(서울고등법원 2015.12.18.선고 2015나2003264 판결)은 "모든 입증책임이 사업주에 있다는 것은 합리적이지 않고 형평에도 맞지 않으므로 적어도 불리한 조치가 있었다는 점은 피해근로자가 입증해야 하고, 그 불리한 조치를 하게 된 다른 실질적인 이유가 있었다는 점은 사업주에게 입증책임이 있다."고 판시하여 논란이 되었다. 그런데 이 사건의 대법원 판결(2017.12.22. 선고 2016다202947 판결(손해배상(기)))은 「남녀고용평등법」의 입증책임 규정은 성희롱 사건에 적용되므로 "직장 내 성희롱으로 인한 분쟁이 발생한 경우에 피해근로자등에 대한 불리한 조치가 성희롱과 관련성이 없거나 정당한 사유가 있다는 점에 대하여 사업주가 증명을 하여야 한다."라고 판시하였다.

현행 「기간제 및 단시간근로자 보호등에 관한 법률」과 「고용상 연령차별금지 및 고령자 고용촉진에 관한 법률」도 사업주에게 입증책임을 부과하고 있다. 그런데 「장애인차별 금지 및 권리구제 등에 관한 법률」은 제47조(입증책임의 배분)에서 "① 이 법률과 관련한 분쟁해결에 있어서 차별행위가 있었다는 사실은 차별행위를 당하였다고 주장하는 자가 입증하여야 한다. ② 제1항에 따른 차별행위가 장애를 이유로 한 차별이 아니라거나 정당한 사유가 있었다는 점은 차별행위를 당하였다고 주장하는 자의 상대방이 입증하여야 한다."라고 규정하고 있다.

5. 사업주의 책임

Section 3. Issues and Related Cases in Handling Workplace Sexual Harassment Incidents

(1) Employer responsibility

The Civil Act stipulates that "the person who uses another person to engage in certain work and the person who supervises such work on behalf of the employer shall be liable for damages caused to a third party in the execution of such work. However, an exception shall be made if the employer exercised reasonable care in the appointment of the person to be used and in the supervision of such work, or if reasonable care was exercised but damages still occurred." (Article 756).

However, in the first sexual harassment lawsuit in South Korea, the trial court (Seoul District Court ruling on Apr. 18, 1994, 93GaHap77840) and the appellate court (Supreme Court ruling on Feb. 10, 1998, 95Da39533 [Claim for Damages (Non-contractual)]), as well as the retrial court (Seoul High Court ruling on June 25, 1999, 98Na12180 [Claim for Damages (Non-contractual)]), all recognized the professor's sexual misconduct as an illegal act, but did not recognize the employer's responsibility for damages. The trial court stated that the professor's sexual harassment was unrelated to his job and that professors must have complete discretion in their research and teaching activities, and even if they are the employer or the supervisor of the person appointed to their position, they are not in a position to directly instruct or supervise the professor's research activities or other personal matters that are not administrative or formal in nature. The Supreme Court stated, "Employment and labor relationships are based on a continuous creditor-debtor relationship that is in turn based on personal trust. Therefore, it is natural for the employer to bear the obligation to provide the employee with a pleasant working environment by respecting and protecting the employee's personality. Also, they should take necessary measures to ensure that the employee does not suffer damages while performing his or her duties, and measures such as granting compensation for the employee's services should be taken by the employer." The Supreme Court further stated, "In this case, it cannot be said that the defendant (the Republic of Korea) did not fulfill its duty to protect and support the employee. The sexual harassment committed by the defendant's professor was completely unrelated to execution of his job. Furthermore the defendant, the Republic of Korea, could not have known about the defendant's sexual harassment as it was secret and personal. Also, the plaintiff did not disclose it to the defendant, the Republic of Korea."

The first court ruling in Korea that recognized employer responsibility was by the Seoul Central District Court (May 3, 2002, 2001GaHap6471) in a dispute related to sexual harassment against female workers by male workers and the employer's responsibility. This ruling stated, "The company, as employer, has an obligation to prevent damage to the dignity of workers and significant obstacles to

(1) 사용자책임

「민법」은 "타인을 사용하여 어느 사무에 종사하게 한 자와 사용자에 갈음하여 그 사무를 감독하는 자는 피용자가 그 사무집행에 관하여 제삼자에게 가한 손해를 배상할 책임이 있다. 다만, 사용자가 피용자의 선임 및 그 사무 감독에 상당한 주의를 한 때 또는 상당한 주의를 하여도 손해가 있을 경우에는 예외로 한다."(제756조)라고 규정하고 있다.

그런데 우리나라 최초의 성희롱 소송에서 1심 법원(서울민사지방법원 1994. 4. 18. 선고 93가합77840 판결 [손해배상(기)]), 3심 법원(대법원 1998. 2. 10. 선고 95다39533 판결 [손해배상(기)]), 파기환송심(서울고법 1999.6.25. 선고 98나 12180 판결 [손해배상(기)])은 모두 교수의 성적 언동을 불법행위로 인정했지만, 피고 총장과 대한민국의 사용자책임은 인정하지 아니하였다. 1심 법원은 교수의 성희롱을 업무관련성이 없다는 것과 교수는 연구 및 강의활동 등에 있어서 전적으로 자유성이 보장되고 있어 그 임용권자인 사용자 또는 그 대리감독자라 하더라도 행정적인 업무나 형식적 사항이 아닌 교수의 연구활동이나 기타 사생활에 대하여 구체적으로 이를 지시, 감독할 수 있는 입장에 아니라고 하며 교수의 언동을 교수의 개인적인 성향에서 비롯된 것으로 보았다. 대법원은 "이 사건 피고 교수의 성희롱 행위가 그의 사무집행과는 아무런 관련이 없을 뿐만 아니라, 또한 기록에 의하면 위 피고의 성희롱 행위 또한 은밀하고 개인적으로 이루어지고 원고로서도 이를 공개하지 아니하여 피고 대한민국으로서는 이를 알거나 알 수 있었다고도 보여지지 아니하므로, 이러한 경우에서까지 사용자인 피고 대한민국이 피용자인 원고에 대하여 고용계약상의 보호의무를 다하지 아니하였다고 할 수는 없다."라고 판시하였다.

우리나라 판례 중에서 사용자 책임을 최초로 인정한 판례는 여성근로자들의 남성근로자에 대한 성희롱과 회사의 사용자책임 관련 분쟁에 관한 서울지방법원(2002. 5. 3. 선고 2001가합6471 판결)이다. 이 판결은 "사용자인 회사는 근로자의 근무환경에 대해 배려하여 성희롱을 통하여 근로자의 인격적 존엄을 해치고, 노무제공에 중대한 지장을 초래하는 것을 방지해야 할 의무가 있으므로 피고들이 원고에게 성희롱을 하였다면 사용자로서 손해배상책임이 있다."라고 판시하였다.

labor supply by showing consideration for the work environment and preventing sexual harassment. If the defendants have sexually harassed the plaintiffs, the company is liable for damages as the employer." Since then, many court rulings in cases of sexual harassment in the workplace have recognized employer responsibility.

However, in the recent highly publicized "R Automotive" sexual harassment case, the first ruling (Seoul Central District Court, Dec. 18, 2014, 2013GaHap536064) recognized the behaviors of the perpetrator (team leader) as sexual harassment, but did not recognize the company's responsibility as employer, as the actions were deemed to be the perpetrator's personal behavior unrelated to work. However, the second court ruling (Seoul High Court, Dec. 18, 2015, 2015Na2003264, Damages (retrial)) recognized partial employer responsibility. The subsequent Supreme Court ruling (Dec. 22, 2017, 2016Da202947, Damages (retrial)) and the appellate court ruling on remand (Seoul High Court, Apr. 20, 2018, 2017Na2076631, Damages (retrial)) recognized broader employer responsibility.

The courts do not easily recognize employer responsibility of universities for sexual harassment by professors against faculty or students. For its part, the National Human Rights Commission often recommends measures such as sanctions against the perpetrator by the head of the department (president, etc.), preventive education for all employees and measures to prevent recurrence and secondary victimization.

(2) Tort liability

Current laws related to sexual harassment, such as the Equal Employment Actand the Framework Act on Gender Equality, impose an obligation on employers to take measures to prevent sexual harassment and to refrain from treating victims unfairly (secondary victimization).

If an employer violates these obligations and causes harm, the employer is liable under Article 393 (Non-performance of Obligation) and Article 750 (Illegal Act) of the Civil Act, rather than under the principle of employer responsibility in Article 756 of the same Act. In addition, the Equal Employment Act stipulates criminal penalties for employers who treat victims of workplace sexual harassment unfairly.

II. Precedents and Decisions related to Workplace Sexual Harassment

1. Disputes involving sexual harassment by male employers[92]

---

[92] Kim El-lim, "Sexual Harassment: Law and Dispute Resolution Cases," Episteme, 2023, pp. 287~290.

그 후 많은 직장 내 성희롱 사건에서 법원은 사용자 책임을 인정하였다. 그런데 근래 가장 많은 주목을 받았던 R자동차 성희롱 사건에서 1심 판결(서울중앙지방법원 2014.12.18., 선고 2013가합536064 판결[손해배상(기)])은 성희롱 행위자(팀장)의 여성근로자에 대한 언동을 성희롱으로 인정하였으나 그 언동은 업무관련성이 없이 행위자의 개인적 행위라며 회사의 사용자책임을 인정하지 아니하였다. 그런데 2심 법원(서울고등법원 2015.12.18. 선고 2015나2003264 판결(손해배상(기))은 일부 조치에 대한 사용자 책임을 인정하였다. 대법원(2017.12.22. 선고 2016다202947 판결 [손해배상(기)])과 파기환송심 판결(서울고등법원 2018. 4. 20. 선고 2017나2076631 판결 [손해배상(기)])은 사용자 책임을 폭넓게 인정하였다.

그러나 한편, 법원은 대학교수가 교직원이나 학생에 대하여 성희롱을 한 행위에 대하여는 교수는 자율적으로 업무 수행을 한다며 대학의 사용자책임을 아직 인정하지 않고 있다. 반면, 국가인권위원회는 행위자의 소속 기관장(총장 등)을 피진정인으로 하거나 시정권고의 대상으로 하여 총장 등에게 행위자에 대한 제재, 전체 직원에 대한 예방교육, 재발방지 대책, 2차 가해 방지 등의 권고를 많이 한다.

(2) 불법행위 책임

현행 「남녀고용평등법」과 「양성평등기본법」 등의 성희롱 관련법은 사업주에게 성희롱 방지를 위한 조치를 하고 피해자 등에게 불리한 처우(2차 가해)를 하지 않을 의무를 부과하고 있다.

사업주가 이러한 의무를 위반하여 피해를 발생시킨 경우에는 사업주는 「민법」 제756조에 따른 사용자책임이 아니라 제393조(채무불이행)와 제750조(불법행위)에 따른 책임을 져야 한다. 또한 「남녀고용평등법」의 경우 사업주가 직장 내 성희롱 피해자 등에 대하여 불리한 처우를 한 경우 형사처벌을 규정하고 있으므로 이를 위반한 사업주는 형사적 제재를 받게 된다.

II. 사업주의 성희롱 사건과 관련 판례·결정례

1. 남성 사업주의 성희롱 관련 분쟁[92]

Section 3. Issues and Related Cases in Handling Workplace Sexual Harassment Incidents

(1) Overview of a case

A, the male CEO (63 years old) of a well-known chicken franchise company was accused of sexual harassment by B, a female secretary (20 years old). The CEO was under non-custodial investigation on June 3, 2017. B claimed that A took her to a restaurant for dinner, saying "You've been working hard, let me buy you a meal," and then made sexual advances towards her while drinking, asking her to take a "love shot" and took her to a hotel lobby. In the hotel lobby, A asked for help from other women, and together they took a taxi to the police station to file a complaint. B stated that she only accompanied A to the hotel because she was worried that she would face dismissal or other disadvantages if she refused the CEO's advances, as she had only been employed for 3 months.

After some time, someone released CCTV footage of B coming out of a hotel and confronting A with several women in a taxi. This was reported in the media, and the police continued to investigate despite B filing a complaint. A claimed that physical contact was consensual with B, and that B was showing physical affection to A by touching him and that they held hands while walking to the hotel lobby, and A did not exert any force. A also claimed that B could not be trusted, since B still filed a complaint after agreeing to receive KRW 300 million from A's family to settle the case, suggesting that B may have conspired with the women in the hotel lobby to extort money from A, like a "gold-digger." As a result of this incident, the franchise store's sales plummeted, and A stepped down from his position as CEO and issued an official apology.

The police referred the case to the prosecution on charges of sexual assault by coercion. However, the prosecution indicted A on December 17, 2018, for violating Article 10 of the Sexual Assault Punishment Act (Sexual Assault by Coercion) on the grounds that A used his position of authority or employment to coerce B. The prosecutor argued that during the trial, A did not show any signs of remorse and instead accused the victim of lying or being a gold-digger, and that the victim clearly expressed a desire for punishment. The prosecutor further argued that the settlement was a means to prevent investigation and did not reflect any apology or remorse towards the victim, and therefore should not be taken into consideration in the sentencing, and requested a sentence of one year and six months.

In arguing that he was innocent, A's defense counsel pointed out "the defendant,

(1) 사건 개요

　　유명 치킨 프랜차이즈 업체 남성 회장 A(63세)는 비서인 여성 B(20세)를 2017.6.3., 단 둘이 저녁 식사한 음식점에서 추행한 혐의로 고소되어 불구속 수사를 받았다.

　　B는 A가 "고생이 많으니 밥을 사주겠다"라고 하여 음식점에 갔더니 맥주를 마시며 "러브샷을 하자"며 자신을 옆에 오게 하여 추행한 후 호텔로 데려가자 로비에 있던 모르는 여성들에게 도움을 요청하고 그 여성들과 함께 택시를 타고 경찰서에 가서 피해 신고를 하였다고 주장하였다. A와 호텔에 동행한 것은 입사한 지 3개월 밖에 안되는데 회장의 제안을 거절하면 해고 등의 불이익을 당할까 염려되었기 때문이라고 하였다.

　　그런데 누군가 B가 호텔에서 나와 여성들과 택시를 타자 A가 쫓아가서 실랑이를 벌이는 CCTV 영상을 인터넷에 공개하였고 이것이 언론에 보도되자 경찰은 B가 고소를 취하하였음에도 수사를 계속하였다.

　　한편, A는 B의 동의를 얻어 신체접촉을 한 것이며 스킨쉽에 B가 더 적극적이었고 호텔에도 손잡고 같이 갔고 강제력을 행사한 적이 없다고 주장하였다. 그리고 회사의 피해를 막기 위해 B의 가족에게 3억 원을 지급하며 사건을 덮기로 합의하자 B가 고소를 취하한 것으로 보아 B를 신뢰할 수 없고 자신에게 돈을 받아내기 위해 호텔 로비에 있던 여성들과 공모했을 가능성도 있어 꽃뱀같다고 하였다. 이 사건으로 가맹점 매출이 급격히 감소되자 A는 회장직에서 물러나고 공식 사과문을 발표하였다.

　　경찰은 강제추행 의견으로 사건을 검찰에 송치하였다. 그런데 검찰은 2017.11.17., A를 업무, 고용으로 인하여 자기의 보호, 감독을 받는 사람을 위력으로 추행하였다며 「성폭력처벌법」 제10조(업무상 위력 등에 의한 추행) 혐의로 기소하였다. 검사는 2018.12.17., "공판과정에서 A는 반성하는 모습을 보이지 않고 피해자를 거짓말쟁이이거나 꽃뱀이라고 몰아가는 등 2차 가해가 심각하게 우려되는 수준"이고 "피해자는 처벌을 원한다고 분명히 밝혔다"며, "합의는 수사를 막기 위한 방편으로, 피해자에 대한 사죄나 반성을 뜻을 전혀 담고 있지 않으므로 이를 선고에 반영해서는 안된다"고 주장하고 1년 6개월을 구형하였다.

---

92) 김엘림, 「성희롱: 법과 분쟁처리사례」, 에피스테매, 2023, 287~290면

Section 3. Issues and Related Cases in Handling Workplace Sexual Harassment Incidents

who was in a settlement state, was unjustly investigated by the police," "the statements of the witnesses were proven to be mistaken, and a significant portion of the victim's statements were revealed to be false," and "A has already suffered immense pain which is difficult for a person to endure."

(2) Court judgment

The court, considering the highly contradictory claims of each party, relied on the victim's statement and rejected the defendant's claims, resulting in a guilty verdict for the defendant with a suspended sentence.

1) First court ruling[93]

<Court Ruling>
The defendant is sentenced to one year of imprisonment. However, execution of the sentence is suspended for a period of two years from the date of this judgment. The defendant is ordered to complete 80 hours of sexual assault lectures.

<Summary of Decision>
- Victim's statement that she complied with the defendant's proposal due to difficulties in resisting the defendant's actions for fear of work-related disadvantages is logically acceptable and credible. The reasons are as follows: considering factors such as the defendant's position and responsibilities within the company, age difference between the defendant and the victim, and the presence or absence of social experience, it is difficult to understand the defendant's claim that the victim consented to physical contact and hotel companionship.
- In the end, it can be concluded that the defendant abused his authority to sexually harass the victim. The defendant took advantage of the victim's inability to resist the defendant's actions due to the defendant's position as the CEO, his age, hierarchical relationship in the workplace, and the plaintiff's lack of social experience.

---

[93] Seoul Central District Court ruling on Feb. 14, 2019, 2017Godan7560, Violation of the Act on Special Cases concerning the Punishment, etc. of Sexual Crimes (Sexual Harassment through Abuse of Occupational Authority)

반면, A의 변호인측은 "합의 상태이던 피고인을 경찰이 무리하게 수사했다" "목격자의 진술은 착각이라는 게 밝혀졌고, 피해자 진술 중 상당수도 거짓으로 드러났다" "A는 이미 인간이 겪기 어려운 고통을 겪고 상당한 피해를 받았다"며 무죄를 주장하였다.

(2) 법원의 판결

법원은 당사자의 주장이 매우 상반되는 상황에서 피해자의 진술을 신뢰하고 피고인의 주장을 배척하여 피고인에 유죄판결을 내리되, 집행유예를 선고하였다.

1) 1심 법원의 판결[93]

< 주문 >
피고인을 징역 1년에 처한다. 다만, 이 판결확정일로부터 2년간 위형의 집행을 유예한다. 피고인에 대하여 80시간의 성폭력치료강의 수강을 명한다.

<판결 요지>
- 사건 당시의 상황에 대하여 당사자의 진술이 크게 상반되지만, 피고인과 피해자의 회사 내에서의 지위와 담당하는 업무 및 나이 차이, 사회경험의 유무 등을 고려할 때, 피해자가 동의하여 신체접촉과 호텔 동행이 이루어졌다는 피고인의 주장은 이해하기 어렵고 업무상 불이익을 우려해 피고인의 행동에 저항하기 어려워 피고인의 제안에 응하였다는 피해자의 진술이 상식적으로 납득이 가고 신빙성이 있다고 판단된다.
- 결국, 피고인은 사업체 회장이라는 업무상 지위를 행사하여 피해자가 피고인의 개인 비서로서 나이, 업무상 상하관계, 사회경험의 일천함 등의 여러 가지 이유로 적극적으로 피고인의 행동에 저항하지 못하는 점을 이용하여 피해자를 추행하였다고 할 것이다.

---

[93] 서울중앙지방법원 2019. 2. 14. 선고 2017고단7560 판결[성폭력범죄의처벌등에관한특례법 위반(업무상위력등에의한추행)]

2) Second court ruling[94]

<Court Ruling>
The appeal of the defendant is dismissed.

<Summary of Decision>
- Considering the coherence of the statements and the consistency with common experience, the credibility of the plaintiff's statements should not be easily rejected due to minor inconsistencies in the expressions or changes in the initial definitive statements to somewhat ambiguous statements. The plaintiff's statements are considered credible, unless the statements of the plaintiff and others are inconsistent or contradictory in a way that is unreasonable or self-contradictory, and also unless there are clear reasons or motives for making false statements that disadvantage the defendant. (Reference: Supreme Court Decision No. 2006do5407, pronounced on November 23, 2006, and others).
- The defendant claims that in the restaurant, he has never used any words or actions or exerted any influence that would disadvantage the plaintiff's status. However, considering the differences in position, age, social experience, and degree of intimacy, the defendant's position or power in relation to the plaintiff can be evaluated as sufficient and intangible influence to suppress the plaintiff's free will. Also, it cannot be said that the exercise of influence is determined solely by the presence or absence of statements regarding the actual work duties or employment relationship.
- In conclusion, the plaintiff's statements are credible. The decision of the trial court is acceptable, and there are no illegalities due to factual errors.

---

[94] Seoul Central District Court ruling on Jan. 16, 2020, 2019no689, Violation of the Act on Special Cases Concerning the Punishment etc. of Sexual Crimes (Sexual Harassment through Abuse of Occupational Status, etc.)

2) 2심 법원의 판결[94]

> **< 주문 >**
> 피고인의 항소를 기각한다.
>
> **<판결 요지>**
> - 피해자 등의 진술은 그 진술 내용의 주요한 부분이 일관되며, 경험칙에 비추어 비합리적이거나 진술 자체로 모순되는 부분이 없고, 또한 허위로 피고인에게 불리한 진술을 할 만한 동기나 이유가 분명하게 드러나지 않는 이상, 표현상의 차이로 인하여 사소한 부분에 일관성이 없는 것처럼 보이는 부분이 있거나 최초의 단정적인 진술이 다소 불명확한 진술로 바뀌었다고 하여 그 진술의 신빙성을 특별한 이유 없이 함부로 배척해서는 안 될 것이다(대법원 2006. 11. 23. 선고 2006도5407 판결 등 참조).
> - 피고인은 음식점 내에서 피해자에게 신분상 불이익을 준다는 어떠한 언사나 거동을 한 적이 없고, 위력을 행사한 바 없다고 주장한다. 그러나 피고인과 피해자의 회사 내에서의 지위와 담당 업무 및 나이 차, 사회경험의 유무, 친밀함의 정도 등을 고려할 때 피해자에 대한 관계에 있어서 피고인의 지위나 권세는 그 자체로 피해자의 자유의사를 제압하기에 충분한 무형적인 세력이라고 평가할 수 있고, 실질적인 업무나 고용관계 등에 영향력을 미치는 내용의 진술 유무에 따라 위력의 행사가 결정되는 것은 아니라고 할 것이다.
> - 결국 이 사건 범행에 관한 피해자의 진술은 신빙할 수 있고, 이를 포함한 검사 제출의 증거를 종합하여 이 사건 공소사실을 유죄로 인정한 원심판결은 수긍할 수 있고 여기에 사실오인의 위법은 없다.

---

[94] 서울중앙지방법원 2020. 1. 16. 선고 2019노689 판결[성폭력범죄의처벌등에관한특례법 위반(업무상위력등에의한추행)]

Section 3. Issues and Related Cases in Handling Workplace Sexual Harassment Incidents

3) Supreme Court ruling[95]

<Disposition>
The appeal is dismissed.

<Summary of Judgment>
- The lower court maintained the first ruling, which found the defendant guilty of the charges based on the same reasons stated in the first ruling. Examination of the relevant legal principles and properly adopted evidence, the lower court's decision did not exceed the limits of the rule of logic and experience. Also, it did not make any errors in understanding the legal principles related to Article 10(1) of the Act on Special Cases concerning the Punishment, etc. of Sexual Crimes(before it was amended by Act No. 15792 on October 16, 2018) (Sexual Harassment through Abuse of Occupational Superiority).

2. Dispute related to sexual harassment by female employer[96]

(1) Overview of the case

The plaintiff, A, is an unmarried male who was employed as a manager at a hospital management consulting company in January 2008. The defendant, B, is a married female owner of the company and A's employer. A claimed to have suffered from harassment by B, who despite being married, engaged in physical contact with him against his stated wishes. For example, she linked arms with him multiple times in front of other employees. She also caused him great distress by sending over 130 text messages and calling him by phone every day, expressing her love, and even asking to meet in front of his house. A resigned from the company after only four months of employment and filed a complaint with the National Human Rights Commission of Korea. A also accused B of attempting to kiss him and engaging in unwanted sexual acts when she took him to her accommodations while on a business trip, and filed a criminal complaint against her.

B denied engaging in any sexual behaviors claimed by A. B also argued that although she did send text messages to A for work-related purposes, the contents

---

[95] May 28, 2020, 2020do1492, on Violation of the Act on Special Cases concerning the Punishment, etc. of Sexual Crimes (Sexual Harassment through Abuse of Occupational Superiority)
[96] Kim El-lim, "Sexual Harassment: Law and Dispute Resolution Cases," Episteme, 2023, pp. 290~291

3) 3심 법원의 판결[95]

<주문>
상고를 기각한다.

<판결 요지>
- 원심은 그 판시와 같은 이유를 들어 이 사건 공소사실을 유죄로 판단한 제1심판결을 그대로 유지하였다. 원심판결 이유를 관련 법리와 적법하게 채택한 증거에 비추어 살펴보면, 원심의 판단에 논리와 경험의 법칙에 반하여 자유심증주의의 한계를 벗어나거나 구 성폭력처벌법(2018. 10. 16. 법률 제15792호로 개정되기 전의 것) 제10조 제1항(업무상 위력 등에 의한 추행)에 관한 법리를 오해하는 등의 잘못이 없다.

2. 여성 사업주의 성희롱 관련 분쟁[96]

(1) 사건 개요

진정인 A는 2008년 1월에 병원경영컨설팅회사에서 과장으로 입사한 비혼 남성이다. 피진정인 B는 회사의 기혼 여성 사장으로 A의 고용주이다.

A는 B가 기혼자이면서 회사 안에서나 출장지 등에서 거부하였는데도 자신에게 신체접촉을 하고 직원들이 보는 앞에서 팔짱을 10여 차례 꼈으며, 휴대전화로 130통 넘게 문자를 보내거나 전화를 하여 사랑한다며 자신의 집 앞까지 만나자고 하여 너무 괴로워 입사한 지 4개월여만에 퇴사하였다고 국가인권위원회에 피해 진정을 하였다. A는 출장지에서 B가 술이 취해 숙소에 데려다 주자 방문을 잠그고 키스하려고 한 행위에 대하여는 그 행위가 계속되었다며 고소도 하였다.

한편, B는 A가 주장하는 성적 행위나 발언을 한 적이 없고, 휴대전화 문자메시지를 보낸 것은 사실이나 그 내용들은 업무에 관한 이야기를 하기 위해서

---
[95] 대법원 2020. 5. 28. 선고 2020도1492 판결[성폭력범죄의처벌등에관한특례법 위반(업무상위력등에의한추행)]
[96] 김엘림, 「성희롱: 법과 분쟁처리사례」, 에피스테메, 2023, 290~291면.

Section 3. Issues and Related Cases in Handling Workplace Sexual Harassment Incidents

were not intended to harass him but rather to express her positive emotions towards him.

(2) Decision of the National Human Rights Commission (Decision No. 08-480, Sexual Harassment, Sept. 22, 2008)[97]

[Decision]
1. The part of the complaint related to sexual assault and confinement shall be dismissed because the investigation by a law enforcement agency is ongoing.
2. It is recommended that the complainant receive special human rights education organized by the National Human Rights Commission. Also, the defendant shall pay KRW 3 million in compensation to the plaintiff.

[Summary of the Decision]
- According to the definition of sexual harassment in Article 2, clause 5 of the National Human Rights Commission Act, the determination of sexual humiliation or disgust should be based not only on the subjective circumstances of the victim, but also on how an ordinary, reasonable person would perceive the actions of the perpetrator.
- A married female employer linked arms with an unmarried employee who had recently been hired, and expressed her affection to him in front of other people, even though he expressed that he did not feel the same. These would be considered actions that cause sexual humiliation or disgust for the male employee. In addition, despite the fact that they have a relationship of employer and employee, the perpetrator repeatedly called, sent text messages, and left voice messages expressing her romantic feelings towards the complainant. These actions constitute sufficient psychological pressure that goes beyond sexual humiliation and causes mental suffering and humiliation, which would be felt by any reasonable person. These actions of the perpetrator caused the victim to involuntarily resign from the company and suffer the resulting loss of income.
- Considering the above circumstances, the actions were sufficient to cause sexual humiliation or disgust for the victim. Therefore, the actions of the perpetrator constitute sexual harassment.

---

[97] Decision made on September 22, 2009, 08 Jincha 480 (Sexual harassment)

또는 여자로서 A에게 좋은 감정이 있었기 때문이지 A를 괴롭히려고 한 것이 아니라고 주장하였다.

(2) 국가인권위원회의 결정[97]

[주문]
1. 진정요지 가.항 부분(강제추행과 감금)은 (현재 수사기관의 수사가 진행 중이므로) 각하한다.
2. 피진정인에게 국가인권위원회가 주최하는 특별인권교육을 받을 것과 진정인에 대하여 손해배상금 300만 원을 지급할 것을 권고한다.

[결정 요지]
- 「국가인권위원회법」 제2조제5호의 성희롱 개념 규정에서 성적 굴욕감 또는 혐오감에 대한 판단은 피해자의 주관적 사정 외에도 보통의 합리적 인간의 관점에서 피진정인의 행위에 대해 피해자가 어떻게 반응하고 느꼈을 것인가를 기준으로 해야 한다.
- 기혼인 여성 고용주가 입사한 지 얼마 되지 않은 미혼인 남성 부하직원에게 본인이 거부의사를 밝혔음에도 다른 사람들 앞에서 팔짱을 끼거나 사랑한다고 하는 등의 언동을 한 것은 보통의 남성이라면 충분히 성적 굴욕감 또는 혐오감을 느끼게 하는 언동이라 할 것이다. 또한 피진정인과 진정인이 사용자와 직원의 관계임에도 불구하고 진정인에게 시도 때도 없이 전화를 하거나 문자 또는 음성메시지를 보내 자신의 이성으로서의 감정을 노골적으로 표현하면서 이를 심리적으로 압박한 점 역시 합리적인 인간이라면 성적 모욕감을 넘어선 정신적 고통과 굴욕감을 느끼게 하기에 충분하다 할 것이다. 피진정인의 이러한 행위는 결과적으로 진정인으로 하여금 비자발적으로 고용관계에서 이탈하게 하고 직장에서 배제되는 경제적 피해를 주었다.
- 위와 같은 내용들을 종합할 때, 피진정인의 언동은 진정인에게 성적 굴욕감 또는 혐오감을 느끼게 하기에 충분한 행위로서 성희롱에 해당하는 것으로 판단된다.

---

[97] 2008.9.22. 결정 08진차480 [성희롱]

Section 3. Issues and Related Cases in Handling Workplace Sexual Harassment Incidents

Ⅲ. Court Rulings and Decisions related to Sexual Harassment by Superiors[98]

1. Dispute related to sexual harassment by male superior

(1) Summary of the case

R Motor Company's female manager A filed a civil lawsuit in June 2013. Allegedly, she had suffered from sexual harassment by her superior, B, and had been subjected to unfavorable treatment by R Company and the employers when she reported it. In June 2014, she also filed a criminal complaint against R Company and the employers for violation of Article 14(2) of the Equal Employment Act, which prohibits disadvantaging alleged victims. In total, the civil lawsuit went through five trials: the court of first instance (Seoul Central District Court, ruling on Dec. 18, 2014, 2013GaHap536064, Damages Claim (Base)), court of second instance (Seoul High Court, ruling on Dec. 18, 2015, 2015Na2003264, Damages Claim (Base)), the Supreme Court (Supreme Court, ruling on Dec. 22, 2017, 2016Da202947, Damages Claim (Base)), the Seoul High Court, where the case was remanded and returned for a new trial (Seoul High Court, ruling on April 20, 2018, 2017Na2076631, Damages Claim (Base)), and finally the Supreme Court, where it went through a retrial (Supreme Court ruling on July 23, 2018, 2018Da232072). Although the defendant, R Company filed for an additional retrial, this was rejected. The main issues in this case and lawsuit can be divided into three categories.

① The first issue is whether the actions of the plaintiff's superior, B, constitute "sexual harassment in the workplace" as prohibited by the Equal Employment Act. This issue was not disputed after the first instance court recognized what occurred as "sexual harassment in the workplace." However, the interpretation of "burden of proof" differed from previous decisions, which drew attention.

② The second issue is the legality of measures taken by the defendant company (hereinafter referred to as "R Company") and the employers towards the alleged victim and the female employee who supported her (hereafter, "supporter"). After the complaint, R company reassigned them to new tasks, suspended them, and imposed disciplinary actions. It was questioned whether these actions constituted legitimate personnel measures or unfavorable measures against alleged victims, etc. prohibited by the Equal Employment Act. The first court ruled them as legitimate personnel measures, while the appellate court denied the legitimacy of some of them. The Supreme Court ruled that not only were the measures taken

---

[98] Kim El-lim, "Sexual Harassment: Law and Dispute Resolution Cases," Episteme, 2023, pp. 293~315

Ⅲ. 상급자의 성희롱 관련 판례·결정례[98]

1. 남성 상급자의 성희롱 관련 분쟁

(1) 사건 개요

R자동차 주식회사 소속 여성 과장 A는 직속 상급자 B로부터 성희롱을 당하여 고충을 신고한 후 R회사와 사용자들로부터 불리한 처우를 받았다며 2013년 6월, 민사소송을 제기하였다.

민사소송은 1심(서울중앙지방법원 2014.12.18., 선고 2013가합536064 판결[손해배상(기)])과 2심 법원(서울고등법원 2015.12.18. 선고 2015나2003264 판결[손해배상(기)]), 대법원(대법원 2017.12.22. 선고 2016다202947 판결[손해배상(기)])을 거쳐 파기환송심(서울고등법원 2018. 4. 20. 선고 2017나2076631 판결 [손해배상(기)]), 재상고심(대법원 2018.7.23. 선고 2018다232072 판결[손해배상(기)])까지 5회의 민사재판으로 진행되었다. 피고 R회사는 재상고심도 제기하였으나 대법원은 심리불속행으로 기각하여 이 사건은 파기환송심 판결로 확정되었다. 이 사건과 소송의 쟁점은 크게 세가지로 구분된다.

① 상급자 B의 원고에 대한 언동이 「남녀고용평등법」이 금지한 '직장 내 성희롱'에 해당되는지 여부이다. 이 쟁점은 1심 법원이 '직장 내 성희롱'을 인정하였기에 2심 법원 이후에서는 쟁점이 되지 못했다. 다만, 2심 법원이 '직장 내 성희롱'과 입증책임 규정에 관하여 현행법과 선행 판결들과 다르게 해석하여 주목이 되었다.

② 원고가 소송을 제기한 후 R회사와 사용자들이 원고와 원고의 소송을 도와 준 여성근로자(이하 "조력자"라 한다)에 대하여 업무분장의 조정, 직무정지와 대기발령, 징계 등의 인사조치를 하였는데 이것이 정당한 인사조치인지, 「남녀고용평등법」이 금지한 '피해자 등에 대한 불리한 조치'인지 여부이다. 1심 법원은 정당한 인사조치로 보았고, 2심 법원은 일부 조치의 정당성을 인정하지 아니하였다. 대법원은 원고에 대한 조치 뿐 아니라 조력자에 대한

---

[98] 김엘림, 「성희롱: 법과 분쟁처리사례」, 에피스테매, 2023, 293~315면.; 김엘림, "[판례평석] 직장 내 성희롱-대상판결 : 대법원 2017.12.22. 선고 2016다202947 판결 손해배상(기) 판결", 「노동판례백선」 제2판, 한국노동법학회 편, 박영사, 2021, 58~61면.

against the plaintiff unfavorable measures against alleged victims, etc, but so were the disciplinary measures against the supporter. The Supreme Court's ruling was in line with the appellate court to dismiss and remand the case.

③ The third issue is whether the defendant company (R Company) bore responsibility for the illegal acts of the employers in this case. The court of first instance did not recognize such liability, while the court of second instance recognized partial liability for some of the disadvantageous measures. The Supreme Court recognized a broad scope of employer responsibility and also agreed with the appellate court to dismiss and remand the case.

Meanwhile, A filed a lawsuit against the company and individuals she claimed had imposed unfair disciplinary measures against her and her supporter, arguing that the company violated the prohibition provisions in Article 14 (6) of Equal Employment Act. The criminal trial proceeded through three instances: the first verdict was by the Suwon District Court, Ruling on Jan. 31, 2020, 2018Godan1046 [Violation of the Equal Employment Act]), the second verdict was also by the Suwon District Court, Ruling on Nov. 13, 2020, 2020Nor816 [Violation of the Equal Employment Act]), and the third verdict was by the Supreme Court. Ruling on July 21, 2021, 2020Do16858 [Violation of the Equal Employment Act]. In the end, Company R was fined KRW 20 million, the head of the personnel department was fined KRW 8 million, and the chairman of the disciplinary committee was fined KRW 4 million. This case is significant because it is the first one that imposed fines for violating the Equal Employment Acton individuals and the company for disadvantaging alleged sexual harassment victims, etc. However, unlike the civil trials, the reassignment of the victim and her supporter to new tasks was deemed justifiable.

This sexual harassment case began in 2012 and took 5 years to end. The related court cases continued from June 11, 2013 to the final appellate trial on July 23, 2018. Furthermore, the litigation process continued for a total of approximately 8 years. The Supreme Court ruled in favor of the plaintiff on July 21, 2021, or 6 years after the victim first filed a lawsuit in 2014. Human rights organizations, labor unions, women's groups, and others formed a joint action committee and provided support to the victim, publicizing her case throughout the process. The media also showed a keen interest in and reported on the case.

징계조치도 '피해자 등에 대한 불리한 조치'가 될 수 있다고 하였다. 파기환송심 판결은 대법원과 같은 취지로 판결하였다.
③ 이 사건 사용자들의 불법행위에 대한 사업주(R회사)의 사용자 책임 유무이다. 1심 법원은 사용자책임을 인정하지 아니하였고, 2심 법원은 일부 조치에 대한 사용자 책임을 인정하였다. 대법원은 사용자책임을 넓게 인정하였다. 파기환송심 판결은 대법원과 같은 취지로 판결하였다.

한편, A는 자신과 조력자에 대하여 부당 징계를 한 사용자들과 회사를 「남녀고용평등법」의 피해자 등에 대한 불리한 조치 금지규정 위반으로 고소하였다. 이 고소로 3회의 형사재판(1심 판결(수원지방법원 2020.1.31.선고 2018고단1046 판결 [남녀고용평등과일·가정양립지원에관한법률위반]), 2심 판결(수원지방법원 2020. 11. 13. 선고 2020노816 판결 [남녀고용평등과일·가정양립지원에관한법률위반]), 3심 법원의 판결(대법원 2021.7.21. 선고 2020도16858 판결 [남녀고용평등과일·가정양립지원에관한법률위반])로 진행되었다. 이 재판으로 R회사는 2천만 원의 벌금형을 받았다. 그리고 인사담당부장은 8백만 원, 징계위원회 위원장은 4백만 원의 벌금형을 받았다. 성희롱 피해자에 대한 불리한 처우를 한 인사 업무관련자들과 회사에 대하여 「남녀고용평등법」 위반을 이유로 한 벌금형을 부과한 첫 번째 판례라는 의의를 가진다. 다만, 민사재판의 경우와 달리 피해자에 대한 업무배치 조정은 무죄로 판정되었다.

2012년에 발생한 이 성희롱 사건에 관한 법적 분쟁은 2013년 6월에 민사소송이 제기된 후 2018년 7월에 재상고심 기각이 이루어질 때까지 5년이 걸렸다. 또한 피해자가 2014년에 고소한 후 6년만인 2020년 1월에 1심 형사 재판이 열렸고, 대법원이 2021년 7월에 원고 승소판결을 할 때까지 소송은 총 약 8년 동안 진행되었다. 이 사건과 분쟁의 진행 과정에 인권단체, 노동단체, 여성단체 등이 연대하여 공동대책위원회를 조직하고 피해자를 지원하며 사건을 공론화시켰다. 이에 언론도 비상한 관심을 보이고 보도하였다.

(2) 여성근로자의 민사소송 제기

A는 2013.6.11. 직속 상급자 B, 소속 부서(R&D 본부 차량성능담당부서) 총책임자인 이사 C, HR본부 인사담당부장 D, 그리고 R회사를 피고로 하여 성희롱과 관련하여 피고들의 행위로 인해 정신적 고통을 당했다며 위자료 청구

Section 3. Issues and Related Cases in Handling Workplace Sexual Harassment Incidents

(2) Female employees file civil lawsuit and related trial

"A" sued her employers and the company for damages. The defendants were B, her immediate superior, C, the head of the department (Vehicle Performance Department of R&D Division) who is also the overall responsible person, D, the head of the HR Division, and R Company itself. Allegedly, she suffered mental distress due to their actions. A's claims are as follows:

① B, her immediate superior (team leader), used his work position to sexually harass her, persistently demanding sexual conversations or meetings with her for about a year, despite knowing that A is married. This has caused her sexual humiliation and disgust.

② C, the head (director) of the department to which A belongs, violated Article 14, paragraph 2 of the Equal Employment Act by advising her not to report the sexual harassment to the personnel department or outside. Instead, C recommended that she resign along with B if she were to continue to create conflict over the sexual harassment. After she reported to the HR division anyways, C isolated her.

③ D, who was head of the HR Division, neglected his duty to manage and supervise, failed to protect the alleged victim when derogatory remarks about A were made by HR team members like F, such as "A is hot-tempered" and "It's A's problem that she did not resist B." Also, D unfairly imposed disciplinary action (a reprimand) against A, causing further harm to A. Moreover, D unfairly suspended A from work, which resulted in disadvantages for A who suffered the sexual harassment.

④ R Company, as an employer, has a responsibility to compensate for damages incurred by third parties due to the actions of its employees in accordance with Article 756 of the Civil Act, which states "if a person uses another person to perform work, the employer shall be liable for damages caused by the execution of the work." Therefore, R Company is responsible for the damages cause by B, C, D, and other personnel department employees for their illegal actions.

(3) Personnel actions taken by Company R after A filed a civil lawsuit

Company R disciplined employee E, who supported A in reporting the sexual harassment, with a one-week suspension for failure to comply with working hours

소송(민사소송)을 제기했다. A의 주장은 다음과 같다.

① 직속 상급 B(팀장)는 배우자가 있음에도 업무상 지위를 이용하여 비혼자인 자신에게 이성 간의 대화나 만남을 약 1년간 지속적으로 요구하고 성적 굴욕감과 혐오감을 느끼게 하는 신체접촉과 성적 발언으로 성희롱을 하는 불법행위를 했다.

② 소속 부서 총책임자 C(이사)는 성희롱 피해 사실을 인사부서나 외부에 하지 말라고 만류하고 계속 성희롱 문제로 분란을 만들꺼면 B와 함께 사직할 것을 권고하였고 그럼에도 자신이 HR본부 인사팀에 신고하자 왕따 분위기를 만들었다. 그리하여 성희롱 피해자에 대하여 불리한 조치를 금지한 「남녀고용평등법」 제14조제2항(현행법의 제14조제6항)을 위반하는 불법행위를 했다.

③ 성희롱 사건의 내부 조사를 담당하는 인사팀 직원 F 등이 다른 부서 동료들에게 자신의 성희롱 피해 신고 사실을 알리고 자신에 대하여 "성격이 보통이 아니더라", "B에 적극 저항하지 않은 것은 문제다" 는 등의 말을 하여 자신의 명예를 훼손하였는데 이는 인사담당부장 D가 직무상 관리·감독을 소홀히 하였기에 발생 된 것이다. 또한 피고 D는 성희롱 피해자인 자신을 보호하지 않고 자신을 비난하는 소문이 유포되는 것을 방치하였으며 B의 비위행위에 대하여 부당하게 경징계 처분(견책)을 하는 등 자신에게 후속 피해를 발생시켰다. 나아가 부당한 대기발령을 핑계로 원고의 신체의 자유를 과도하게 제한하고 압박하는 등으로 성희롱 피해자인 자신에게 불리한 조치를 하였다.

④ R회사는 "타인을 사용하여 어느 사무에 종사하게 한 자는 피용자가 그 사무집행에 관하여 제삼자에게 가한 손해를 배상할 책임이 있다."라고 규정한 「민법」 제756조(사용자 배상책임)에 따라 B, C, D 및 F 등 인사팀 직원들의 불법행위에 관하여 손해배상 책임을 져야 한다.

(3) 소송 제기 후 인사조치와 대응

R회사는 A의 민사소송 제기 후 A의 성희롱 문제 제기에 도움을 준 조력자 E에 대하여 유연근무제가 실시되고 있음에도 근무시간 미준수를 이유로 정직 1주일의 징계를 했다. 또한 A에 대하여 부하 직원을 과격한 발언으로

Section 3. Issues and Related Cases in Handling Workplace Sexual Harassment Incidents

despite her being subject to a flexible working hours system. Company R also issued a disciplinary warning to employee G, a subordinate of A, for making aggressive remarks and spreading rumors related to sexual harassment. A included these actions as additional grounds for damages in the civil lawsuit. In addition, A and E filed a relief application for unfair disciplinary action with the Gyeonggi Provincial Labor Relations Commission, and received a decision of unfair disciplinary action against the company (dated December 4, 2013) and a similar decision from the National Labor Relations Commission (dated March 17, 2014).

Meanwhile, on October 17, 2013, Company R adjusted A's duties and excluded her from specialized tasks, assigning only common tasks to her. They also suspended A and E from work, arguing that they possessed confidential company documents that they were not authorized to possess. E requested for A's help to quickly transport these documents off company premises, eventually turning them over to the police when the company attempted to retrieve them. Immediately thereafter, on December 11, 2013, Company R filed a criminal complaint with the Suwon District Prosecutors' Office against A for theft and E for defamation, insult, and violation of the Act on Promotion of Information and Communications Network Utilization and Information Protection, Etc. The prosecutor decided to suspend the indictment for the theft charge against E and a decision of no charges for the remaining accusations against A, citing that it was difficult to conclude that A was aware of E's act of taking the documents from company premises. \E filed a constitutional appeal with the Constitutional Court against the prosecutor's decision to suspend indictment, and the Constitutional Court (2014Hunma574, ruling on Feb. 26, 2015) overturned the prosecutor's decision of suspension of indictment, stating that it was difficult to conclude that E intended to steal or illegally acquire the documents in question.

In response to A's civil lawsuit, all the defendants refuted A's claims, arguing that the duties and disciplinary action given to A were legitimate and reasonable exercises of personnel authority, not retaliatory measures against her for the sexual harassment lawsuit. They also argued that B's actions were personal misconduct unrelated to official duties, for which the employer had no liability.

(4) Civil litigation trial
1) Judgment from the court of first instance[99]

협박하여 자신에 대한 성희롱 관련 소문 유포에 관한 진술서를 받았다며 견책의 징계를 하였다.

　A는 이러한 조치들을 민사소송의 손해배상 청구사유에 추가로 포함시켰다. 그리고 E와 함께 경기지방노동위원회에 부당징계 구제신청을 하여 부당징계 판정(2013.12.4. 결정)을 받았고 중앙노동위원회의 부당징계 판정(2014.3.17. 결정)도 받았다.

　한편, R회사는 2013년 10월, A의 업무를 조정하여 전문업무를 배제하고 비전문업무(공통업무)를 많이 부여했다. 또한 A와 E가 노동위원회에 제출한 서류 중 이들이 정상적으로는 소지할 수 없는 회사기밀 서류가 있다는 의심을 하고 이들에 대하여 직무정지와 대기발령 처분을 하였다. E는 소지한 서류들을 회사로부터 압류당할까봐 A에게 도움을 요청하여 둘이 급히 외부로 반출하려다가 회사 측이 막자 경찰서에 이 서류들을 반환하였다. R회사는 2013년 12월, A를 절도방조죄, E를 명예훼손·모욕·「정보통신망법」 위반(정보통신망 침해등)·절도 혐의로 수원지방검찰청에 고소하였다. 검사는 2014년 6월, E의 절도 혐의에 대하여는 기소유예 처분을, 나머지 혐의에 대하여는 혐의없음 처분을 하고, A에 대하여는 E의 서류 반출행위를 알고 있었다고 보기 어렵다는 이유로 '혐의없음' 처분을 하였다. 그런데 E는 헌법재판소에 검사의 기소유예 처분에 대하여 헌법소원을 제기하였다, 헌법재판소(2015. 2. 26. 선고 2014헌마574호)는 E에게 절도의 고의나 불법영득의 의사가 있다고 보기 어렵다며 검사의 기소유예 처분을 취소하였다.

　한편, A의 민사소송 제기에 대하여 피고들은 모두 A의 주장이 사실이 아니라고 반박하며, A가 문제 삼는 업무조정이나 징계는 성희롱 소송 제기에 대한 보복적인 불리한 조치가 아니라 인사권의 정당하고 합리적 행사이며, B의 언동은 사무집행과 관계없는 개인적 일탈이기 때문에 「민법」 제756조(사용자 배상책임)에 따른 손해배상 책임이 발생하지 않는다고 주장했다.

(4) 민사소송의 재판
1) 1심 법원의 판결의 요지[99]

---

[99] 서울중앙지방법원 2014.12.18. 선고 2013가합536064 판결[손해배상(기)]

Section 3. Issues and Related Cases in Handling Workplace Sexual Harassment Incidents

> <Court Ruling>
> 1. Defendant B shall pay the Plaintiff KRW 10,000,000. Between Nov. 1, 2014 and to Dec. 18, 2014, he must pay an annual interest rate of 5%, which will increase to 20% per annum, calculated on a pro-rata basis, thereafter until the date of full payment.
> 2. The remaining claims against Defendant B by the Plaintiff and claims against Defendants C, D, and R Company are dismissed.
> 3. The Plaintiff shall bear 1/4 of the litigation costs incurred by the Plaintiff and Defendant B, and Defendant B shall bear the remaining costs. The Plaintiff shall also bear the costs incurred between the Plaintiff and Defendants C, D, and R.
> 4. The first clause may be provisionally executed.

The court of first instance determined that Defendant B's behavior was sexual harassment, as an ordinary and average person would have felt sexual humiliation or shame. However, regarding Defendant C's behavior, the Court recognized that there were attempts to resolve the issue in a reasonable manner as a manager or person in charge of the organization, and did not consider the conduct illegal. As for Defendant D's behavior, it was only a brief explanation of his personal impression of the plaintiff in a private setting without mentioning specific facts, so it is difficult to consider it an illegal act that damaged the Plaintiff's reputation. There was no evidence to support the claim that Defendant D violated his obligation to take protective measures for the Plaintiff as the head of the personnel team or unfairly disciplined Defendant B. It also ruled that the disciplinary action against the Plaintiff and E were legitimate personnel actions unrelated to the sexual harassment incident, and therefore, the Court did not recognize it as illegal conduct. Furthermore, the Court did not hold R Company responsible for Defendant B's sexual harassment because it felt this not a responsibility of R Company and held the same view of Defendant C and D's actions.

2) Judgment of the Court of Second Instance[100]

The plaintiff appealed, this time with only Company R as the defendant. The court of second instance made the following ruling, which differed from the previous court's decision and was in accordance with the provisions of the current Equal Employment Act regarding sexual harassment:

---

[99] Seoul Central District Court, ruling on Dec. 18, 2014, 2013GaHap536064 for Damages (Basic)
[100] Seoul High Court, Dec. 18, 2015, 2015Na2003264) (Compensation for Damages (Civil Case))

> <주문>
> 1. 피고 B는 원고에게 10,000,000원 및 이에 대하여 2014. 11. 1.부터 2014. 12. 18.까지는 연 5%의, 그 다음날부터 다 갚는 날까지는 연 20%의 각 비율에 의한 금원을 지급하라.
> 2. 원고의 피고 B에 대한 나머지 청구 및 피고 C, D, R에 대한 각 청구를 각 기각한다.
> 3. 소송비용 중 원고와 피고 B 사이에 생긴 부분 중 1/4은 원고가, 나머지는 피고 B가 각 부담하고, 원고와 피고 C, D, R 사이에 생긴 부분은 원고가 부담한다.
> 4. 제1항은 가집행할 수 있다.

1심 법원은 피고 B의 언동에 대하여 객관적으로 상대방과 같은 처지에 있는 일반적이고 평균적인 사람이 성적 굴욕감이나 수치심을 느꼈을 것으로 판단한다며 성희롱으로 인정하였다. 그러나 피고 C의 언동에 대하여는 조직의 관리·책임자로서 원만하게 문제를 해결하려는 시도가 인정된다며 불법행위로 인정하지 않았다. 피고 D의 언동에 대하여는 F 등의 인사팀 직원이 구체적인 사실관계에 관해 언급한 것이 아니었고 단순히 자신의 개인적인 인상을 사적인 자리에서 간략하게 설명한 것에 불과하여 원고의 명예를 훼손하는 불법행위를 하였다고 보기는 어렵고, 인사부장으로서 원고에 대한 보호조치를 취할 의무를 위반했다거나 부당하게 피고 B에 대해 경징계를 하였다는 점을 인정할 증거가 없으며 원고와 E를 징계한 것은 성희롱 사건과는 관련이 없는 정당한 인사조치였다며 불법행위를 인정하지 아니하였다. 그리고 피고 B의 성희롱 행위가 R회사의 사무집행에 관하여 발생한 것이 아니라 개인적으로 이루어진 것이라며 R회사의 사용책임을 인정하지 아니하였다. 또한 피고 C, D에 대한 판단에 기초하여 R회사의 불법행위와 사용자책임도 인정하지 않았다.

2) 2심 법원의 판결[100]

원고는 R회사만을 피고로 하여 항소하였다. 2심 법원은 다음과 같이 판시하였다. 이 판시에는 성희롱에 관한 현행 「남녀고용평등법」의 규정과 다른

---

[100] 서울고등법원 2015.12.18. 선고 2015나2003264 판결[손해배상(기)]

Section 3. Issues and Related Cases in Handling Workplace Sexual Harassment Incidents

<Decision>
1. The portion of the plaintiff's claim for which the court of first instance ordered the defendant to pay money is hereby cancelled.
   The defendant shall pay the plaintiff KRW 10,000,000. Between Nov. 1, 2014 and to Dec. 18, 2014, he must pay an annual interest rate of 5%, which will increase to 20% per annum, calculated on a pro-rata basis, thereafter until the date of full payment.
2. The remaining appeals of the plaintiff against the defendant are dismissed.
3. The total litigation costs between the plaintiff and the defendant shall be divided by 10, with 9/10 to be borne by the plaintiff and the remaining by the defendant.
4. The part regarding the payment of money from paragraph (1) may be provisionally executed.

① The definition of sexual harassment in the workplace was interpreted broadly to include not only actions with sexual connotations, but also discriminatory remarks based on gender such as "doing household chores at home" directed at female employees.

② Unlike the first-instance judgment, the joint responsibility of Company R and Defendant B for the illegal actions was recognized. However, the responsibility of R was extinguished as B had already compensated the plaintiff for damages after the first trial,

③ Unlike the first-instance judgment, the actions of the director in charge were recognized as disadvantageous towards the plaintiff which are prohibited under Article 14(2) of the Equal Employment Act. These actions included assigning the plaintiff only common duties after she had reported the sexual harassment, and giving negative evaluations to the plaintiff for the report. Company R was recognized as responsible for these unfair actions.

④ The court of second instance stated that current law stipulates that the burden of proof lies with the employer. However in this case, it is reasonable for the employee and the employer to share the burden of proof collectively, and therefore, the burden of proof provision was not applied in this case. Meanwhile, the court also ruled that the disciplinary actions against the plaintiff and the supporter were legitimate personnel actions unrelated to the sexual harassment report, in line with the first judgment.

법원의 판결과 다른 판단이 포함되어 있다.

> <주문>
> 1. 제1심 판결의 피고 R회사에 대한 부분 중 다음에서 지급을 명하는 돈에 해당하는 원고 패소부분을 취소한다.
>   피고는 원고에게 1천만 원 및 이에 대하여 2014년 11월 1일 부터 2015년 12월 18일 까지는 연 5%의, 그 다음 날부터 다 갚는 날까지는 연 20%의 각 비율로 계산한 돈을 지급하라.
> 2. 원고의 피고에 대한 나머지 항소를 기각한다.
> 3. 원고와 피고 사이의 소송 총비용은 이를 10분하여 그 9는 원고가, 나머지는 피고가 각 부담한다.
> 4. 제1항 중 돈의 지급 부분은 가집행할 수 있다.

① 성희롱에 관한 다른 판결들과 달리, 직장 내 성희롱의 의의에 관하여 성적인 성질을 가지는 언동뿐 아니라 여성 근로자에게 "집에서 살림이나 하지" 등의 성차별적 발언과 성별에 기반한 비하 등을 포함하여 폭넓게 해석하였다.

② 1심과 다르게 성희롱 행위자 B의 불법행위에 대하여 R회사의 공동책임을 인정하였다. 다만, B가 1심 재판에서 손해배상액을 변제했으므로 R의 책임은 소멸했다고 판결하였다.

③ 1심과 다르게 원고가 성희롱 피해 사실을 신고한 후 원고에게 전문업무에서 배제하고 공통업무만을 배정한 담당이사의 업무조정 조치, 원고의 신고 사실과 이에 관한 부정적인 평가를 한 조사담당자의 행위를 「남녀고용평등법」 제14조제2항이 금지한 불리한 조치로 인정하고 이에 대하여 R회사의 사용자 책임을 인정하였다.

④ 입증책임에 관하여 현행법이 사용자가 부담한다라고 규정하고 있지만, 근로자, 사용자가 공동으로 부담하는 것이 타당하다며 입증책임 규정을 이 사건에 적용하지 않았다.

한편, 2심 법원은 1심 법원과 같이 원고와 그 조력자에 대한 징계조치는 성희롱 신고와 무관한 정당한 인사조치라고 판결하였다.

Section 3. Issues and Related Cases in Handling Workplace Sexual Harassment Incidents

3) Judgment of the Supreme Court[101]

<Decision>
1. The portion of the lower court's judgment that dismissed the plaintiff's claim for damages related to the disciplinary action taken against the plaintiff on September 4, 2013, the suspension and placement on standby on December 11, 2013, and the disciplinary action against the plaintiff's co-worker on July 19, 2013, is set aside, and this portion of the case is remanded to the Seoul High Court.
2. The defendant's (R company) appeal is dismissed.

Both the plaintiff and the defendant appealed the judgment of the court of second instance. The Supreme Court annulled and remanded the original judgment, recognizing the employer's liability for unfavorable treatment under Article 14(2) of the Equal Employment Act, and illegal acts (sexual harassment) by its employees. The main points of the Supreme Court's decision are as follows:

① The provisions of the Equal Employment Act prohibit unfavorable measures against victims of sexual harassment. Its purpose is not only to promptly and appropriately redress workplace sexual harassment, but also to prevent workplace sexual harassment. It encourages the employer to take appropriate measures against a perpetrator, such as taking disciplinary action without the victim having to fear secondary victimization. If an employer dismisses or takes other unfavorable action against a victim of workplace sexual harassment, this constitutes an illegal act under Article 750 of the Civil Act and also violates Article 14(2) of the Equal Employment Act.

② Whether the employer's actions against the victim are considered illegal, depends on whether the unfavorable measures were taken around the time of the victim's report of the workplace sexual harassment. The following should be considered as well: the circumstances and process surrounding the unfavorable measures; whether the reasons for unfavorable measures stated by the employer existed prior to the victim reporting the harassment; the extent to which the rights or interests of third parties were infringed upon by the actions of the victim; whether the unfavorable measures were exceptional or discriminatory compared to previous practices or similar cases; and whether the victim filed a request for relief related to the unfavorable measures. In determining whether the unfavorable measures are illegal, such factors should be considered

---

[101] Supreme Court, Dec. 22, 2017, 2016Da202947 (Damages Claim (Tort))

3) 3심 법원의 판결[101]

> <주문>
> 1. 원심판결의 원고 패소 부분 중 원고에 대한 2013.9.4일자 견책처분, 2013.12.11일자 직무정지와 대기발령, 소외 1(조력자)에 대한 2013.7.19일자 정직처분에 관한 손해배상청구 부분을 파기하고, 이 부분 사건을 서울고등법원에 환송한다.
> 2. 피고(R회사)의 상고를 기각한다.

제2심 법원의 판결에 대하여 원고와 피고 모두 상고하였다. 대법원은 피고회사의 「남녀고용평등법」 제14조제2항의 불리한 처우와 종사자의 불법행위(성희롱)에 관한 사용자책임을 인정하여 원심을 파기 환송하였다.
대법원의 주요 판결 요지는 다음과 같다.
① 「남녀고용평등법」이 피해자 등에 대한 불리한 조치를 금지한 규정을 둔 것은 직장 내 성희롱 피해를 신속하고 적정하게 구제할 뿐만 아니라 직장 내 성희롱을 예방하기 위한 것으로, 피해자가 직장 내 성희롱에 대하여 문제를 제기할 때 2차적 피해를 염려하지 않고 사업주가 가해자를 징계하는 등 적절한 조치를 하리라고 신뢰하도록 하는 기능을 한다. 사업주가 피해근로자등에게 해고나 그 밖의 불리한 조치를 한 경우에는 「남녀고용평등법」 제14조제2항을 위반한 것으로서 「민법」 제750조의 불법행위가 성립한다.
② 사업주의 조치가 피해근로자 등에 대한 불리한 조치로서 위법한 것인지 여부는 불리한 조치가 직장 내 성희롱에 대한 문제 제기 등과 근접한 시기에 있었는지, 불리한 조치를 한 경위와 과정, 불리한 조치를 하면서 사업주가 내세운 사유가 피해근로자 등의 문제제기 이전부터 존재하였던 것인지, 피해근로자 등의 행위로 인한 타인의 권리나 이익 침해 정도와 불리한 조치로 피해근로자등이 입은 불이익 정도, 불리한 조치가 종전 관행이나 동종 사안과 비교하여 이례적이거나 차별적인 취급인지 여부, 불리한 조치에 대하여 피해근로자 등이 구제신청 등을 한 경우에는 그 경과

---
[101] 대법원 2017.12.22. 선고 2016다202947 판결[손해배상(기)]

comprehensively.

③ According to Article 14, paragraph 2 of the Equal Employment Act, it is difficult to consider it as a direct violation of the law, if an employer takes unfavorable actions against the supporter who provided assistance to the victim.

④ However, when the unfavorable measures taken by the employer against the supporter are unfair and have caused mental distress to the victim as a result, the victimized employee may hold the employer liable for illegal conduct under Article 750 of the Civil Act. The victim can hold the employer liable for illegal conduct even if the unfavorable actions were not directly taken against the victim.

⑤ In cases where a dispute related to sexual harassment arises, the employer must prove that unfavorable actions taken against the victimized employee are unrelated to sexual harassment or that there were justifiable reasons to do so (Article 30 of the Equal Employment Act).

4) Reversed and Remanded Judgment[102]

The reversed and remanded judgment ruled in favor of the plaintiff and supporter, ordered the defendant (R company) to pay KRW 30 million in damages for unfavorable actions taken against them, in line with the ruling of the Supreme Court.

<Decision>
1. The portion of the first-stage (regional) court's judgment concerning the defendant (R), excluding the portion that has been separately determined by the remand decision, which corresponds to the amount specified below for payment, is hereby canceled.
    The defendant is ordered to pay the plaintiff 30 million won, and for this amount, interest shall be calculated at a rate of 5% per annum from November 1, 2014, until April 20, 2018, and at a rate of 20% per annum from the following day until the full amount is paid.
2. The plaintiff's remaining appeal against the defendant is dismissed.
3. The plaintiff shall bear 1/3 of the total litigation costs between the plaintiff and the defendant, while the remaining costs shall be borne by the defendant.
4. The monetary payment portion in Paragraph 1 may be enforced.

---

[102] Seoul High Court, ruling on April 20, 2018, 2017Na2076631) [Compensation for Damages]

등을 종합적으로 고려하여 판단해야 한다.
③ 「남녀고용평등법」 제14조제2항의 법문상 사업주가 피해근로자 등이 아니라 그에게 도움을 준 동료 근로자에게 불리한 조치를 한 경우에 위법행위를 하였다고 보기는 어렵다. 그러나 사업주가 피해근로자 등을 가까이에서 도와준 동료 근로자에게 불리한 조치를 한 경우에 그 조치의 내용이 부당하고 그로 말미암아 피해근로자 등에게 정신적 고통을 입혔다면, 피해근로자 등은 불리한 조치의 직접 상대방이 아니더라도 사업주에게 「민법」 제750조에 따라 불법행위책임을 물을 수 있다.
④ 「남녀고용평등법」 제30조에 따라 성희롱으로 인한 분쟁이 발생한 경우에 피해근로자등에 대한 불리한 조치가 성희롱과 관련성이 없거나 정당한 사유가 있다는 점에 대하여 사업주가 증명을 하여야 한다.

4) 파기환송심의 판결[102]

파기환송심 판결은 피고 R회사에 대하여 대법원과 같은 취지로 원고와 그 조력자에 대한 징계, 직무정지와 대기발령을 '피해자 등에 대한 불리한 조치'를 인정하고 3천만 원의 손해배상을 명하는 판결을 하였다.

> <주문>
> 1. 제1심 판결의 피고(R)에 대한 부분(환송판결에 의하여 분리 확정된 부분 제외) 중 아래에서 지급을 명하는 금액에 해당하는 원고 패소 부분을 취소한다.
>   피고는 원고에게 3천만 원 및 이에 대하여 2014. 11. 1.부터 2018. 4. 20.까지는 연 5%, 그 다음날부터 다 갚는 날까지는 연 20%의 각 비율로 계산한 돈을 지급하라.
> 2. 원고의 피고에 대한 나머지 항소를 기각한다.
> 3. 원고와 피고 사이의 소송총비용 중 1/3은 원고가, 나머지는 피고가 각 부담한다.
> 4. 제1항 중 금전지급 부분은 가집행할 수 있다.

---

[102] 서울고등법원 2018. 4. 20. 선고 2017나2076631 판결[손해배상(기)]

Section 3. Issues and Related Cases in Handling Workplace Sexual Harassment Incidents

5) Significance and impact of the civil lawsuit

① In order to provide practical and definite protection for victims of sexual harassment in the workplace, Article 14 (Action in the Event of Sexual Harassment in the Workplace) of the Equal Employment Actwas significantly amended on November 28, 2017, coming into effect on May 29, 2018. With this amendment, measures for the protection of victims and alleged victims ("workers who have suffered harm due to workplace sexual harassment" or "workers who claim to have suffered harm," respectively) during related investigations were newly established (paragraph 3). Sanctions against perpetrators (paragraph 4) were also specified once sexual harassment is confirmed by the investigation. In addition, the scope of protection against unfavorable actions against (alleged) victims was expanded to include "workers who have reported the occurrence of sexual harassment" (paragraph 6). Furthermore, the types of unfavorable measures that employers must not take were specified into seven categories.

② The Supreme Court's ruling on this case was the first to provide criteria for determining whether unfavorable measures taken against (alleged) victims and reporters of sexual harassment are unfair. It was also the first time that the court ruled disciplinary action against the supporter is an unfair unfavorable action taken indirectly against the victim.

③ Furthermore, this is the first ruling to state the duties of the sexual harassment investigator and the liability of the employer for taking unfavorable actions against (alleged) victims. Paragraph 7 was added to the Equal Employment Actin November 2017, and states, "Persons who have learned confidential information during the investigation process shall not disclose such information to others, against the will of the victim and etc., except for when reporting to the employer or providing necessary information requested by relevant agencies."

(5) Accusation, criminal lawsuit, and trial

This criminal lawsuit holds significance in that it is the first ruling to impose fines on HR personnel and the company for engaging in discriminatory treatment of the victim of sexual harassment, which violates the Equal Employment Act.

5) 이 사건 민사소송과 재판의 의의와 영향

① 이 사건 성희롱 소송과 재판의 영향으로 직장 내 성희롱 피해자에 대한 실질적이고 구체적인 보호를 위해 2017년 11월 28일, 「남녀고용평등법」 제14조(직장 내 성희롱 발생 시 조치)가 크게 개정되어 2018년 5월 29일부터 시행되었다. 이 개정으로 "직장 내 성희롱과 관련하여 피해를 입은 근로자 또는 피해를 입었다고 주장하는 근로자"에 대한 성희롱 사건의 조사기간 중의 보호조치 규정(제3항)이 신설되었고, 조사 결과 직장 내 성희롱 발생 사실이 확인된 때의 피해자에 대한 보호조치 규정(제4항)과 행위자에 대한 제재 규정(제5항)이 구체화되었다. 또한 피해자 등에 대한 불리한 조치 규정(제6항)의 보호 대상에 "성희롱 발생 사실을 신고한 근로자"가 포함되었고, 사업주가 해서는 안 되는 불리한 조치가 일곱 가지로 세분화되어 명시되었다.

② 이 사건 대법원의 판결은 성희롱 피해자와 신고자에 대한 불리한 조치의 판단기준을 제시하였고 피해자의 조력자에 대한 부당 징계를 피해자에 대한 불리한 조치로 해석한 최초의 판결이다.

③ 또한 성희롱 조사담당자의 조리상의 직무와 그 직무위반에 대한 사업주의 사용자 책임을 원심과 함께 판시한 최초의 대법원 판결이다. 이로 인해 2017년 11월 28일의 「남녀고용평등법」 개정 시에 "직장 내 성희롱 발생 사실을 조사한 사람, 조사 내용을 보고 받은 사람 또는 그 밖에 조사 과정에 참여한 사람은 해당 조사 과정에서 알게 된 비밀을 피해 근로자 등의 의사에 반하여 다른 사람에게 누설하여서는 아니 된다. 다만, 조사와 관련된 내용을 사업주에게 보고하거나 관계 기관의 요청에 따라 필요한 정보를 제공하는 경우는 제외한다."라는 제7항이 신설되었다.

(5) 고소와 형사소송 및 재판

이 사건의 형사소송에 관한 재판은 성희롱 피해자에 대한 불리한 처우를 한 인사 업무관련자들과 회사에 대하여 「남녀고용평등법」 위반을 이유로 한 벌금형을 부과한 첫 번째 판례라는 의의를 가진다.

Section 3. Issues and Related Cases in Handling Workplace Sexual Harassment Incidents

1) Judgment of the court of first instance[103]

The main points of the first-instance judgment are as follows:

<Decision>
1. Defendant J (Head of HR Department) shall be fined KRW 8 million, Defendant K (Deputy Head of R&D Department) shall be fined KRW 4 million, and Defendant R company shall be fined KRW 20 million.
2. If the defendants fail to pay the above fines, they shall be detained in a labor camp for a period calculated at KRW 100,000 per day. The defendants shall be ordered to make a significant portion of the fines as a contribution.
3. Defendant J (mediator for labor dispute concerning the plaintiff) is found not guilty.
4. The summary of the part of the judgment concerning Defendant J shall be made public.

① Employers, corporate representatives, officers, and other employees of a corporation or their agents shall not dismiss or take other unfavorable actions against employees who have suffered (or claimed to have suffered) from workplace sexual harassment. However, Defendant D, as the chairman of the disciplinary committee, and Defendant H, as the vice chairman of the disciplinary committee, imposed unfair disciplinary measures, suspensions from duty, and job suspensions and instigated prosecution against the victims and supporters of the sexual harassment claim. These defendants have conspired to take unfavorable actions against an alleged victim of sexual harassment.
② Defendant R Company neglected to manage and supervise to prevent the illegal acts of Defendants D and H.
③ Defendant J (Operations Manager of the System Engineering Division at R&D Department of the Defendant Company) is accused of taking unfavorable actions by excluding the victim from specialized tasks and assigning only common tasks. However, he was not actually excluding the victim from specialized tasks, and the actual number of common tasks was only 3 instead of 5. Therefore, it is difficult to consider it as a discriminatory work assignment or unfavorable measures taken against an alleged victim of sexual harassment.

---

[103] Suwon District Court ruling on Jan. 31, 2020, 2018godan1046 [Violation of the Equal Employment Act]

1) 1심 판결[103]

1심 판결의 요지는 다음과 같다.

> < 주문 >
> 1. 피고인 D(HR본부인사 담당 부장)를 벌금 8백만 원에, 피고인 H(R&D 본부 부소장, 징계위원회 위원장)을 벌금 4백만 원에, 피고인 R회사를 벌금 2천만 원에 처한다.
> 2. 피고인들이 위 벌금을 납입하지 아니하는 경우 각 10만 원을 1일로 환산한 기간 위 피고인들을 노역장에 유치한다. 피고인들에 대하여 위 벌금에 상당한 금액의 가납을 명한다.
> 3. 피고인 J(원고에 대한 업무조정자)는 무죄.
> 4. 이 판결 중 피고인 J에 대한 부분의 요지를 공시한다.

① 사업주 및 법인의 대표자나 법인 또는 대리인, 사용인 그 밖의 종업원은 직장 내 성희롱과 관련하여 피해를 입은 근로자 또는 피해를 입었다고 주장하는 근로자, 성희롱 사건을 신고한 근로자에게 해고나 그 밖의 불리한 조치를 하여서는 아니 된다. 그런데 피고인 D는 인사업무를 총괄하는 부장, 피고인 H는 징계위원회 위원장으로서 직장 내 성희롱의 피해자와 조력자에 대하여 부당한 징계와 대기발령, 직무정지 처분, 고소를 주도하였다. 그리하여 피고인들은 공모하여 성희롱 피해자에 대하여 불리한 조치를 하였다.

② 피고 R회사는 피고인 D와 H의 위법행위를 방지하기 위한 상당한 주의와 감독을 게을리 하였다.

③ 그런데 피고인 J는 피고인 회사 R&D본부 시스템엔지니어링 담당 오퍼레이션장으로서 피해자에게 전문업무에서 배제하고 공통업무만을 부여하여 불리한 조치를 하였다는 혐의를 받고 있으나 실제 조사한 결과 피해자가 기존에 맡고 있던 전문 업무에서 배제되지 않았고 공통업무가 실질적으로는 5개가 아니라 3개이어서 그 자체로는 기형적인 업무분장이라고 보기 어려우므로 공소사실이 적시한 '성희롱 피해 관련 불리한 조치'는 인정될 수 없다.

---

[103] 수원지방법원 2020. 1. 31. 선고 2018고단1046 판결 [남녀고용평등과일·가정양립지원에관한법률위반])

Section 3. Issues and Related Cases in Handling Workplace Sexual Harassment Incidents

2) Judgment of court of second instance[104]

The second-instance judgment regarding the appeals of Defendant J, H, and R Corporation and the appeals of the prosecutor against Defendant J and C was as follows.

<Decision>
1. The part of the original judgment that pertains to Defendant R Corporation is annulled.
2. Defendant R Corporation is fined KRW 20 million.
3. Defendant R Corporation is ordered to deposit the significant amount of the fine.
4. Defendant J of Defendant R Corporation is acquitted of the charge of unfairly changing job assignments.
   The acquittal of this charge is publicly announced.
5. The appeals of Defendants D and H, and the appeals of the prosecutor against Defendant J and C are all rejected.

---

3) Judgment of the Supreme Court[105]

Defendants D and H, R Corporation, and the prosecutor appealed the judgment, but the appeal was rejected by the Supreme Court, thereby confirming the ruling of the Suwon District Court (court of second instance).

2. Dispute regarding sexual harassment by a female superior[106]

(1) Case Overview

The plaintiff, A, is a female manager at B Research Institute, while the defendant, C, is a female director in her 60s at B.

A alleges that C would often kiss employees on the lips while intoxicated. During a department workshop, while having dinner and drinking with colleagues, C forcefully kissed A after grabbing her face. A also claims that during subsequent department gatherings, she refused C's advances, yet C still attempted to kiss her. As a result of C's actions, A experienced sexual humiliation and decided to resign, filing a complaint with the National Human Rights Commission.

On the other hand, C admits to hugging A but denies engaging in the alleged actions, such as the kisses claimed by A. C argues that A's complaint seems to be motivated by retaliatory intent stemming from work-related dissatisfaction and incidents where she felt slighted by A's behavior at other social gatherings.

---

[104] Suwon District Court ruling on Nov. 13, 2020, 2020no816 [Violation of the Equal Employment Act]
[105] Supreme Court ruling on July 21, 2021, 2020do16858 [Violation of the Equal Employment Act]
[106] Kim El-lim, "Sexual Harassment: Law and Dispute Resolution Cases," Episteme, 2023, pp. 315-316.

2) 2심 판결[104]

2심 판결은 피고인 D, H, R회사의 항소 및 검사의 피고인 J의 무죄에 대한 항소에 대하여 주문과 같이 판결하였다.

> < 주문 >
> 1. 원심판결 중 피고인 R회사에 대한 부분을 파기한다.
> 2. 피고인 R회사를 벌금 2천만 원에 처한다.
> 3. 피고인 R회사에 대하여 위 벌금에 상당한 금액의 가납을 명한다.
> 4. 피고인 R회사의 피고인 J 업무 변경 조치 부분에 대하여는 무죄. 이 부분 무죄판결의 요지를 공시한다.
> 5. 피고인 D, H의 항소 및 검사의 피고인 J의 무죄에 대한 항소를 모두 기각한다.

3) 3심 법원의 판결[105]

피고인 D와 H, R회사 그리고 검사가 상고하였는데 대법원은 이를 모두 기각하여 원심이 확정되었다.

2. 여성 상급자의 성희롱 관련 분쟁[106]

(1) 사건 개요

진정인 A는 리서치 전문기관인 B연구소의 여성 과장이며, 피진정인 C는 B의 60대 여성 이사다.

A는 C가 술을 마시면 직원들을 안고 입술에 키스를 하곤 했는데 부서 워크숍에서 직원들과 저녁식사를 하며 술을 마시던 중 자신에게도 얼굴을 잡고 강제로 키스를 하였고, 그 후의 부서 회식자리에서도 거부하였는데도 키스를 하여 성적 굴욕감을 느껴 퇴사를 하였다고 국가인권위원회에 진정하였다.

한편, C는 A를 껴안은 것은 기억하지만, A가 주장하는 키스 등의 언동은 하지 않았다며, A가 업무상의 불만과 다른 술자리에서 자신이 술을 끼얹은 일 등으로 서운한 감정에서 보복으로 진정을 제기한 것 같다고 주장하였다.

---

104) 수원지방법원 2020. 11. 13. 선고 2020노816 판결 [남녀고용평등과일·가정양립지원에관한법률위반]
105) 대법원 2021. 7. 21. 선고 2020도16858 판결 [남녀고용평등과일·가정양립지원에관한법률위반]
106) 김엘림, 「성희롱: 법과 분쟁처리사례」, 에피스테메, 2023, 315-316면.

Section 3. Issues and Related Cases in Handling Workplace Sexual Harassment Incidents

(2) Decision of the National Human Rights Commission of Korea[107]

<Decision>
1. Respondent is ordered to receive special human rights education organized by the National Human Rights Commission.
2. President of B institution is recommended to take disciplinary action against the perpetrator, and to take measures for the perpetrator to attend the special human rights education organized by the National Human Rights Commission. Also, it is recommended to establish measures to prevent recurrence of the sexual harassment, such as managing the sexual harassment prevention education program in a substantial manner.

<Summary of Decision>
① Whether a certain behavior constitutes sexual harassment should be determined by comprehensive consideration of many factors, such as the relevance of the behavior to work, the factual relationship between the parties, the place and circumstances of the behavior, explicit or implicit reactions of the other party, whether the other party did not want such behavior and felt discomfort, whether the behavior involved sexual implications, and whether it constitutes behavior that would cause sexual humiliation or disgust from the perspective of a reasonable and ordinary person.
② The perpetrator is in a higher position than the victim, and they work in the same department. The perpetrator's behaviors are work-related because it occurred at a department workshop and a work-related dinner gathering.
③ Both the victim and the perpetrator are female. However, sexual harassment can be established even between members of the same sex if the perpetrator's behavior involves sexual implications and causes sexual humiliation or disgust for the victim.
④ The act of the perpetrator forcibly kissing the victim at a department workshop and dinner gathering exceeds the permissible level of behavior in the workplace, even between members of the same sex. It is sufficient to cause sexual humiliation or disgust from the perspective of a reasonable person. Therefore, this constitutes sexual harassment as defined in Article 2, Clause 3 of the National Human Rights Commission Act.

---

[107] Decision made on July 30, 2014, 14 Jinjung 480 (Sexual harassment)

(2) 국가인권위원회의 결정[107]

<주문>
1. 피진정인에게, 국가인권위원회가 주관하는 특별인권교육을 수강할 것을 권고한다.
2. ㈜ B연구소 회장에게, 피진정인에 대하여 징계조치를 할 것, 피진정인이 국가인권위원회가 주관하는 특별인권교육을 수강할 수 있도록 조치를 취할 것, 직장 내 성희롱 예방교육을 내실 있게 운영하는 등 재발 방지를 위한 대책을 마련할 것을 권고한다.

<결정 요지>
- 어떠한 행위가 성희롱인지 여부는 당사자 간의 업무관련성, 언동의 사실관계, 언동이 행해진 장소 및 상황, 그 언동에 대한 상대방의 명시적 또는 추정적 반응 등을 구체적으로 종합하여 상대방이 그러한 행위를 원치 않았고 불쾌감을 느꼈는지, 성적 함의가 있으며, 합리적 피해자의 관점에서 성적 굴욕감이나 혐오감을 줄 만한 행위에 해당하는지 여부에 의하여 판단하여야 할 것이다.
- 피진정인은 진정인과 같은 부서에서 근무하는 상위 직급자이고, 이 사건 관련 피진정인의 언동이 부서전체 워크숍 및 업무의 연장선상인 회식 자리에서 발생한바 그 업무 관련성을 인정할 수 있다.
- 이 사건은 진정인과 피진정인이 모두 여성이나, 성희롱의 당사자가 반드시 이성 간이어야 할 필요는 없고 동성 간에도 성적 함의가 담긴 피진정인의 언동으로 인하여 성적 굴욕감 또는 혐오감을 느꼈을 경우 성희롱이 성립된다.
- 피진정인이 부서 워크숍 및 회식자리에서 진정인에게 강제로 키스를 한 것은, 아무리 동성 간이라 하더라도 직장 내에서 허용되는 수준을 넘어 합리적인 사람의 관점에서 성적인 굴욕감 또는 혐오감을 불러 일으키기에 충분한 행위라 할 것이다. 따라서, 이는 「국가인권위원회법」 제2조제3호 라목이 정한 성희롱에 해당한다.

---

[107] 2014.7.30. 결정 14 진정0294500 [성희롱]

Section 3. Issues and Related Cases in Handling Workplace Sexual Harassment Incidents

IV. Court Rulings and Decisions related to Sexual Harassment of Employees[108]

1. Dispute related to sexual harassment by male employee

(1) Overview of the case

Female worker A who works at F Steel Works, is the only woman in her 20s in a department where about 50 male employees work. On June 7, 2022, she filed a complaint against four male coworkers in the same department for alleged sexual harassment and sexual assault. One senior coworker, a department manager, allegedly came to her home after drinking and sexually assaulted her in a manner similar to rape, and the other three coworkers allegedly touched specific parts of her body against her will and coerced her to drink alcohol at a company dinner, and sexually harassed her during work.

A reported the incidents of workplace and sexual harassment to the audit office of F Company, but the perpetrator only received a three-month suspension. A, who was transferred to another department as a measure of separation from the perpetrator, claimed that she was forced to return to her original department after three months against her will by the department manager. On the other hand, the department manager argued that he was only trying to console her. When this dispute was reported in the media, the Ministry of Employment and Labor recognized that the environment in which female workers can work without anxiety was seriously violated in light of the recent cases of sexual harassment and sexual assault in F Steel Works on June 27, 2022. It issued a press release stating that they were conducting a joint investigation with the police. It was also conducting an investigation on whether there has been any violations of the provisions of the Equal Employment Act, since June 21, 2022. On the same day, the Ministry also began a diagnostic assessment of the organizational culture regarding employment equality in F Steel Works, in order to identify risk factors in the workplace that could allow for sexual harassment and employment discrimination.

(2) Results of the official investigation by the Ministry of Employment and Labor

On August 5, 2022, the Ministry of Employment and Labor announced the results of an official investigation.

> <Results of the Ministry of Employment and Labor Investigation and Diagnosis of Organizational Culture at F Steel Works>
> - Male workers identified by the victims have violated Article 12 of the Equal Employment Act, by engaging in acts of sexual harassment in the workplace.

---

108) Kim El-lim, "Sexual Harassment: Law and Dispute Resolution Cases," Episteme, 2023, pp. 316~318.

Ⅳ. 근로자의 성희롱 사건과 관련 판례·결정례[108]

1. 남성 근로자의 성희롱 관련 분쟁

(1) 사건 개요

F제철소 여성근로자 A는 직원 50여명이 근무하는 해당 부서에서 유일한 여성이며 20대이다. 그런데 2022.6.7., 같은 부서의 4명 남성근로자들을 성희롱·성폭력의 혐의로 고소하였다. 선배 1명은 술을 먹고 막무가내로 집에 들이닥쳐 폭력을 하며 자신을 유사강간했고 나머지 직원 3명도 회식 자리에서 자신에게 특정 신체 부위를 만지거나 억지로 술을 마시도록 강요하고 업무 때 성희롱을 하였다고 주장했다.

A는 피해 사실을 F회사 감사실에 직장 내 괴롭힘과 성희롱 사건을 신고했다. 그런데 가해자에 대한 징계는 3개월 감봉에 그쳤다. 가해자와의 분리조치로 다른 부서로 이동했던 A씨는 원하지 않았는데도 부소장이 복귀를 종용해 석 달 만에 원래 부서로 돌아와야 했다고 주장했다. 반면, 부소장은 피해자를 위로하고자 방문한 것이라고 반박했다. 이러한 분쟁이 언론에 보도되자, 고용노동부는 2022년 6월 27일, 최근 문제되고 있는 F제철소 직장 내 성희롱·성폭력 사건에 대해 여성 근로자가 안심하고 일할 수 있는 환경이 심각하게 침해된 상황임을 엄중하게 인식, 경찰과 긴밀한 조사 협조체계를 구축하는 동시에 「남녀고용평등법」 관련 규정 위반 여부에 대해서는 2022년 6월 21일부터 직권조사 중이며, 또 직장 내 성희롱과 고용상 성차별 등 위험요인을 확인하기 위해 이날부터 F제철소 근로자들을 대상으로 사업장 고용평등 조직문화 진단에 착수했다는 보도자료를 배포하였다.

(2) 고용노동부의 직권조사결과

고용노동부는 2022년 8월 5일, 다음과 같은 취지의 직권조사 결과를 발표하였다.

■ 피해자가 지목한 남성근로자들은 「남녀고용평등법」 제12조(직장 내 성희롱의 금지)를 위반하여 직장 내 성희롱 행위를 하였다.

---

[108] 김엘림, 「성희롱: 법과 분쟁처리사례」, 에피스테메, 2023, 316~318면.

Section 3. Issues and Related Cases in Handling Workplace Sexual Harassment Incidents

- F Steel Works is scheduled to be fined KRW 5 million for violating Article 14, paragraph 4 of the Equal Employment Act. This is because they have failed to take prompt action despite the victim's request for a department transfer after confirming the fact of sexual harassment in the workplace. This eventually resulted in the victim's unavoidable frequent contact with the perpetrator for a considerable period of time. In addition, there is a suspicion of violating Article 14, paragraph 6 of the Equal Employment Act, for secondary victimization. Therefore, the representative director of F Steel Works will be prosecuted and enter legal proceedings.

(3) Result of organizational culture diagnosis by the Ministry of Employment and Labor

The Ministry of Employment and Labor conducted an online survey of all employees working for F Steel Works, from June 27 to July 4, 2022, to diagnose the organizational culture of equal employment, in conjunction with the official investigation.

< Results of the Ministry of Employment and Labor Investigation of Organizational Culture at F Steel Works >

- There are differences in sensitivity regarding organizational culture between male and female workers. Also, there are differences between workers in their 20s and 30s and those in their 40s and above. The responses which indicated that confidentiality is not well maintained when incidents of sexual harassment occur, were higher than the average. Also, it was confirmed that effective sexual harassment prevention education is not being conducted in the workplace. The main reasons for not taking any action despite the occurrence of workplace sexual harassment were mainly about potential disadvantages after reporting, and lack of trust in the company's internal handling system.
- On August 4, 2022, the Ministry of Employment and Labor explained the specific results of the organizational culture diagnosis to the management of F Steel Works and instructed them to inform their employees of the results. They also directed them to prepare improvement measures through detailed self-diagnosis, such as improving organizational culture related to sexual harassment and discrimination in the workplace, improving the internal grievance handling system, improving the response system in the event of incidents, taking measures to prevent secondary damages, and enhancing the effectiveness of sexual harassment prevention education by August 31, 2022.
- The Ministry of Employment and Labor will continuously monitor and check the contents and implementation of the improvement measures to prevent recurrence of workplace sexual harassment and ensure that the

- F제철소는 직장 내 성희롱 사실이 확인된 이후 피해자가 근무부서 변경을 요청하였음에도 지체없이 조치하지 않아 행위자와 빈번한 접촉이 불가피한 상황이 상당 기간 지속된 점에 관하여 「남녀고용평등법」 제14조제4항 위반으로 보아 과태료 500만 원을 부과할 예정이다. 또한 피해자에 대한 불리한 처우 등의 2차 가해 행위에 대하여 「남녀고용평등법」 제14조제6항 위반 혐의가 있는 것으로 보고 대표자를 입건하여 수사를 통해 사법처리할 예정이다.

(3) 고용노동부의 조직문화진단

한편, 고용노동부는 직권조사와 병행하여 2022.6.27.부터 7.4.까지 F제철소 소속 전 직원을 대상으로 온라인 설문조사를 통해 해당 사업장의 고용평등 조직문화 진단을 실시하였다.

- 조직문화 진단 결과, 남성과 여성, 20~30대 근로자와 40대 이상 근로자 사이에 조직문화에 대한 민감도 차이가 존재하며 직장 내 성희롱 사건 발생시 비밀유지가 잘 안된다는 답변이 평균 이상으로 나타났고 실효적인 직장 내 성희롱 예방교육이 이루어지지 못하는 것으로 확인되었으며 직장 내 성희롱 관련 경험이 있더라도 아무런 대응을 하지 않은 주요 사유는 신고 후에 불이익이 우려되거나 회사 내 처리제도를 신뢰하지 못하기 때문인 것으로 나타났다.
- 고용노동부 F지청은 2022.8.4., F 제철소 경영진을 상대로 구체적인 조직문화 진단 결과를 설명하면서, 이를 소속 근로자에게 주지시키도록 하는 한편, 2022.8.31.까지 직장 내 성희롱·성차별 관련 조직문화 개선, 사내 고충처리제도 개선, 사건 발생 시 대응체계 개선, 2차 피해 예방대책, 직장 내 성희롱 예방교육 실효성 제고 등에 대해 면밀한 자체진단을 통해 개선대책을 마련하여 제출할 것을 지도하였다.
- 고용노동부는 향후 해당 사업장에 직장 내 성희롱 재발을 방지하고 예방 및 대응 체계가 확실히 개선될 수 있도록 개선대책 내용 및 이행상황을 지속적으로 점검하고 사업주의 개선의지가 부족하다고 판단되는 경우에는 근로조건 전반에 대한 심층 점검을 위해 특별감독 실시를 적극 검토할 계획이다.

Section 3. Issues and Related Cases in Handling Workplace Sexual Harassment Incidents

> prevention and response system is substantially improved. If it is found out that the employer is not working to make improvements, special inspections will be considered for in-depth examination of overall working conditions at the workplace.

2. Dispute related to sexual harassment by female workers[109]

(1) Overview of the case

A, a male worker (28 years old, unmarried), was employed as an assistant machine repairman by B Company, which is engaged in clothing manufacturing and sales. The company had 200 female workers and 7 male. A alleges that when he went to repair machines in the production department of B Company, two married female workers (Defendant 1, 40 years old, and Defendant 2, 35 years old), who were working as sewing machine operators and sewing machine assistants, intentionally touched his nipples and buttocks and made comments such as "You have a nice body," "You look like a young chicken," and "You are mine," despite his discomfort which was clearly expressed.

A approached the production manager and the director of general affairs of B Company for consultation, and demanded action to resolve the situation. The production manager, C, scolded A for making a fuss over a trivial matter and for not being enough of a "man" to handle some women's jokes. Also, the manager threatened to press defamation charges against A and fire him if he couldn't bring a signed statement from the women admitting to the sexual harassment. When A strongly protested, C reported him to the police station and had him detained.

In March 2001, A submitted a resignation letter stating that he wished to resign due to personal reasons, and then visited the local labor office to file an application for unemployment benefits. When applying for the benefits, he stated that he had been forced to quit by the company's coercion and threats. After he turned in the application, the labor inspector suggested that A's case could be considered as sexual harassment in the workplace. Subsequently, A filed a lawsuit against the female workers who had harassed him and B Company. He sought compensation for damages and invalidation of the unfair dismissal. His case was represented by women's rights lawyers.

(2) Court ruling[110]

For the first time, the court recognized the occurrence of sexual harassment by female workers against a male worker. The court also acknowledged the employer responsibility of Company B.

---

109) Kim El-lim, "Sexual Harassment: Law and Dispute Resolution Cases," Episteme, 2023, pp. 318~321.
110) Seoul District Court ruling on May 3, 2002, 2001 Gahap 6471 [compensation for damages]

2. 여성 근로자의 성희롱 관련 분쟁[109]

(1) 사건 개요

A는 여성근로자 2백 명, 남성근로자 7명을 고용하여 의류제조·판매업 등을 하는 B주식회사의 기계수리기사 보조사원으로 입사한 신입 미혼 남성근로자(28세)이다. A는 B회사의 생산부에 기계를 수리하러 갈 때마다 미싱사, 미싱보조로 일하는 기혼여성 2명(피고1(40세), 2(35세))이 자신에게 "덩치가 있어 좋다", "영계 같아 좋다", "너는 내 꺼야"라는 등의 말을 하며 젖꼭지와 둔부를 만지기도 하는 등 의도적으로 신체 접촉을 하여 거부의사를 밝혔는데도 그러한 언동을 지속하였다고 주장하였다.

A는 B회사의 생산부장과 총무이사를 찾아가 상담하고 대책을 요구하였다. 생산부장 C는 여성들이 장난한 것 가지고 남자답지 못하게 문제 삼는다며 핀잔을 주고 여성들로부터 성희롱을 하였다는 자인서를 받아오지 못하면 무고죄로 고소하고 퇴사시키겠다고 하였다. 이에 A가 강하게 항의하자 C는 파출소에 신고하여 A가 연행되게 하였다.

A는 2001년 3월, 개인사정으로 사직한다는 내용의 사직서를 제출한 후, 지방노동사무소에 찾아가 "사직할 의사가 없었음에도 회사 측의 강요와 협박에 의해 회사를 그만뒀으니 실업급여를 청구한다."며 신청서를 제출하였다.

그런데 근로감독관은 A의 피해는 성희롱 사건으로 인정될 수 있다고 하였다. 이에 A는 여성인권변호사들을 소송대리인으로 하여 성희롱을 한 여성들과 B회사를 피고인으로 하여 손해배상을 청구하고 아울러 해고무효확인을 구하는 소송을 제기하였다.

(2) 법원의 판결[110]

법원은 여성근로자들에 의한 남성근로자의 성희롱 피해를 최초로 인정하였고 또한 B회사의 사용자책임도 인정하였다.

---

109) 김엘림, 「성희롱: 법과 분쟁처리사례」, 에피스테매, 2023, 318~321면.
110) 서울지방법원 동부지원 2002.5.3. 선고 2001가합6471 판결[손해배상(기)]

Section 3. Issues and Related Cases in Handling Workplace Sexual Harassment Incidents

<Decision>
1. The Defendants shall each pay the plaintiff KRW 3,000,000, along with interest at an annual rate of 5% from March 28, 2001 to May 3, 2002, and interest at an annual rate of 25% from May 4, 2002 until the date of full payment.
2. The dismissal of the plaintiff by Company B on March 28, 2001 is invalid. Company B shall pay the plaintiff KRW 848,600, along with monthly wages at the rate of KRW 839,687 from March 28, 2001 until the Plaintiff is reinstated.
3. The remaining claims against the Defendants by the Plaintiff are dismissed.
4. The Plaintiff shall bear 1/2 of the litigation costs incurred between the Plaintiff and Company B, and the remaining costs shall be borne by the Defendants. The Plaintiff shall bear 7/10 of the litigation costs incurred between the Plaintiff and Defendant 1, and the remaining costs shall be borne by the Defendants.
5. Paragraphs 1 and 2 of this order shall be enforced immediately.

<Summary of Decision>
1. Judgment on Defendants 1 and 2
- The actions of the defendants clearly show a sexual motive and intention. Such sexual behavior goes beyond the category of ordinary jokes or friendly gestures that are socially acceptable. It caused the plaintiff to feel sexual humiliation or disgust, lowered the plaintiff's social evaluation, and deteriorated the plaintiff's working environment, thereby infringing upon the plaintiff's personal rights. Such actions constitute workplace sexual harassment as defined in the Equal Employment Act. Based on common experience, it is clear that the plaintiff suffered mental anguish as a result of the defendants' actions.
- Therefore, the defendants' sexual behavior constitutes joint illegal conduct, and the defendants have an obligation to compensate the plaintiff for the mental damages suffered by the plaintiff. Considering the plaintiff's age, gender, occupation, and the circumstances of how the physical contact occurred in this case, including the method and degree, the appropriate amount of compensation for damages to be awarded to the plaintiff by the defendants is determined to be KRW 3 million.

2. Judgment against Company B
A. Claim for Damages

[주문]
1. 피고들은 각자 원고에게 금 3,000,000원 및 이에 대한 2001.3.28. 부터 2002.5.3.까지 연 5%, 2002.5.4. 부터 완제일까지 연 25%의 각 비율에 의한 금원을 지급하라.
2. 피고 주식회사 B가 원고에 대하여 한 2001.3.28.자 해고는 무효임을 확인한다. B는 원고에게 금 848,600원 및 2001.3.28.부터 원고를 복직시킬 때까지 월 금 839,687원의 비율에 의한 금원을 지급하라.
3. 원고의 피고들에 대한 각 나머지 청구를 기각한다.
4. 소송비용 중 원고와 B 사이에 생긴 부분은 그 1/2은 원고의, 나머지는 위 피고의 각 부담으로 하고, 원고와 피고 1, 피고 2 사이에 생긴 부분은 그 7/10은 원고의, 나머지는 위 피고들의 각 부담으로 한다.
5. 제1항 및 제2의 나.항은 가집행할 수 있다.

< 판결 요지>
1. 피고 1, 2에 대한 판단
- 피고들의 행동은 분명한 성적인 동기와 의도를 가진 것으로 보여지고, 그러한 성적인 언동은 사회통념상 일상적으로 허용되는 단순한 농담 또는 호의적인 언동의 범주를 넘어 원고로 하여금 성적 굴욕감이나 혐오감을 느끼게 함과 동시에 원고에 대한 사회적 평가를 저하시키고 원고의 근무환경을 악화시켜 원고의 인격권을 침해한 것이며, 이러한 침해행위는 「남녀고용평등법」에서 정한 직장 내 성희롱에 해당하는 위법한 행위로서 원고가 위와 같은 위 피고들의 행위로 인하여 정신적 고통을 받았을 것임은 경험칙상 명백하다.
- 따라서 피고들의 이와 같은 성적인 언동은 공동불법행위를 구성한다 할 것이므로 피고들은 원고에게 각자 원고가 입은 정신적 손해를 금전으로나마 위자할 의무가 있다고 할 것인바, 원고의 나이, 성별, 직업 및 이 사건 신체접촉이 이루어진 경위와 그 방법 및 정도 등 여러 사정을 종합하여 보면 피고들이 원고에게 배상할 위자료는 금 300만 원으로 정함이 상당하다.

2. 피고 회사에 대한 판단
가. 손해배상 청구

Section 3. Issues and Related Cases in Handling Workplace Sexual Harassment Incidents

- An employee must not engage in "work-related behavior" which causes another employee to feel humiliation or disgust due to sexual gestures or other sexual harassment-related actions. "Work-related behavior" includes not only the employee's work itself or actions necessary to complete the work, but also the actions generally perceived as related to the work, even if it is intended for the benefit of the employee. Company B, as an employer of the victim, has an obligation to prevent sexual harassment which undermines the dignity of the employee and seriously violates labor law by deteriorating the working environment of the employee. Therefore, if employees of Company B sexually harassed another employee who came to repair the machine, the company is subject to employer's liability for damages.
- In addition, the employer has a duty to take prompt and appropriate actions in accordance with the Equal Employment Act. The employer could transfer the perpetrator to another department, impose disciplinary action, or take other equivalent actions, when it is confirmed that sexual harassment has occurred in the workplace. The employer also has the duty not to take any disadvantageous actions against the victim. If the company was aware or could have been aware of the occurrence of sexual harassment in the workplace through the plaintiff, the company must take prompt and appropriate action. However, there are cases where the company failed to do so in accordance with the relevant law. If a company neglects the situation and tries to maintain workplace order through forced concessions and sacrifice by the plaintiff such as his resignation, the company is liable for illegal actions as an employer.
- Therefore, the defendant company also has an obligation to pay compensatory damages of KRW 3 million to the plaintiff as joint illegal co-actors with the other defendants.

B. Confirmation of Invalid Dismissal
- The plaintiff submitted a resignation letter due to the defendant company's coercion to resign, which itself was because of the plaintiff's report of sexual harassment in the workplace. However, the plaintiff had no intention to resign and his submission of a resignation letter should actually be considered a dismissal. There is no evidence to acknowledge that the dismissal is just. The defendant company's dismissal of the plaintiff on March 28, 2001 is invalid. As long as the defendant company is currently disputing the validity of the dismissal, there is also an interest for the company in seeking confirmation of the relevant matter.

- 근로자는 업무와 관련하여 다른 근로자에게 성적인 언동 등으로 성적 굴욕감 또는 혐오감을 느끼게 하여서는 아니된다. 여기서 '업무와 관련하여'라 함은 근로자의 업무 그 자체 또는 이에 필요한 행위뿐만 아니라 이와 관련된 것이라고 일반적으로 보여지는 행위는 설사 그것이 근로자의 이익을 도모하기 위한 경우라도 이에 포함된다고 보아야 할 것이며, 사용자인 회사는 근로자의 근무환경에 대해 배려하여 성희롱을 통하여 근로자의 인격적 존엄을 해치고, 노무제공에 중대한 지장을 초래하는 것을 방지해야 할 의무가 있으므로 위 피고들이 그들이 사용하는 기계를 수리하러 온 다른 근로자인 원고에게 성희롱을 하였다면 피고 회사는 사용자로서 손해배상책임이 있다.
- 또한, 사업주에게는 「남녀고용평등법」상 직장 내 성희롱 발생이 확인된 경우 지체 없이 행위자에 대하여 부서 전환, 징계 기타 이에 준하는 조치를 취하고 그 피해근로자에게 고용상 불이익한 조치를 하여서는 아니 될 법령상의 주의의무가 있는바, 회사가 원고의 신고를 통하여 직장 내 성희롱의 발생 사실을 알았거나 알 수 있는 상황에서 이에 대해 위 법령의 취지에 부합하는 신속하고도 적절한 개선책을 실시하지 아니한 채 오히려 이를 방치하고 원고의 퇴직이라는 양보와 희생을 통한 부적절하고 불공평한 방법으로 직장질서를 유지하려고 한 점에서도 피고 회사는 사용자로서의 불법행위책임을 면할 수 없다.
- 따라서 피고 회사도 위 피고들과 공동불법행위자로서 각자 원고에게 위에서 지급을 명한 금 300만 원의 위자료를 지급할 의무가 있다.

나. 해고무효확인

원고는 사직할 의사가 없음에도 불구하고 원고의 직장 내 성희롱 신고를 이유로 한 피고 회사의 사직강요에 의하여 어쩔 수 없이 사직서를 제출한 것이므로 이러한 원고의 사직서 제출은 실질상 해고로 보아야 할 것인데, 이와 같은 해고에 정당한 이유가 있었음을 인정할 아무런 증거가 없으므로 피고 회사의 원고에 대한 2001. 3. 28.자 해고는 무효라 할 것이고, 피고 회사가 해고의 효력을 다투고 있는 이상 그 확인을 구할 이익도 있다고 할 것이다.

Chapter 4. Case Studies for Workplace and Sexual Harassment (Bongsoo Jung)

Section 1. **Cases Studies for Workplace Harassment (MOEL)**

Section 2. **Labor Cases relate to Workplace Harassment**

Section 3. **Sexual Harassment Case and Procedures for Handling this Case (for Sales Workers)**

Section 4. **Sexual Harassment Case in the Workplace & Lessons Learned (for Production Workers)**

Section 5. **Labor cases related to Sexual Harassment**

제4장 직장 내 괴롭힘과 성희롱 사건 사례와 판단(정봉수)

제1절 고용노동부의 직장 내 괴롭힘 판단 사례

제2절 직장 내 괴롭힘 관련 주요 사례

제3절 직장 내 성희롱 사건사례 (영업직 직원)

제4절 직장 내 성희롱 사건사례 (사무직 직원)

제5절 직장 내 성희롱 관련 주요 사례

Section 1. Cases Studies for Workplace Harassment (MOEL)[111]

I. Determining Workplace Harassment Example 1 (Recognized Case)

1. Content of Harassment and Matters of Fact

Clerk and assistant administration jobs were given to an employee who returned after maternity leave instead of her original duties (handling deposits at the counter), and a direction to exclude her was given to persuade her to leave the company. In a meeting attended by other employees excluding the victim, a direction was given to exclude her in an attempt to drive her out of the company. Directions were then given to remove her desk and disallow her from sitting at the counter, with remarks that the victim was no longer considered as an employee. The victim suffered depression and left the company as a result.

2. Determination of Harassment in the Workplace

① Harasser: an executive director (managing director)
② Victim: an employee who had returned from childcare leave
③ Place of harassment: inside a business establishment
④ Requirements for harassment
④-1. Use of superiority in position or relations in the workplace
  ○ The harasser used position as an executive to direct other employees to exclude the victim
④-2. Exceeding occupationally bearable limits
  ○ Despite the legal obligation to reinstate an employee returning from childcare leave to the same work as before the leave or any other work paying the same level of wages (Article 19(4) of the EEO Act), assistant work was assigned and the employee's desk was removed with the intent of coercing the returning employee to leave the company.

---

[111] Ministry of Employment and Labor, 「Workplace Bullying Determination, Prevention and Response Manual, February 2019

제1절 고용노동부의 직장 내 괴롭힘 판단 사례[111]

I. 직장 내 괴롭힘 판단례 1 : 인정 사례

1. 행위내용 및 사실관계

육아휴직 후 복직한 직원에게 전에 담당하던 업무(창구 수신업무)가 아닌 창구 안내 및 총무 보조업무를 주고, 직원을 퇴출시키기 위한 따돌림을 지시함. 피해자를 제외한 다른 직원들만 참석한 회의에서 피해자를 내쫓기 위하여 따돌림을 할 것을 지시하는 취지의 내용을 전달하였음. 이후 책상을 치우고 창구에 앉지 못하게 할 것을 지시, 그를 직원으로 생각하지 않는다는 취지의 발언을 하는 등 행위를 하여 피해자는 우울증을 앓았고, 결국 퇴사함

2. 직장 내 괴롭힘 판단

① 행위자: 회사 임원 (전무)
② 피해자: 육아휴직 후 복직한 직원
③ 행위장소: 사업장 내
④ 행위요건
④-1. 직장에서의 지위 또는 관계 등의 우위 이용 여부
 ○ 회사 임원이라는 지위를 이용하여 다른 직원들에게 따돌림을 지시하는 등 행위를 함
④-2. 업무상 적정범위를 넘었는지 여부
 ○ 육아휴직 후 복귀한 직원에게는 휴직 전과 같은 업무 또는 같은 수준의 임금을 지급하는 직무에 복귀시켜야 하는 법적 의무가 있음에도 (「남녀고용평등법」 제19조제4항), 이를 무시하고 오히려 육아휴직 후 복귀한 직원을 퇴출시킬 목적으로 보조업무를 부여하고 책상을 치우는 등의 행위를 한 것은 업무상 필요성이 없는 행위에 해당

---

[111] 고용노동부,「직장 내 괴롭힘 판단 및 예방, 대응 매뉴얼」, 2019. 2.

Section 1. Cases Studies for Workplace Harassment (MOEL)

- ○ Directing others to exclude an employee who returns from childcare leave, removing a victim's desk, and using humiliating or insulting words are inappropriate in view of social norms

④-3. Inflicting physical or mental suffering or aggravating work environment

- ○ The victim suffered depression due to extreme mental stress and consequentially left company.

➡ **Comprehensive Determination**
- ○ The act was determined to constitute workplace harassment.

3. Other Issues to Consider

- ○ The act in question is punishable as a violation of Article 19(4) of the EEO Act.
- * In the actual case, the harasser was punished due to the violation of the EEO Act.

Ⅱ. Determining Workplace Harassment Example 2 (Recognized Case)

1. Content of Harassment and Matters of Fact

The harasser, a senior employee, repeatedly threatened a junior employee with personnel disadvantages if the victim refused to meet and drink alcohol. Demands were repeatedly given to "organize a drinking meeting," and the victim was questioned why he "had not set a date." The harasser insisted that the victim "write a statement of reasons," as well as apologies, and insisted that the junior member "should spend 30% of incentives in treating a senior."

2. Determination of Harassment in the Workplace

① Harasser: a senior employee
② Victim: a junior employee
③ Place of harassment: inside and outside the business establishment
④ Requirements for harassment

o 육아휴직 후 복귀한 직원을 상대로 다른 직원들에게 따돌림을 지시하거나 직접 나서 책상을 치우거나 비하·모욕하는 발언을 하는 등의 행위는 사회통념상 상당 하지 않은 행위

④-3. 신체적·정신적 고통을 주거나 근무환경을 악화시켰는지 여부

o 피해자는 극심한 정신적 스트레스로 인한 우울증을 앓았으며, 결국 퇴사함

➡ **종합적 판단**

o 직장 내 괴롭힘에 해당되는 것으로 판단

3. 기타 참고사항

o 「남녀고용평등법」 제19조제 4항 위반으로 처벌 가능
  * 실제 사안에서도 「남녀고용평등법」 위반으로 인한 처벌을 받음

Ⅱ. 직장 내 괴롭힘 판단례 2 : 인정 사례

1. 행위내용 및 사실관계

가해자인 선배가 후배인 피해자에게 술자리를 마련하지 않으면 인사상 불이익을 주겠다고 반복하여 말한 사건. "술자리를 만들어라", "아직도 날짜를 못 잡았느냐", "사유서를 써와라", "성과급의 30%는 선배를 접대하는 것이다" 등 반복적으로 술자리를 갖자는 발언을 하고 시말서, 사유서를 쓰게 한 행위

2. 직장 내 괴롭힘 판단

① 행위자: 선배 직원
② 피해자: 후배 직원
③ 행위장소: 사업장 내, 외
④ 행위요건

④-1. Use of superiority in position or relations in the workplace
- ○ Superiority in relations between a senior and a junior within the company was used.

④-2. Exceeding occupationally bearable limits
- ○ Acts inappropriate in view of social norms—coercing another to organize a drinking meeting and demanding a written statement of reasons—were committed.

④-3. Inflicting physical or mental suffering or aggravates work environment
- ○ Coercion from the harasser inflicted mental distress on the victim

➡ **Comprehensive determination**
- ○ The act was determined to constitute workplace harassment.

Ⅲ. Determining Workplace Harassment Example 3 (Recognized Case)

1. Content of Harassment and Matters of Fact

A chairman continuously used abusive language and swear words with his chauffeur because he did not like the chauffeur's driving. The chairman also hit the chauffeur's head from behind, and forced him to drive the vehicle with the rear- and side-view mirrors folded, causing the victim to drive under extreme stress.

2. Determination of Harassment in the Workplace

① Harasser: a chairman
② Victim: a chauffeur
③ Place of harassment: inside the vehicle with which the chauffeur was performing his duties
④ Requirements for harassment
④-1. Use of superiority in position or relations in the workplace
- ○ The chairman used his status as a chairman (an employer).

④-2. Exceeding occupationally bearable limits

④-1. 직장에서의 지위 또는 관계 등의 우위 이용 여부
　　ㅇ 직장 내 입사 선·후배라는 관계의 우위를 이용
④-2. 업무상 적정범위를 넘었는지 여부
　　ㅇ 술자리를 마련하도록 강요하고, 불응하는 경우 시말서 등을 쓰게 하는 등 사회 통념상 상당하지 않은 행위를 함
④-3. 신체적·정신적 고통을 주거나 근무환경을 악화시켰는지 여부
　　ㅇ 피해자는 선배 직원의 이 같은 강요로 인하여 정신적 고통을 당함

➡ **종합적 판단**
　　ㅇ 직장 내 괴롭힘에 해당되는 것으로 판단

Ⅲ. 직장 내 괴롭힘 판단례 3 : 인정 사례

1. 행위내용 및 사실관계

　회장이 운전기사에게 운전이 마음에 들지 않는다며 지속적으로 폭언, 욕설을 하고, 때로는 운전 중인 운전기사의 머리를 뒤에서 가격하며 마구 때리기도 함. 룸미러와 사이드미러를 접은 상태에서 운전하도록 하여 피해자는 극도의 스트레스 속에서 운전 업무를 함

2. 직장 내 괴롭힘 판단

① 행위자: 회장
② 피해자: 고용된 운전기사
③ 행위장소: 운전기사가 업무 수행 중인 자동차 안
④ 행위요건
④-1. 직장에서의 지위 또는 관계 등의 우위 이용 여부
　　ㅇ 회장이라는 (사용자로서의) 지위를 이용함
④-2. 업무상 적정범위를 넘었는지 여부
　　ㅇ 지속적인 폭언·욕설, 머리를 폭행하는 등 사회 통념상 상당하지 않은

Section 1. Cases Studies for Workplace Harassment (MOEL)

- ○ Abusive language, including swear words, was continuously used, and the chauffeur was forced to drive with the rear- and side-view mirrors folded, thereby hindering him from safely performing his duties. These acts can be considered inappropriate in view of social norms.

④-3. Inflicting physical or mental suffering or aggravating work environment
- ○ The victim suffered physical pain from his head being assaulted and mental distress due to abusive language and demands drive the vehicle in an unusual way.

➡ **Comprehensive determination**
- ○ The act was determined to constitute workplace harassment.

3. Other Issues to Consider

- ○ The act is also punishable as assault under the LSA, as well as under the Criminal Act.

Ⅳ. Determining Workplace Harassment Example 4 (Recognized Case)

1. Content of Harassment and Matters of Fact

A lead held up a glass soju bottle threatened to strike the victim during a company dinner. The lead also committed physical violence by squeezing the victim's neck in front of customers. The harasser continuously bullied the victim and humiliated him by throwing paper at him at a gathering with a general manager and other colleagues, as well as by making him stand still and vow repeatedly.

2. Determination of Harassment in the Workplace

① Harasser: a lead
② Victim: a subordinate
③ Place of harassment: company dinner venue, within the establishment
④ Requirements for harassment

행위를 하였으며, 룸미러와 사이드미러를 접은 상태에서 운전하도록 한 행위 역시 피해자가 안전 하게 업무 수행하는 것을 방해한 것으로서 사회 통념상 상당하지 않은 행위에 해당

④ -3. 신체적·정신적 고통을 주거나 근무환경을 악화시켰는지 여부
   ㅇ 피해자는 머리를 폭행당한 것에 대한 신체적 고통 및 폭언·욕설, 비정상적인 방식의 운전업무 지시에 따른 정신적 고통을 당함

➡ **종합적 판단**
   ㅇ 직장 내 괴롭힘에 해당되는 것으로 판단

3. 기타 참고사항

   ㅇ 「근로기준법」상 폭행, 형법상 폭행으로도 처벌 가능

Ⅳ. 직장 내 괴롭힘 판단례 4 : 인정 사례

1. 행위내용 및 사실관계

회식자리에서 직장상사가 소주병을 거꾸로 쥐어 잡고 피해자를 가격하려고 위협하고, 고객들 앞에서도 피해자의 목을 짓누르는 신체적 폭력을 가하기도 함. 또한 부장님과 다른 직장동료가 한자리에 모인 자리에서 피해자에게 종이를 던지며 모욕을 주는 행위를 가하기도 하고, 차렷 자세로 인사를 반복적으로 시키는 등 지속적인 괴롭힘을 가함.

2. 직장 내 괴롭힘 판단

① 행위자: 상사
② 피해자: 부하 직원
③ 행위장소: 회식 장소, 사업장 내
④ 행위요건

④-1. Use of superiority in position or relations in the workplace
○ The position as a lead was used.

④-2. Exceeding occupationally bearable limits
○ Assaults including threatening to strike the victim with a glass soju bottle, squeezing the victim's neck, etc. were inappropriate acts in view of social norms. Publicly insulting someone in front of other managers and employees is also considered inappropriate in view of social norms.

④-3. Inflicting physical or mental suffering or aggravating work environment
○ Physical pain due to injuries from an assault and mental distress due to insulting behavior can be recognized.

➡ **Comprehensive determination**
○ The act was determined to constitute workplace harassment.

3. Other Issues to Consider

○ The act is also punishable for assault under the LSA, and under the Criminal Act.

V. Determining Workplace Harassment Example 5 (Recognized Case)

1. Content of Harassment and Matters of Fact

In addition to their original duties, employees were tasked with the CEO's personal errands, including being asked to serve as of chauffeur and personal assistant. One victim was also made to remove snow from the vehicle of the CEO's wife after a heavy snowfall with bear hands. Employees were even asked to harvest and sell corn from the CEO's personal field, but the conservative corporate culture has prevented anyone from speaking out.

2. Determination of Harassment in the Workplace

④-1. 직장에서의 지위 또는 관계 등의 우위 이용 여부
   o 상사라는 지위를 이용
④-2. 업무상 적정범위를 넘었는지 여부
   o 회식자리에서 피해자에게 소주병으로 가격을 하려고 위협, 목을 짓누르는 등의 폭행을 하여 사회 통념상 상당하지 않은 행위를 함
   o 다른 임·직원이 있는 자리에서 공개적으로 모욕을 주는 행위를 한 것도 사회 통념상 상당하지 않은 행위에 해당
④-3. 신체적·정신적 고통을 주거나 근무환경을 악화시켰는지 여부
   o 폭행 피해로 인한 신체적 고통 및 모욕적 행위로 인한 정신적 고통 인정 가능

➡ **종합적 판단**
   o 직장 내 괴롭힘에 해당되는 것으로 판단

3. 기타 참고사항

   o 「근로기준법」 상 폭행, 형법상 폭행으로도 처벌 가능

V. 직장 내 괴롭힘 판단례 5 : 인정 사례

1. 행위내용 및 사실관계

본래 업무에 더하여 대표의 개인적인 일까지 보며 운전기사, 수행비서 역할까지 하였고, 눈이 많이 온 날 맨손으로 대표의 부인 자동차 눈 제거 작업까지 시킴. 직원을 동원해 대표 개인 밭의 옥수수 수확과 판매까지 시키지만, 회사 분위기가 워낙 보수적인 곳이라 이에 대한 문제제기도 할 수 없는 분위기임.

2. 직장 내 괴롭힘 판단

① Harasser: a CEO
② Victim: employees
③ Place of harassment: inside and outside establishment
④ Requirements for harassment
④-1. Use of superiority in position or relations in the workplace
○ Position as an employer was used.
④-2. Exceeding occupationally bearable limits
○ Mobilizing employees for the CEO's personal affairs is an act not relevant to work.
④-3. Inflicting physical or mental suffering or aggravating work environment
○ The work environment was aggravated by the CEO's behaviors as victims were forced to carry out jobs irrelevant to their work.

➡ **Comprehensive determination**
○ The act was determined to constitute workplace harassment.

VI. Determining Workplace Harassment Example 6 (Unrecognized Case)

1. Content of Harassment and Matters of Fact

Prior to a new design presentation, an apparel company team leader directed team members to report new product designs. Though employee responsible for designs reported drafts several times, the leader kept asking for additions, saying the drafts were not in line with new product concepts of the season. This resulted in workload increase and mental distress of the employee in question.

2. Determination of Harassment in the Workplace

① Harasser: a design team head
② Victim: a design responsible person
③ Place of harassment: inside establishment

① 행위자: 회사 대표
② 피해자: 직원
③ 행위장소: 사업장 내, 외
④ 행위요건
④-1. 직장에서의 지위 또는 관계 등의 우위 이용 여부
　　ㅇ 사용자로서의 지위를 이용함
④-2. 업무상 적정범위를 넘었는지 여부
　　ㅇ 대표의 개인적 용무에 동원 시키는 등 업무상 필요성이 없는 행위를 함
④-3. 신체적·정신적 고통을 주거나 근무환경을 악화시켰는지 여부
　　ㅇ 피해자는 대표의 행위로 인하여 업무와 무관한 일을 해야 하는 등 근무환경이 악화됨

➡ **종합적 판단**
　　ㅇ 직장 내 괴롭힘에 해당되는 것으로 판단

Ⅵ. 직장 내 괴롭힘 판단례 6 : 불인정 사례

1. 행위내용 및 사실관계

의류회사 디자인팀장은 조만간 있을 하계 신상품 발표회를 앞두고, 소속 팀원에게 새로운 제품디자인 보고를 지시함. 디자인 담당자가 수차례 시안을 보고하였으나, 팀장은 회사의 이번 시즌 신제품 콘셉트와 맞지 않는다는 이유로 보완을 계속 요구하였고, 이로 인해 디자인 담당자는 업무량이 늘어났으며 스트레스를 받음

2. 직장 내 괴롭힘 판단

① 행위자: 디자인팀장
② 피해자: 디자인 담당자
③ 행위장소: 사업장 내

④ Requirement of conduct

④-1. Use of superiority in position or relations in the workplace
○ Superiority of position as team leader was used.

④-2. Exceeding occupationally bearable limits
○ Repeatedly giving team members work criticism, assessment, and directions for improving the design of products was necessary for work, and the pattern of behavior was not deemed inappropriate in view of social norms.

④-3. Inflicting physical or mental suffering or aggravating work environment
○ The employee in concern was placed under occupational stress.

➡ **Comprehensive determination**
○ The act was determined to not constitute workplace harassment.
- Regarding acts "exceeding occupationally bearable limits," the alleged harasser, as a team leader responsible for the overall designs of the company, holds the occupational authority to give criticism and directions regarding work to improve performance before a new product presentation, and did not commit inappropriate behaviors to that end. Therefore, even if some team members were placed under occupational stress, such acts do not constitute workplace harassment under the LSA.

VII. Determining Workplace Harassment Example 7 (Unrecognized Case)

1. Content of Harassment and Matters of Fact

Mr. Kim, a sales branch manager who had spent ten years at this company, was the sole employee from among those who joined the company in the same year, who had not been promoted to a sales branch head. Though an A grade in efficiency rating was required for promotion, an executive director who rates efficiency again gave him a B grade for his performance following the previous year. Considering that his branch head had also received a B grade from the executive director, it seemed that performance of the branch had fallen short of other branches. Mr. Kim, however, felt that the executive director had intentionally blocked his promotion with the B grade, as he expected that his superior would be considerate of the fact that he was awaiting promotion.

④ 행위요건
④-1. 직장에서의 지위 또는 관계 등의 우위 이용 여부
   ○ 직속 관리자라는 지위의 우위를 이용
④-2. 업무상 적정범위를 넘었는지 여부
   ○ 신제품의 디자인 향상을 위해 부서원에 대해 업무 독려 및 평가, 지시 등을 수 차례 실시하는 정도의 행위는 업무상 필요성이 있으며, 그 양태가 사회 통념상 상당하지 않다고도 보기 어려운 상황
④-3. 신체적·정신적 고통을 주거나 근로환경을 악화시켰는지 여부
   ○ 해당 근로자로서는 업무상 스트레스를 받음

➡ **종합적 판단**
○ 직장 내 괴롭힘에 해당되지 않는 것으로 판단
- '업무상 적정범위를 넘었는지 여부'와 관련하여 행위자인 팀장은 회사의 디자인을 총괄하는 담당자로서 새로운 제품 발표회를 앞두고 성과 향상을 위하여 부서원의 업무에 대해 독려 및 지시를 할 수 있는 업무상 권한이 존재하며, 이를 수행하기 위해 다른 부적절한 행위를 한 바도 없으므로 일부 업무상 부서원이 스트레스를 받았다 하더라도 이는 「근로기준법」 상 직장 내 괴롭힘에 해당한다고 볼 수 없음

Ⅶ. 직장 내 괴롭힘 판단례 7 : 불인정 사례

1. 행위내용 및 사실관계

입사 10년차의 영업소 매니저 김씨는 입사 동기 중 유일하게 아직 영업소장으로 승진하지 못함. 다음 인사에서 승진하기 위해서는 이번 근무평정에서 A등급이 꼭 필요하나, 평정자인 본부장은 김씨의 근무성적을 지난번에 이어 B등급으로 통보함. 김씨의 영업소장도 본부장 평가에서 B등급으로 통보받은 것으로 보아 영업소 실적이 다른 지점에 비해 어지는 건 사실로 보이지만, 승진을 앞둔 자신에 대한 상사의 배려를 기대하였던 김씨는 B등급이 나오자 본부장이 본인의 승진을 고의적으로 막는 게 아닐까하는 생각으로 괴로움

Section 1. Cases Studies for Workplace Harassment (MOEL)

2. Determination of Harassment in the Workplace

① Harasser: an executive director
② Victim: a sales branch manager
③ Place of harassment: inside establishment
④ Requirements for harassment
④-1. Use of superiority in position or relations in the workplace
   ○ Superiority in position as an executive director who has an authority in rating efficiency was used.
④-2. Exceeding occupationally bearable limits
   ○ Due to their poor performance in managing a sales branch, the executive director gave B grades (a grade lower than the highest grade A) to the head and manager of a sales branch. This is a weak basis for being considered unnecessary for work or inappropriate.
④-3. Inflicting physical or mental suffering or aggravating work environment
   ○ The victim suffered mental distress after being excluded as a candidate for promotion due to the efficiency grade.

➡ Comprehensive determination
   ○ The act was determined to not constitute workplace harassment. Giving a low grade to an individual responsible for the management of a sales branch in response to the objective fact of the poor performance of that sales branch falls under the justifiable scope of the assessor's work responsibilities and authority. Unless other facts that can be deemed unreasonable assessment or intentional harassment, such as the giving of low grades to high performers, exist, even though the employee suffered as a result of the act, it does not constitute harassment in the workplace under the LSA.

2. 직장 내 괴롭힘 판단

① 행위자: 본부장
② 피해자: 영업소 매니저
③ 행위장소: 사업장 내
④ 행위요건
④-1. 직장에서의 지위 또는 관계 등의 우위 이용 여부
ㅇ 근무평정권한이 있는 본부장으로서의 지위의 우위를 이용
④-2. 업무상 적정범위를 넘었는지 여부
ㅇ 영업소의 실적 부진에 대하여 영업소 관리책임이 있는 영업소장과 매니저에 대하여 최우수 등급(A등급)의 하위인 B등급을 부여한 것에 대하여 업무상 필요성이 없거나 상당하지 않다고 볼 근거가 미약함
④-3. 신체적·정신적 고통을 주거나 근로환경을 악화시켰는지 여부
ㅇ 근무평정 결과로 인하여 승진 대상에서 누락되어 정신적으로 괴로움

➡ **종합적 판단**
ㅇ 직장 내 괴롭힘에 해당되지 않는 것으로 판단
- 영업소 실적 부진이라는 객관적 사실을 이유로 영업소의 관리책임자에 대하여 근무평정에서 상위등급 이하의 평정을 부과한 것은 평정자의 정당한 업무범위(권한)에 속하는 사항임
- 성과우수자에 대한 평가 저하 등 불합리한 평가 또는 의도적 괴롭힘으로 볼 수 있는 다른 사실관계가 존재하지 않는 이상, 근로자 입장에서 승진 누락에 대한 괴로운 심정은 있다고 하더라도 이를 「근로기준법」 상 직장 내 괴롭힘으로 볼 수 는 없음

Section 2. Labor Cases relate to Workplace Harassment[112]

⟨ Reference Examples of Verified and Possible Workplace Harassment ⟩

It is impossible to uniformly enumerate acts recognizable as workplace harassment as such acts vary widely in form, and a determination requires a comprehensive consideration of a variety of circumstances. However, examples from actual cases reported in the media, court decisions, and cases counseled by private organizations for public rights are provided below.
➡ When an act of potential harassment is actually committed, whether the act meets the respective legal requirements to be considered as workplace harassment should be determined based on a detailed account of the act and the facts surrounding it.

❖ For professors to realize and be able to fulfill their personality rights, they must be able to lecture on their major disciplines and conduct further academic study. However, one incorporated educational institute assigned an employed professor to give lectures on subjects irrelevant to that professor's major discipline—without any special circumstances necessary to exercise its right to supervise operations—with the sole intent of excluding the professor from his original duties. This resulted in the professor failing to deliver lectures. (Supreme Court Decision 2006da30730 Delivered on June 26, 2008: Recognition of an Incorporated Education Institute's Accountability for Damages)

❖ Assistant jobs were given to an employee upon her return from maternity leave rather than her original duties. In a meeting excluding the victim, other employees were also directed to exclude her to drive her out of the company. Following that order, directions were given to remove the victim's desk and disallow her from sitting at the counter, with remarks being made that the victim was no longer considered an employee, all actions which constitute discriminatory treatment. (Gwangju District Court Decision 2012na10375 Delivered on Oct 246, 2008: Recognition of Accountability for Damages)

---

[112] Ministry of Employment and Labor, 「Workplace Bullying Determination, Prevention and Response Manual, February 2019

제2절 직장 내 괴롭힘 관련 주요 사례[112]

〈 직장 내 괴롭힘으로 볼 수 있는 사례 〉

> 직장 내 괴롭힘은 그 양태가 매우 다양하고 여러 가지 사정을 종합적으로 판단해야 하는 만큼 직장 내 괴롭힘을 볼 수 있는 행위를 일률적으로 열거하는 데에는 한계가 있으나, 언론 보도, 판례 사안, 민간공익단체(직장갑질119) 상담사례 등 우리나라에서 실제 발생한 사례를 토대로 법상 직장 내 괴롭힘으로 볼 수 있는 행위를 예시하면 아래와 같음(단, ➡ 해당 행위가 실제 발생되면 법상 직장 내 괴롭힘의 개별 요건에 부합하는지에 대하여 구체적인 행위 내용, 사실관계 등을 토대로 판단되어야 함)

❖ 대학교수는 자신의 전공분야에 대해 강의하고 이를 통해 자신의 학문 연구를 보다 발전시키는 것이 인격권 실현의 본질적 부분에 해당하므로, 대학교수의 사용자인 학교 법인이 그 업무지휘권 등의 행사에 지장을 초래하는 등의 특별한 사정이 없는데도, 오로지 소속 대학교수를 본연의 업무에서 배제하려는 의도하에 그 의사에 반하여 전공분야와 관련 없는 과목의 강의를 배정함으로써 결국 강의할 수 없게 함(대법원 2008. 6. 26. 선고 2006다30730 판결: 학교법인의 손해배상책임 인정)

❖ 육아휴직 후 복직한 직원에게 전에 담당하던 업무가 아닌 보조업무를 주고, 직원을 퇴출시키기 위한 따돌림을 지시한 사건. 피해자를 제외한 다른 직원들만 참석한 회의에서 피해자를 내쫓기 위하여 따돌림을 할 것을 지시하는 취지의 내용을 전달하였으며, 이후 책상을 치우고 창구에 앉지 못하게 할 것을 지시, 그를 직원으로 생각하지 않는다는 취지의 발언을 하는 등 차별적인 대우를 함(광주지방법원 2012. 10. 24 선고 2012나10375 판결: 손해배상책임 인정)

---

[112] 고용노동부, 「직장 내 괴롭힘 판단 및 예방, 대응 매뉴얼」, 2019. 2.

Section 2. Labor Cases relate to Workplace Harassment

- ❖ A senior employee repeatedly harassed a junior employee, saying that unless the victim held a drinking meeting, he would ensure personnel disadvantages. The senior employee insisted that the junior employee "organize a drinking meeting," and questioned why that employee "had not set a date?" The harasser also insisted that the victim "write a statement of reasons," and stated that the junior employee "should spend 30% of incentives in treating a senior." Such demands were repeatedly handed down and the victim was made to write apologies and explanations. (District Court Decision 2014gohap207 Delivered on Aug 28, 2015: Recognition of Attempted Coercion)

- ❖ An employee who opposed being excluded from a list of promotion candidates was harassed while protesting against the recommendation for voluntary retirement. The victim was ostracized in the workplace, and given discriminatory treatment including assault while protesting against the change in his duties, having work-related materials and his ID card taken, being made to work from a meeting room and then removing the desk and chairs form the meeting room, being prohibited from using a computer, and being excluded from an e-mail distribution list. (Seoul Administrative Court Decision 2006gu34224Delivered on Aug 14, 2000: Recognition of Industrial Accident Compensation for Consequential Mental Illness)

- ❖ A disabled individual who worked for a school library under a public job program was physically punished. The victim was prohibited from touching electronic devices such as computers, was hit with a plastic ruler on the palm, or made to keep his arm raised when violating instructions. (NHRCK representation case: 17jinjeong0169100)

- ❖ An employee was ostracized by colleagues. Harassers intentionally ignored the victim and frequently committed verbal violence including sneering, reproach, and swearing. Furthermore, the victim was not provided with air-conditioning in the summer or heating in the winter. (NHRCK representation case: 16jinjeong0186100)

- ❖ A deputy principal of a school used swear words and other abusive language which intimidated teachers. When a request was made to approve a formal document, the harasser smashed a table, yelled, and referred to teachers simply as "You!" The harasser also intentionally refused approvals, thereby interrupting work, and intimidated with disadvantages including dismissal. When one teacher

❖ 가해자인 선배가 후배인 피해자에게 술자리를 마련하지 않으면 인사상 불이익을 주겠다고 반복하여 말한 사건. "술자리를 만들어라", "아직도 날짜를 못 잡았느냐", "사유서를 써와라", "성과급의 30%는 선배를 접대하는 것이다" 등 반복적으로 술자리를 갖자는 발언을 하고 시말서, 사유서를 쓰게 한 행위 (대전지방법원 2015. 8. 28. 선고, 2014고합207 판결: 강요미수죄 인정)

❖ 승진대상에서 누락되어 반발한 직원이 명예퇴직 권고대상자로 선정된 후 이에 항변하는 과정에서 괴롭힘을 당한 사건. 업무변경과 관련한 문제를 따지는 과정에서 폭행, 업무용 물품 및 ID를 회수, 자리를 회의용 탁자로 이동시키고 이후 회의용 탁자와 의자 회수, 피해자가 컴퓨터를 쓰지 못하게 하고, 직원들에게 전자우편 동시 발송 시 피해자를 제외하도록 지시하는 등 직장 내에서의 따돌림, 차별적 대우(서울행법 2000.8.14. 선고2000구 34224판결: 이로 인한 정신적 질환에 대한 산재보상 인정)

❖ 공공일자리 사업으로 학교도서관에 근무하는 장애인에 대한 체벌 사건. 피해자에게 컴퓨터 등 전자기기를 만지지 못하게 하고, 이를 어기면 피해자의 손바닥을 플라스틱 자로 때리고 손을 들어 벌을 서게 함(인권위 진정사건: 17진정0169100)

❖ 동료 간 피해자에 대한 따돌림 사건. 피해자를 의도적으로 무시하고, 피해자 면전 에서 비웃음, 비난, 욕설 등 수시로 언어폭력을 가하고, 겨울, 여름에는 피해자에게 보일러나 에어컨 등을 제공하지 않고 가해자들 끼리만 사용함 (인권위 진정사건: 16진정0186100)

❖ 학교 교감이 같은 학교 소속 교사들을 상대로 욕설, 위협 등을 행한 사건. 학교 교감이 교사들에게 결재요 청을 받자 책상을 내리치고 고함을 지르며, '야', '너' 등의 호칭을 사용하거나, 결재서류를 고의적으로 반려하고 지연시켜 업무를 방해하고, 해고 등을 언급하며불이익으로 위협하는 등 폭언을 가함. 컨설팅을 받지 않겠다는 의견을 말하는 교사의 팔을

refused to undertake consulting, the harasser attempted intimidation by grabbing the teacher's arm and yelling. (NHRCK representation case: 12jinjeong0974000)

- ❖ A vice-chair continuously used abusive language including swear words to his chauffeur because he did not like the chauffeur's driving. He also hit the chauffeur's head from behind while being driven and forced the chauffeur to drive with the rearview and side-view mirrors folded, causing the victim extreme stress.

- ❖ A company-level direction was handed down to place the desks of office workers who refused voluntary retirement to face lockers (the so-called work-facing-the-wall). One employee, from among twenty individuals the company selected as voluntary retirement candidates, refused voluntary retirement. The work-facing-the-wall direction was given, and the victim was made to report any time he was out of his position for over ten minutes. He was also prohibited from smoking or making personal calls at times other than during recesses. His wages were reduced as punishment for using his personal laptop, and his duties were changed to include material management, which was not related with his usual office work.

- ❖ For more than six decades since being established, a company has maintained the practice of forcing female employees to leave upon getting married. Female employees who refused to leave were coerced to quit through a hostile work environment and inappropriate personnel measures.

- ❖ Company-level "measures to manage reinstated employees" were developed and used against an employee who had been reinstated following an unfair dismissal decision. The victim's work environment was systematically aggravated with the victim being made to work in front of restroom, placed under concentrated absenteeism and tardiness management, and given highly intense work directions.

- ❖ A boss held up a soju bottle and threatened to strike an employee at a company dinner and also squeezed the victim's neck in front of customers. The harasser continuously bullied the victim, humiliating him by throwing paper at him at a gathering attended by a general manager and other colleagues, and by forcing him to stand still and vow repeatedly.

잡아끌고 고함을 지르는 등 위협을 함(인권위 진정사건: 12진정097
4000)

❖ 부회장이 운전기사에게 운전이 마음에 들지 않는다며 지속적으로 폭언, 욕설을 하고, 때로는 운전 중인 운전기사의 머리를 뒤에서 가격하며 마구 때리기도 함. 룸 미러와 사이드미러를 접은 상태에서 운전하도록 하여 피해자는 극도의 스트레스 속에서 운전업무를 함

❖ 기업 차원에서 명예퇴직을 거부하는 사무직 직원에게 사물함만 바라보도록 자리를 배치하는 일명 면벽근무를 지시함. 피해자는 회사가 명예퇴직 대상자로 통보한 20명 중 한 명이었으나, 피해자가 명예퇴직을 거부하자 이러한 면벽근무를 지시하였으며, 10분 이상 자리를 비우면 상급자에게 보고, 쉬는 시간 이외에 흡연, 개인 전화 등을 금지 시킴. 개인 노트북 사용을 이유로 보안규정 위반으로 감봉 징계를 하기도 하고, 사무업무와 아무런 관련 없는 자재관리로 배치전환을 하기도 함

❖ 창사 이래 60여 년 동안 결혼하는 여성 직원을 예외 없이 퇴사시키는 관행을 유지. 결혼으로 인한 퇴사를 거부하는 여성 직원에게는 근무환경을 적대적으로 만들거나 부적절한 인사 조치를 통해 퇴사를 강요함

❖ 부당해고 판정으로 받고 복직한 직원에 대해 기업 차원에서 '복직자 관리 방안'을 만들어 화장실 앞에서 근무하도록 지시, 다른 근로자들에 비하여 집중적인 근태 관리, 고강도의 업무지시를 시키는 계획을 수립하고 실제 해당 방안과 유사하게 피해자의 근무환경을 악화시키는 조치를 취함

❖ 회식자리에서 직장 상사가 소주병을 거꾸로 쥐어 잡고 피해자를 가격하려고 위협하고, 고객들 앞에서도 피해자의 목을 짓누르는 신체적 폭력을 가하기도 함. 또한 부장님과 다른 직장동료가 한자리에 모인 자리에서 피해자에게 종이를 던지며 모욕을 주는 행위를 가하기도 하고, 차렷 자세로 인사를 반복적으로 시키는 등 지속적인 괴롭힘을 가함

Section 2. Labor Cases relate to Workplace Harassment

- ❖ While receiving on-the-job training from the owner, a new restaurant employee was punched in the chest and arm and choked until he was out of breath because the owner did not like the victim's attitude for learning. The owner demanded that 10,000 won be subtracted from the victim's salary whenever he threw away what the victim cooked, saying it tasted horrible, leading to the victim having to remit 490,000 won to the owner from his salary.

- ❖ While being reported, a boss demanded, "Why? Is it wrong? Put your hand on the table." The boss then held the victim's left middle finger while pretending to cut it with a box cutter, creating a frightening atmosphere.

- ❖ A regional headquarters manager responsible for decisions on contract renewal often used violent and intimidating words on a whim. He was heard to exclaim "If you are not capable enough, you have to lobby with your body, Fxxx," "Fxxx, don't you have a brain? Do I have to swear to get things done?" and "Crazy bitxx, you can't work nowhere but here."

- ❖ A director gave work directions and nagged foreign and Korean workers with abusive language including swear words. He also verbally insulted workers by saying they needed to work with windows open because of their body odor. The harasser drank outside of the office during working hours, returned to the office, and told one employee to quit while swearing at him. When the victim refused, he smashed a glass table in the office and called in all workers using swear words and other abusive language, making them clean up the broken glass. The harasser committed his abnormal acts including cutting stairs using an oxygen cutter and hammer to intimidate the victim, as well as destroying an office while driving a company fork lift under the influence of alcohol.

- ❖ A boss posted whiny messages in his team's mobile messenger group chat room while drunk after office hours or on weekend evenings. When nobody replied, he demanded replies and asked why none were replying, thereby causing suffering to his team members. Furthermore, when his opinions were not accepted, he yelled at and bullied employees, causing mental distress.

- 요식업에 취업하여 사장에게 일을 배우던중 사장은 피해자의 배우는 태도가 마음에 들지 않는다며, 주먹으로 흉부나 팔 부분을 폭행하고 숨이 넘어갈 정도로 목을 조르기도 함. 사장은 피해자가 만든 요리를 못 보고 맛이 없어 버릴 때마다 월급에서 만 원씩 제한다고 하면서 실제로 월급에서 49만 원을 다시 사장 계좌로 보내라고 하여 그렇게 한 적도 있음

- 상사에게 업무를 보고하던 중 "왜 틀렸어?, 손 올려봐"라고 하면서 피해자의 왼손 중지를 잡고 커터칼로 피해자의 왼손중지를 자르려는 행동을 하는 등 공포 분위기를 조성함

- 재계약 결정권을 갖고 있는 지역본부 매니저는 기분에 따라 "능력 안 되면 몸빵이 라도 해야지 씨○~~", "씨○, 대가리 안 쓰냐? 내가 입에 걸레를 물어야 돌아가냐?", "미친○ 너네들 어차피 갈 데 없잖아"라는 등의 잦은 폭언과 협박을 함

- 사내이사는 현장에 근무하는 외국인 근로자와 내국인 근로자에게 폭언과 욕설로 업무지시와 잔소리를 함. 뿐만 아니라 직원에게 몸에서 냄새가 난다고 근무할 때 창문을 활짝 열어놓고 근무하라고 모욕을 주는 등 폭언은 점점 심해짐 또한 근무시간에 외부에서 술을 먹고 사무실에 와서 욕설을 하며 피해자에게 그만두라고 하고, 이에 반박하자 사무실 유리 테이블을 박살 내고 모든 근로자를 욕설과 폭언으로 불러서 깨진 유리를 청소시킴. 또한 피해자를 위협하기 위해 산소절단기와 해머를 이용해 계단을 절단하거나, 음주상태에서 회사 포크레인을 직접 몰고 사무실을 손괴하는 등 비정상적인 행동을 함

- 상사가 퇴근 이후 주말, 저녁 시간에 술에 취해서 팀 모바일메신저단체 채팅방에 하소연하는 글을 올리고 대답 안하면 대답 왜 안하냐고 답을 요구하여 팀원들이 힘들어 함. 상사 본인 의지대로 안 되면 직원들에게 소리를 지르고 윽박지르는 등의 행위로 정신적 고통을 유발함

Section 2. Labor Cases relate to Workplace Harassment

- ❖ With other employees present, a branch head told a victim, "You used to be gorgeous and slender. If I had not been married, I could have done something to you," and "Let's have a romantic relationship." He also repeatedly sexually harassed and molested other young female employees. The victim requested that the regional headquarters take measures, but was ignored, and when the victim raised the issue at corporate headquarters, the harasser threatened to sue the victim over false accusations and continued to harass her, causing her continued suffering from secondary victimization.

- ❖ In addition to their original duties, employees were tasked with carrying out the CEO's personal errands and given roles such as chauffeur and personal assistant. One employee was made to remove snow from the vehicle of the CEO's wife following a heavy snowfall with bear hands. Employees were even mobilized to harvest and sell corn from the CEO's personal fields, but the conservative corporate culture prevented the issue from being raised.

- ❖ A CEO poured different types of alcohol into a large bowl and coerced employees—regardless of gender—to binge drink. Regardless of their personal affairs, employees were required to go at the CEO's bidding, and he retaliated against employees' refusal by making their office lives difficult. During a company dinner at a Chinese restaurant, female workers were forced to drink soju and beer mixed in the bowls of jajangmyeon that they had finished.

- ❖ Employees were forced to prepare a talent show for every company event, and were directed to practice during recesses including lunch breaks. On one occasion, they were instructed to prepare a talent show in the style of "The King of Mask Singer," a popular singing competition program. Employees were coerced to sing in masks and costumes that they had personally prepared in front of the chair of directors, a director general, and other employees.

- ❖ A CEO directed five employees to explain a mistake in front of all employees. Notes were also circulated to other employees, asking them to choose measures they thought should be taken from amongst several choices: advising them to resign, assigning them to a production line and giving them a pay cut, giving them a pay-cut for six months, and finding them not guilty (10% pay-cut for the CEO and all employees). The CEO had the results posted on the employee's mobile messenger group chat room, humiliating the concerned employees. He

❖ 지점장은 직원들이 있는 자리에서 피해자에게 "예전에 엄청 이쁘고 날씬했었는데 내가 결혼만 안했으면 너 어떻게 해보고 싶었는데", "연애하자" 등의 발언을 하고, 어린 여직원에게도 손에 꼽을 수 없을 정도로 성희롱과 추행을 일삼음. 피해자는 지사에 조치를 취해줄 것을 요구했지만 묵살됐고, 본사에 문제를 제기하자 지점장은 무고죄로 고소할 것이라고 협박하고, 계속해서 괴롭히는 등 피해자는 신고를 이유로 2차 피해를 당함

❖ 본래 업무에 더하여 대표의 개인적인 일까지 보며 운전기사, 수행비서 역할까지 하였고, 눈이 많이 온 날 맨손으로 대표의 부인 자동차 눈 제거 작업까지 시킴. 직원을 동원해 대표 개인 밭의 옥수수 수확과 판매까지 시키지만, 회사 분위기가 워낙 보수적인 곳이라 이에 대한 문제제기도 할 수 없는 분위기임

❖ 회사 대표가 냉면사발에 술을 섞어서 마시도록 하는 등 직원들에게 폭음을 강요함. 이는 성별에 상관없이 무조건적임. 직원들의 개인 사정은 상관없고 무조건으로 오라고 하면 가야하고, 거절하면 회사생활을 힘들게 하는 등 어떤 식으로든지 보복을 하여 어쩔 수 없이 불려나갈 수밖에 없음. 실례로 중국집 회식에서 여직원들에게 짜장면을 먹고 난 그릇에 소주와 맥주를 섞어 마시도록 강요한 적도 있음

❖ 회사에서 행사가 있을 때마다 직원들에게 장기자랑 준비를 강요. 이를 위해 점심시간 등 휴게시간까지 연습을 지시하고, 복면가왕과 같은 장기자랑을 준비하라며 가면이나 복장까지도 개인적으로 준비하도록 함. 이를 입고 이사장, 국장, 직원들 앞에서 노래를 부르도록 강요함

❖ 대표는 5명의 직원들에게 전직원 앞에서 무엇을 잘못했는지 설명하라는 지시를 하고, 이후 다른 직원들에게 쪽지를 나눠주면서 5명의 직원에 대해 권고사직, 생산직 발령 및 급여 강등, 6개월감봉, 무죄(대표이사, 전직원 10% 감봉) 중 어떠한 처분이 적절한지 적어 내라고 함, 그 결과를 직원들 모바일메신저단체채팅방에 올려 공유하도록 지시하는 등 해당

Section 2. Labor Cases relate to Workplace Harassment

frequently used swear words and other abusive language, and he sometimes even claimed that if he died, he would kill them all before he died.

❖ A boss continuously harassed an employee wearing outer clothing or a mask because of the cold, and used insults such as "Did you ever wash your padding?" and "Your clothing stinks." He also pointed out the victim's clothing and bags in front of others, asking "Did you buy it for 3,000 won?" and saying "All the things you use are cheap."

❖ A newly transferred director did not like an employee and ordered all employees, including the victim's subordinates, to ostracize the victim. As a result, the victim had to eat lunch alone, feeling pressure to voluntarily quit.

❖ After the CEO of a customer company set up a blind date for an employee of the primary company, her boss accused her of being "a female worker who played around with the customer company CEO." The CEO demanded that she break up with her new boyfriend arguing, "you risk revealing corporate secrets to the customer company, and I will not take the risk of continuing to employee you." The harasser also threatened to have her boyfriend fired using personal connections, and spread rumors, leading to her becoming ostracized.

❖ A boss repeatedly requested written apologies from an employee even though that employee had not committed any unlawful act or violation of company rules. Though the victim inevitably wrote such apologies, the harasser continued asking for additional written apologies and coerced the victim to involuntarily write statements such as "I will take any punishment." Under the pretext of capacity building, the harasser asked the victim to write book reports, to which the victim agreed, but then continued giving unreasonable peremptory demands, including the instruction to watch an entire drama series (episode 1-20) and write a report. Such demands consumed both the victim's working and personal time and continued to cause suffering to the victim.

직원들을 모욕함. 수시로 직원들에게 욕설을 하고, 본인이 죽게 되면 너희들을 먼저 다 죽이고 죽겠다는 등 입에 담을 수 없는 막말을 함

❖ 피해자가 감기에 걸려 겉옷을 입거나 마스크를 착용하는 것에 대해 상사가 지속적인 비난을 하고, 직원들 앞에서 "패딩은 세탁해서 입고는 다니냐", "옷에서 냄새가 난다"는 등의 모욕적 발언을 함. 또한 직원들 앞에서 피해자가 입고 다니는 옷과 가방 등을 지적하며 "3천원 주고 산거냐", "시장에서 산 물건만 쓴다"는 등의 모욕 감을 줌

❖ 새로운 부임한 상무는 피해자가 마음에 들지 않는다면서 피해자의 부하직원들을 포함하여 회사 직원들로 하여금 피해자를 왕따 시키도록 하고, 이로 인해 피해자는 점심식사도 혼자하게 됨. 사실상 자발적으로 퇴사하도록 압박하는 것으로 느껴짐

❖ 거래처 사장으로부터 소개팅을 받았다는 이유로 상사가 "거래처 사장과 놀아난 여직원"이라며 회사 내에서 말하고, "거래처에 회사 기밀을 노출 시 킬 위험이 있다. 그런 위험을 감수하면서까지 널 데리고 있을 수 없다."라고 하며 애인과 헤어질 것을 요구 함. 또한 인맥을 이용해서 애인을 해고당하게 하겠다는 등의 협박도 하고, 직원들에게 실제 있지도 않은 얘기를 퍼뜨림으로써 회사에서 따돌림을 당하게 함

❖ 상사가 특별한 위법행위나 회사 내규를 위반한 사항이 없음에도 시말서를 요구하고, 이에 부득이 시말서를 작성했음에도 추가적인 시말서 작성을 계속 요구하거나, '어떠한 처벌도 감수하겠다'는 등의 비자발적인 문장을 기재할 것을 강요함. 역량강화라는 이유로 독후감 작성을 요구하여 이에 따라 왔으나, 피해자에게만 드라마 전편(1~20화)을 시청하고 독후감을 작성해 오라는 등 이해할 수 없는 독단적 지시를 계속함. 이러한 지시는 업무시간 외 집에서 개인적인 시간을 할애해야 하는 것으로 계속된 지시에 괴로움

Section 2. Labor Cases relate to Workplace Harassment

- ❖ A company tried to coerce an employee to sign a labor contract with degraded working conditions. After the victim refused, company representatives ostracized the victim by unilaterally changing the office passcode and the victim's personal computer password to block access. The victim was also kicked out of the work messenger service.

- ❖ After pointing out unreasonable issues when adjusting work duties, the head of a team assigned an employee with duties that were completely different from what that person had previously done. Without allowing for discussion on the issue, and despite the difficult situation this change caused, the irrelevantly assigned duty assignment was upheld, resulting in the victim leaving the company.

- ❖ After an employee's shift changed from a night-day rotation to day-time, the team leader began to ostracize him within the company, arguing that the change resulted in increased work intensity for colleagues. The victim was then kept on stand-by without working for three days, and was forced to sit at his table without any work. Though the victim requested that he be assigned work, he was excluded from carrying out his actual duties, instead being assigned miscellaneous work and cleaning duties.

- ❖ An employee was forced to do chores irrelevant to duties, including plucking the boss' grey hair, grilling and peeling corn and sweet potatoes, cooking ramyeon, and giving massages. The victim was forced to eat any food leftover by the boss and to eat it in its entirety simply because the victim was the youngest.

- ❖ An employee who worked at a gas station suffered from abusive language and violence from customers, but the employer neglected this issue and forced the victim to sign an agreement in relation to a criminal case. The employer also made the victim work in a vegetable garden or on his personal land, and used abusive language, including swear words, when the victim refused. He also called the victim in to work on holidays, and when the victim arrived after such a call, the employer swore and used violent language with the employee for being late by as little as three minutes.

- ❖ CCTVs were installed inside a company and were monitored by a middle manager. Despite not being assigned with monitoring the entrance, and having an

❖ 근로조건을 하향하는 근로계약을 강요하여 이를 거절하자, 회사는 사무실 비밀번호와 피해자 개인 컴퓨터의 비밀번호를 일방적으로 바꾸어 접근을 막고, 업무용 메신저에서 피해자를 강퇴 시키는 등 노골적으로 따돌림

❖ 업무 조정 시 불합리한 점을 제기하자, 부서장이 그간에 하지 않던 전혀 다른 업무를 아무런 협의 없이 부여하고, 이로 인해 힘든 상황에서도 피해자가 수행할 수 없는 본래 업무와 관련 없는 직무를 계속해서 부여하여 피해자가 이를 견디지 못하고 사직함

❖ 주야간 근무를 하다가 상시주간업무로 변경되었는데, 이로 인해 다른 동료들의 업무강도가 강해졌다며 팀장이 회사 내에서 왕따를 시키기 시작함. 이후 일을 시키지 않다가 출근대기를 3주 시키고 그 이후에는 아무런 기약도 없이 책상에만 앉아 있게 함. 업무부여를 요청하였으나, 업무에서 배제된 채 청소나 잡일 등만을 지시함

❖ 상사의 지시로 상사의 흰머리 뽑기, 옥수수와 고구마 껍질 까고 굽기, 라면 끓이기, 안마 등 업무와 관련 없는 온갖 잡일을 해야 했음. 상사가 먹고 남은 음식을 모두 먹으라고 했고, 막내라는 이유로 음식을 남기지도 못하게 함

❖ 주유소 주유원인 피해자는 별다른 잘못 없이 고객에게 폭언, 폭행을 당하였으나, 사업주는 이를 방치하고 이와 관련한 형사사건에서 피해자에게 형사 합의서를 작성 할 것을 종용함. 또한 사업주의 텃밭이나 개인 땅에서 막노동을 시키고, 이를 거절 하면 폭언과 욕을 함. 휴일에 전화해서 출근하라고 하고, 이에 갑자기 출근하면서 약 3분 정도만 늦어도 폭언과 욕을 함

❖ 회사 내에 CCTV가 설치되어 있고 해당 모니터가 중간관리자의 자리에 설치되어 있음. 출입구 등에 사람이 지키고 있지 않아 CCTV 외에는

office layout that did not allow for the direct monitoring of employee movement, the harasser observed employees from the screen and sent warning emails or messages in real-time. After observing employers having refreshments, the harasser would ask "Did you enjoy your refreshments?" thereby keeping them constantly aware that they were being watched.

- ❖ A sudden instruction for employees to come to work early in the morning was given by a boss via mobile messenger group chat early in the morning. Workers hurriedly came to work, but just before their arrival, the boss sent another message instructing them to come at the usual time. The boss sent group chat messages like this regardless of time — morning, noon, after office hours, 12 o'clock in the morning — but most of the messages were simply meant to nitpick and explain why his feelings had been hurt. He took out his aggressions on one employee who had not replied to a certain group chat message.

- ❖ An employee who performed personnel, administrative, and procurement duties at a subsidiary of a public corporation made an occupational error, which led to an aggravated relationship with the boss. The boss responded by using abusive language, including curses, and ostracized the employee in the workplace; the victim was excluded both internally and externally, and essential information was not provided. Furthermore, the victim was addressed simply as "You" rather than with the proper official title, and the boss publicly swore at the victim and threatened actions such as dismissal from the company trade union.

- ❖ An employee who worked for a mid-sized electronic parts company was recognized for good performance and selected to work in the headquarters sales department, but was at the same time under continuous pressure to recover the falling market share. The boss' grilling about performance went beyond ordinary levels to include abusive behavior and language. When a business trip did not produce good results, the boss continued the intimidating behavior including using abusive language and tearing up and throwing reports.

- ❖ Employees used in-house SNS to make sexually harassing remarks and smutty jokes about victims over a long period of time. Despite the imposition of sanctions against them, the harassers continued the behavior through SNS.

직원들의 움직임을 확인할 수 없는 구조임에도, 간식을 먹고 난 후 "간식은 맛있었냐"는 등 실시간으로 모니터로 직원들을 관찰하고, 경고메일, 메시지 등을 보내는 방식으로 감시 사실을 직원들에게 주지시킴

❖ 상사가 아침 일찍 갑자기 모바일메신저단체채팅으로 아무런 설명 없이 ○시까지 조기 출근하라고 지시하여 직원들이 급하게 출근하고 있었으나, 회사 도착 직전에 단체채팅으로 그냥 다음에 얘기하자며 정시 출근시간에 출근하라고 함. 이와 같이 아침, 점심, 퇴근 후, 밤 12시 할 것 없이 단체채팅을 하는데, 대부분 급한 전달상 황도 아니고 본인 감정이 상한 일들을 하나하나 따지는 말임. 이에 응답하지 않는 직원에 대하여는 모바일메신저 단체채팅 등을 통해 화풀이를 함

❖ 공기업 자회사에서 인사, 총무, 구매 등의 업무를 수행하던 피해자는 업무상 실수를 계기로 상사와 관계가 악화. 이후 상사로부터 욕설 등의 폭언뿐만 아니라 다른 직원들로부터도 따돌림을 당함. 구체적으로는 업무 내·외적으로 피해자를 의도적으로 배제하거나 필요한 정보를 제공하지 않기, 피해자를 부를 때 사내에서 부적절한 호칭(공식 직함이 아닌 "야! 너!" 등) 사용하기, 공개적인 자리에서 욕설하기, 노동조합으로부터의 해고에 대한 협박 등 다양한 행위가 있었음

❖ 중견 전자부품 회사에서 근무하던 피해자는 우수한 실적으로 본사 영업부로 발탁될 만큼 회사에서 인정을 받았으나, 시장 내에서 회사 점유율이 어지면서 시장점유율을 회복시키라는 압박을 지속적으로 받아 옴. 상사의 실적 추궁은 일반적인 수준 이상을 넘어 폭력적인 행동과 폭언을 동반함. 출장을 다녀온 후 결과가 좋지 않으면 폭언을 하고, 보고서를 찢고 집기를 던지는 등의 위협적인 행동을 지속함

❖ 가해자들은 장기간에 걸쳐 사내 SNS를 이용하여 피해자들에 대한 성희롱적 발언, 음담패설을 함. 다른 직원들로부터 제재를 받은 바 있음에도 SNS를 통한 가해자들의 행위는 지속됨

Section 2. Labor Cases relate to Workplace Harassment

- ❖ A preceptor (a kind of mentor) was assigned to a newly hired nurse. The preceptor began the practice of so-called "taeum," or burn-to-ashes culture, from the third day after the nurse began work. The preceptor made abusive statements such as "if you are going to quit, quit soon," "I really want to beat you up," and "can't you see? do I have to pull out your eyes and wash them?" Swear words were also used when the victim failed to finish work despite the fact that an inadequate amount of time was given to complete the work.

- ❖ While working in an operation room, a surgeon yelled at and talked down to nurses, threw surgical instrument, and swore (including the f-word), with more severe abuse being directed at newer nurses. As nurses began to quit because of the surgeon, the work loads of remaining nurses increased, and they were required to take on more night duties due to a shortage of nurses. Nurses requested resolution from the hospital due to the high demands, but the hospital sided with the surgeon and did not resolve the situation.

- ❖ A boss ordered a subordinate to write his doctoral thesis, and made the victim do his personal work—such as preparing presentations, gathering material for his outside lectures, and writing and marking tests—during office hours. As a result, the victim was required to complete work at home when he was unable to finish within working hours.

- ❖ An administration general manager directed an irregular cleaner worker to clean his house because he was moving. Though the work fell outside of the victim's regular duties, as the harasser held a superior position, the victim was forced to accept the task.

- ❖ A newly transferred boss selected several employees to use as personal trainers in the company gym. He also ordered them to massage him during and after workouts.

- ❖ A boss directed subordinates to secretly teach him English. The English lessons were not part of their regular duties, and were given in secret in company meeting rooms during office hours at the boss's direction and without consultation with executives or the HR team. The employees were forced to

❖ 신규간호사로 입사하자 업무를 가르쳐주는 프리셉터(일종의 멘토)가 배정됨. 프리셉터로부터 입사 3일째부터 태움이 시작됨. "그만 둘 거면 빨리 그만둬라.", "쥐어 팰 수도 없고", "이게 눈에 안보이냐? 눈깔을 빼서 씻어줄까?" 등 폭언을 하고, 시간 내에 완료할 수 없는 양의 업무를 부과하고는 못했다고 욕을 하기도 함

❖ 수술실 간호사로 근무 중인데, 한 수술의사는 수술할 때마다 간호사에게 소리를 지르거나 반말을 하고, "씨×, 씨×"하면서 욕하고 수술기구 던짐. 신참 간호사일수록 그 정도는 더욱 심함. 간호사들이 그 의사로 인해 퇴직을 많이 하다 보니 간호사 부족으로 남은 간호사는 업무가 더욱 가중되고 당직수도 늘어남 너무 힘들어 병원에 해결해 달라 요구했지만 병원은 의사 편만 들어 이를 제대로 해결해 주지 못함

❖ 상사가 본인의 대학원 박사 학위 논문 작성을 직원에게 시키고, 개인적인 외부 강의를 위한 프리젠테이션 자료 작성, 자료수집, 시험문제 출제, 채점 등의 업무를 근무시간에 직원에게 시킴. 이로 인해 직원은 근무시간도 부족하여 집으로 가져가 해야 하는 경우도 있었음

❖ 비정규직으로 청소업무에 근무 중에 행정부장이라는 상급자가 자신의 집이 이사를 하니 본인 집에 와서 집안 소를 지시함. 거절하기가 어려워 받아들일 수밖에 없었음

❖ 새로 부임한 상사가 직원들 몇 명을 뽑아 회사 내 체력단련장에서 개인 운동 트레이너 역할을 시키고, 운동 중간 그리고 운동이 끝난 후에 자신의 몸을 마사지하도록 지시함

❖ 상급자가 하급자에게 자신들에게 영어를 가르쳐 해줄 것을 지시함. 영어 교육에 사실에 대해서는 다른 사람에게 누설하지 말 것을 지시. 영어 교육은 업무 분장에도 없으며, 임원 및 다른 인사부서의 협의도 없이 상사의 지시만으로 회사 회의실에서 몰래 업무시간 중 진행함. 그 과정에

come to work an hour earlier than other employees when the boss directed them to scan over a 400-page English textbook.

- An owner operated a hotel which was situated nearby a restaurant owned by his father. The owner sent hotel employees on rotation to his father's restaurant and asked them to carry out jobs irrelevant to their original duties. The owner kept the hotel employees working in the other establishment (his father's restaurant) stating that he needed his father's financial assistance.

- The chair of a hospital board invited an outside training provider to provide training for nurses and doctors after working hours. Though participation was at first voluntary, as time went on, the training became mandatory, and many abusive words were spoken during the course. Employees had to pay between three and ten million won as educational costs, and employees who failed to pay were ostracized and received disadvantageous treatment regarding personal transfers.

- A company de facto coerced employees into running a marathon. Employees were required to exercise twice a week (with fines for being late or absent), write training logs, and submit group photos to prove the number of participants, and had to attend two-day overnight training programs in the spring and winter. Finally, employees were required to pay their own entry fees to take part in the marathon tournament.

- After a CEO turned down an employee's request to return after childcare leave, the employee complained to the MOEL and was reinstated. However, the employee was not reinstated with her previous bookkeeping duties, which she had performed for ten years before taking leave, but with marketing work under the technical sales department. In addition, a computer was not provided despite a promise to provide one after a month. When the victim arrived to work before 9:00, she was not allowed to go inside the office, and lunch break was from 12:00 to 13:00, but the victim was not allowed to come in before 13:00. Other employees were instructed to not have personal or work-related talk, and to record every conversation with her.

400페이지가 넘는 영어 교재를 스캔하도록 지시한 적도 있는 등 영어 교육을 위한 준비 때문에 다른 직원보다 1시간 일찍 출근할 수밖에 없었음

❖ 호텔에서 근무 중인데 사장의 아버지가 근처에서 식당을 하고 있음. 사장은 호텔 직원들을 돌아가면서 아버지 식당에 보내 숯불 올리는 일 등 본래 업무와 전혀 관련 없는 식당 일을 시킴. 사장은 아버지로부터 도움을 받아야 한다는 핑계로 직원들을 계속해서 다른 사업장(아버지 식당)에서 근무하도록 함

❖ 병원 이사장은 외부 교육기관을 불러 간호사, 의사 등을 대상으로 근무 시간 외에 교육을 실시함. 자율 참석이라고 하나 후반으로 갈수록 교육 참여가 강제가 되었고 그 과정에서 많은 폭언들이 있었음. 직원들은 교육비 명목으로 300만 원에서 많게는 1000만 원 이상을 냈는데 교육비를 내지 못한 직원은 왕따를 당하고 낸 직원들은 차기 인사에서 이익을 보았음

❖ 회사에서 마라톤을 사실상 강제로 실시함. 일주일에 주2회 참여(지각 및 결석 시 벌금 부과)해야 하고, 훈련일지 작성 및 참여인원 수 파악을 위한 인증사진을 제출 해야 함. 마라톤대회 출전 시에는 개인 사비로 출전해야 함. 1년에 1~2번씩 동계·춘계훈련 이름으로 1박2일 훈련을 강행함

❖ 육아휴직 후 복직하려 했으나, 사장은 복직시킬 의사가 없다고 하였고 이에 노동부에 진정을 제기한 결과 복직하게 됨. 복직 이후 10년간 해왔던 기존 경리업무가 아닌 기술영업부에 속해 마케팅 업무를 하도록 하고 업무용 컴퓨터 등은 한 달 후에 지급하겠다고 하고 지급하지 않음. 9시 이전에 출근해도 사무실에는 들어오지 못하게 하고, 점심시간도 12시부터 13시까지로 하되 13시 이전에는 사무실에 들어오지 못하게 함. 다른 직원들과 사적으로도, 업무적으로도 얘기하지 말라며, 모든 대화는 직원을 통해 녹취하겠다고 함

Section 2. Labor Cases relate to Workplace Harassment

❖ An employee began work as a deep learning research engineer as his three-year alternative service after obtaining a master's degree. In violation of the Military Service Act, the company used the knowledge that, if he left the company he would have to serve in the military, to coerce the employee into carrying out administrative duties. The research center head frequently threatened the employee in front of others saying, "I will not renew your contract, so leave."

❖ An employee became a whistle-blower by proxy after being asked to report by a colleague who had been sexually harassed by her direct boss. The victim told the harasser's boss about the sexual harassment but the harasser was informed of the whistle-blowing. Following the incident, the harasser frequently browbeat or wagged fingers at the victim, excluded the victim from team meetings, and made remarks that plainly disregarded the victim in front of other employees. Team members also took part in the harassment by ostracizing the victim.

❖ While working as a fixed-term irregular worker, a worker's boss frequently made humiliating remarks such as questioning "Will I give you a contract renewal or not?" or "We need to make an opening, who shall I fire, OO? or XX?" The victim politely asked the harasser not to make such remarks because they were humiliating. On the contrary, the harasser continued talking behind the victim's back to other employees, and as a result, the victim was the only fixed-term employee in the establishment whose contract was not renewed.

❖ At a company drinking party, the CEO forced all employees to drink alcohol by delivering it mouth-to-mouth. A male employee was disgusted and secretly spat out what he had received, so the CEO ordered that employee to repeat the same act and this time swallow the alcohol.

❖ A senior worker who was assisting in the delivery of home electronic appliances frequently swore at and physically assaulted him. When a customer provided water or other beverages, the senior employee drank by himself and did not allow the victim a sip, forcing the victim to drink tap water from the restroom. The senior employee also threw cigarettes he had been smoking and a lighter at the victim's face.

❖ 전문연구요원으로 대체복무 중이며 석사학위 취득 후 복무를 시작하여 복무기간은 총 3년임. 회사는 퇴사 할 경우 군 복무를 해야 한다는 약점을 이용하여 병역법에 위반되는 행정업무 등을 강요함. 연구소 책임자는 다른 사람들 앞에서 "재계약을 안해줄테니 나가라."라고 수시로 퇴사를 위협함

❖ 직속상사로부터 성추행을 당하곤 했던 직원의 부탁에 의해 대리자로서 내부고발을 함. 가해자의 성추행 사실을 가해자의 상사에게 얘기하였으나, 도리어 내부고발 한 사실을 가해자에게 바로 전달. 이후 그 상사는 수시로 피해자에게 윽박지르거나 삿대질하고, 회의에서 배제하거나 직원들 앞에서 대놓고 무시하는 발언을 계속함. 팀원들도 피해자를 따돌리는 등 상사의 괴롭힘에 동참함

❖ 기간제 비정규직으로 근무하고 있음. 직속상사인 부장은 수시로 '재계약을 해줄까 말까', '티오를 한 명 줄여야 하는데 ○○씨 자를까 아니면, ○○씨 자를까?'라고 비인격적인 발언을 수시로 함. 부장에게 그런얘기를 들을 때마다 비참한 생각이 드니 시정해달라고 정중히 요청하였으나, 해당 부장은 도리어 다른 직원들에게 피해자에 대한 험담을 계속하였고, 결과적으로도 피해자는 사업소의 기간제 근로자 중 유일하게 재계약 탈락함

❖ 회사 뒤풀이 술자리에서 사장은 술자리에 참여한 전 직원에게 술을 입에서 입으로 넘겨 전달해서 마시게 하는 행위를 강요함. 한 남직원이 너무 역겨워 입으로 넘겨 받은 술을 몰래 뱉자 사장은 왜뱉냐며 똑같은 행위를 다시 시켜 마시게 함

❖ 가전 배송일을 하는 부기사로 일을 하고 있는 피해자의 사수는 업무 미숙을 이유로 수시로 욕을 하고, 발길질에 손찌검까지 함. 배송 가서 고객이 물이나 음료수를 줘도 혼자 다 마시고 피해자는 마시지도 못하게 하여 목이 너무 말라 화장실에 가서 수돗물을 마신 적도 있음. 피우던 담배나 라이터를 얼굴로 던진 적도 있음

❖ When a senior manager came to work feeling upset about personal issues, he criticized and harassed anyone around him. He also repeated abnormal behavior and insults such as "What's on your lips? It looks like blood from a live mouse you ate," (in reference to a female employee's red lipstick). He also chided others asking "Do you behave like that at home? Is that the way your parents taught you?" and "I say this because I feel like your own brother. Wear a condom when you do it with your boyfriend." He frequently threw documents, and retaliated whenever a victim reported it to upper management

Section 3 Sexual Harassment Case and Procedures for Handling this Case (for Sales Workers)

I. Summary (Introduction)[113]

Incidents of sexual harassment occurred in a Korean branch office (hereinafter referred to as "the Company") of a foreign company. The female employee victimized by the sexual harassment (hereinafter, "the victim-employee") submitted a petition to the National Human Rights Commission over the incidents. The victim-employee then informed the company of the petition she had submitted, and details within her statement to the Human Rights Commission. From this, the Company investigated the senior sales manager concerned (hereinafter, "Offender A"), estimated that his actions were sexual harassment, and then took appropriate disciplinary action against him. Shortly after, the Human Rights Commission transferred this case to the Gangnam Labor Office of the Ministry of Employment and Labor. On June 16, 2011, the Company received a written notice from the Labor Inspector in charge of sexual harassment cases, that there would be an investigative hearing. The Labor Inspector also informed the Company that there were two more alleged offenders that the victim-employee had not mentioned to the Company. After being informed of the additional alleged sexual harassment, the Company investigated the sales director (hereinafter, "Offender B") and the country manager (hereinafter, "Offender C"), and after evaluation, determined their behaviors were also sexual harassment, based upon their statements and the victim's, and took

---

[113] A sexual harassment petition case at GangNam Labor Office from Apr to Jun 2011

❖ 회사 차장은 개인적인 일로 기분이 나쁘면 출근해서 아무나 걸려라 하고 트집을 만들어내서 괴롭힘. 수시로 "주둥이에 그게 뭐냐, 쥐잡아 먹었냐", "너는 집에서 그렇게 하냐, 부모가 그렇게 가르치더냐", "내가 오빠 같아서 걱정되서 그러니 남친을 만나면 꼭 콘돔을 써라"와 같은 상식에서 벗어난 언행을 반복함. 서류를 집어던 지는 건 기본이며, 상부에 보고해봐야 차장은 다시 보복성 공격을 퍼붓곤 함

제3절 직장 내 성희롱 사건사례 (영업직 직원)

I. 사건개요[113]

모 외국계 회사의 국내지사 (이하 "회사"라 함)에서 직장 내 성희롱 사건이 발생하였고, 2011.5.23. 성희롱 피해를 당한 여직원(이하 '피해자'라함)은 국가인권위원회에 진정서를 제출하였다. 또한 피해자는 본 사건과 관련하여 진정서를 제출한 사실과 그 내용을 회사에 통보하였다. 이에 회사는 해당 영업부장 (이하 "가해자 A")과 피해자를 조사한 후, 성희롱 여부를 판단하여 가해자 A에게 적절한 징계조치를 하였다. 그런데, 국가인권위원회는 본 사건을 관할 노동사무소인 고용노동부 서울강남지청으로 이관하였고, 2011.6.16. 본 성희롱 진정사건에 담당 근로감독관으로부터 출석요구를 통지 받았고, 여기에 피해자가 진술하지 않았던, 추가적으로 2명의 성희롱 가해자가 있다는 사실을 확인하였다. 이러한 추가적인 성희롱 사실을 통보 받은 회사는 영업이사(이하 "가해자 B")와 지사장(이하 "가해자 C")에 대해 조사하였으며 피해자의 진술서도 받아 성희롱 여부를 판단한 후, 가해자 B와 C에 대해 적절한 징계조치를 하였다. 2011.6.28. 상기 노동사무소에 출석한 회사는 회사가 취한 법령에 따른 적절한 조치 내용을 설명하였고, 또한 담당 근로감독관도 회사의 조치에

---
[113] 2011. 4월 ~ 6월 간 고용노동부 서울강남지청 진정사건 (강남노무법인)

Section 3. Sexual Harassment Case and Procedures for Handling this Case (for Sales Workers)

appropriate disciplinary actions against Offenders B and C. On June 28, 2011, the Company attended the investigative hearing at the Labor Office and explained the measures that it had taken appropriately according to related law. The Labor Inspector in charge agreed that the Company had taken the proper actions and closed the petition. However, the Labor Inspector discovered that the Company had not given any education to its employees to prevent sexual harassment at work in 2008 and 2009, but had started only in 2010. For this non-fulfillment of the Company's legal duty to provide education on sexual harassment prevention, the Company was fined 2 million won.

According to the 'Equal Employment and Work-Home Balance Assistance Act,' sexual harassment at work refers to "a situation where a person's superior or colleague harasses him/her with sexually-charged behavior or language," and it is the employer who is responsible to prevent sexual harassment at work and take appropriate measures if such harassment occurs. I would like to review the appropriate measures taken by the Company.

II. Details of the Sexual Harassment Case at Work

1. Sexual Harassment by Offender A

On April 27, 2011, during a team-building event at a company workshop with all employees (about 30), the victim-employee had to do something as a penalty in a game. The penalty was that she had to write her name with her backside. Before doing so, she told everybody that they couldn't take any video with their cameras or cell phones. The sales manager (Offender A) took a video of her with his cell phone secretly, saved it, and forgot about it. On May 19, 2011, at a company dinner, Offender A remembered the video he had secretly recorded and showed the video to his colleagues in turn. The conversation among those employees was sexually humiliating for the victim-employee, and included such expressions as "It would be fun to show this as a highlight at a Sales Kick-Off event," and "Since we can't see her face, send her ID picture to me with the video." The victim-employee demanded Offender A to delete the video, but Offender A did not do so. At this, the victim-employee informed the personnel team of her displeasure and requested a formal apology from him. Offender A would not offer a formal apology and simply showed his displeasure at her informing the personnel team.

2. Sexual Harassment by Offender B

대해 긍정적으로 수긍하였다. 다만, 직전 3년간의 직장 내 성희롱예방교육 실시 여부를 확인한 결과, 회사는 작년도에는 교육을 실시하였으나 2008년과 2009년에 대해 직장 내 성희롱예방 교육을 실시하지 않아 200만 원의 과태료 처분을 받고 납부하면서, 본 사건은 종결되었다.

「남녀고용평등법」에 따르면 직장 내 성희롱은 직장 내에서 상급자나 직장 동료가 다른 동료를 성적 언동 등으로 괴롭히는 것이기 때문에 사업주에게 직장 내 성희롱 예방의무를 부여하고, 성희롱 발생시 적절한 조치를 취할 것을 요구하고 있다. 그러면 본 사건과 관련하여 회사가 취한 적절한 조치사항에 대해 구체적으로 살펴보도록 하겠다.

Ⅱ. 사건 내용

1. 가해자 A의 성희롱

2011.4.27. 회사의 전 직원(30여명)이 참석한 워크숍에서 피해자는 엉덩이로 이름쓰기 하는 벌칙에 걸렸다. 피해자는 엉덩이로 이름을 쓰기 전에 카메라 및 핸드폰 촬영을 하지 말라고 당부하였다. 영업부장인 가해자 A는 몰래 핸드폰으로 촬영하였고, 그것을 자신의 핸드폰에 저장해 둔 채 잊고 지냈다. 2011. 5. 19. 가해자 A는 회사의 전체회식에서 회사의 워크숍에서 피해자 몰래 촬영한 핸드폰 동영상을 남자직원들과 돌려보면서, "Sales Kick Off 때 하이라이트로 틀면 재미있겠다.", "얼굴이 돌아서서 잘 안보이니 증명사진 붙여서 보내라." 등 피해자에게 성적수치심을 일으키는 대화가 오갔다. 피해자는 그 자리에서 가해자 A에게 그 동영상의 삭제를 요구했지만, 가해자 A는 아무런 조치를 취하지 않았다. 이에 피해자는 인사부에 불쾌함을 알리면서 가해자 A가 정식으로 사과해야 한다고 통보했다. 이에 가해자 A는 정식 사과도 하지 않고 인사부에 통지한 것에 대해 불쾌함을 표시했다.

2. 가해자 B의 성희롱

2011년 5월 19일 직원전체 회식자리에서 가해자 B는 직원들에게 전통주를

Section 3. Sexual Harassment Case and Procedures for Handling this Case (for Sales Workers)

On May 19, 2011, at the same company dinner, Offender B wandered around, pouring traditional wine for his colleagues. When he came to the victim-employee's seat, he said to her, "Ms. Lee, you sat in my seat. You must like me" and sat beside her. He then said, "Shall we have a love shot?" The victim-employee was humiliated as he was suggesting that she was a "bar hostess" (a position which sometimes involves sexual behavior). The victim-employee very obviously did not like his suggestion, saying "That is a very dangerous thing to say." To which Offender B replied, "I'm not dangerous."

On March 29, 2011, at a company dinner, all the employees went to a Singing Room after dinner. There, while the victim-employee was singing a song by Sym Subong at someone's request, Offender B approached the victim-employee with a gesture in blue dancing, but the victim-employee avoided looking at him. After the song was finished, she sang another song by Ju Hyunme, which talked about a 'confession of love' many times. When she returned to her seat, Offender B said to her, "You were talking to me. That story was about me, right?"

On February 11, 2011, at a company dinner, Offender B approached the victim-employee and said, "Let's hug each other!" It was hard for the victim-employee to refuse in front of all her colleagues, so she patted his shoulder from a distance. The victim-employee began to wonder seriously how she could continue working with her manager (Offender B) who, without hesitation, had shown sexually-charged behavior and caused this humiliation to a married employee at a company dinner with their colleagues.

3. Sexual Harassment by Offender C

On March 29, 2011, the victim-employee was trying to get out of the company dinner because she was humiliated by Offender B's sexual behavior, but after giving it more thought, she went to the country manager (Offender C) to say 'good-bye'. When she said to him, "I have to go home early," Offender C offered his hand to shake hers. Shortly after they shook hands, Offender C said goodbye again, wanted to shake hands again, and attempted to kiss her hand. Surprised, the victim-employee took her hand back quickly, but some of her fingers touched Offender C's lips. The victim-employee was very embarrassed, shocked, and humiliated.

한 잔씩 직원들에게 따라 주면서 피해자가 앉은 자리로 오면서 "이 대리가 내 자리 앉았네. 나를 좋아하나 보다."라고 말하며 옆에 앉아 "러브샷 한번 할까?"라고 말하는 것에 대해 피해자는 술집접대부로 여기는 것 같아서 수치심을 느꼈고, 그 자리에서 "위험한 행동입니다."라고 거부의사를 표시하였다. 이에 가해자 B는 "나는 안 위험한데?"라고 말했다.

2011년 3월 29일 직원전체 회식자리에서 2차로 노래방에 가게 되었다. 피해자가 심수봉씨의 노래를 요청하여 불렀는데, 가해자 B는 '블루스춤'을 추는 시늉을 하며 피해자에게 다가왔고 피해자는 이를 외면하였다. 노래가 끝나자 직원들이 앵콜 요청이 있어 주현미의 노래를 불렀고 그 가사에 '사랑고백' 관련된 단어가 많이 포함되어 있었다. 피해자가 노래를 마치고 자리로 돌아오는데, 가해자 B는 "나한테 하는 얘기지? 내 이야기지?"하는 식으로 이야기를 했다.

2011년 2월 11일 회사의 전체 회식자리에서 가해자 B는 피해자에게 "허그 한번하자."고 다가왔다. 피해자는 전 직원들이 있는 자리에서 거절하는 것이 어려웠고, 대신 최대한 어깨를 두드리는 수준에서 마무리했다. 피해자는 다른 직원들이 있는 회식자리에서 결혼까지 한 유부녀에게 이런 수치심을 유발하는 행동을 스스럼없이 하는 직원이 상급자로 있는 회사를 다녀야 하는지 고민이 빠졌다.

3. 가해자 C의 성희롱

2011년 3월 29일 회식자리에서 가해자 B에게 성희롱을 당한 것에 기분이 좋지 않아 서둘러 그 자리를 빠져 나오려고 하였으나, 지사장 (가해자 C)에게 인사라도 하고 가야 할 것 같아서 가해자 C에게로 갔다. "먼저 들어가야 할 것 같다."고 인사를 하자 가해자 C는 악수를 청했고, 이에 악수에 응했다. 그런 후 바로 가해자 C는 피해자에게 다시 한 번 인사를 하고 악수를 청하면서 자신의 입술을 피해자의 손에 갖다 대려 하였다. 피해자는 놀라서 손을 급히 빼려 했는데 그 순간 자신의 손가락 일부가 가해자 C의 입술에 닿게 되었다. 이에 피해자는 너무 당황하였고 어이가 없고 수치스러움을 느꼈다.

Section 3. Sexual Harassment Case and Procedures for Handling this Case (for Sales Workers)

III. Company Recognition of Sexual Harassment and Handling Procedures

1. Employer procedures in dealing with sexual harassment complaints

Upon receiving a complaint of sexual harassment, the employer will conduct interviews, investigate the facts, implement appropriate measures such as disciplinary punishment, etc. and then inform the victim-employee.

- **1st Stage: Receipt of the sexual harassment complaint** (HR or Labor Department)
- **2nd Stage: Interview and investigation**
  Upon receiving the complaint, the person-in-charge is to quickly set up an interview and begin a thorough investigation. If necessary, the investigator can hear the defendant's testimony instead by organizing a face-to-face meeting between him/her and the victim.
  The person-in-charge shall weigh the collected information obtained during the investigation. As soon as the person-in-charge reaches a final conclusion, it shall be reported to the employer.
- **3rd Stage: Confirmation and disciplinary measures**
  If it is confirmed that sexual harassment has occurred, the employer shall take appropriate action against the offender, such as a transfer to another department or position, warning, reprimand, work suspension, or dismissal, etc.
- **4th Stage: Report of the results**
  Upon closing the investigation, the company shall notify the victim and the offender of the results.
- **5th Stage: Preventative action**
  The employer shall pay special attention to the victim-employee after the closure of the sexual harassment case to prevent further sexual harassment of that employee.

2. The Company's handling of the above cases of sexual harassment

When it recognized the victim-employee's accusations regarding sexual harassment, the Company immediately requested statements from the victim-employee and the alleged offenders. As the country manager (Offender C) was involved in this case, the Company used a labor attorney to interview the

Ⅲ. 회사의 사건인지 및 처리 과정

1. 사업주의 직장 내 성희롱문제 처리절차

직장 내 성희롱 관련 내용이 접수되면 사업주는 당사자 상담과 조사를 통하여 사실관계를 확인하고, 징계 등 적절한 조치와 함께 처리 결과를 피해 근로자에게 통보하는 순서로 처리한다.

- 1단계 : **성희롱 접수** (인사부서, 노무부서)
- 2단계 : **상담과 조사**
  사건 접수를 하면 피해자와 성희롱 용의자에게 신속하게 성희롱 사건 전모를 듣고 공정하고 세심하게 조사한다. 필요한 경우에는 피해자의 입장을 성희롱 용의자와의 대면 대신 증인의 증언을 통해 들을 수 있다. 담당자는 조사 과정에서 취득한 개인정보를 양자의 사생활 보호 측면에서 비밀로 지켜야 한다. 공식 조사된 결과가 직장 내 성희롱이라고 판단하면 담당자는 사업주에 보고한다.
- 3단계 : **확인과 징계절차**
  사업주는 성희롱 사실이 확인되면 성희롱 행위자에 대해 부서 이동, 경고, 견책, 전직, 대기발령, 정직, 해고 등의 적절한 조치를 취해야 한다.
- 4단계 : **결과 통지**
  조사를 종결 할 때에는 피해자와 성희롱 행위자 모두에게 조사 결과를 통지한다.
- 5단계 : **사후 재발 방지**
  사업주는 성희롱 사건에 대한 조치 후에도 향후 피해 근로자에 대한 성희롱 문제가 재발하지 않도록 관심을 가져야 한다.

2. 회사의 성희롱 사건처리

회사가 성희롱 사건에 대해 인지하였을 때, 지체 없이 피해자와 가해자들의 진술서를 확보하였다. 이 과정에서 가해자 C(지사장)가 관련되어 있어서, 공정한 판단을 위해 외부의 공인노무사를 통해 피해자, 그리고 가해자들과

Section 3. Sexual Harassment Case and Procedures for Handling this Case (for Sales Workers)

victim-employee and the alleged offenders and receive their statements, to ensure fair conclusions. After receiving their statements and witness accounts, the Company determined the related behaviors were sexual harassment according to the criteria for evaluating whether certain behavior is sexual harassment at work. In this process, the Company handled the investigations quickly and confidentially, in order to protect the alleged offenders and the victim-employee at the same time. The alleged offenders resisted this investigation, saying they did not intend to harass her sexually. However, the Company explained to them seriously of the criteria for determining the existence of sexual harassment, "In evaluating whether certain behavior is sexual harassment or not, the victim's subjective conditions must be considered. As a socially accepted idea, how a reasonable person evaluates or copes with a situation against the particular controversial behaviors involved must also be considered in the victim's case." The Company concluded that the three men's behaviors were sexual harassment and they were disciplined in accordance with the level of their violations. After this, the Company invited an external expert, (a labor attorney), and implemented training for all employees towards preventing sexual harassment at work. The Company also strove to prevent the reoccurrence of any sexual harassment by posting a notification on the bulletin board, detailing ways to prevent any further sexual harassment in the work environment.

The Company held a Disciplinary Action Committee composed of three members designated by the Company in accordance with the disciplinary regulations in the Rules of Employment, and took disciplinary action after reviewing the disciplinary details. There are five types of discipline: ① written warning, ② wage reduction, ③ suspension from work, ④ recommended resignation, and ⑤ dismissal. The Company decided the level of discipline according to the level of violation as follows.

Offender A: ① 10% wage reduction from one month's salary;
② Suspension of promotion for six months;
③ Official apology to the victim in front of company directors

Offender B: ① Written warning;
② 2.5% wage reduction from one month's salary (July)

Offender C: Written warning

상담한 후 진술서를 받았다. 회사는 이 진술서와 당시 목격자들의 의견을 들어 성희롱 여부에 대해 직장 내 성희롱 판단기준에 따라 판단하였다. 또한 이 과정에서 피해자와 가해자들을 보호하기 위해 보안을 유지하면서 사건 처리를 신속하게 진행하였다. 가해자 A, B, C는 자신들이 특정한 의도를 가진 성희롱이 아니었다고 반발하였다. 그러나 회사는 이들에게 성희롱 판단의 기준은 "피해자의 주관적 사정을 고려하되, 사회 통념상 합리적인 사람이 피해자의 입장이라면 문제가 되는 행동에 대하여 어떻게 판단하고 대응하였을 것인가를 함께 고려하여야 한다."라는 기준으로 판단한다고 설명을 해주었다. 회사는 가해자 A, B, C의 행위가 모두 성희롱에 해당된다는 결론을 내리고, 그 위반 정도에 따라 징계조치를 하였다. 또한 외부전문가인 공인노무사를 통해 회사 전체직원들에게 직장 내 성희롱예방 교육을 실시하였으며, 직원들 간에 이와 같은 환경형 성희롱이 더 이상 확산되지 않도록 직원 전체에 대해 '공고물' 게시함으로써 성희롱 재발방지를 위해 노력하였다.

회사는 취업규칙의 징계규정에 따라 회사가 지명하는 3인으로 징계위원회를 구성하고, 징계내용을 심의한 후 징계조치를 취했다. 회사의 징계의 종류는 ① 서면견책, ② 감봉, ③ 정직, ④ 권고사직, ⑤ 해고의 5가지가 있고, 회사는 위반정도에 따라 다음과 같이 징계 수위를 결정하였다.

(1) 가해자 A의 경우:

① 1개월 감봉 – 월급의 10%;

② 6개월간 진급연기;

③ 회사 경영진 앞에서 피해자에게 공식사과

(2) 가해자 B의 경우:

① 서면견책;

② 1개월 감봉 – 7월 평균임금의 2.5%

(3) 가해자 C의 경우: 서면견책

IV. Conclusion

These cases of sexual harassment at work were related to environmental sexual harassment, and the employees recognized that their behavior at company dinners could be interpreted as sexual harassment even if they didn't think much about it. These cases brought some educational benefit to the Company. And the employees also realized that their unintentional behavior could be interpreted as sexual harassment because the criteria for determining sexual harassment is partly judged from the victim's perspective, rather than the offender's intention. In addition, this case contributes to the building of healthy relationships between employees. The Company was able to protect the victim from being further humiliated, through appropriate measures against sexual harassment. The Company also took appropriate action to prevent a repeat of sexual harassment by determining acceptable discipline for the offenders, carrying that discipline out, and providing education to prevent sexual harassment of other employees.

Due to the victim-employee's complaint of sexual harassment to the Labor Office, the Company was investigated to determine whether or not it had followed the employer procedures for handling sexual harassment complaints. The Labor Office found that the Company had carried out its duties as employer very well according to the Equal Employment Act, except for one, which was skipping its obligation for two years before setting up sexual harassment education last year. As already mentioned, the Company was fined 2 million won for two occurrences of failing to provide education to prevent sexual harassment. Beyond this, the victim-employee's petition to the Labor Office was concluded without any further penalty or demand.

Sexual Harassment Case in the Workplace & Lessons Learned (for Production Workers)

I. Introduction

The most important step to handling workplace sexual harassment is to prevent it in advance. When it happens in reality, it is also important to deal with it appropriately in accordance with on-the-spot situations. There is a legal procedure

Ⅳ. 의견

이번 직장 내 성희롱 사건은 환경형 성희롱으로서 회사 영업부 직원들이 회식자리에서 일상적으로 대수롭지 않게 생각하고 한 행동들이 성희롱이 될 수 있다는 사실을 인식하게 한 교육적인 효과가 있었다. 이 사건으로 말미암아 회사는 물론 회사의 모든 직원들에게도 '성희롱 판단기준이 가해자의 입장이 아닌 피해자의 관점에서 판단하기 때문'에 가해자의 의도와 관계없이 성희롱이 될 수 있다는 사실을 인식하도록 해 주었다. 아울러 이 사건은 직원들의 건전한 대인관계 형성에도 기여하였다고 할 수 있다.

회사는 성희롱 사건에 대한 적절한 조치를 통해, 피해자에게 더 이상의 피해가 발생하지 않도록 보호할 수 있었고, 또한 성희롱 가해자들에게 수긍할 수 있는 징계 수위를 결정·부과하였고 성희롱에 대한 예방교육을 통해 성희롱 사건이 재차 발생하지 않도록 적절한 조치를 이행하였다.

회사는 이번 성희롱 사건을 통해 성희롱 관련 사업주의 이행 의무 사항에 대하여 관할 노동사무소의 조사를 받았다. 그 결과로 근로감독관은 회사가 최근 3년 동안 (금년 제외) 성희롱 예방교육을 2번 누락한 것에 대한 200만 원의 과태료를 부과하였으며, 그 밖에 사항에 대해서는 회사가 「남녀고용평등법」에 의한 사업주의 의무를 모두 이행하였으므로 별도의 명령이나 제재 없이 이번 성희롱사건을 종결하였다.

제4절 직장 내 성희롱 사건사례 (사무직 직원)

Ⅰ. 사건개요

실제로 직장 내 성희롱은 예방이 가장 중요하다. 다만 성희롱이 발생했을 때 상황에 맞는 적절한 대응도 중요하다. 성희롱 사건의 해결에 대한 법적

for handling sexual harassment cases, but the particular case in this article was greatly influenced by the emotional state of the victim and the offending employee. Accordingly, it is necessary to seek a reasonable solution through appropriate actions, rather than only following the legal procedures by the letter.

The case discussed herein was not well handled and resulted in resignation of both the victim and the offending employee, causing direct loss to the related parties through the loss of their jobs, and to the company through the loss of the personnel in question. In the interest of preventing this kind of disruptive outcome, we will look at the problem-solving procedures in the case, review the lessons learned and consider methods of improvement.

II. Sexual Harassment Case

1. Summary of the case

On August 5, 2014, a woman who had been employed by the company in April 2012 and had worked at the company's Suwon site since then submitted a written complaint of sexual harassment by her supervisor. The Personnel Manager asked for legal opinion from a labor attorney who read the female employee's statement and advised problem-solving procedures for the company to follow.
The labor attorney did not recognize the seriousness of the case, and focused upon prevention of recurrence through protection of both the offender and the victim. In the meantime, the female employee and her colleague submitted their resignations as they were afraid of revenge from the offending supervisor (the site manager). Then, because of their resignations, the offending supervisor was also forced to resign. As a result, the company lost significant resources: two female staff employees and one site manager.

2. Details of sexual harassment

The sexual harassment consisted of physical and verbal harassment, as detailed in the female employee's statement as follows.

A. Physical sexual harassment
At the end of 2013, my hair was down and hanging to my shoulders, and the site manager, saying my hair needed trimming, touched my neck with

절차는 있다. 하지만, 성희롱 사건은 피해자와 가해자(행위자)의 심리상태에 큰 영향을 미친다. 이에 단순히 법적 절차를 따를 것이 아니라, 적절한 대응으로 원만한 해결 방안을 모색해야 한다.

이번 성희롱 사건은 적절하게 대응하지 못해 결국 피해자와 가해자 모두가 퇴사함으로써 당사자들에게는 직장을 잃는 직접적인 손해를, 회사에게는 인적자원을 잃는 막대한 손해를 끼쳤다. 이러한 불행한 결과를 사전에 예방하는 차원에서 직장 내 성희롱과 관련한 해결 과정을 살펴본 후, 그 교훈과 개선방안을 검토하고자 한다.

Ⅱ. 사건내용

1. 사건의 개요

2014년 8월 5일, 수원의 A사업장에서 피해 여직원은 2012년 4월에 입사해 2년 4개월째 사업장에서 사무직으로 근무하면서 특정 상급자로부터 지속적으로 성희롱을 당했다며, '성희롱 내용'을 회사에 제기하였다. 그러자 인사담당자는 자문노무사에게 자문을 의뢰하였고, 노무사는 여직원의 '진술서'를 바탕으로 성희롱 사실관계를 확인한 후 회사의 처리방안을 제시하였다.

노무사는 성희롱 사건의 심각성을 인지하지 못한 채, 가해자와 피해자 보호를 통한 재발방지에 초점을 두었다. 그런데 피해 여직원과 동료 여직원은 가해 상급자(소장)의 보복이 두려워 사직서를 제출하였고, 이로 인해 가해자도 권고사직 하였다. 결국, 이에 회사는 업무에 중요한 여직원 2명과 담당 소장을 잃게 되어 큰 인적자원의 손해를 보게 되었다.

2. 성희롱 내용

피해 여직원의 구체적인 성희롱 내용(신체적/언어적 성희롱)은 다음과 같다.

가. 신체적 성희롱
2013년도 말, 한번은 머리가 풀어진 상태로 어깨 앞에 늘어져 있었는데

his fingers and combed them through my hair. It felt instantly creepy and I felt sexually humiliated.

B. Verbal sexual harassment
- Not long time after being hired by the company, a male colleague and I were sweeping the building in preparations for auditing, when the site manager came over to us, looked at me and said to my colleague, "You guys are sweeping like feeling a virgin's breast." His remark really shocked me.
- The site manager often commented about my make-up "You need to put on more make-up and wear more lipstick." Recently he said to me in front of some other colleagues, "You seem to have let everything go. I mean since you got married, you really don't put on make-up nor dress well at all. Put on some make-up before you come to work." He even said to other female colleagues with a laugh, "Please teach her how to put on make-up properly." I felt very displeased and angry.
- Two months ago, while a female worker in the same office was listening, the site manager said smilingly to a male worker, "Women in the US air force do everything by themselves. In the hot summer some women only wear undershirts, moving oil drums and swinging their full breasts."
- On August 5, 2014, while the female employees were talking to each other, the female victim of the harassment said to her supervisor, "I have a headache and feel sick." The site manager responded, "You must feel sick because you're having your period." Both my colleague and I were shocked at his statement.

III. Handling of the Case by the Company

1. Questions and answers regarding the issue

The company asked three questions of the advising labor attorney regarding this sexual harassment on August 6, 2014.

<Question 1> Can sexual language or unnecessary physical contact used by this site manager be considered workplace sexual harassment?
<Response> Judgment of sexual harassment (Supreme Court ruling on June 14, 2007, 2005 du 6461): 'Sexual language and behaviors in becoming 'workplace sexual harassment' in accordance with Article 2(2) of the

답답해 보인다며, 소장이 본인 손가락으로 제 목에 손을 대면서 머리를 쓱 넘기시는 겁니다. 순간 정말 소름이 끼쳤고 성적 수치심을 느꼈습니다.

나. 언어적 성희롱

- 입사한 후 검열준비로 한 팀원과 청소하는 중에 소장님이 다가오셔서 저를 쳐다보더니 팀원에게 "숫처녀 젖가슴 만지듯이 빗자루질한다."라는 표현에 정말 기겁했다.
- 소장님은 2012년 입사후 최근까지 제 얼굴 화장에 관해 꾸준히 "립스틱도 좀 진하게 바르고 화장도 제대로 하고 다녀라"고 말했다. 얼마 전에 다른 직원들 앞에서 "결혼하더니 다 포기했나봐, 화장도 안하고 꾸미는 것도 안하네. 화장 좀 하고 다녀." 또한 다른 여직원한테 "00씨 언니한테 화장 하는 법 좀 알려줘" 라고 웃으면서 말하는데, 정말 불쾌했고 화가 났다.
- 2개월 전에, 사무실에 다른 여직원이 듣는데, 소장은 다른 남직원에게 "미국 여군들은 스스로 알아서 다한다. 어떤 미국 여군들은 여름에 런닝 셔츠만 입고 젖가슴 덜렁덜렁하면서 드럼통 옮기는 걸 봤다."라고 웃으면서 얘기했다.
- 2014년 8월 5일 한 여직원이 소장과 대화중 '머리도 아프고 몸이 안 좋다.' 라고 말하자 소장은 "그건 ○○씨가 생리 중이라 그런 거야."라고 말했다. 저와 다른 여직원들은 그 대화를 듣고 충격을 받았다.

III. 처리과정

1. 문의와 자문내용

회사는 2014년 8월 6일 사건이 발생하자 자문 노무사에게 3가지 자문을 하였다.

<문의 1> 성적 언어문제와 불필요한 신체적 접촉이 직장 내 성희롱에 해당 되는지?
<자문내용> 성희롱 판단 (대법원 2007.6.14. 선고, 2005두6461 판결):

Section 4. Sexual Harassment Case in the Workplace & Lessons Learned (for Production Workers)

Equal Employment Act refer to physical relations between a man and a woman or physical, linguistic and visual behaviors in relation to the male or female physical appearance. These behaviors mean that a normal and average person would feel sexually humiliated or offended if that person were in the victim employee's situation in view of the social community's healthy common sense and socially accepted notions. The condition in which these behaviors are considered sexual harassment does not require the offender's sexual motivation or intention, but shall consider the relation with the victim employee, place and situation where such behaviors happened, the counterpart's explicit and presumptive reactions and details of such behaviors, characteristics and degree of the behavior, whether such behavior was one time only or repeated, and other concrete situations. So, such behaviors should be ones which a normal and average person in the same situation would also feel sexually humiliated or offended objectively. In such cases, these behaviors should be admitted as sexual harassment that resulted in the counterparty feeling sexually humiliated and offended.

In this sexual harassment case, the victim employee felt humiliated by her supervisor's sexual language and behavior, which furthermore caused a feeling of inferiority and disgust by the victim. In considering a normal person's reaction, such language and physical behavior would cause similar feelings. Therefore, the sexual language and other details mentioned by the female employee would be considered workplace sexual harassment.

<Question 2> How can the company deal with a reported case of workplace sexual harassment?

<Response> According to the Equal Employment Act, "1) An employer shall take without delay disciplinary measures or other equivalent actions against the sexual harasser if an occurrence of sexual harassment at work has been verified. 2) No employer shall dismiss or take any other disadvantageous measures against a worker who has been the victim of sexual harassment at work or has claimed to have been sexually harassed (Article 14). If the Company violates the aforementioned

「남녀고용평등법」 제2조제2호에서 규정한 '직장 내 성희롱'의 전제 요건인 '성적 언동 등'이란 남녀 간의 육체적 관계나 남성 또는 여성의 신체적 특징과 관련된 육체적, 언어적, 시각적 행위로서 사회 공동체의 건전한 상식과 관행에 비추어 볼 때 객관적으로 상대방과 같은 처지에 있는 일반적이고도 평균적인 사람으로 하여금 성적 굴욕감이나 혐오감을 느끼게 할 수 있는 행위를 의미한다. 위 규정상의 성희롱이 성립하기 위해서는 행위자에게 반드시 성적 동기나 의도가 있어야 하는 것은 아니지만, 당사자의 관계, 행위가 행해진 장소 및 상황, 행위에 대한 상대방의 명시적 또는 추정적인 반응의 내용, 행위의 내용 및 정도, 행위가 일회적 또는 단기간의 것인지 아니면 계속적인 것인지 여부 등의 구체적 사정을 참작하여 볼 때, 객관적으로 상대방과 같은 처지에 있는 일반적이고도 평균적인 사람으로 하여금 성적 굴욕감이나 혐오감을 느낄 수 있게 하는 행위가 있고, 그로 인하여 행위의 상대방이 성적 굴욕감이나 혐오감을 느꼈음이 인정되어야 할 것이다.

본 사안의 직장 내 성희롱 사건에서 직장 상사의 성적인 언어나 행동이 피해자에게 성적 수치심을 느끼게 했고, 이로 인해 성적 굴욕감이나 혐오감으로 주어서 피해자의 업무에 부정적 영향을 미쳤다고 본다. 또한 이러한 성적 언어나 신체적 접촉을 하였을 때, 일반인도 불쾌한 감정을 느꼈을 것이라 짐작할 수 있다. 따라서 피해자가 제시한 성적 언어 등은 직장 내 성희롱에 해당된다고 할 수 있다.

<문의 2> 직장 내 성희롱 문제 제기시 사업주는 어떻게 해야 하는지?
<자문내용> 「남녀고용평등법」에서는 "1) 사업주는 직장 내 성희롱 발생이 확인된 경우 지체없이 행위자에 대하여 징계, 그 밖에 이에 준하는 조치를 취해야 한다. 2) 사업주는 직장 내 성희롱과 관련해 피해주장을 제기한 근로자 또는 피해를 입은 근로자에게 해고 그 밖의 불이익한 조치를 취해서는 안 된다"(제14조). 이를 위반시 500만 원 이하의 과태료에 처하게 된다(제39조). 따라서 직장 내

items, the employer shall be punished by a fine for negligence not exceeding 5 million won (Article 39)." Accordingly, when receiving information on sexual harassment at work, the employer shall interview the parties concerned, investigate the case, confirm the actual facts, and then take appropriate measures such as disciplinary action and report the outcome to the employee who was sexually harassed.

<Question 3> How can the company deal with this case in a reasonable manner?

<Response> The company shall take appropriate action for cases of sexual harassment in which the victim employee shall be protected from any further damage and the offender punished through acceptable disciplinary action. The company shall also work to prevent recurrence through employee education on sexual harassment.

I would like to suggest a level of disciplinary action for this case as salary reduction (10% of one month's salary) and a written warning letter stipulating that any repeat will result in serious disciplinary action like dismissal. It is also advisable to have the labor attorney who is handling this case to give a presentation on prevention of sexual harassment at your Suwon site.

2. Email conversations between the victim employee and the Labor Attorney

> *From:* **Victim employee;** *To:* **Labor Attorney;** *Sent:* **August 20, 2014 (Wednesday)**
>
> On August 12 I submitted my resignation, and on Thursday, August 14, the site manager held a general meeting in an attempt to excuse his behaviors and said to all attending employees that he did not have any intention to harass the female employees. At that meeting, he outlined point by point what I explained in my statement, explaining that he did not mean to harass me.
>
> What angered me is that the site manager apologized to me and even sent a message that he was a stupid man and he was so sorry for his behaviors, but in front of other employees, he excused himself by skipping over the worst incidents and telling people that I was hypersensitive about nothing out of the ordinary.

성희롱의 내용이 접수되면, 사업주는 당사자 상담과 조사를 통하여 사실관계를 확인하고, 징계 등 적절한 조치와 함께 처리결과를 피해 근로자에게 통보해야 한다.

<문의3> 이번 사건에 대한 회사의 합리적인 처리방법은?
<자문내역> 회사는 성희롱 사건에 대한 적절한 조치를 통해, 피해자에게 더 이상의 피해가 발생하지 않도록 보호하고, 행위자에게도 수긍할 수 있는 징계 수준을 결정·처벌해야 할 것이다. 그리고 성희롱에 대한 예방교육을 통해 성희롱 사건이 재발생하지 않도록 적절한 조치를 이행해야 한다.

본 사안에 대한 징계의 수준은 1개월에 걸친 10%의 감봉과 "재발시 해고할 수 있다"는 문구가 기재된 서면 경고장의 발급이 바람직하다고 판단된다. 또한 이번 수원사업장에 실제로 성희롱 사건을 처리한 노무사에게 성희롱 예방교육을 맡기는 것이 필요하다고 생각한다.

2. 피해자와 노무사의 이메일 대화 내용

From: **피해 근로자** ; To: **노무사**; Sent: 2014-08-20 (수)

지난 8월 12일 제가 사직서를 제출한 후 14일(목) 07:30에 소장님이 전체회의에서 진실을 밝히고 싶다면서 전 직원들 앞에서 본인은 그런 의도로 한 게 아닌데 억울하다고 해명했다고 하시네요.

그 때 제 진술서의 성희롱 내용을 일일이 사례를 들어가며 '이건 이런 의도였었고 저건 저런 의도였었다. 절대 성희롱을 하려는 의도가 아니었다' 라고 하셨답니다.

제가 무엇보다 화가 나는 이유는 제 앞에서는 진심으로 미안했다고 사과까지 하시고, 본인이 못난 놈이란 것에 많은 자책을 하고 크게 미안했다고 문자도 보내시더니 제가 없을 때 사람들 앞에서 사실을 교묘히 포장해 본인한테 불리한 이야기는 쏙 빼놓고, 흡사 제가 별일도 아닌 일에 민감하게 반응한 것처럼 이야기를 몰고 가셨다는 점입니다.

Section 4. Sexual Harassment Case in the Workplace & Lessons Learned (for Production Workers)

From: **Labor Attorney;** *To:* **Victim employee;** *Sent:* **August 20, 2014 (Wednesday)**

I apologize that I have been unable to protect you better. I think the company made mistakes in handling this case. First of all, the most important thing is to protect the victim employee…. I wish you had contacted me before submitting your resignation.

From: **Victim employee;** *To:* **Labor Attorney;** *Sent:* **August 20, 2014 (Wednesday)**

The Personnel Team continuously recommended that I not submit my resignation. However, frankly speaking, I was disappointed to hear that the level of punishment would only be salary reduction (10% of one month's pay). I was not sure whether I could continue to work with the site manager, so, after discussing it with my family, I decided to resign.

From: **Labor Attorney;** *To:* **Victim employee;** **August 20, 2014 (Wednesday)**

It is very sad. Now, the site manager has resigned and you also quit. So, everyone related to this has become a victim. My expectations were that I could protect both him and you, but I was unable to protect anyone at all. I think that I should take more preventive action to avoid a repeat of this case.

As time passes, it will be difficult for people to adjust to the changed environment. I would like to recommend that you reconsider your decision to quit.

From: **Victim employee;** *To:* **Labor Attorney;** *Sent:* **August 26, 2014 (Tuesday)**

The reason why I quit was not because the Labor Attorney could not protect me. When I officially submitted my statement to the Personnel Team, the other female employee was also planning to submit her statement, but the Head Office persuaded me not to make this case public until obtaining more tangible evidence, because the company needed the site manager during contract-renewal with the client company. As I understood the company's situation, I felt it would be hard to continue to work for this company.

From: **노무사** ; To: **피해 근로자** ; Sent: 2014-08-20 (수)

　　노무사로써 ○○○님을 보호해 드리지 못해점에 대해 죄송스러움을 통감합니다. 회사의 처리 절차상 실수가 있었던 것 같습니다. 우선, 피해자를 보호할 의무가 중요한데… 사직서 제출 전에 저에게 연락을 한번 주셨으면 좋았지 않았나 하는 생각이 듭니다.

From: **피해 근로자**; To: **노무사**; Sen: 2014-08-20 (수)

　　인사부에서 끝까지 사직서를 내지 말라고 하셨습니다. 하지만 아마도 징계수위가 감봉 10% 정도가 될거라고 말하신 걸 듣고 나니 솔직히 실망이 되는 건 사실이었습니다. 그리고 소장님과 얼굴 보면서 같이 일할 자신도 없었구요. 그래서 가족과 상의 후 회사를 그만둬야겠다는 결정을 하게 됐습니다.

From: **노무사**; To: **피해 근로자** ; Sent: 2014-08-20 (수)

　　안타깝네요. 소장님도 그만 두시고, ○○○님도 그만두시고, 모두가 피해자가 되었네요.
　　전 두 분 다 지켜드리려고 했다가 결국 모두를 지켜드리지 못한 셈이 되었네요. 앞으로 이러한 일이 발생하지 않으려면 사전예방이 중요한 것 같습니다. 요즈음, 시대가 바뀐 만큼 이에 대해 적응하는데 모두가 어려운 것 같습니다. 사직할 마음을 바꿔 다시 근무하는 것도 생각해 보면 어떠실지 모르겠습니다.

From: **피해 근로자** ; To: **노무사** ; Sent: 2014-08-26 (화)

　　제가 그만둔 건 노무사님이 못 지켜주셔서가 아닙니다. 처음에 이 일을 공론화 시키려고 할 때 다른 여직원들도 함께 진술서를 낼 예정이었지만, 본사에서는 회사가 재계약 시점이라 소장님이 필요하다고 생각해 이번엔 그냥 참고, 다음 번에 좀더 확실한 증거를 모아서 신고하는게 어떻겠는가 라는 식으로 회유를 하시더군요. 어쩌면 그때부터 이번 일이 끝나고 나서 계속해 회사를 다니기 힘들겠구나 라는 생각을 하게 되었습니다.

Section 4. Sexual Harassment Case in the Workplace & Lessons Learned (for Production Workers)

> *From:* **Labor Attorney;** *To:* **Victim employee;** *Sent:* **August 26, 2014 (Tuesday)**
>
> I feel very unhappy to see the tragic results of this sexual harassment case. I have always thought that the offender should be given a chance and punished lightly, but now I think this is not always best. Because of this case, I realize I need to consider the victim employee's situation and try to help the victim employee more.

IV. Lessons Learned & Opportunities for Improvement

Sexual harassment cases cause considerable damage not only to the individual employees concerned, but also to the company. This company has also turned to annual education to prevent sexual harassment, but this has not prevented it effectively. Rather, this company spent energy on covering up the case more than on dealing with it appropriately.

The labor attorney in charge could not give sufficient advice as he did not fully understand the situation. His advice was designed to protect both the victim and the offender together, but he could not protect anyone as three people related to this case resigned. As the company failed to adequately consider the victim's position and requests, two victim employees resigned. The offender was forced to resign due to his moral responsibility. As can be seen by reviewing the email conversations between the victim employee and the labor attorney handling the case, it is regrettable that the company failed to handle things effectively, and that the labor attorney did not fully appreciate the victim employee's situation.

On August 27, 2014, the labor attorney in the case above gave a presentation on prevention of workplace sexual harassment at the Suwon site where the sexual harassment occurred. He explained the definition, the types, the judgment criteria for determining sexual harassment, and the employer's legal obligations, all of which was taken very seriously in light of the case the participants all knew about. As the outcome of this case reveals, preventive action through education on sexual harassment is the best policy.

> From: **노무사** ; To: **피해 근로자** ; Sent: **2014-08-26 (화)**
>
> 이번 성희롱 사건이 비극적으로 종결되게 되어 참으로 답답합니다. 가해자를 약하게 벌주고 한 번 더 기회를 주는 것이 가장 바람직하다고 생각했는데, 늘 그것이 옳지만은 않은 것이라는 생각도 드는군요. 이번 계기를 통해 피해자 입장에서 좀더 진지하게 처리하고, 피해자를 돕도록 하겠습니다.

Ⅳ. 교훈 및 개선방안

성희롱 사건의 발생시 개인문제를 떠나 회사에도 상당한 업무상 손해를 끼친다. 이 사건의 사업장도 매년 성희롱 교육을 실시하였지만, 성희롱을 적절하게 예방하지 못했다. 오히려 회사는 사건을 제대로 대처하지 못하고 덮으려는 데에 초점을 두었다.

위의 자문내용에서 담당 노무사는 당시 상황을 제대로 파악하지 못해 미흡한 자문을 할 수밖에 없었다. 또한 피해자와 가해자를 동시에 보호하려고 하였다가 3명의 직원이 퇴직(사직)함으로 말미암아 모두를 보호하지 못한 결과를 가져왔다. 결국 회사가 피해자의 입장을 충분히 반영하지 못하자, 피해 여직원 2명이 퇴사하고, 가해자도 도의적 책임을 지고 권고사직하였다. 또한, 피해 여성 근로자와 담당 노무사의 이메일의 내용에서 사건 성희롱 피해자의 심리상태에 대한 이해와 회사와 노무사의 대응조치가 미흡한 부분이 있었다.

담당 노무사는 그 후 2014년 8월 27일 수원사업장에서 실시되었던 성희롱 예방 교육에서 이번 사례를 기초로, 성희롱의 정의/유형/판단기준, 사용자의 법적 책임을 따지는 교육을 실시해 노사로부터 큰 공감을 얻었다. 직장 내 성희롱은 철저한 사전 예방교육을 통해 방지 가능한 부분으로 유비무환(有備無患)의 자세가 필요하다.

Section 5. Labor cases related to Sexual Harassment

Section 5. Labor Cases related to Sexual Harassment[114]

I. Questions and Answers concerning Sexual Harassment at Work

1. Q&A designed to understand the concept of sexual harassment at work

Q) Does sexual behaviors of the customer's agents or employees from the affiliate company constitute sexual harassment at work?
A) It is difficult to define sexual harassment by people, that is, by those related to customers' companies or by those within the company in which one works. However, if an employer, a senior, or an employee makes the environment conducive for sexual harassment or demands the victimized employee to tolerate sexual harassment, it can constitute sexual harassment at work and the employer may be held liable.

Q) Is it possible for sexual harassment to occur in the process of job interview before an employee is formally hired?
A) Yes, it is possible. An interviewee in the process of job interview for employment is a potential employee. It can thus constitute sexual harassment when the interviewer causes the interviewee to feel sexually humiliated, makes any verbal or physical conduct of a sexual nature to the interviewee, or makes sexual approaches or requests to the interviewee.

Q) Is it possible for a female to be a sexual harasser?
A) Generally, sexual harassment at work is committed by men rather than women, but it may also be possible at times for such offences to be committed by a female to a male, a female to a female, and a male to a male. For example, it can constitute sexual harassment when a female superior sexually harasses a male subordinator against his wishes.

Q) Can an hourly or daily rated employee be protected against sexual harassment at work?
A) The Equal Employment Act is applicable to all employees, including hourly and daily rated employees working at a business or workplace with five or

---

[114] Ministry of Labor & Employment, 『Sexual Harassment at Work, from its preventions to countermeasures』, June 2019.

제5절 직장 내 성희롱 관련 주요 사례[114]

I. 직장 내 성희롱에 관한 Q&A

1. 직장 내 성희롱 개념의 이해를 위한 Q & A

Q) 거래처 관계자나 계열사 직원 등의 성적 추근거림도 직장 내 성희롱으로 성립될 수 있는가?
A) 거래처 관계자나 계열사 직원에 의한 성희롱은 직장 내 성희롱으로 인정하기가 어렵다. 다만 사업주, 직장 내 상사 또는 동료가 거래처나 계열사 직원에 의한 성희롱이 일어날 수 있는 상황을 유도하거나 감수하도록 피해자에게 요구한 경우에는 직장 내 성희롱으로 성립되어 사업주에게 책임을 물을 수 있다.

Q) 정식으로 채용되기 전인 면접과정에서도 성희롱이 성립될 수 있는가?
A) 성립될 수 있다. 채용을 위한 면접 과정에 있는 피면접인은 잠정직 피고용인의 지위를 가지므로 면접자가 피면접인에게 성적 굴욕감을 느끼게 하거나 성적 행위 등을 요구하는 성적 언동은 성희롱으로 성립될 수 있다.

Q) 여자도 성희롱의 행위자가 될 수 있는가?
A) 직장 내 성희롱은 일반적으로 남자가 여자에게 하는 행위가 대부분이지만 경우에 따라서 여자가 남자에게, 여자가 여자에게, 남자가 남자에게 하는 행위도 있을 수 있다. 예를 들어 여자 상사가 남자 부하직원에게 원하지 않는 성적 행위를 통해서 괴롭히는 경우도 직장 내 성희롱이 될 수 있다.

Q) 시간제, 일용직 근로자도 직장 내 성희롱과 관련하여 보호를 받을 수 있는가?
A) 시간제, 일용직 근로자라고 할지라도 상시 5인 이상의 사업 또는 사업장

---
114) 고용노동부,『직장 내 성희롱 예방에서 대응까지』2019.6

Section 5. Labor cases related to Sexual Harassment

more employees. As such, hourly or daily rated employees working in a workplace with five or more employees can be protected against sexual harassment at work. For hourly or daily rated employees working in a workplace with four or less employees, the 'Gender Discrimination Prohibition and Remedy Act' which applies to workplace with four or less employees provides them with such protection.

Q) If the victimized employee reacts to verbal or physical conducts of sexual nature passively / silently, can it still be regarded as sexual harassment?
A) Yes, it can. For an example, due to lack of social experience, a victimized employee may be under the impression that sexual harassment is generally acceptable and thus tolerated passively without apparent signs of rejection. As he/she gradually felt sexually humiliated and raised contention against such acts, it can still be regarded as sexual harassment. However, it may not be regarded as sexual harassment if the victimized employee explicitly permits the continuance of such verbal or physical conducts of a sexual nature.

Q) If a senior employee displays pictures of overly exposed women on his desktop computer screen, is it regarded as sexual harassment?
A) Except for special circumstances, visual conduct of sexual nature is also regarded as sexual harassment as long as there is a victim resulting from such conducts. Having obscene pictures on one's own desktop computer screen placed on one's own table is a personal inclination. Although such a personal lifestyle shows inconsideration to others and hence immaturity, it does not suffice for relation to sexual harassment. However, when such behaviors cause others to feel uneasy and when the harasser pays no heed to victim's explicit expression of such uneasiness but continues with such behavior, it can be regarded as sexual harassment at work. In that respect, hanging an obscene calendar at a location meant to be seen by women is definitely regarded as sexual harassment.

Q) Does sexual harassment exists only when the harasser carries intention of causing sexual harassment?
A) No, even though the sexual harasser may not be conscious of his sexual harassment act, the victim may feel sexually harassed. Hence, whether sexual harassment exists or not should not be judged based on the harasser's intention but from the point of view of the victim. However, since the victim's response differs from person to person, the standard of judgment should therefore be based on the socially accepted norm of how a reasonable

에서 근무하는 경우라면 「남녀고용평등법」의 적용을 받으므로 상시 5인 이상의 사업장에 근무하는 시간제, 일용직 근로자도 직장 내 성희롱과 관련하여 보호를 받을 수 있다. 남녀차별금지및구제에관한법률은 4인 이하의 사업장에 적용되므로 4인 이하의 사업장의 시간제, 일용직 근로자는 이 법에 의하여 보호를 받을 수 있다.

Q) 피해자가 성희롱 행위자의 성적 언동을 묵시적으로 용인한 경우에도 성희롱으로 성립될 수 있는가?
A) 성립될 수 있다. 예컨대 피해자의 사회경험 부족으로 성희롱 상황을 당연히 받아들여야 하는 것으로 간주하여 명시적인 거부를 못하고 묵시적으로 용인하였으나 점차 성적 굴욕감을 느껴 성희롱으로 주장하는 경우에 성희롱으로 성립될 수 있다. 다만, 성희롱 피해자의 적극적 동의로 성적 언동을 주고 받는 관계가 지속된 경우에는 성립될 수 없다.

Q) 직장상사가 자신의 컴퓨터 바탕화면에 노출이 심한 여자 사진을 실어 놓고 있는 경우 그 자체로서도 성희롱이 성립될 수 있는가?
A) 시각적 행위에 의한 성희롱 성립의 문제는 특별한 사정이 없는 한 대상이 있어야 한다. 즉, 자신의 책상위에 자신이 즐기기 위하여 야한 사진을 컴퓨터 바탕화면을 실어 놓는 것은 개인 취향의 문제이고, 그 개인적 생활이 타인을 고려하지 않은 미숙한 것이라 할 수 있을지라도 그것이 바로 성희롱으로 연결되는 것은 아니다. 그러나 그 행위가 타인에게 성적 불쾌감을 초래하고 그 감정을 표현했는데도 그러한 행위가 지속된다면 이는 직장 내 성희롱이 된다. 또한 여직원을 대상으로 보이는 곳에 야한 달력을 걸어놓는 행위는 당연히 성희롱으로 성립될 수 있다.

Q) 성희롱 행위자가 성희롱하려는 의도를 가져야 성희롱으로 성립되는가?
A) 그렇지 않다. 성희롱 행위자가 스스로는 성희롱으로 인식하지 못하여도 피해자는 성희롱으로 받아들일 수 있으므로 성희롱 행위자의 성희롱 의도 여부보다는 피해자의 입장에서 살펴보아야 한다. 다만, 피해자의 반응은 사람에 따라 다양하므로 사회통념상 합리적인 사람이 피해자의 입장이라면

Section 5. Labor cases related to Sexual Harassment

person would react towards such verbal and physical conduct of a sexual nature if he or she were in the victim's situation.

Q) If there is no specifically targeted person for sexual jokes, does it still constitute sexual harassment?

A) Yes, it does. Even though verbal and physical conduct of sexual nature may not be targeted at specific person, it still constitutes sexual harassment if it invokes sexual humiliation or contributes to hostile environment.

Q) Does demand for errands such as delivery of beverages and photocopying of document targeted restrictively at female employees constitute sexual harassment?

A) Sexual discrimination acts, as below, may be regarded as sexual harassment ① Degrading female employees by addressing them as 'Halmony(grand mother)', 'Ajumma', 'Yah', etc. ② Discrimination of roles between the genders such as degrading females' roles to homemaking, husband-supporting or child-raising whilst glorifying males' roles as master and authority of home ③ Restricting certain task to be performed by a certain sex, for instance, only female employees are demanded to perform errands such as delivery of tea and photocopying of document.

Notwithstanding the type of job the victimized employee is engaged in, 'sexual discrimination type of sexual harassment' basically affects the victim's will to work and her work efficiency by degrading female employees to roles of home-making and child-raising whilst glorifying male employees to more superior status as home master.

Whether such acts constitute sexual harassment or not very much depends subjectively on the victim's individual feelings in addition to a standard of judgment based on a socially accepted norm of how a reasonable person would react towards such sexual discrimination if he/she were in the victim's situation. With such a perspective, it remains difficult for Koreans to perceive sex discrimination as a form of sex harassment because until now, sex discrimination has been our nation's socially accepted norm.

Q) Does a one-time verbal abuse of sexual nature constitute sexual harassment?

A) Yes, it does. Under conditional sexual harassment, when such one-time verbal abuse of sexual nature resulted in the victimized employee showing rejection or expressing feeling of displeasure or suffering disadvantages in personnel-related matters, it undoubtedly constitutes sexual harassment. Also, even if the verbal abuse is trivial but if such unwanted behavior is repeated to the extent of causing sexual humiliation or affecting work efficiency, it can constitute sexual harassment.

문제가 되는 언동에 대하여 어떻게 판단하고 대응하였는가 하는 점이 판단 기준이 되어야 할 것이다.

Q) 특정인을 대상으로 하지 않은 성적 농담도 성희롱으로 성립될 수 있는가?
A) 성립될 수 있다. 특정인을 염두해 두지 않은 성적 언동이라도 하더라도 성적으로 불쾌감을 주고 거부감을 주는 환경(적대적 환경: hostile environment)을 조성하였다면 성희롱으로 성립될 수 있다.

Q) 차나 복사 심부름 등을 여성에게만 강요하는 것도 성희롱이 될 수 있는가?
A) ① 여성을 '할머니', '아줌마', '야' 등으로 부르는 행위, ② '여성에게는 가사나 내조, 양육'을, '남성에게는 가장의 역할, 힘'을 강조하는 행위, ③ 차 심부름, 복사 심부름 등을 한 성 에게만 강조하는 등의 행위는 이른바 성역할에 기반한 성희롱(Gender Harassment)이라고 볼 수 있다. '성역할에 기반한 성희롱'이라 함은 업무와 상관없이 여성에게는 가사일과 육아를, 남성에게는 가장의 역할을 강조함으로써 근로의욕을 감퇴시키고 원활한 업무수행을 방해하는 것을 말한다.
성희롱 여부의 판단은 피해자의 주관적인 사정을 고려하되 사회통념상 합리적인 사람이 피해자의 입장이라면 문제가 되는 행동에 대하여 어떻게 판단하고 대응하였을 것인가를 감안하여 판단기준으로 삼아야 할 것이다. 이런 관점에서 볼 때 '성역할에 기반한 성희롱'의 경우는 아직까지 우리나라의 사회통념에 비추어 직장 내 성희롱으로 보기 어려울 것이다.

Q) 단 1회의 성적 언동이라도 성희롱이 성립되는가?
A) 성립된다. 조건형 성희롱의 경우 행위자의 한번의 성적 언동에 대하여 피해자가 거부하거나 불쾌감을 표시하여 인사상의 불이익을 받은 경우 당연히 직장 내 성희롱으로 성립된다. 또한 경미한 성적 언동이라도 상대방이 원하지 않는 행위가 반복되어 굴욕감을 유발하여 업무 능률을 저해시켰다면 성희롱으로 성립될 수 있다.

Section 5. Labor cases related to Sexual Harassment

2. Q&A concerning employer's duties in relation to sexual harassment at work

Q) Does distribution of company's papers or brochures suffice as training on preventing sexual harassment?

A) In implementing training on preventing sexual harassment, it is a good method to create awareness about sexual harassment to company's managers or employees by distributing company's papers or brochures. However, such method should be used as a supplementary measure. At the very least, there should be various forms of training such as employee seminars, regular meetings, department-level training, and audiovisual educational training. If possible, it is also important to have many dialogue and discussion sessions for sharing and exchange of opinions with one another.

Q) As trivial sexual jokes may also be regarded as sexual harassment at work, should employer adopt personnel measures such as department transfer and disciplinary punishment when such harassment occurs?

A) There should at least be measures such as written warnings. Even if a verbal or physical conduct of sexual nature appears trivial from a third party's objective point of view but from the point of view of the victim, it may be felt as a severe sexual humiliation. As such, so long as the employer agrees that the offence constitutes sexual harassment, the employer should pursue it and serve disciplinary warnings to the harasser in order to prevent the recurrence of such harassment. Accordingly, the employer should, through the use of punishments such as warnings, try to ensure that harassments akin do not recur.

Q) Can an employer impose heavy disciplinary punishment such as dismissal for trivial sexual harassment offence?

A) If a light disciplinary punishment such as warning fails to stop sexual harassment behaviors, the employer may impose heavier disciplinary punishment. However, if heavy disciplinary punishment is resorted without attempting light disciplinary punishment for even once or if heavy disciplinary punishment is resorted after the harasser has already stopped its sexual harassment behaviors after a light disciplinary warning, it would then have to be deemed as not acting in line with socially accepted norm.

Q) In the event there are harasser and victim parties to a case of sexual harassment, is it regarded as unfair to transfer only the victimized employee?

A) In general, workplace transfer can be used as a disciplinary punishment against the sexual harasser. However, if the victimized employee voluntarily requests for or agrees to the transfer and there is no problem arising from doing so, transfer of victimized employee may also be the case. However,

2. 직장 내 성희롱에 관한 사업주의 의무와 관련된 Q & A

Q) 직장 내 성희롱 예방교육은 사보 또는 홍보물의 발간으로도 충분한가?
A) 직장 내 성희롱 예방교육을 실시함에 있어 수시로 사보 또는 홍보물을 발간하여 기업의 관리자나 근로자에게 관련사항을 알리는 것은 좋으나 이러한 방법은 보조적인 수단으로 사용되어야 할 것이다. 최소한 직원 연수교육, 정례회의, 부서별교육, 시청각교육 등의 다양한 형태로 진행하고 가능한 한 많은 대화와 토론을 통하여 서로간의 생각을 공유하는 것이 중요하다.

Q) 경미한 성적 농담도 직장 내 성희롱으로 성립되면 사업주는 부서전환, 징계 조치 등의 인사조치를 취하여야 하는가?
A) 적어도 가벼운 경고 등의 조치는 취하여야 한다. 객관적 혹은 제3자가 보아 경미한 성적 언동이라고 판단할 수 있는 경우에도 피해자가 처한 입장에서는 심한 성적 굴욕감을 느낄 수 있으므로 일단 직장 내 성희롱으로 성립되면 사업주는 성희롱 행위자에 대해 성희롱 재발을 방지할 수 있는 일정한 경고 조치를 취하여야 한다. 따라서 경고 등의 경징계로 더 이상 유사한 행동이 발생하지 않을 것을 담보할 수 있도록 해야 한다.

Q) 경미한 성희롱 사건에 대하여도 사업주는 해고 등의 강력한 징계조치를 취할 수 있는가?
A) 경고 등의 경징계 조치로 성희롱 행위가 중단되지 않는다면 사업주는 중징계 조치를 취할 수 있다. 다만, 사업주가 한번의 경미한 사건에 대하여 처음부터 중징계 조치를 취하거나 성희롱 행위자가 가벼운 경고로 성희롱 행태를 중단하였는데도 중징계 조치를 취하는 것은 사회통념상 인정되지 않는다고 보아야 할 것이다.

Q) 성희롱의 행위자와 피해자가 발생한 경우 피해자를 전직하는 것은 부당전직에 해당하는가?
A) 일반적으로 전직은 성희롱의 행위자에 대한 징계라고 할 수 있는데, 피해자를

if there is no business necessity in making such transfer or if there is no consideration to the victimized employee's opinion, or if it is done against the victim's will, such transfer would be treated as transfer without appropriate reason according to Article 30 of the Labor Standards Act.

Q) When a dispatched employee committed sexual harassment at work, does the employer who uses his/her services have to impose disciplinary punishment?

A) In the event a dispatched employee initiates sexual harassment at work, the employer who uses his/her services will have to take the responsibility to conduct fact-finding and organize the formation of dispute dissolution committee. However, as such employer does not have the authority to discipline the dispatched employee, direct disciplining would be impossible. Nevertheless if the dispatched staff's sexual harassment act is confirmed to be true, the employer who uses his/her services may recommend to the employer who dispatched him/her to take disciplinary punishment against him/her. If the dispatched employer does not respond, the using employer can request for termination of seconding contract.

3. Q&A concerning the rights of the victimized employee to seek help

Q) Is it possible to punish sexual harasser by the Equal Employment Act?

A) It is not possible to directly punish sexual harassers by the Equal Employment Act. This is because in order to punish the sexual harasser by an act that does not differentiates between his/her acts inside and outside of the company, it would have to be regulated by a general law that apply to all nationals instead of a law, such as the Equal Employment Act, which is specific to employment. As the Equal Employment Act entrusts employers with the responsibility of prohibiting and preventing discrimination, there is no provision stipulated in the administrative legal structure to punish the sexual harasser. However, as there are provisions for employer to implement measures, such as department transfer, disciplinary punishment, etc. against sexual harassers, the victimized employee may therefore request to a grievance handling committee for help to resolve problems of sexual harassment and may also request for disciplinary punishments to be imposed on the sexual harasser. If such requests are not accepted by the employer, the employee may lodge with the Labor Office for remedial action against the employer. In addition, the victimized employee may also bring a civil suit against the sexual harasser so as to claim for compensation.

Q) For sexual harassment case happened 2 years ago, is it still possible to appeal for an internal solution by the company or to lodge complaint with

전직하는 경우 피해자가 자진하여 요구하거나 또는 전직에 동의하는 경우는 문제가 발생하지 않으나 업무상 필요성이 없음에도 피해자의 의사를 확인하지 않거나 반하여 전직발령을 하는 경우 이는 「근로기준법」 제30조의 정당한 이유 없는 전직에 해당 된다.

Q) 파견근로자가 직장 내 성희롱을 가했을 경우 사용사업주가 징계 등의 조치를 취하여야 하는가?
A) 파견근로자에 의한 직장 내 성희롱이 발생하였을 경우, 사실규명 및 분쟁처리절차 회부 등은 사용사업주가 담당하여야 할 것이다. 그러나 사용사업주는 파견근로자에 대한 징계권한이 없기 때문에 직접적인 징계는 불가능하고 파견근로자의 직장 내 성희롱이 명확해지면 파견사업주에게 징계 조치할 것을 권고할 수 있다. 만약 파견사업주가 이에 응하지 않은 경우에는 파견계약의 해지 등을 요구할 수 있을 것이다.

3. 피해자의 권리구제에 관한 Q & A

Q) 직장 내 성희롱 행위자를 「남녀고용평등법」으로 처벌할 수 있는가?
A) 「남녀고용평등법」에서 성희롱 행위자를 직접 처벌할 수는 없다. 그 이유는 성희롱 행위자에 대한 처벌문제는 직장 내외를 불문하고 일반적으로 적용하기 위해 「남녀고용평등법」이 아닌 모든 국민에게 적용되는 법에 규정되어야 할 사항이며, 「남녀고용평등법」은 사업주에게 차별금지 및 예방의무를 부여하고 있기 때문에 성희롱 행위자에 대한 처벌규정은 두고 있지 않다. 그러나 사업주가 성희롱 행위자를 부서전환, 징계 등 조치를 취하도록 규정하고 있기 때문에 성희롱 피해자는 사내의 고충처리기구 등에 성희롱 문제 해결요청을 하여 성희롱 행위자에 대한 조치 요구를 할 수 있으며, 이러한 요구가 받아들여지지 않는다면 지방노동관서에 사업주를 대상으로 진정을 제기할 수 있다. 또한 피해자는 성희롱 행위자를 상대로 손해배상을 요구하는 민사소송을 제기할 수 있다.

Q) 2년 전에 발생한 성희롱 사건에 대해서도 사내 해결을 요구하거나 지방

Section 5. Labor cases related to Sexual Harassment

the Labor Office?

A) Yes, it is possible. Extinctive prescription of labor laws generally allows for three years, and extinctive prescription of general rights in the Equal Employment Act also allows for three years. As such, for sexual harassment occurring within three years, the Equal Employment Act is absolutely applicable, and the victimized employee may lodge such complaint with the Labor Office.

Q) When there is sexual harassment, must the victimized employee personally lodge her appeal or complain in order for her right to seek help to be effective?

A) No. In the event an employer disadvantages an employee in her employment or did not take appropriate measures against the sexual harasser, it is also possible for a third party such as a consulting body to seek redress or to complain to the Labor Office. However, as sexual issues are likely to infringe on characters and rights of both the victimized employee and the sexual harasser, the representing third party will have to sufficiently consider the victimized employee's opinion before appealing or complaining to the labor office

II. Cases of Sexual Harassment at Work

[Case 1] This was a case affirmed as sexual harassment at work as the assistant manager demanded his subordinate to fill the glass of the managers with liquor.

■ **Details of the case**
❖ The victimized employee (A), a nurse of a hospital supervised by a Manager of Nurse of the same hospital, attended a company's dinner on March 26 1999 and was told by an Assistant Manager of the General Affairs team (B) at the company's dinner to fill the glass of the Director of General Affairs and that of the General Manager of Treatment team with liquor. When (A) rejected that suggestion, (B) grasped her arm and took her to the table of the director and the general manager, and forced her to fill the glass with liquor. Because of this incident, the victimized employee (A) felt severely humiliated.

■ **Judgment**
❖ Sexual harassment at work can occur in a company's dinner related to work. This case was in relation to work as the company's dinner was held under

노동관서에 진정·고소 등을 할 수 있는가?
A) 할 수 있다. 노동관계법상의 소멸시효는 통상 3년이므로 「남녀고용평등법」 상의 제 권리에 대한 소멸시효도 3년이다. 따라서 3년 이내에 발생한 성희롱 사건에 대해서는 「남녀고용평등법」이 전면적으로 적용되므로 지방노동관서에 진정·고소 등을 제기할 수 있다.

Q) 직장 내 성희롱 발생시 반드시 피해자가 직접 진정·고소 등을 제기하여야 권리를 구제받을 수 있는가?
A) 아니다. 사업주가 근로자에게 고용상의 불이익을 주거나 성희롱 행위자에 대하여 조치를 취하지 않는 경우 상담기관 등 제3자에 의한 진정 및 고발도 가능하다. 그러나 성에 관련된 사항은 오히려 제3자에 의해 피해근로자나 성희롱 행위자의 인격 및 권리가 침해될 소지가 크므로 성희롱 사건의 특성상 피해근로자의 진정 및 고발여부에 대한 의사가 충분히 고려되어야 한다.

II. 직장 내 성희롱 노동사건 사례

[사례1] 중간관리자가 하급직원에 대하여 관리자에게 술 따르기를 강요한 것을 직장 내 성희롱으로 인정한 사례

■ 사건의 경위
❖ 피해자 A는 병원의 간호사로 99년 3월 26일 동 병원 간호과장이 주재하는 전체회식 자리에서 총무계장 B로부터 원장과 진료부장에게 술따르기를 권유하였으나, 피해자가 이를 거부하자 총무계장 B가 피해자의 팔을 잡고 원장과 진료부장이 있는 테이블로 끌고가 술을 따르도록 하였고 이로 인하여 피해자 A는 심한 굴욕감을 느낀 사건이다.

■ 판단
❖ 직장 내 성희롱은 업무와 관련이 있는 회식장소에서도 발생할 수 있는바, 본사건에서의 회식자리는 병원의 간호과장이 주재하는 회식자리라는 점에서

the supervision of the Manager of Nurse.

❖ position as a superior in the company to verbally compel the victimized employee (A) to fill the glass regardless of her dislike. From the perspective that the employee felt sexually humiliated, such an act therefore constitutes sexual harassment at work.

[Case 2] Disciplinary dismissal due to sexual harassment behavior at work is an exercise of justifiable rights of personnel, but disciplinary dismissal out of sympathy for the offender is unfair dismissal.

■ **Details of the case**
❖ Applicant A and B worked as Manager and Assistant Manager of the Planning team in a hospital respectively and attended the department's dinner at a restaurant near the hospital. At the dinner, applicant A went to the extent of making physical abuse of a sexual nature by fumbling the thigh of a female employee and touching her breast, but applicant B just looked on such sexual harassment behaviors and somewhat expressed sympathy.

❖ After this incident, the employer dismissed applicant A on grounds of sexual harassment and also dismissed applicant B for not upholding morals at work. Both applicants A and B sought remedial help to the Labor Relations Commissions against unfair dismissal by the employer.

■ **Judgment**
❖ Depending on the severity of the sexual harassment and the continuity of such acts, the employer would have to take reasonable disciplinary measures such as department transfer, warning, reprimand, salary reduction, job transfer, suspension from work, being placed on the waiting list, suspension from office, etc.,

❖ Article 10 of enforcement decree of the Equal Employment Act regulates that 'in cases where the employer takes disciplinary measures such as department transfer, disciplinary punishment, etc., he shall consider the severity of sexual harassment and its continuity. Accordingly, the employer shall determine a reasonable level of disciplinary punishment, considering ① whether the sexual harasser is aware of the fact that the victim employee did not want the behavior? ② were the behaviors repeated somehow? (for example, the level

업무와의 관련성이 있고

❖ 총무계장 B는 직장 내 상사라는 지위를 이용하여 피해자 A가 싫어하는 술 따르기를 강요하는 언어적인 성희롱을 함으로써 근로자의 성적 굴욕감을 유발했다는 점에서 직장 내 성희롱이 성립한다고 할 수 있다.

[사례 2] 직장 내 성희롱 행위로 인한 징계해고는 정당한 인사권의 행사이나 이에 동조한 행위는 부당해고라는 사례

■ 사건의 경위
❖ 신청인 A와 B는 각각 병원 기획예산과의 과장과 계장으로 99년 9월 7일 퇴근 후 병원 인근 식당에서 회식을 하는 도중, 신청인 A는 여직원의 허벅지를 더듬고 가슴을 만지는 등 성추행에 가까운 신체접촉을 하였으며, 신청인 B는 다만 성희롱 행위를 방관하고 일부 동조하는 행위를 하였다.

❖ 그 후 피신청인(사용자)은 성희롱을 자행하였다는 이유로 신청인 A와 B에 대하여 품위유지 위반을 이유로 징계해고를 하였고 이에 신청인 A, B는 피신청인을 대상으로 지방노동위원회에 부당해고구제신청을 제기한 사건이다.

■ 판단
❖ 사업주는 성희롱 행위자에 대하여 성희롱의 정도, 지속성 등을 감안하여 부서전환이나 경고, 견책, 감봉, 전직, 정직, 대기발령, 휴직, 해고 등의 적절한 징계 조치를 하여야 한다.

❖ 「남녀고용평등법」 시행규칙 제10조에 의하면 '직장 내 성희롱을 한 자에 대한 부서 전환, 징계 등의 조치를 하는 경우에는 성희롱의 정도 및 지속성 등을 고려하여야 한다.'고 규정하고 있는바, 사업주는 ① 성희롱 행위자는 피해자가 그 행동을 원치 않았다는 사실을 알았는가? ② 어느 정도 확산된 행동인가? (예: 성희롱의 정도, 지속성 등) ③ 성희롱 행위자와 피해자

of sexual harassment, its continuity, etc.) ③ Is there any difference in power (authority) between the sexual harasser and the victimized employee? and ④ the legal ambit which the victimized employee comes under.

- In this respect, as dismissal is the heaviest disciplinary punishment causing severe threat of the employee's survival right, Article 30 (1) of the Labor Standards Act regulates that it shall be implemented only in the case where there is a reasonable grounds. In this case, reasonable grounds imply that the employee's violation was so severe that it would be difficult to continue his employment with the company. The employer will have to consider the gravity of the employee's violations and equality compared with other employees, and shall not abuse the rights of employer in imposing punishment.

- It follows that the disciplinary dismissal imposed on A, who had at the dinner gone to the extent of physical sexual abuse by fumbling the thigh of the female employee and touching on her breast, was an appropriate exercise of personnel management's rights as it had considered the severity of applicant A's sexual harassment conducts. However, for applicant B who had just looked on such sexual harassment behaviors and who somewhat showed sympathy, the imposing of disciplinary dismissal similar to the punishment received by applicant A would be deemed as an abuse of the employer's right in considering the severity of the employee's violations and in maintaining equality amongst employees.

[Case 3] **A case difficult to be affirmed as sexual harassment based on the harasser's verbal and physical conduct.**

■ **Details of the case**
- The applicant and the defendant were both hospital employees. The applicant worked as a Service Manager in charge of receiving patients, while the defendant worked as a Planning Director in charge of personnel management of all employees and was a senior manager to the applicant.

- On August 16 2000, the applicant was waiting for an elevator together with her superior, a Nursing Manager, on their way to work. The defendant got on the elevator at the underground first floor, and the applicant and her superior joined in from the first floor to the fifth floor. On the way to the fifth floor, the defendant said to the applicant "Ms. Kim, you should try to

❖ 아울러 해고란 근로자의 생존권에 중대한 위협을 초래하는 중징계이므로 「근로기준법」 제30조제1항에 의거 정당한 이유가 있는 경우에만 행하도록 규정하고 있고, 여기서 정당한 이유란 근로자의 귀책사유가 더 이상 고용관계의 지속이 곤란할 정도의 중대한 것이어야 하며, 이 경우 징계양정을 선택함에 있어서도 귀책사유의 정도, 다른 근로자의 형평성 등을 고려하여 징계권이 남용되지 않도록 하여야 할 것이다.

❖ 따라서 회식자리에서 여직원의 허벅지를 더듬고 가슴을 만지는 등 성추행에 가까운 신체접촉을 행한 신청인 A에 대한 징계해고는 성희롱의 정도 등을 고려해 볼 때 정당한 인사권의 행사라고 할 수 있으나, 신청인 B는 다만 성희롱 행위를 방관하고 일부 동조하는 행위를 하였을 뿐인데 A와 동일하게 징계해고를 하는 것은 귀책사유의 정도, 다른 근로자와의 형평성 등을 고려해 볼 때 징계권의 남용이라고 할 것이다.

[사례 3] 성적인 언어나 행동으로 보기 어려워 직장 내 성희롱이 성립 하지 않는다고 본 사례

■ 사건의 경위

❖ 신고인과 피신고인은 병원 소속 직원이고 신고인은 수납업무를 담당하는 원무팀장이고, 피신고인은 직원관리를 담당하는 기획실장으로서 피신고인은 신고인의 상급자이다.

❖ 2000년 8월 16일 신고인이 출근하기 위하여 직장상사인 간호과장과 같이 엘리베이터 탑승을 위해 기다리고 있을 때 피신고인이 지하에서 올라와 신고인과 동승하여 1층에서 5층으로 엘리베이터를 타고 올라가는 동안 피신고인이 신고인에게 '김주임 인사 좀 하지'라고 하며 신고인의 옆 엉덩이를 접혀진 신문지로 두 번 이어서 때리자 간호과장이 피신고인의

greet" and he tapped the hip of the applicant twice with a folded newspaper. The Nursing Manager got himself involved at this juncture, but the defendant said, "I wonder whether people still know their workplace manners after marriage." The applicant felt embarrassed and sexually humiliated to have her hip tapped in the presence of many employees working together in the same building and therefore claimed this incident to be a case of sexual harassment rather than a case of plain assault.

■ **Judgment**

❖ In judging sexual harassment, the victim's subjectivity should be considered. At the same time, socially accepted norms on how a reasonable person, in the victim's circumstances, would evaluate or react to such a controversial situation should also be considered.

❖ The applicant claimed that she felt embarrassed and sexually humiliated when the right-hand side of her hip was hit by the defendant's newspaper.

❖ Even though she was tapped on the hip, it was only an indirect contact with the newspaper held by the defendant. There was no verbal abuse of a sexual nature except for an advisory remark," Ms. Kim, you should try to greet" and there was also no disadvantage in employment to the applicant. The main fault lies with the defendant's behavior in using an advisory method in front of other people. As it was hard to find sexual factors in the incident, what the applicant felt was judged as plain humiliation rather than sexual humiliation. As such, it could not constitute sexual harassment.

[Case 4]

1. Adjudicated to compensate 30 million won for compelling a subordinate to drink[115]

A married male manager at an internet game development company had very often organized drinking sessions after work on the reason of promoting teamwork, and he also included the female unmarried employees. At such drinking sessions, he would compel female employees who could not drink

---

[115] (May 5, 2007, Seoul Appellate Court 2006 na 109669)

행동을 말렸고 이후 피신고인이 신고인에게 '결혼을 했으면 직장예절 등을 알고 있을 것인데'라는 등의 말을 하였는 바, 이에 신고인은 같은 건물에 근무하고 있는 다른 사람이 있는 앞에서 엉덩이 부위를 맞았기 때문에 모멸감과 부끄러움을 느꼈고 맞은 부위가 엉덩이 옆이기 때문에 단순폭행이기보다는 성희롱이라고 주장한 사건이다.

■ 판단
❖ 성희롱 여부의 판단에 있어서는 성희롱 피해자의 주관적인 사정을 고려하되, 사회통념상 합리적인 사람이 피해자의 입장이라면 문제가 되는 행동에 대하여 어떻게 판단하고 대응하였는가를 함께 고려하여야 한다.

❖ 동 사안에서 신고인은 피신고인에게 신문지로 오른쪽 옆 엉덩이 부위를 맞고 모멸감과 부끄러움을 느껴 성희롱이라고 주장하고 있으나

❖ 엉덩이 부위를 맞았다고 하지만 이는 피신고인이 들고 있던 신문으로 툭 쳤던 간접적인 접촉이었으며 '김주임 인사 좀 하지'라는 훈계성 발언 외에 다른 성적인 언동이 전혀 없었을 뿐만 아니라 신고인에게 아무런 고용상의 불이익도 없었던 점으로 보아 타인이 보는 앞에서 훈계방법이 좋지 않아 신고인에게 수치심을 주었던 것으로 사건과정에서 성적 함축성이 있었다고 보기 어려우므로 사건 발생 이후 신고인의 감정은 성적 굴욕감이라기보다는 단순 수치심에 가깝다고 판단되어 「남녀고용평등법」에 의한 직장 내 성희롱이라고 보기 어렵다 할 것이다.

[판례 사례 4]

1. 부하직원에 '술 강요' 3천 만 원 배상 판결[115]

이 사건 판결은 온라인게임을 개발하는 어느 회사의 기혼 남자 상사가 미혼의 부하 여직원에 대하여 직원들의 단합을 도모한다는 명목으로 술자리를 자주

---
[115] 서울고등법원 2007.05.03. 선고, 2006나109669 판결.

Section 5. Labor cases related to Sexual Harassment

alcoholic liquor for physical and health reasons to drink. Such drinking events often went on till dawn, disabling the female employees from returning home early. He had also often used sexual remarks of sexual harassment nature to the female employees at the drinking place or office. The manager's aforementioned behaviors, which are infringement of the autonomous expression of opinion and behavior of his younger employees and violations of their personality freedom, are damage to others' humane dignity. If their behaviors were confirmed to have caused others severe sufferings in their state of mind, it can also constitute illegal behavior.

2. Vice-Principal's verbal and physical conduct at official dinner meeting of expecting female teachers to fill the glass of the male principal did not constitute sexual harassment.[116]

The dinner meeting was arranged by the 3rd grade elementary school teachers to welcome a newly appointed vice-principal (plaintiff), and they invited the principal and vice-principal. So, it was a place where the plaintiff and the teachers met for the first time. At the dinner meeting, participants were mainly discussing about teachings when some female teachers were given liquor-filled glasses by the principal and were suggested to toast. However, neither did they empty their glass nor did they reciprocate by filling the glass of the principal. The plaintiff, on seeing this situation, suggested that the female teachers should fill the glass of the principal. The plaintiff claimed that it would be more correct to view his verbal and physical conduct in this case as a recommendation for subordinates to reciprocate their superior's toasting rather than an intention to discriminate against the female and asking them to pour liquor for the principal just because they are females. Other female teachers who heard the plaintiff's suggestion to those female teachers about pouring the liquor for the principal felt unpleasantness but did not feel a sense of sexual humiliation or dislike. Integrating all the points in this testimony about the characteristics of the dinner meeting, relationships of the participants, place, the situation under which the plaintiff's remarks were made, and whether there had been any sexual motives or intention, etc., the verbal and physical conduct of the plaintiff in this case, strictly speaking, is in line with our nation's common sound knowledge and customary practices. So, it is difficult to conclude his remarks and behaviors as intolerable or are violations of kind mannerism or social order.

---

[116] (Feb. 11, 2004, Seoul Administrative Court 2003 guhap 23387)

만들어 그 술자리에서 체질상, 건강상의 이유로 술을 거의 못 마시는 여직원에게 음주를 강요하고, 술자리를 새벽까지 이어가며 일찍 귀가도 못하게 하고, 술자리나 사무실 등지에서 수시로 여직원에게 성희롱에 해당하는 성적 언동을 한 사건이다. 위와 같은 직장 상사의 행동들이, 자기의 의사와 행위를 자율적으로 결정하는 인격적 자율성을 침해하는 행위로서 상대방의 인간으로서의 존엄성을 훼손하는 행위가 될 뿐만 아니라 이로 인하여 상대방이 심한 정신적 고통을 느꼈다면 불법행위를 구성한다는 취지이다.

2. 회식자리에서 교감이 여자교사들에 대하여 남자교장에게 술 한 잔씩 따라 드리라는 언행을 한 것은 성희롱에 해당하지 않는다[116].

이 사건 회식은 초등학교 3학년 교사들이 새로 교감으로 부임한 원고를 환영한다는 의미에서 자신들의 전체회식에 교장 및 원고 등을 초대하여 이루어졌다. 원고가 교사들과 처음으로 개별적으로 접촉하는 자리였으며 위 회식에서 참석자들이 주로 학습에 관한 대화를 나누었고, 여자교사들이 교장으로부터 술을 한 잔씩 받은 다음 건배제의 후에도 술잔을 비우지 아니하고 교장에게 답례로 술을 권하지도 아니한 상황에서 원고가 교장에게 술을 따라 드리라는 취지의 이 사건 언행을 하였다. 이 언동에 대해 원고는 여자교사들은 여성이므로 교장에게 술을 따라야 한다는 성적 의도를 가지고 이 사건 언행을 한 것이라기보다는 회식장소에서 부하직원이 상사로부터 술을 받았으면 답례로 상사에게 술을 권하여야 한다는 차원에서 이 사건 언행을 한 것으로 보여 진다. 다른 여자교사들은 원고가 교장에게 술을 따라드리라는 취지의 말을 하여 불쾌하게 생각하였으나 그로 인하여 성적인 굴욕감 또는 혐오감을 느끼지는 않았다고 진술하고 있다. 이 사건 회식의 성격, 참석자들의 관계, 장소 및 원고가 이 사건 언행을 할 당시의 상황, 성적 동기 또는 의도의 유무 등의 구체적인 사정을 종합하여 보면, 원고의 이 사건 언행이 우리 사회공동체의 건전한 상식과 관행에 비추어 볼 때 용인될 수 없는, 선량한 풍속 또는 사회질서에 위반되는 것이라고 보기 어렵다.

---

116) 서울행정법원 2004.02.11. 서고, 2003구합23387 판결.

<References>

Ministry of Employment and Labor, "Manual for Workplace Bullying Prevention and Response," 2019.2.

Ministry of Employment and Labor, "Manual for Workplace Sexual Harassment Prevention and Response," 2021.

Kim, El-Im, "Sexual Harassment: Law and Dispute Resolution Cases," Episteme, 2023.

Kim, El-Im, "(Case Commentary) Workplace Sexual Harassment - Subject Ruling: Supreme Court Decision 2016DA202947 Damage Compensation, Decision on December 22, 2017," Labor Law 100 Cases, 2nd Edition, edited by the Korean Labor Law Association, Parkyoungsa, 2021.

Kim, El-Im, "Trends in Case Law on Employer's Responsibility in Sexual Harassment Cases," Gender Law Journal, Vol. 14, Korean Gender Law Association, 2016.

Kim, El-Im, "(Case Commentary) Workplace Sexual Harassment and employer's Responsibility - Subject Ruling: Supreme Court Decision 95DA39533 Damage Compensation, Decision on February 10, 1998," Labor Law 100 Cases, 1st Edition, edited by the Korean Labor Law Association, Parkyoungsa, 2015.

Kim, El-Im, "Formation and Evolution of Legal Concept of Sexual Harassment," Gender Law Journal, Vol. 11, Korean Gender Law Association, 2015.

Kim, Jin, "Remedies for Gender Discrimination in Employment and Related Cases," Gender and Law, Parkyoungsa, 2022.

Park, Gwi-Cheon, "Judgment and Remedies for Workplace Sexual Harassment," Gender and Law, Parkyoungsa, 2022.

Lee, Jong-Hee, "Workplace Sexual Harassment and Secondary Harm: What is Employer's Responsibility? (Renault Samsung Case)," The Groundbreaking Gender Equality Ruling, Pureunsangsa, 2020.

Jung, Bong-Soo, "Interpretation of Korean Labor Law," Joongang Economy, 2021.

Jung, Bong-Soo, "Termination Manual," K-labor press, 2022.

Jung, Bong-Soo, "Personnel and Labor Management," Time Travel, 2022.

〈주요 참고문헌〉

고용노동부	「직장 내 괴롭힘 판단 및 예방, 대응 매뉴얼」, 2019. 2.
고용노동부	「직장 내 성희롱 예방·대응 매뉴얼」, 2021.
김엘림	「성희롱: 법과 분쟁처리사례」, 에피스테매, 2023.
김엘림	"(판례평석) 직장 내 성희롱 - 대상판결 : 대법원 2017.12.22. 선고 2016다202947 손해배상(기) 판결" 「노동판례백선」제2판, 한국노동법학회 편, 박영사, 2021.
김엘림	"성희롱 사건의 사용자 책임론에 관한 판례의 동향", 「젠더법학」 통권 제14호, 한국젠더법학회, 2016.
김엘림	"(판례평석) 직장 내 성희롱과 사용자 책임-대상판결 : 대법원 1998.2.10.선고 95다39533 손해배상(기)", 「노동판례백선」제1판, 한국노동법학회편, 박영사, 2015.
김엘림	"성희롱의 법적 개념의 형성과 변화", 「젠더법학」 통권 제11호. 한국젠더법학회. 2015.
김진	"고용상 성차별 구제제도와 사례", 「젠더와 법」, 사단법인 올 엮음, 박영사, 2022.
박귀천	"직장 내 성희롱의 판단과 구제", 「젠더와 법」, 사단법인 올 엮음, 박영사, 2022.
이종희	"직장 내 성희롱과 2차 피해, 사용자의 책임은 무엇인가?" (르노삼성 사건)", 「세상을 바꾼 성평등 판결」, 푸른사상, 2020.
정봉수	"한국노동법 해설", 중앙경제, 2021.
정봉수	"해고 매뉴얼", K-labor press, 2022.
정봉수	"인사노무실무", 시간여행, 2022.

< Index >

(A)
A Case Analysis ································ 2
Administrative appeals ···················· 119
administrative lawsuit ····················· 122
Administrative lawsuits ·················· 120

(B)
Basic Understanding of Sexual Harassment ··········· 2
Basic Understanding of Workplace
Harassment ···································· 2
Burden of proof ······························ 97

(C)
Civil lawsuit ·································· 122
compliance status reports ················ 110
Concept & Criteria of Determining
Workplace Harassment ···················· 2
corrective orders ····························· 108
criminal lawsuit ······························ 121

(D)
Disciplinary Committee Decisions ······ 74
disclosure of confidential information ········· 97
discriminatory nature of sexual harassment ········· 38
Discriminatory Treatment ················ 103
Disputes related to sexual harassment ········· 43

(E)
Emergency relief ····························· 119
Employer's Obligation to Protect ······· 2

(G)
gap-jil ·· 34

(H)
Handling of Incidents by the Labor
Relations Commission ····················· 3
Handling of Incidents by Investigative
Agencies and the Courts ·················· 3
Handling of Incidents by the Minister of
Employment and Labor ···················· 3
Handling of Incidents by the National Human
Rights Commission of Korea ············ 3
honorary supervisor for employment equality 92

(I)
Industrial Accident Compensation
Insurance Act ·························· 21, 23
Industrial Safety and Health Act ········ 21, 23

(J)
Judgment by Courts and National Human
Rights Commissions ························ 3

(L)
Labor cases related to Sexual Harassment ···· 3
Labor Cases related to Workplace Harassment ······ 3
Legal sanctions ······························· 88

(M)
Measures to Prevent Workplace Sexual
Harassment ···································· 3

(O)
Obligation to consider safety ············ 10
Occupational Accident ····················· 55
organizational culture ······················ 41

(P)
Patriarchal social structures ·············· 41
Personnel measures ························· 99
Preventing Workplace Sexual Harassment ·········· 3
Primary harm ································· 46
Prohibiting Workplace Sexual Harassment ········· 3

(R)
Recognizing Consequent Mental Illness as an
Occupational Accident Related to Work ············· 2
Recommending conciliation ············· 117
Responding to Reported Incidents of Workplace
Sexual Harassment ·························· 3

(S)
Secondary harm ······························ 46
secondary victimization ···················· 99
Sexual Harassment and Its Relationship to
Workplace Harassment, Sexual Assault, and Gender
Discrimination ································ 2
Sexual Harassment Case and Procedures for
Handling this Case (for Sales Workers) ············ 3
Sexual Harassment Case in the Workplace &
Lessons Learned (for Production Workers) ········· 3
Sexual Language and Behaviors ······· 32

(T)
The Workplace Harassment Prevention Law
and the Employer's Duty ················· 2
Tort liability ·································· 131

(U)
unfavorable treatment ······················ 22

(W)
When Workplace Harassment Occurs, What
Measures Should an Employer Take? ············· 2
Workplace Harassment against a New
Employee ······································ 2
Workplace Harassment Prevention Law ········· 20, 23
Workplace Harassment Resolved through
Recognition of an Accident as Related to Work ··· 2

〈찾아보기〉

(ㄱ)
갑질 ·· 34
고객 등의 성적 언동에 대한 고충 신고 ······· 95
고용노동부의 직장 내 괴롭힘 판단 사례 ········ 3
고용노동부장관의 사건 처리 ···························· 3
괴롭힘 관련 주요 사례 ······································ 3
괴롭힘 방지법과 사업주의 의무 ······················ 2
괴롭힘 사례와 산재인정 요건 ························ 55
괴롭힘, 성희롱 사건과 기각 결정 사례 ········ 74
괴롭힘에 대한 원인 제거를 위한 산재신청 ··· 52
괴롭힘으로 인한 정신질환 ······························ 56
괴롭힘의 기본적 이해 ·· 2
국가인권위원회의 성희롱 관련 사건처리 ····· 116
근로자의 성희롱 ·· 149
긴급구제 ·· 119

(ㄴ)
남녀고용평등법 ··· 100
남녀고용평등법 시행규칙 ······························ 32
남성 근로자의 성희롱 ··································· 149
남성 사업주의 성희롱 ··································· 132

(ㅁ)
명예고용평등감독관 ·· 92

(ㅂ)
불이익(2차 가해)금지조치 ······························ 99
비밀누설금지 ·· 97

(ㅅ)
사업주의 성희롱 사건 ······························ 3, 132
사용자의 보호의무 ·· 2
사용자책임 ··· 129
산재보험법의 정신질병에 대한 인정기준 ····· 58
산재신청 ·· 52
상급자의 성희롱 ·· 137
성폭력범죄 ·· 36
성희롱 관련 분쟁 ·· 43
성희롱 관련 주요 사례 ···································· 3
성희롱 금지와 예방조치 ································ 48
성희롱 발생 사업장의 종사자 ······················ 48
성희롱 발생 시 조치와 사건 처리 ·················· 3
성희롱 사건사례 (사무직 직원) ······················ 3
성희롱 사건사례 (영업직 직원) ······················ 3
성희롱 여부의 판단기준 ······························ 122
성희롱 피해자 등의 보호조치 ······················ 99
성희롱의 기본적 이해 ······································ 2
성희롱의 인권문제 ·· 41

손해배상청구 ·· 153
수사기관과 법원의 사건 처리 ························ 3
시정명령 ··· 108
시정명령 불이행 ·· 111
시정명령 이행상황 ·· 110
신체적 성희롱 ··· 180
신체적 정신적 고통 ·· 69

(ㅇ)
안전을 배려할 의무 ·· 10
양성평등기본법 ·· 27
언어적 성희롱 ··· 181
업무관련성 ·· 34
업무상 부상 ·· 50
업무상 적정 범위 ·· 69
업무일탈 ·· 15
여성 근로자의 성희롱 ··································· 151
여성 사업주의 성희롱 ··································· 135
여성 상급자의 성희롱 ··································· 147
여성편향성 ·· 36
예방교육의 위탁 ·· 91
인권문제 ·· 41
인권침해 ·· 41

(ㅈ)
정신질병 업무관련성 ······································ 58
정신질병의 대상 ·· 59
조사 관여자의 비밀누설금지 ························ 97
조직문화 ·· 41
지위 또는 관계 등의 우위 ···························· 68
직장 내 괴롭힘 처리 사례 (신입직원) ········ 67
직장 내 괴롭힘·성폭력·성차별과의 관계 ········ 2
직장 내 성희롱의 예방교육 ·························· 89
직장 내 괴롭힘 방지법 ·································· 19
직장 내 괴롭힘 원인제거 ······························ 50
집단 따돌림 ·· 52
징계위원회 ·· 79

(ㅍ)
피해자 등에 대한 보호조치 ·························· 96
피해자다움 ··· 126

(ㅎ)
합의의 권고 ··· 117
행정소송 ·· 120, 122
행정심판 ··· 119
형사소송 ··· 121

Manual on Bullying and Sexual Harassment in the Workplace
직장 내 괴롭힘과 성희롱 예방 매뉴얼

발 행 일 : 2023년 6월 1일 초판발행

지 은 이 : 김 엘 림, 정 봉 수

펴 낸 이 : 정 봉 수

펴 낸 곳 : 강남노무법인 출판부 (K-Labor Press)

편집,디자인 : 정 영 철

주　　소 : 서울시 강남구 대치동 테헤란로 406 A-1501 (대치동, 샹제리제센터)

전　　화 : 02-539-0098

팩　　스 : 02-539-4167

홈페이지 : www.k-labor.com

출판등록 : 강남, 바00177

I S B N : 979-11-85290-25-6

정　　가 : 30,000원

＊ 이 책자는 저작권법에 따라 보호받는 저작물이므로 무단전재와 복제를 금합니다.